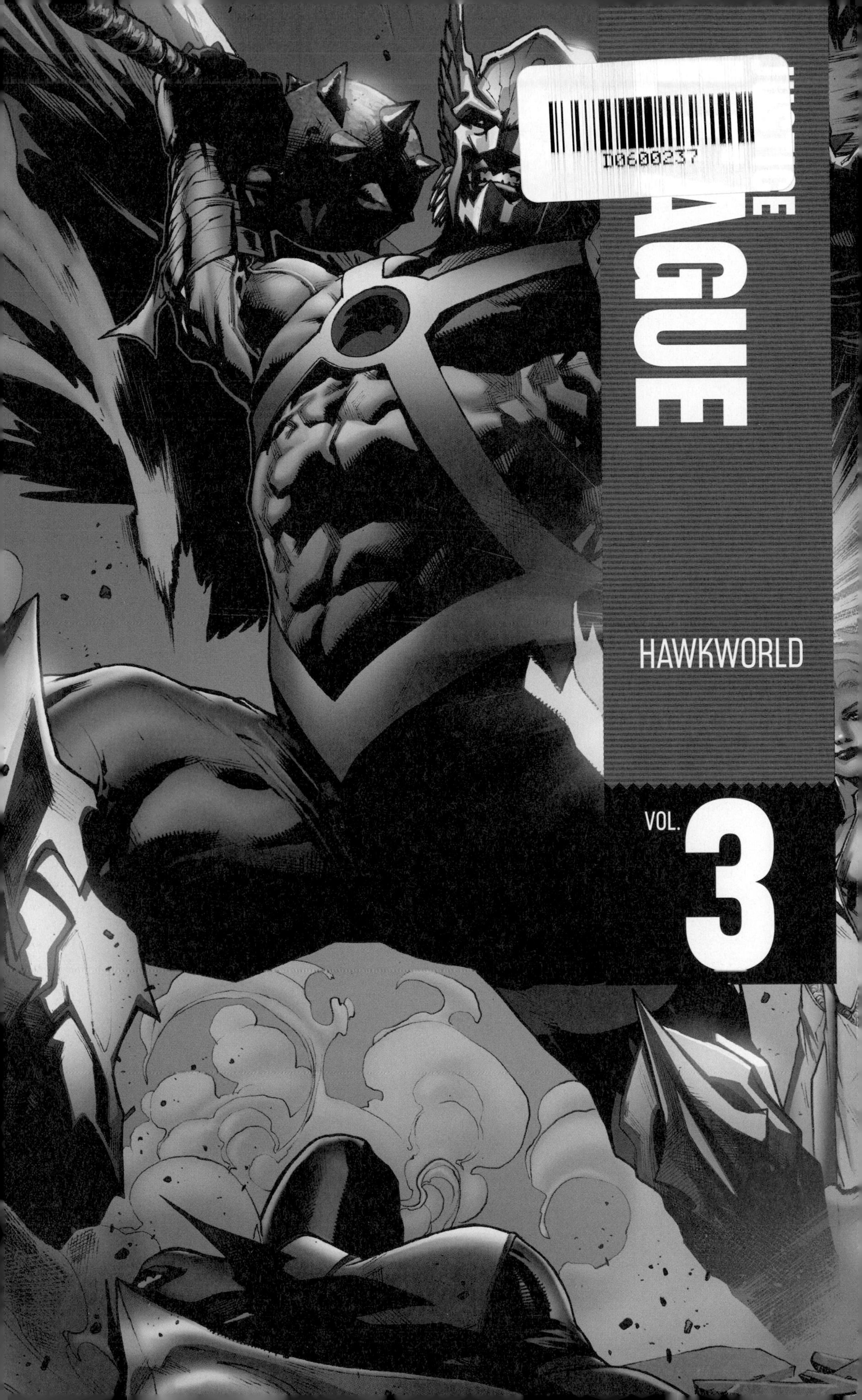
E
AGUE
HAWKWORLD
VOL. 3

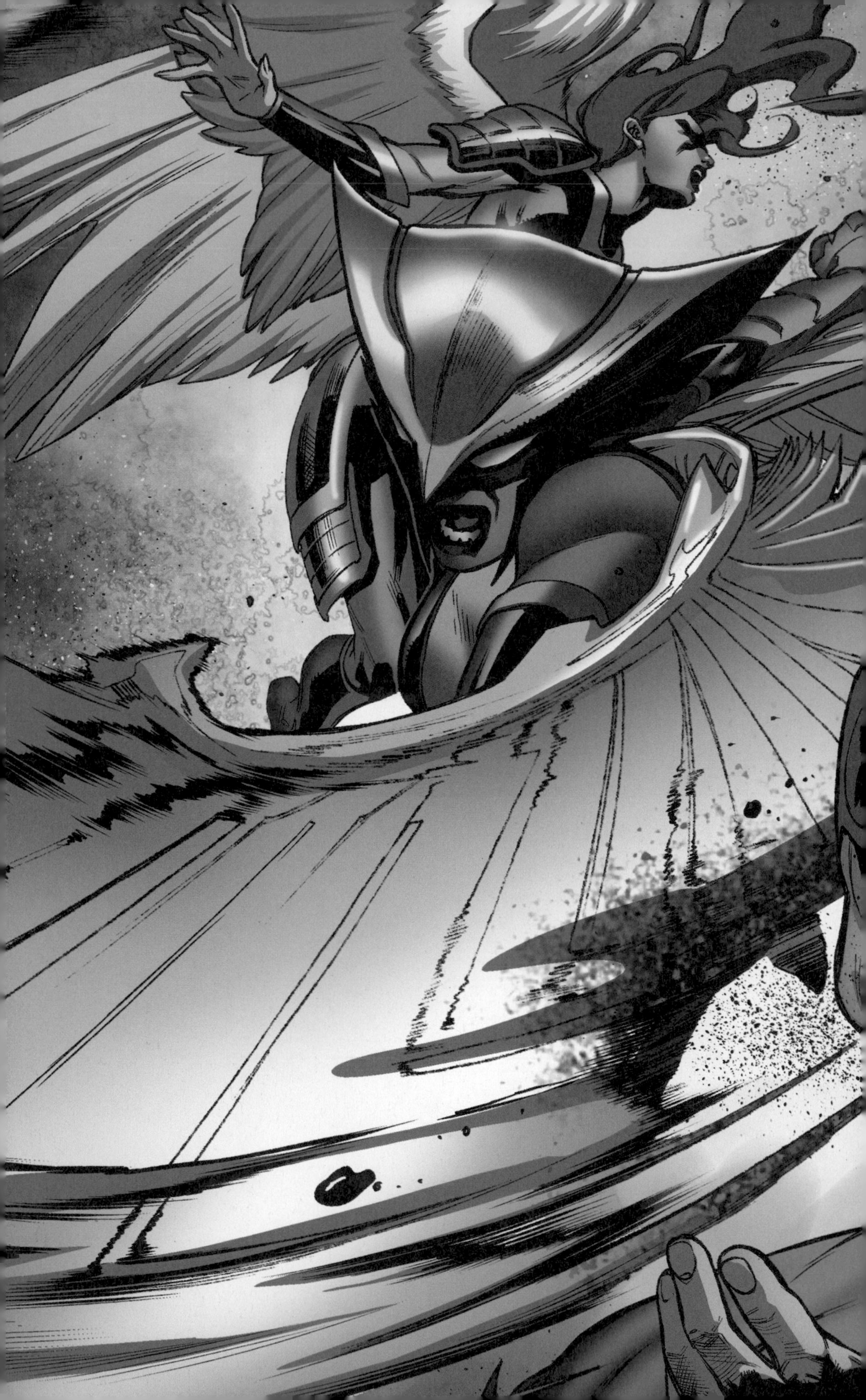

JUSTICE
LEAGUE
HAWKWORLD

writers
SCOTT SNYDER
JAMES TYNION IV

artists
JIM CHEUNG / STEPHEN SEGOVIA
GUILLEM MARCH / DANIEL SAMPERE
PASQUAL FERRY / MARK MORALES
JUAN ALBARRAN / WALDEN WONG

colorists
TOMEU MOREY / WIL QUINTANA
ARIF PRIANTO / ADRIANO LUCAS
HI-FI

letterer
TOM NAPOLITANO

collection cover artists
JIM CHEUNG and TOMEU MOREY

SUPERMAN created by **JERRY SIEGEL** and **JOE SHUSTER**
By special arrangement with the Jerry Siegel family

VOL.
3

MARIE JAVINS **PAUL KAMINSKI** Editors – Original Series
ROB LEVIN Associate Editor – Original Series
ANDREW MARINO Assistant Editor – Original Series
JEB WOODARD Group Editor – Collected Editions
ROBIN WILDMAN Editor – Collected Edition
STEVE COOK Design Director – Books
MONIQUE NARBONETA Publication Design
ADAM RADO Publication Production

BOB HARRAS Senior VP – Editor-in-Chief, DC Comics
PAT McCALLUM Executive Editor, DC Comics

DAN DiDIO Publisher
JIM LEE Publisher & Chief Creative Officer
BOBBIE CHASE VP – New Publishing Initiatives & Talent Development
DON FALLETTI VP – Manufacturing Operations & Workflow Management
LAWRENCE GANEM VP – Talent Services
ALISON GILL Senior VP – Manufacturing & Operations
HANK KANALZ Senior VP – Publishing Strategy & Support Services
DAN MIRON VP – Publishing Operations
NICK J. NAPOLITANO VP – Manufacturing Administration & Design
NANCY SPEARS VP – Sales
MICHELE R. WELLS VP & Executive Editor, Young Reader

JUSTICE LEAGUE VOL. 3: HAWKWORLD

Published by DC Comics. Compilation and all new material Copyright © 2019 DC Comics. All Rights Reserved.
Originally published in single magazine form in JUSTICE LEAGUE 13-18, JUSTICE LEAGUE ANNUAL 1. Copyright ©
2018, 2019 DC Comics. All Rights Reserved. All characters, their distinctive likenesses and related elements
featured in this publication are trademarks of DC Comics. The stories, characters and incidents featured in this
publication are entirely fictional. DC Comics does not read or accept unsolicited submissions of ideas, stories
or artwork. DC – a WarnerMedia Company.

DC Comics, 2900 West Alameda Ave., Burbank, CA 91505
Printed by LSC Communications, Owensville, MO, USA. 6/14/19. First Printing.
ISBN: 978-1-4012-9138-9

Library of Congress Cataloging-in-Publication Data is available.

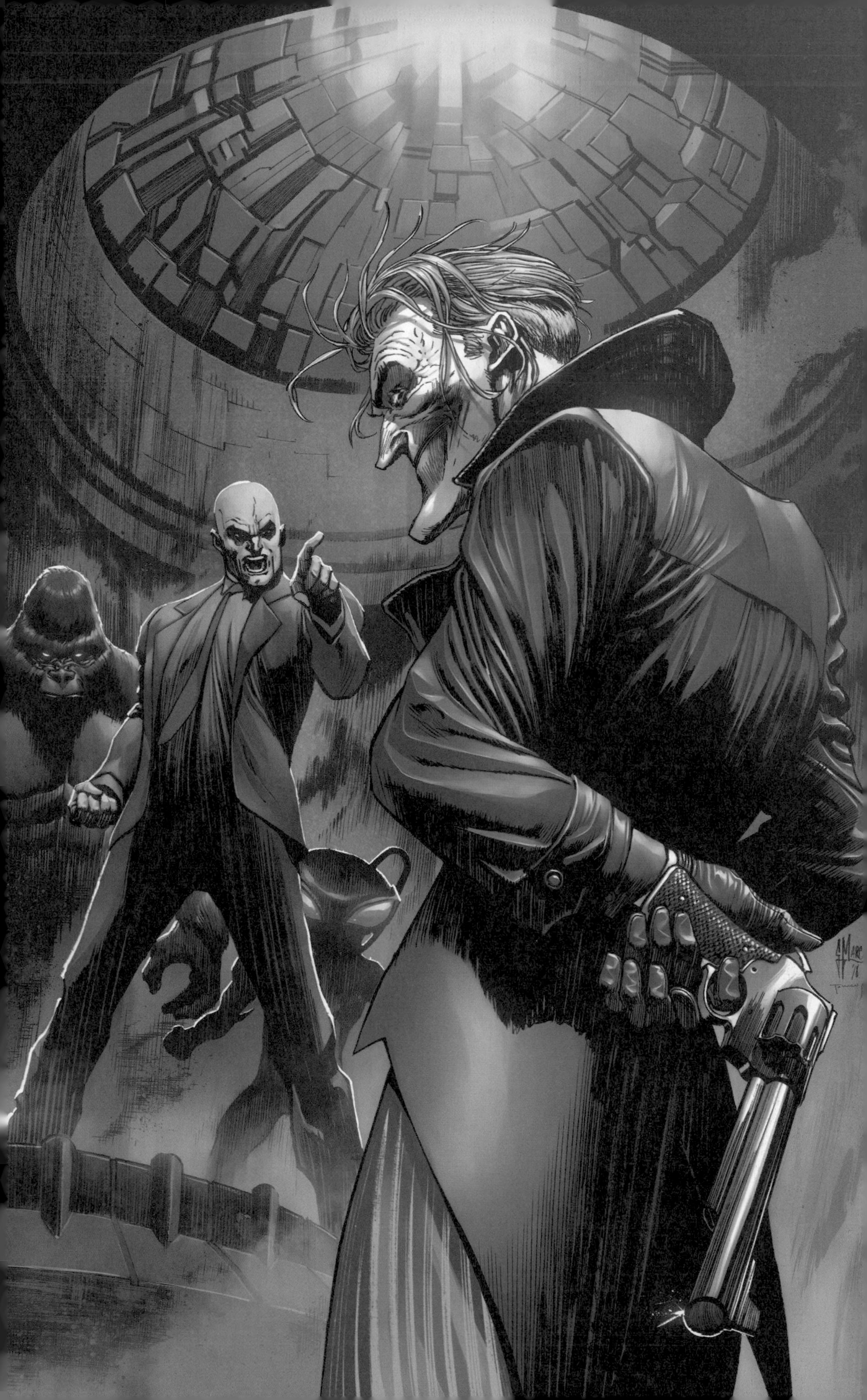

JUSTICE
LEAGUE
#13

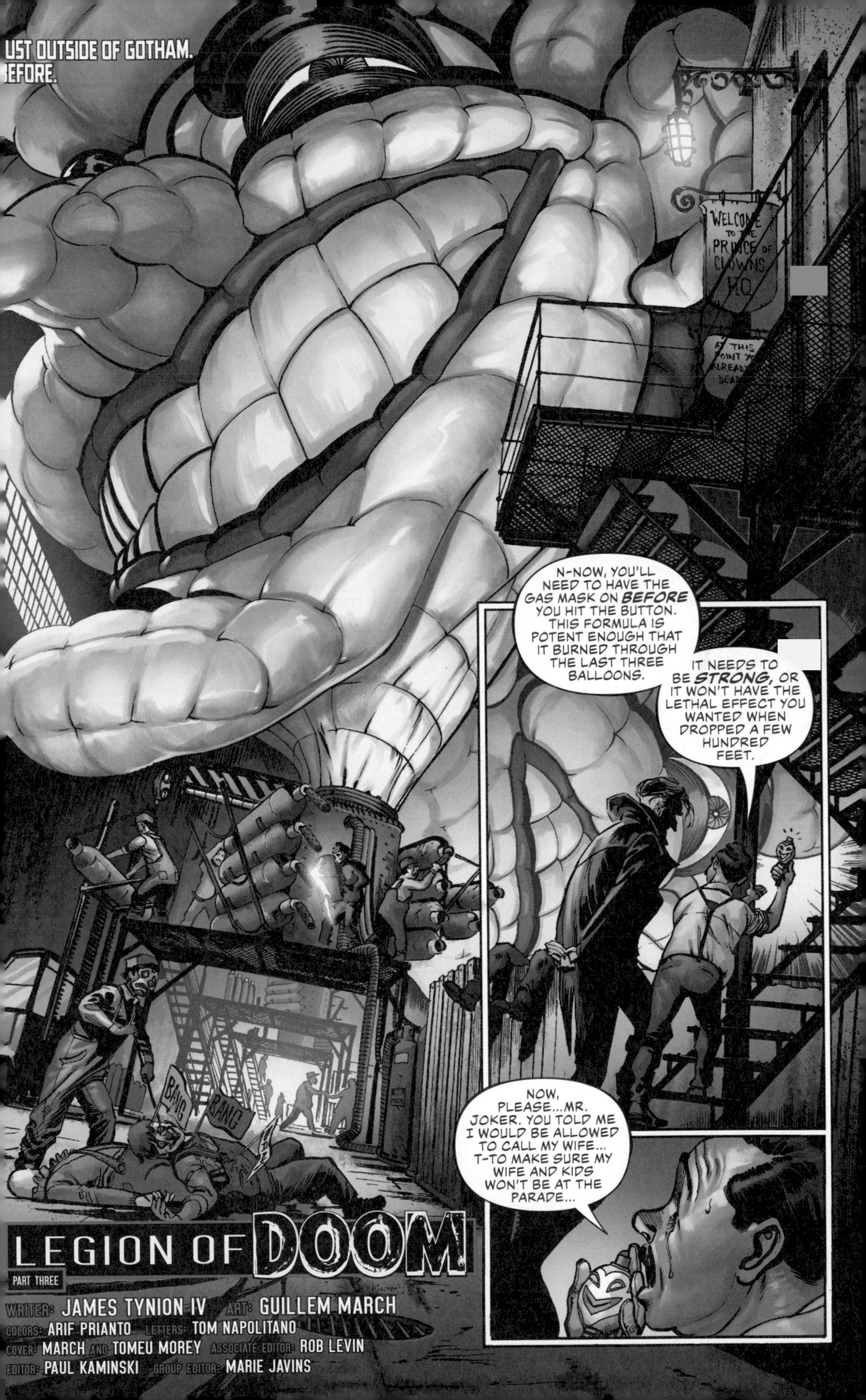
UST OUTSIDE OF GOTHAM.
EFORE.
WELCOME TO THE PRINCE OF CLOWNS HQ
N-NOW, YOU'LL NEED TO HAVE THE GAS MASK ON BEFORE YOU HIT THE BUTTON. THIS FORMULA IS POTENT ENOUGH THAT IT BURNED THROUGH THE LAST THREE BALLOONS.
IT NEEDS TO BE STRONG, OR IT WON'T HAVE THE LETHAL EFFECT YOU WANTED WHEN DROPPED A FEW HUNDRED FEET.
NOW, PLEASE...MR. JOKER. YOU TOLD ME I WOULD BE ALLOWED TO CALL MY WIFE... T-TO MAKE SURE MY WIFE AND KIDS WON'T BE AT THE PARADE...
LEGION OF DOOM
PART THREE
WRITER: JAMES TYNION IV ART: GUILLEM MARCH
COLORS: ARIF PRIANTO LETTERS: TOM NAPOLITANO
COVER: MARCH AND TOMEU MOREY ASSOCIATE EDITOR: ROB LEVIN
EDITOR: PAUL KAMINSKI GROUP EDITOR: MARIE JAVINS

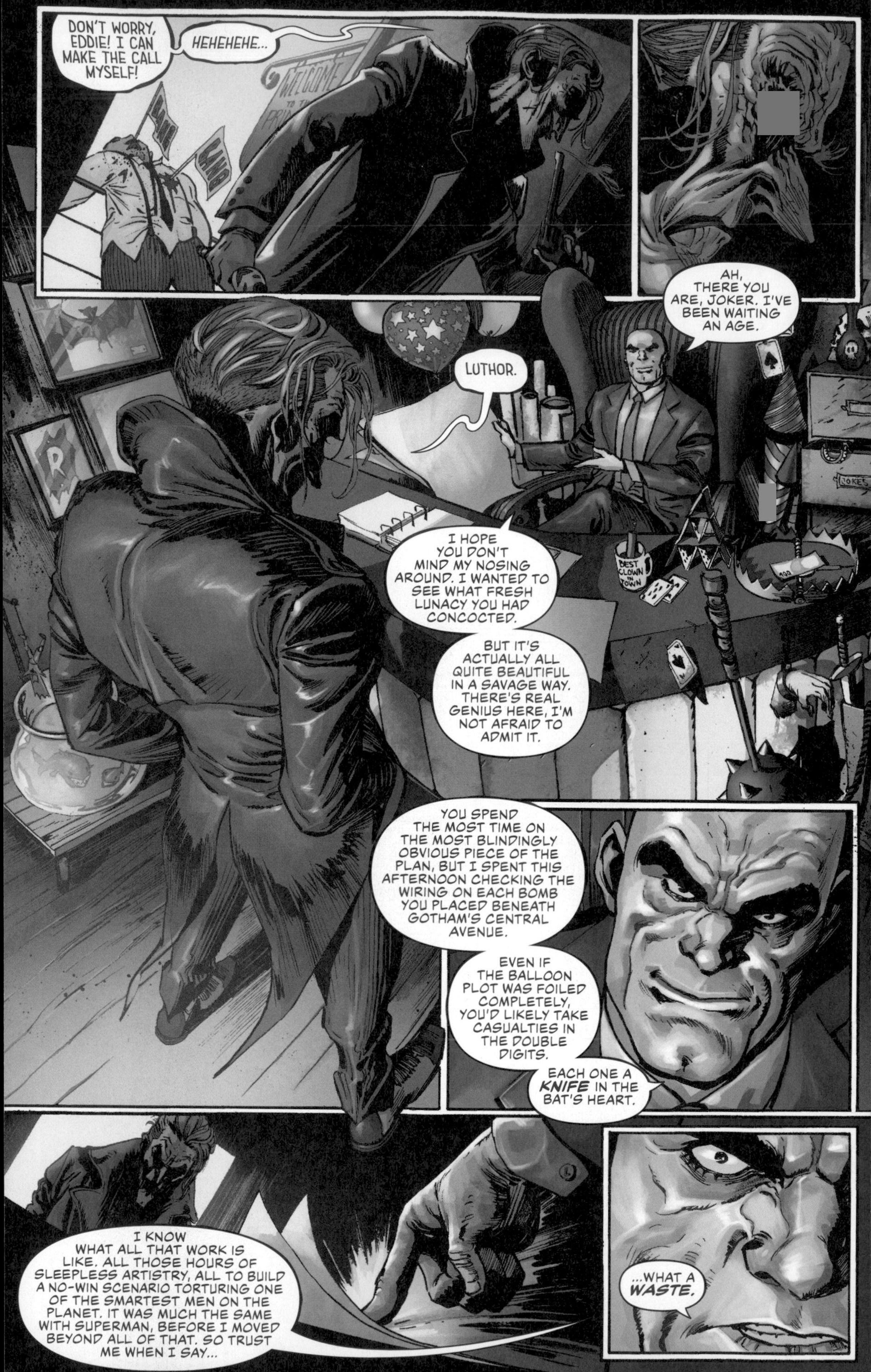
DON'T WORRY, EDDIE! I CAN MAKE THE CALL MYSELF!
HEHEHEHE...
WELCOME
AH, THERE YOU ARE, JOKER. I'VE BEEN WAITING AN AGE.
LUTHOR.
I HOPE YOU DON'T MIND MY NOSING AROUND. I WANTED TO SEE WHAT FRESH LUNACY YOU HAD CONCOCTED.
BEST CLOWN IN TOWN
JOKES
BUT IT'S ACTUALLY ALL QUITE BEAUTIFUL IN A SAVAGE WAY. THERE'S REAL GENIUS HERE, I'M NOT AFRAID TO ADMIT IT.
YOU SPEND THE MOST TIME ON THE MOST BLINDINGLY OBVIOUS PIECE OF THE PLAN, BUT I SPENT THIS AFTERNOON CHECKING THE WIRING ON EACH BOMB YOU PLACED BENEATH GOTHAM'S CENTRAL AVENUE.
EVEN IF THE BALLOON PLOT WAS FOILED COMPLETELY, YOU'D LIKELY TAKE CASUALTIES IN THE DOUBLE DIGITS.
EACH ONE A KNIFE IN THE BAT'S HEART.
I KNOW WHAT ALL THAT WORK IS LIKE. ALL THOSE HOURS OF SLEEPLESS ARTISTRY, ALL TO BUILD A NO-WIN SCENARIO TORTURING ONE OF THE SMARTEST MEN ON THE PLANET. IT WAS MUCH THE SAME WITH SUPERMAN, BEFORE I MOVED BEYOND ALL OF THAT. SO TRUST ME WHEN I SAY...
...WHAT A WASTE.

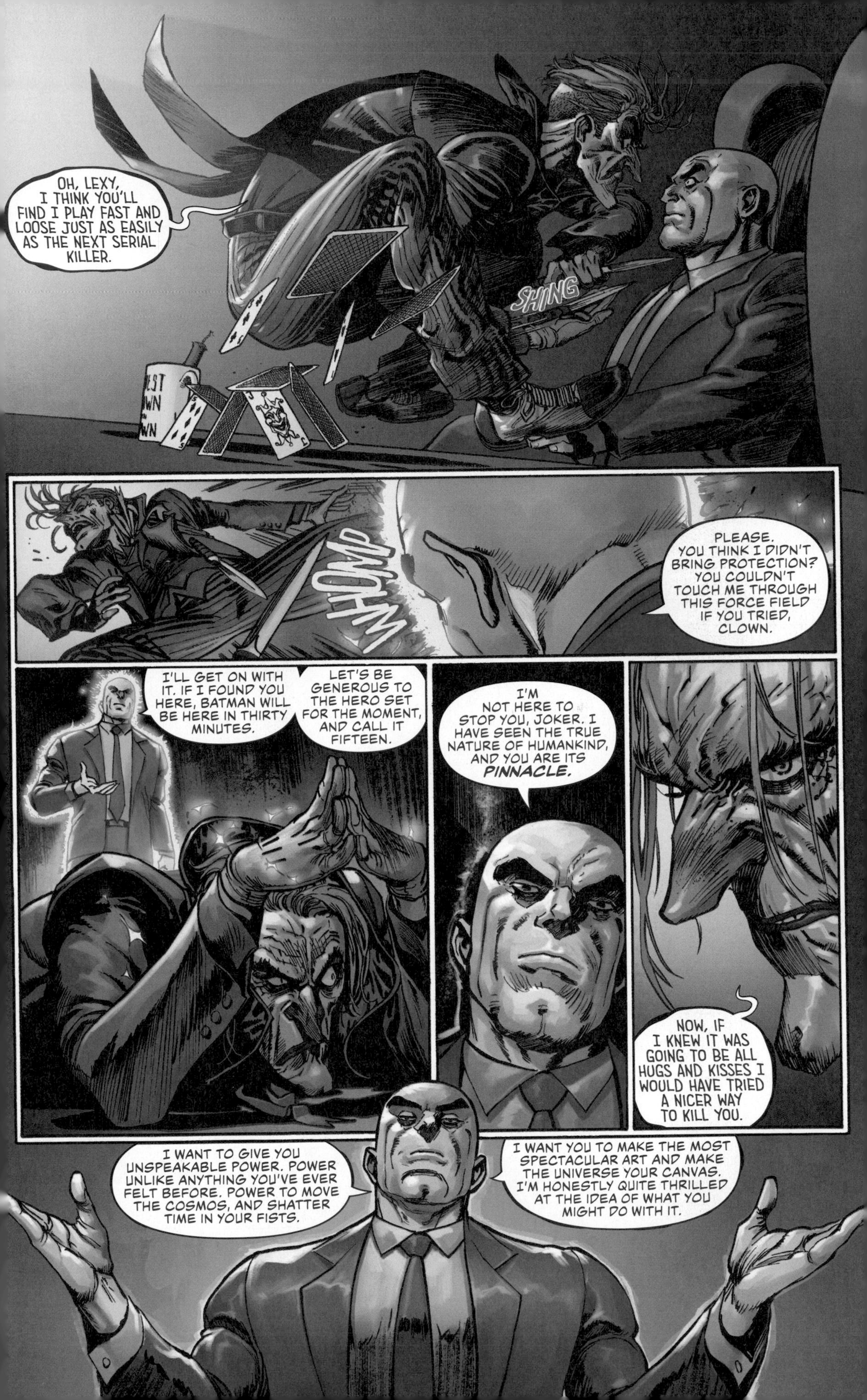
OH, LEXY, I THINK YOU'LL FIND I PLAY FAST AND LOOSE JUST AS EASILY AS THE NEXT SERIAL KILLER.
SHING
WHOMP
PLEASE. YOU THINK I DIDN'T BRING PROTECTION? YOU COULDN'T TOUCH ME THROUGH THIS FORCE FIELD IF YOU TRIED, CLOWN.
I'LL GET ON WITH IT. IF I FOUND YOU HERE, BATMAN WILL BE HERE IN THIRTY MINUTES.
LET'S BE GENEROUS TO THE HERO SET FOR THE MOMENT, AND CALL IT FIFTEEN.
I'M NOT HERE TO STOP YOU, JOKER. I HAVE SEEN THE TRUE NATURE OF HUMANKIND, AND YOU ARE ITS PINNACLE.
NOW, IF I KNEW IT WAS GOING TO BE ALL HUGS AND KISSES I WOULD HAVE TRIED A NICER WAY TO KILL YOU.
I WANT TO GIVE YOU UNSPEAKABLE POWER. POWER UNLIKE ANYTHING YOU'VE EVER FELT BEFORE. POWER TO MOVE THE COSMOS, AND SHATTER TIME IN YOUR FISTS.
I WANT YOU TO MAKE THE MOST SPECTACULAR ART AND MAKE THE UNIVERSE YOUR CANVAS. I'M HONESTLY QUITE THRILLED AT THE IDEA OF WHAT YOU MIGHT DO WITH IT.

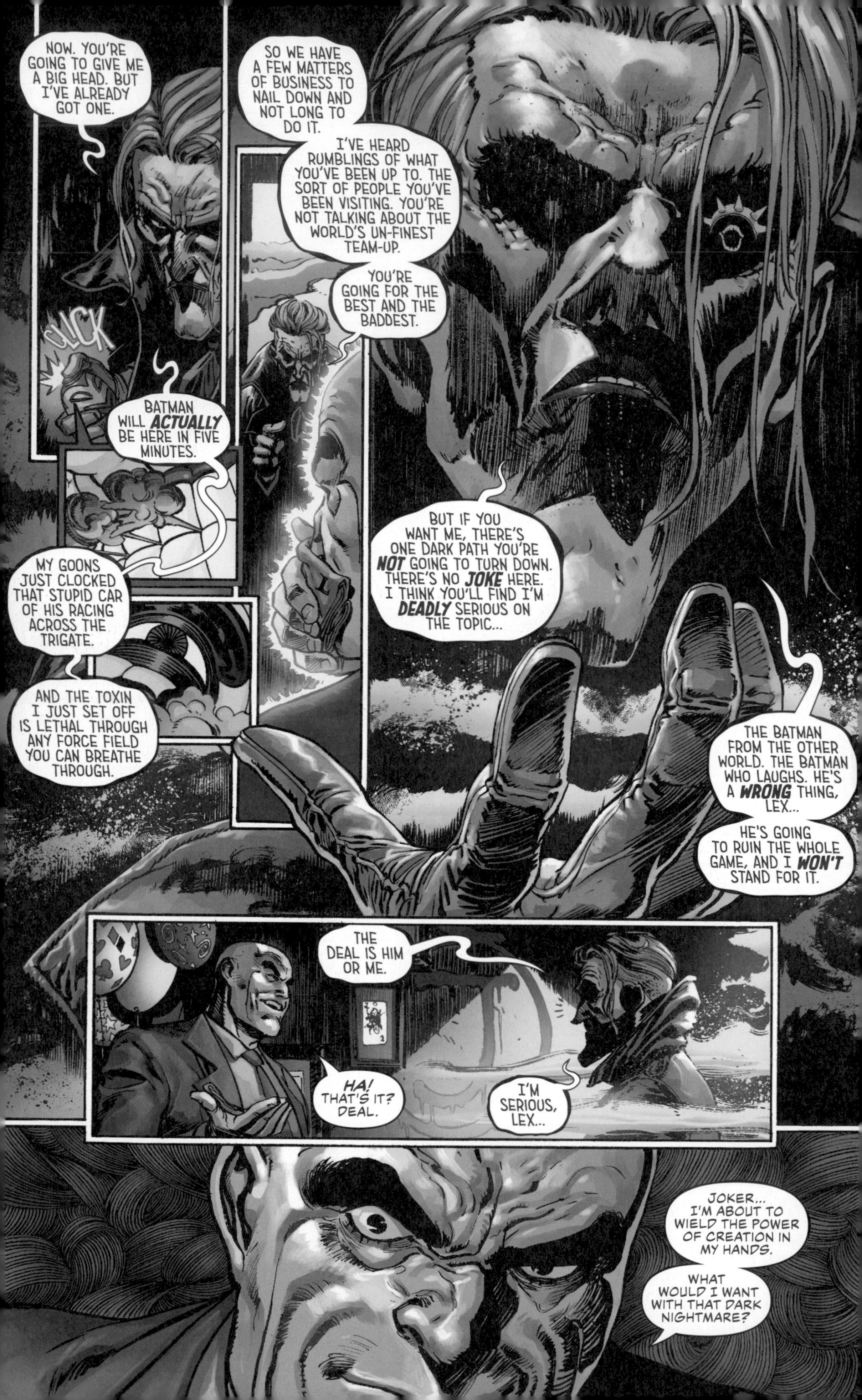
NOW. YOU'RE GOING TO GIVE ME A BIG HEAD. BUT I'VE ALREADY GOT ONE.
SO WE HAVE A FEW MATTERS OF BUSINESS TO NAIL DOWN AND NOT LONG TO DO IT.
I'VE HEARD RUMBLINGS OF WHAT YOU'VE BEEN UP TO. THE SORT OF PEOPLE YOU'VE BEEN VISITING. YOU'RE NOT TALKING ABOUT THE WORLD'S UN-FINEST TEAM-UP.
YOU'RE GOING FOR THE BEST AND THE BADDEST.
CLICK
BATMAN WILL ACTUALLY BE HERE IN FIVE MINUTES.
MY GOONS JUST CLOCKED THAT STUPID CAR OF HIS RACING ACROSS THE TRIGATE.
AND THE TOXIN I JUST SET OFF IS LETHAL THROUGH ANY FORCE FIELD YOU CAN BREATHE THROUGH.
BUT IF YOU WANT ME, THERE'S ONE DARK PATH YOU'RE NOT GOING TO TURN DOWN. THERE'S NO JOKE HERE. I THINK YOU'LL FIND I'M DEADLY SERIOUS ON THE TOPIC...
THE BATMAN FROM THE OTHER WORLD. THE BATMAN WHO LAUGHS. HE'S A WRONG THING, LEX...
HE'S GOING TO RUIN THE WHOLE GAME, AND I WON'T STAND FOR IT.
THE DEAL IS HIM OR ME.
HA! THAT'S IT? DEAL.
I'M SERIOUS, LEX...
JOKER... I'M ABOUT TO WIELD THE POWER OF CREATION IN MY HANDS.
WHAT WOULD I WANT WITH THAT DARK NIGHTMARE?

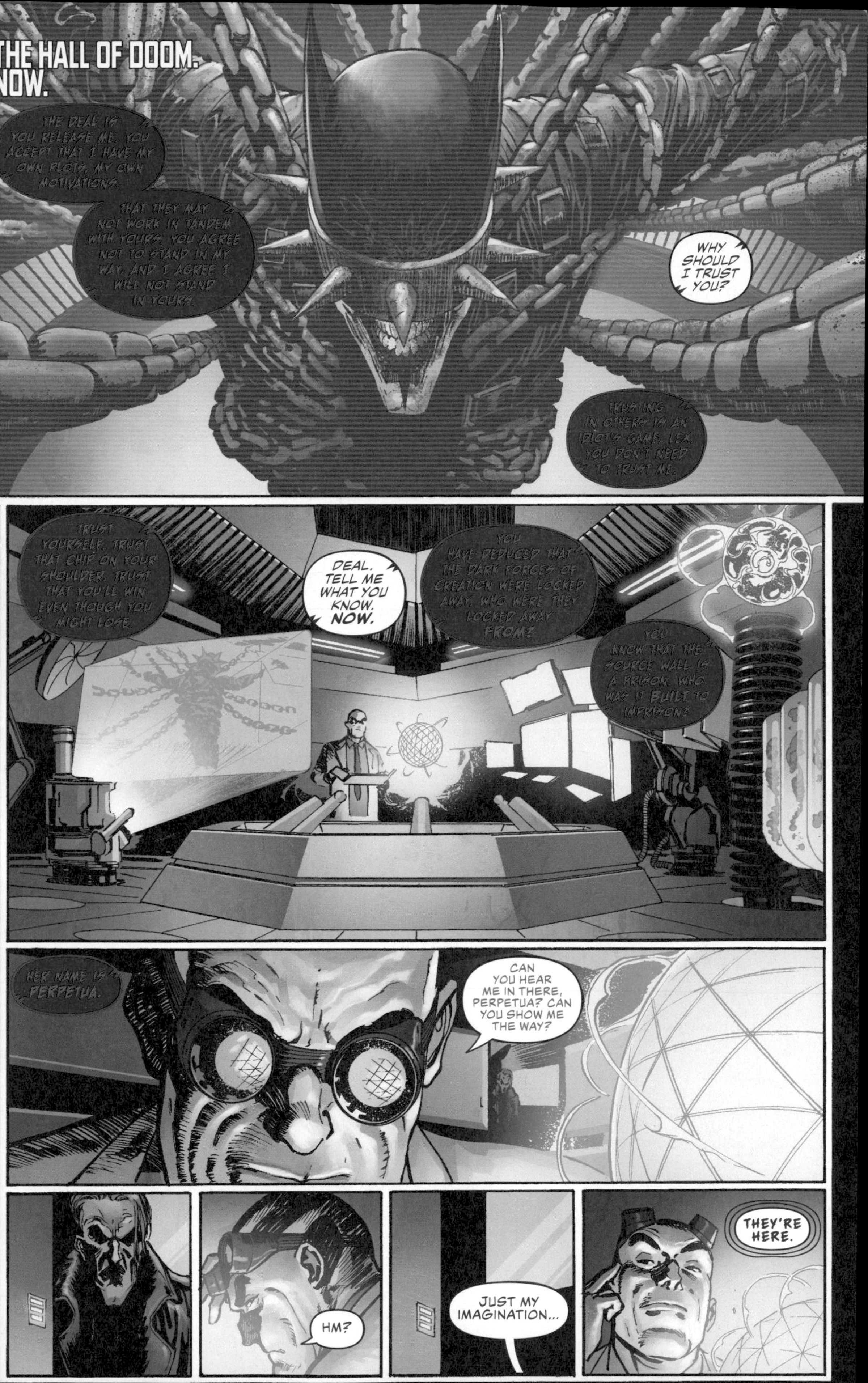
THE HALL OF DOOM. NOW.
THE DEAL IS YOU RELEASE ME. YOU ACCEPT THAT I HAVE MY OWN PLOTS, MY OWN MOTIVATIONS.
THAT THEY MAY NOT WORK IN TANDEM WITH YOURS. YOU AGREE NOT TO STAND IN MY WAY. AND I AGREE I WILL NOT STAND IN YOURS.
WHY SHOULD I TRUST YOU?
TRUSTING IN OTHERS IS AN IDIOT'S GAME, LEX. YOU DON'T NEED TO TRUST ME.
TRUST YOURSELF. TRUST THAT CHIP ON YOUR SHOULDER. TRUST THAT YOU'LL WIN EVEN THOUGH YOU MIGHT LOSE.
DEAL. TELL ME WHAT YOU KNOW. NOW.
YOU HAVE DEDUCED THAT THE DARK FORCES OF CREATION WERE LOCKED AWAY. WHO WERE THEY LOCKED AWAY FROM?
YOU KNOW THAT THE SOURCE WALL IS A PRISON. WHO WAS IT BUILT TO IMPRISON?
HER NAME IS PERPETUA.
CAN YOU HEAR ME IN THERE, PERPETUA? CAN YOU SHOW ME THE WAY?
HM?
JUST MY IMAGINATION...
THEY'RE HERE.

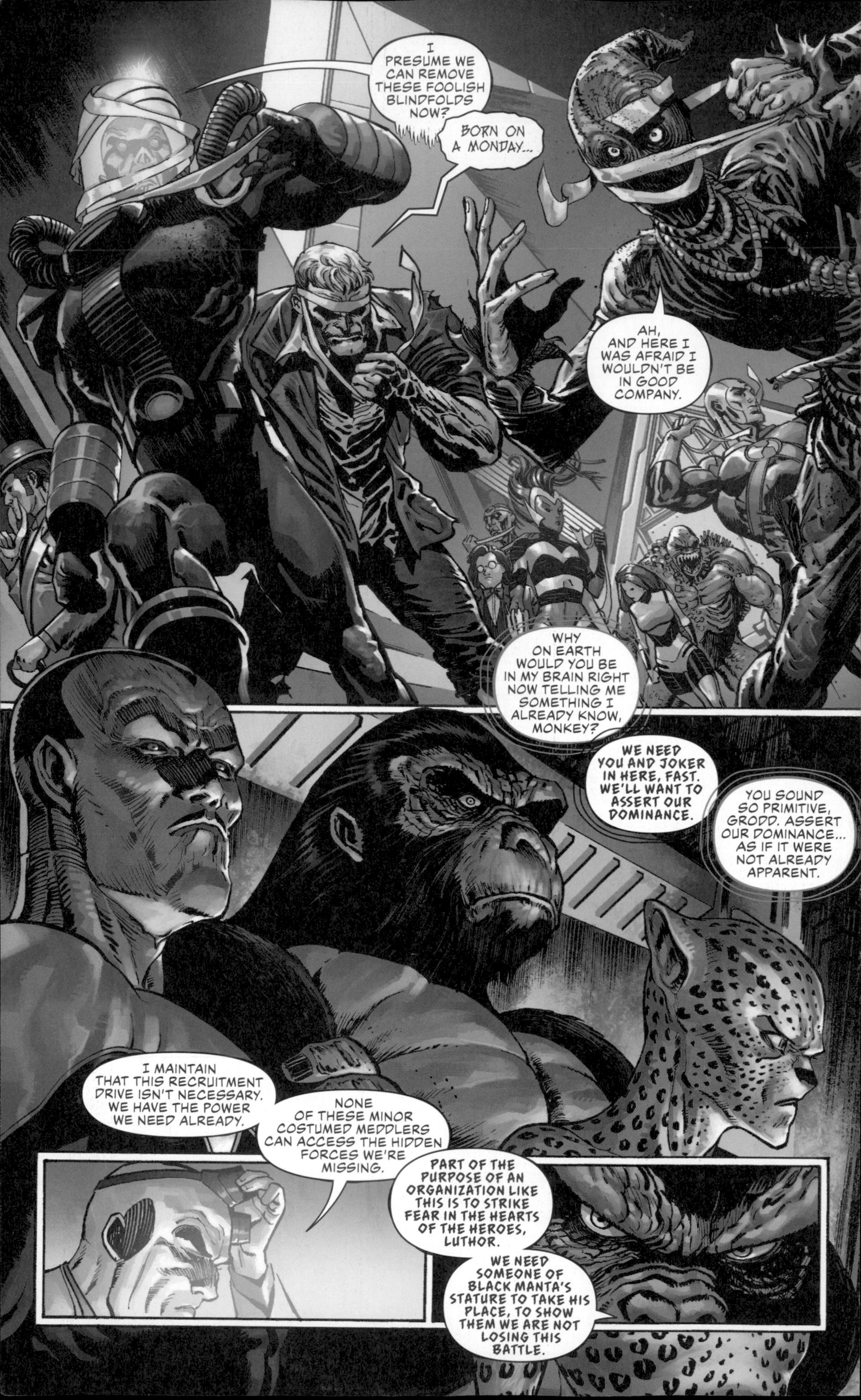
I PRESUME WE CAN REMOVE THESE FOOLISH BLINDFOLDS NOW?
BORN ON A MONDAY...
AH, AND HERE I WAS AFRAID I WOULDN'T BE IN GOOD COMPANY.
WHY ON EARTH WOULD YOU BE IN MY BRAIN RIGHT NOW TELLING ME SOMETHING I ALREADY KNOW, MONKEY?
WE NEED YOU AND JOKER IN HERE, FAST. WE'LL WANT TO ASSERT OUR DOMINANCE.
YOU SOUND SO PRIMITIVE, GRODD. ASSERT OUR DOMINANCE... AS IF IT WERE NOT ALREADY APPARENT.
I MAINTAIN THAT THIS RECRUITMENT DRIVE ISN'T NECESSARY. WE HAVE THE POWER WE NEED ALREADY.
NONE OF THESE MINOR COSTUMED MEDDLERS CAN ACCESS THE HIDDEN FORCES WE'RE MISSING.
PART OF THE PURPOSE OF AN ORGANIZATION LIKE THIS IS TO STRIKE FEAR IN THE HEARTS OF THE HEROES, LUTHOR.
WE NEED SOMEONE OF BLACK MANTA'S STATURE TO TAKE HIS PLACE, TO SHOW THEM WE ARE NOT LOSING THIS BATTLE.

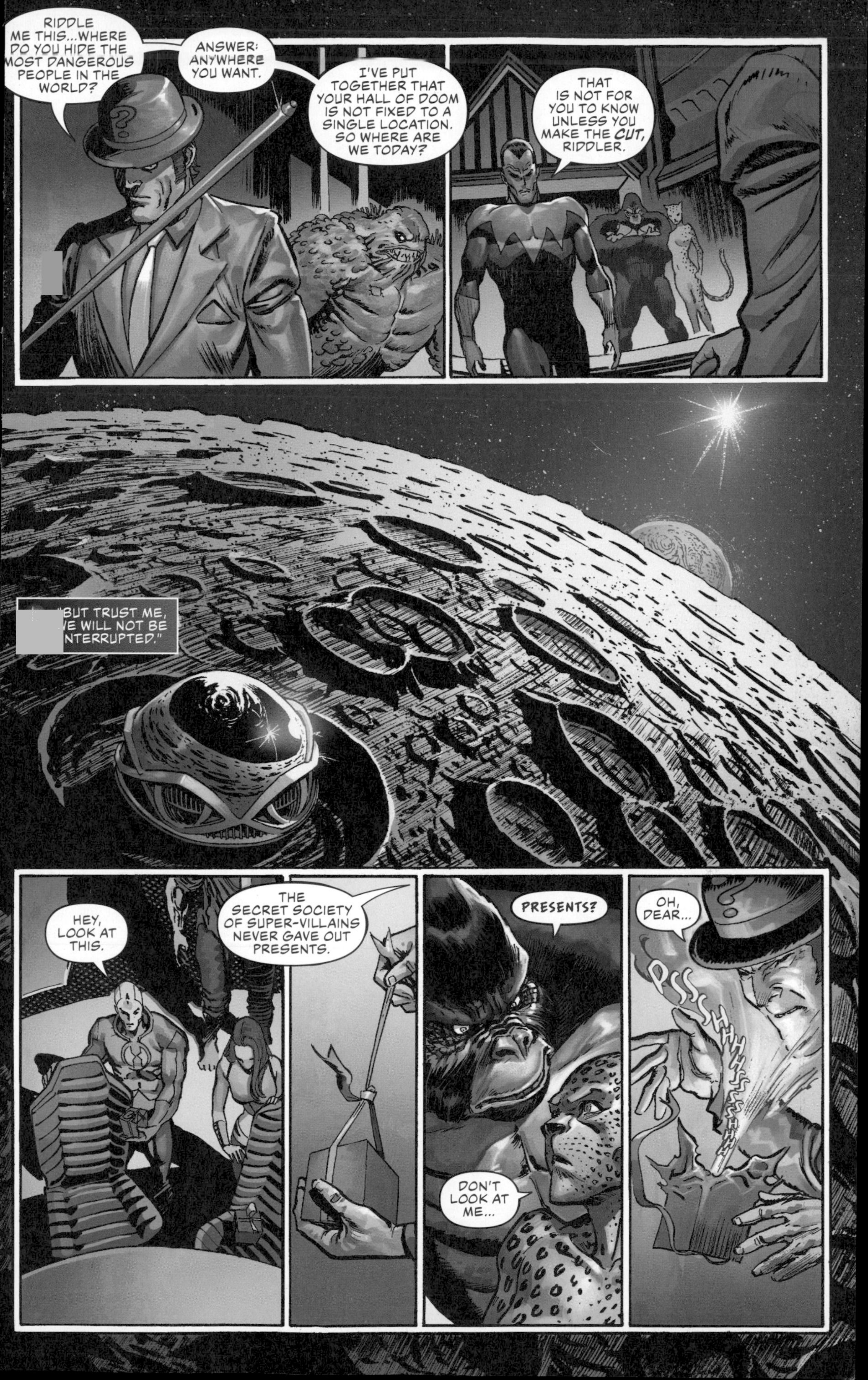
RIDDLE ME THIS...WHERE DO YOU HIDE THE MOST DANGEROUS PEOPLE IN THE WORLD?
ANSWER: ANYWHERE YOU WANT.
I'VE PUT TOGETHER THAT YOUR HALL OF DOOM IS NOT FIXED TO A SINGLE LOCATION. SO WHERE ARE WE TODAY?
THAT IS NOT FOR YOU TO KNOW UNLESS YOU MAKE THE CUT, RIDDLER.
"...BUT TRUST ME, WE WILL NOT BE INTERRUPTED."
HEY, LOOK AT THIS.
THE SECRET SOCIETY OF SUPER-VILLAINS NEVER GAVE OUT PRESENTS.
PRESENTS?
DON'T LOOK AT ME...
OH, DEAR...
PSSSHHHHSSSSHHHH

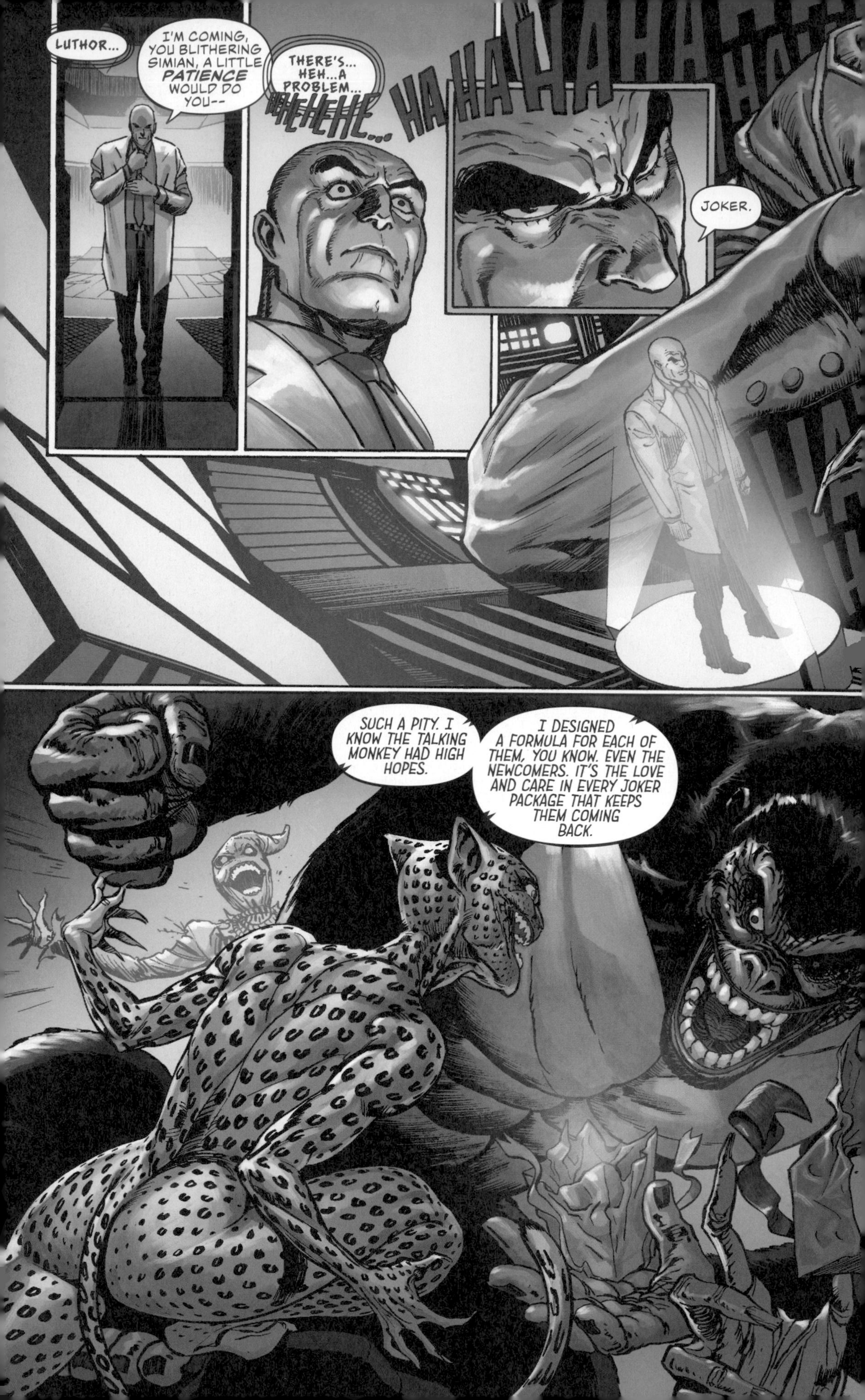
LUTHOR...
I'M COMING, YOU BLITHERING SIMIAN, A LITTLE PATIENCE WOULD DO YOU--
THERE'S... HEH...A PROBLEM...
HEHEHE...
HAHAHAHAHAHA
JOKER.
SUCH A PITY. I KNOW THE TALKING MONKEY HAD HIGH HOPES.
I DESIGNED A FORMULA FOR EACH OF THEM, YOU KNOW. EVEN THE NEWCOMERS. IT'S THE LOVE AND CARE IN EVERY JOKER PACKAGE THAT KEEPS THEM COMING BACK.

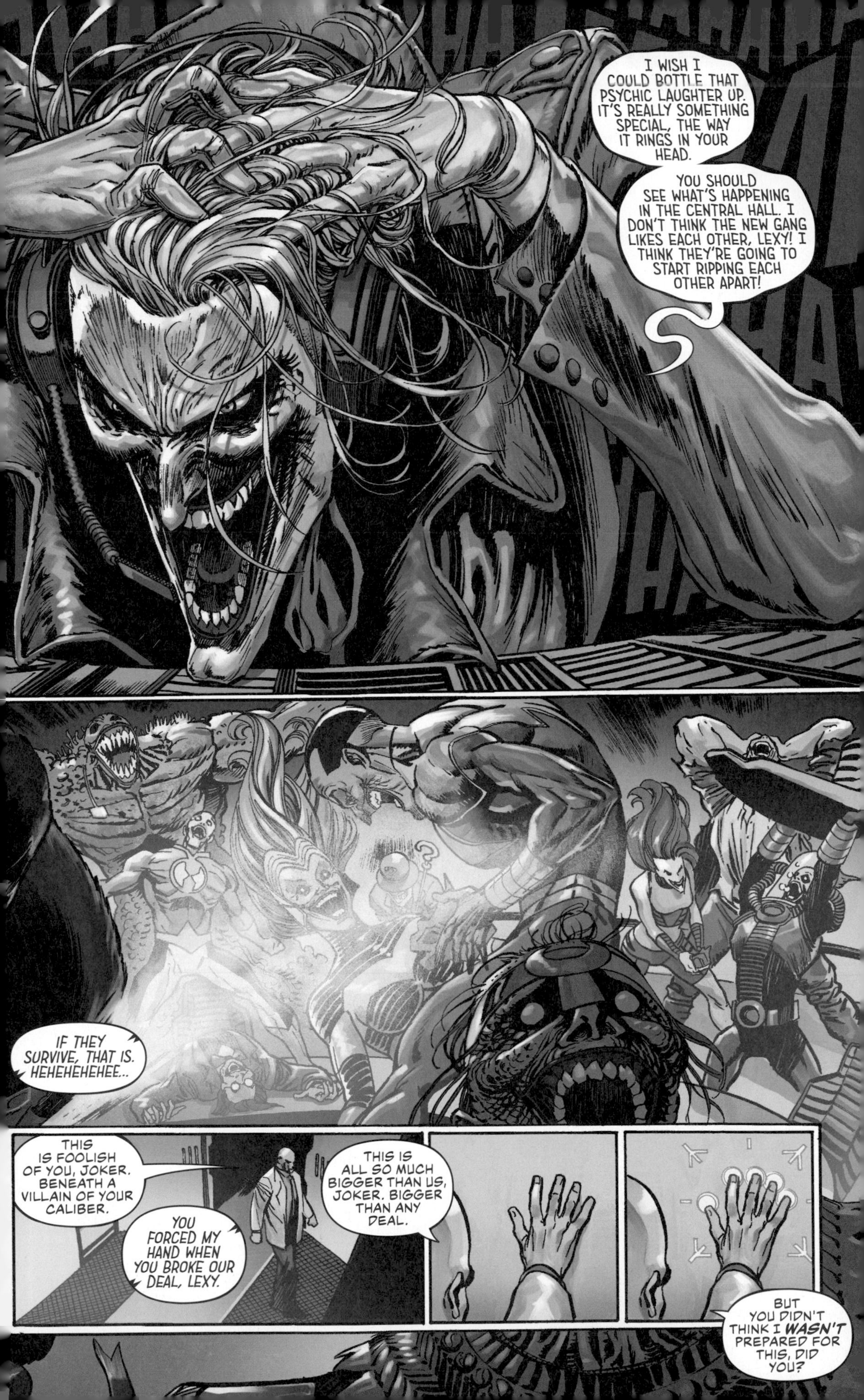
I WISH I COULD BOTTLE THAT PSYCHIC LAUGHTER UP. IT'S REALLY SOMETHING SPECIAL, THE WAY IT RINGS IN YOUR HEAD.
YOU SHOULD SEE WHAT'S HAPPENING IN THE CENTRAL HALL. I DON'T THINK THE NEW GANG LIKES EACH OTHER, LEXY! I THINK THEY'RE GOING TO START RIPPING EACH OTHER APART!
IF THEY SURVIVE, THAT IS. HEHEHEHEHEE...
THIS IS FOOLISH OF YOU, JOKER. BENEATH A VILLAIN OF YOUR CALIBER.
YOU FORCED MY HAND WHEN YOU BROKE OUR DEAL, LEXY.
THIS IS ALL SO MUCH BIGGER THAN US, JOKER. BIGGER THAN ANY DEAL.
BUT YOU DIDN'T THINK I ***WASN'T*** PREPARED FOR THIS, DID YOU?

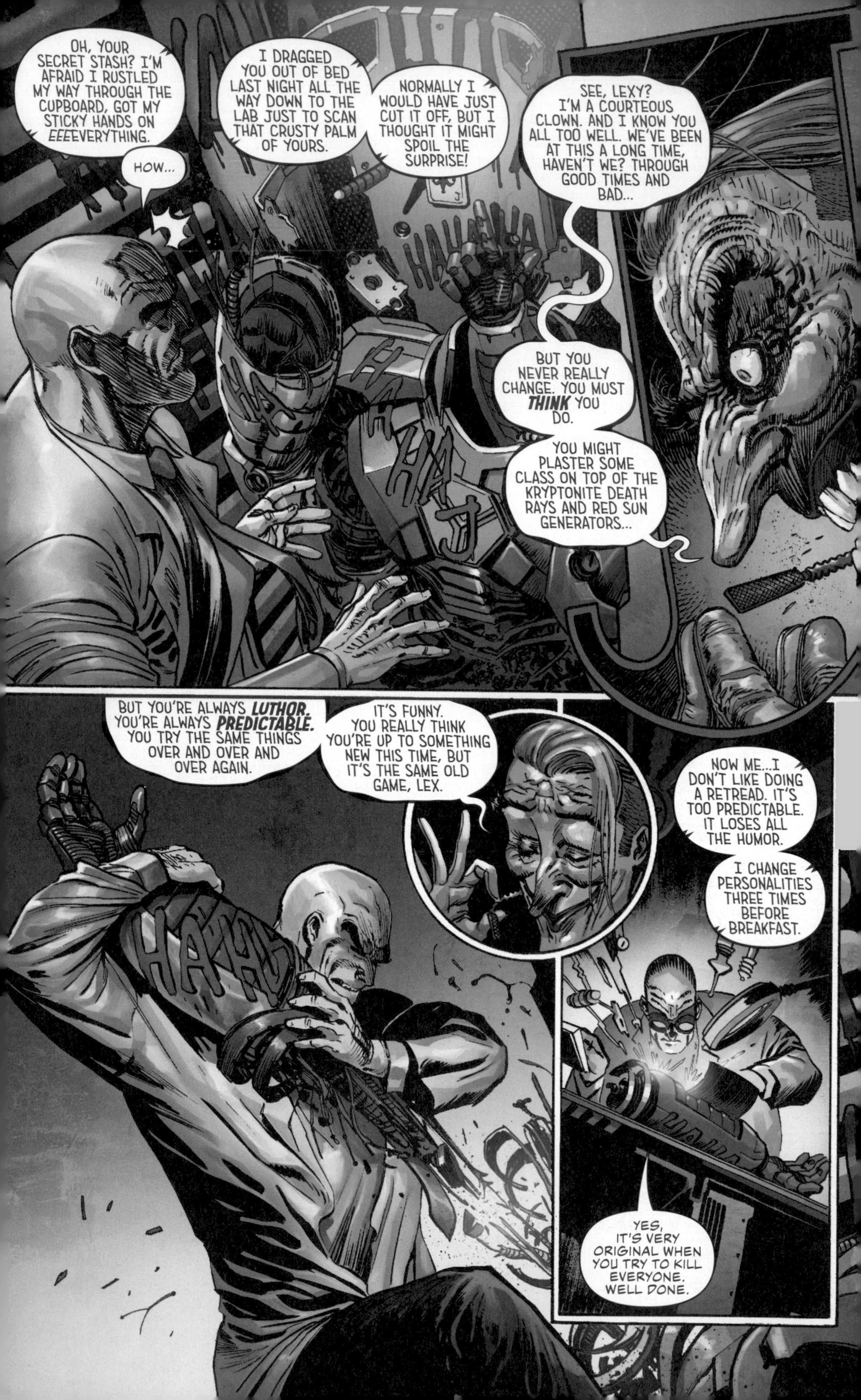
OH, YOUR SECRET STASH? I'M AFRAID I RUSTLED MY WAY THROUGH THE CUPBOARD, GOT MY STICKY HANDS ON *EEE*EVERYTHING.
HOW...
I DRAGGED YOU OUT OF BED LAST NIGHT ALL THE WAY DOWN TO THE LAB JUST TO SCAN THAT CRUSTY PALM OF YOURS.
NORMALLY I WOULD HAVE JUST CUT IT OFF, BUT I THOUGHT IT MIGHT SPOIL THE SURPRISE!
SEE, LEXY? I'M A COURTEOUS CLOWN. AND I KNOW YOU ALL TOO WELL. WE'VE BEEN AT THIS A LONG TIME, HAVEN'T WE? THROUGH GOOD TIMES AND BAD...
BUT YOU NEVER REALLY CHANGE. YOU MUST ***THINK*** YOU DO.
YOU MIGHT PLASTER SOME CLASS ON TOP OF THE KRYPTONITE DEATH RAYS AND RED SUN GENERATORS...
HAHAHA!
BUT YOU'RE ALWAYS ***LUTHOR.*** YOU'RE ALWAYS ***PREDICTABLE.*** YOU TRY THE SAME THINGS OVER AND OVER AND OVER AGAIN.
IT'S FUNNY. YOU REALLY THINK YOU'RE UP TO SOMETHING NEW THIS TIME, BUT IT'S THE SAME OLD GAME, LEX.
NOW ME...I DON'T LIKE DOING A RETREAD. IT'S TOO PREDICTABLE. IT LOSES ALL THE HUMOR.
I CHANGE PERSONALITIES THREE TIMES BEFORE BREAKFAST.
YES, IT'S VERY ORIGINAL WHEN YOU TRY TO KILL EVERYONE. WELL DONE.

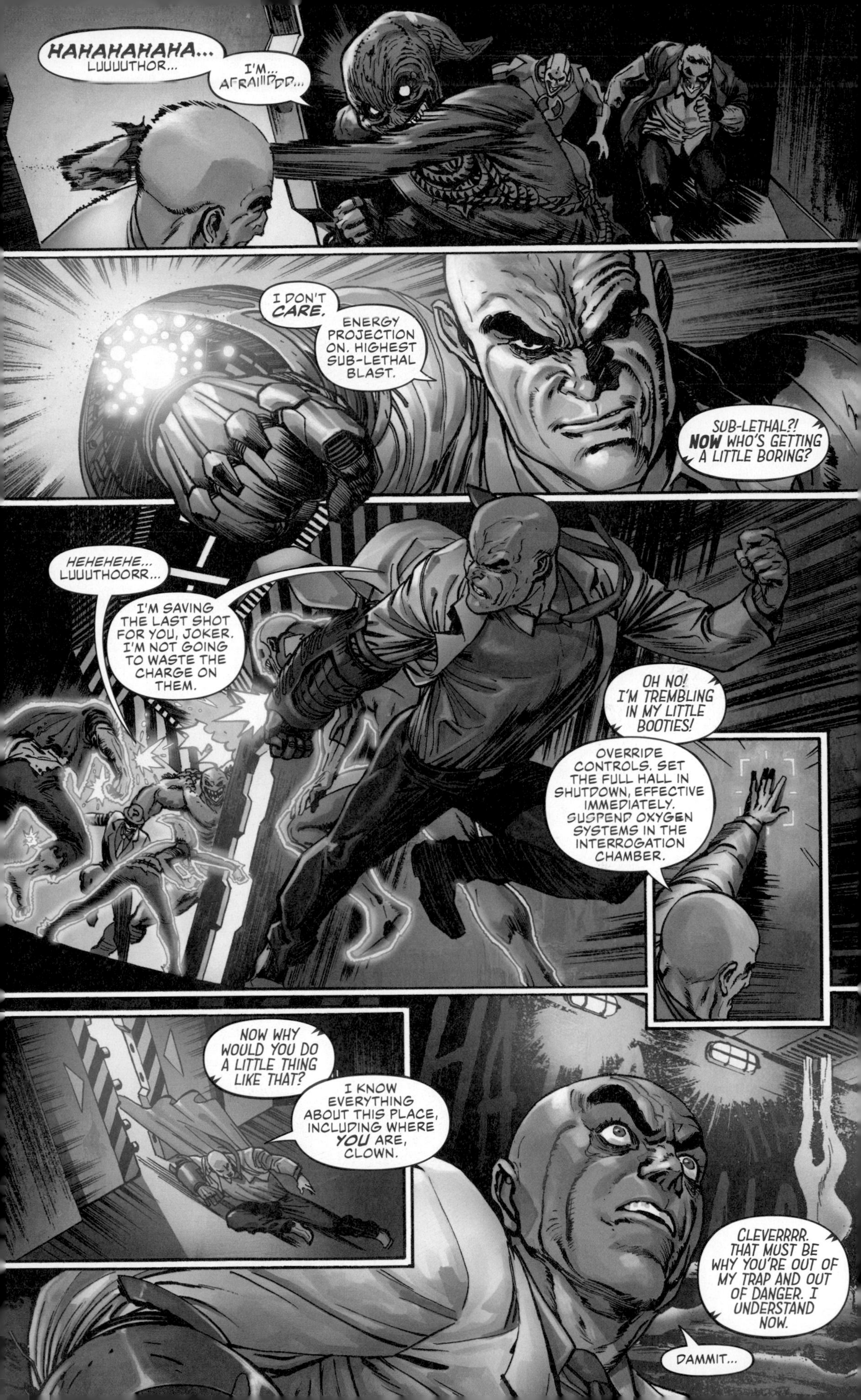
HAHAHAHAHA... LUUUUTHOR...
I'M... AFRAIIIIDDD...
I DON'T CARE.
ENERGY PROJECTION ON. HIGHEST SUB-LETHAL BLAST.
SUB-LETHAL?! NOW WHO'S GETTING A LITTLE BORING?
HEHEHEHE... LUUUTHOORR...
I'M SAVING THE LAST SHOT FOR YOU, JOKER. I'M NOT GOING TO WASTE THE CHARGE ON THEM.
OH NO! I'M TREMBLING IN MY LITTLE BOOTIES!
OVERRIDE CONTROLS. SET THE FULL HALL IN SHUTDOWN, EFFECTIVE IMMEDIATELY. SUSPEND OXYGEN SYSTEMS IN THE INTERROGATION CHAMBER.
NOW WHY WOULD YOU DO A LITTLE THING LIKE THAT?
I KNOW EVERYTHING ABOUT THIS PLACE, INCLUDING WHERE YOU ARE, CLOWN.
CLEVERRRR. THAT MUST BE WHY YOU'RE OUT OF MY TRAP AND OUT OF DANGER. I UNDERSTAND NOW.
DAMMIT...

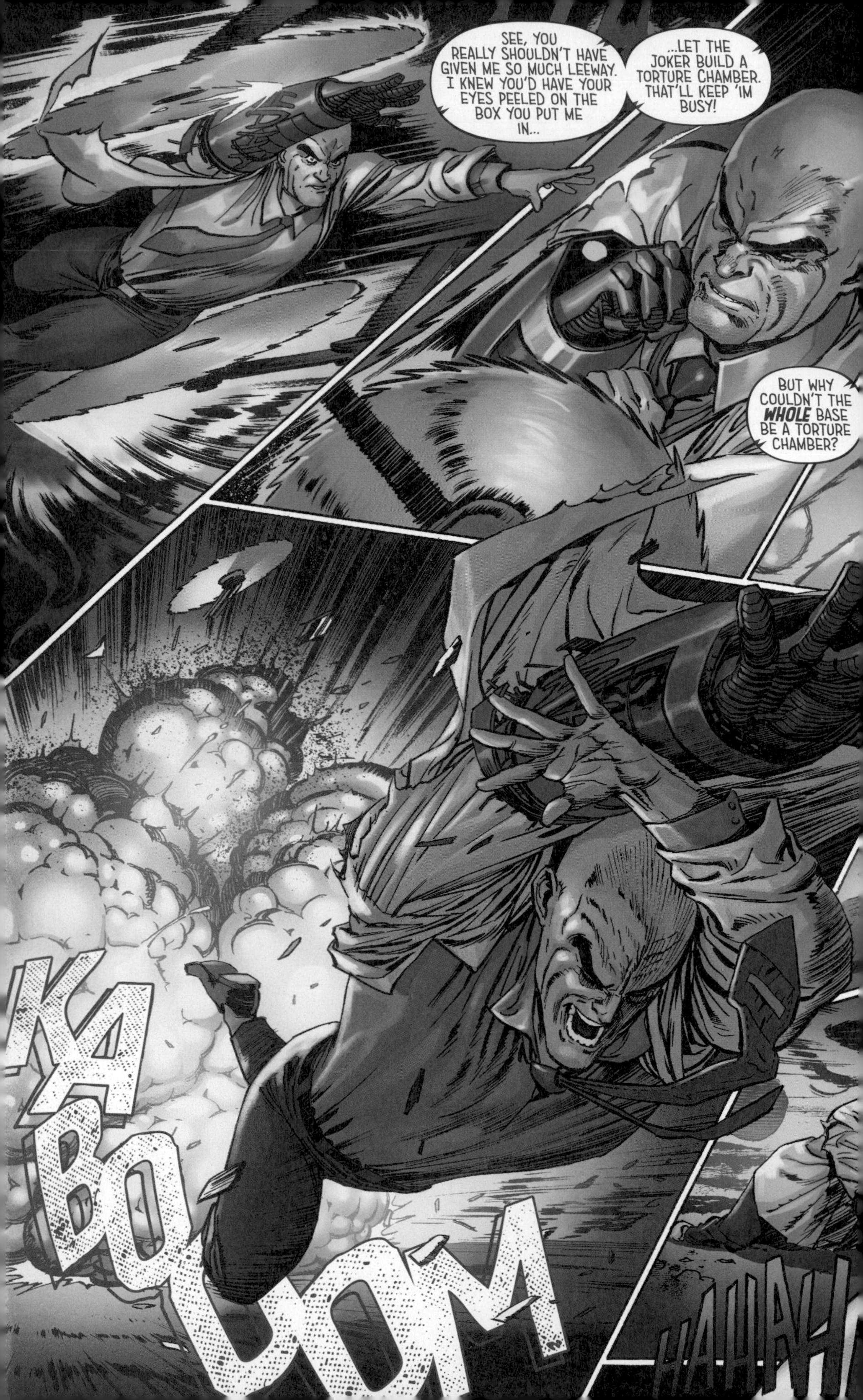
SEE, YOU REALLY SHOULDN'T HAVE GIVEN ME SO MUCH LEEWAY. I KNEW YOU'D HAVE YOUR EYES PEELED ON THE BOX YOU PUT ME IN...
...LET THE JOKER BUILD A TORTURE CHAMBER. THAT'LL KEEP 'IM BUSY!
BUT WHY COULDN'T THE WHOLE BASE BE A TORTURE CHAMBER?
KA BOOOM
HAHAH

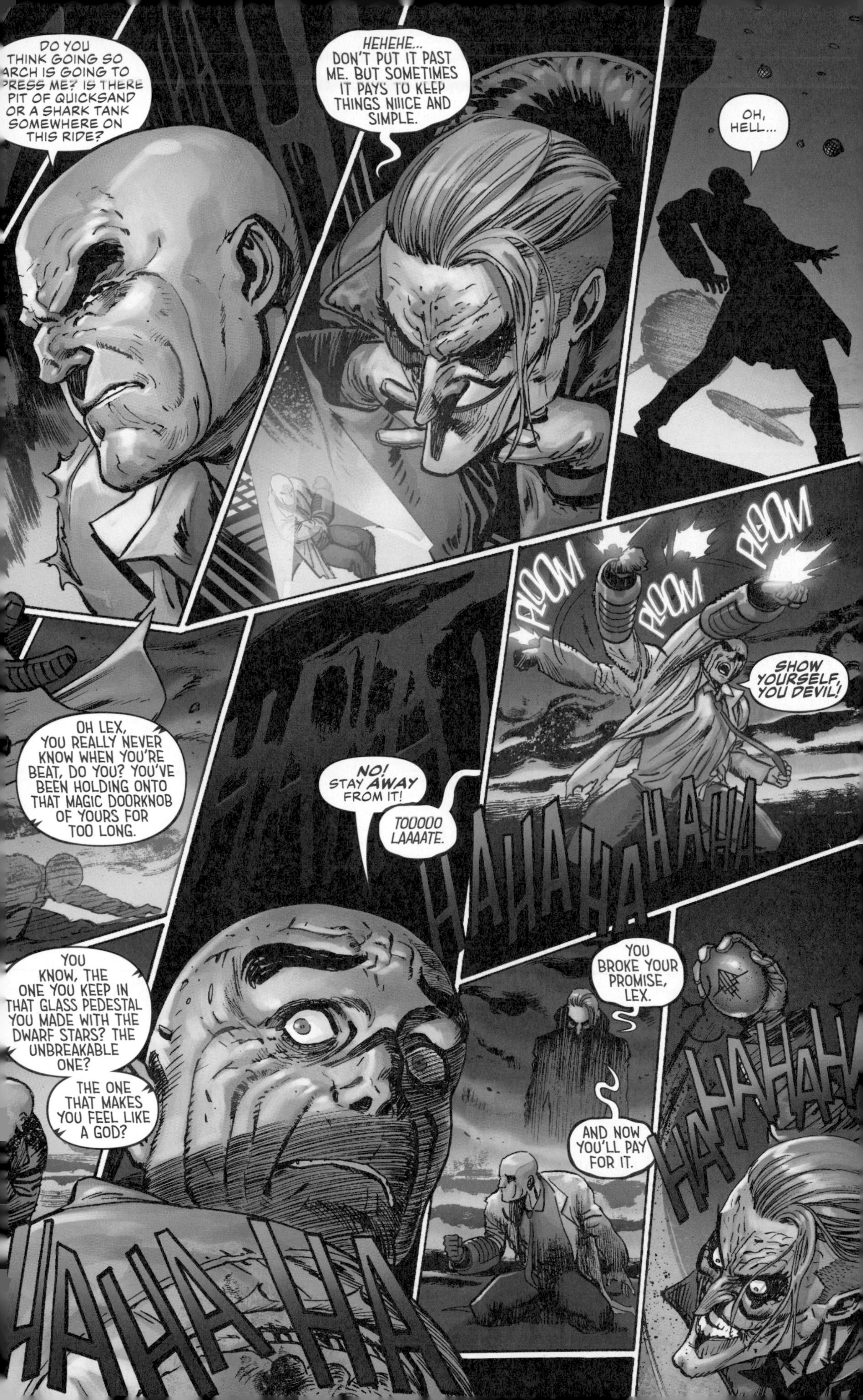
DO YOU THINK GOING SO ARCH IS GOING TO PRESS ME? IS THERE PIT OF QUICKSAND OR A SHARK TANK SOMEWHERE ON THIS RIDE?
HEHEHE... DON'T PUT IT PAST ME. BUT SOMETIMES IT PAYS TO KEEP THINGS NIIICE AND SIMPLE.
OH, HELL...
PLOOM
PLOOM
PLOOM
SHOW YOURSELF, YOU DEVIL!
OH LEX, YOU REALLY NEVER KNOW WHEN YOU'RE BEAT, DO YOU? YOU'VE BEEN HOLDING ONTO THAT MAGIC DOORKNOB OF YOURS FOR TOO LONG.
NO! STAY AWAY FROM IT!
TOOOOO LAAAATE.
HAHAHAHAHAHA
YOU KNOW, THE ONE YOU KEEP IN THAT GLASS PEDESTAL YOU MADE WITH THE DWARF STARS? THE UNBREAKABLE ONE?
THE ONE THAT MAKES YOU FEEL LIKE A GOD?
HAHAHAHA
YOU BROKE YOUR PROMISE, LEX.
AND NOW YOU'LL PAY FOR IT.
HAHAHAHA

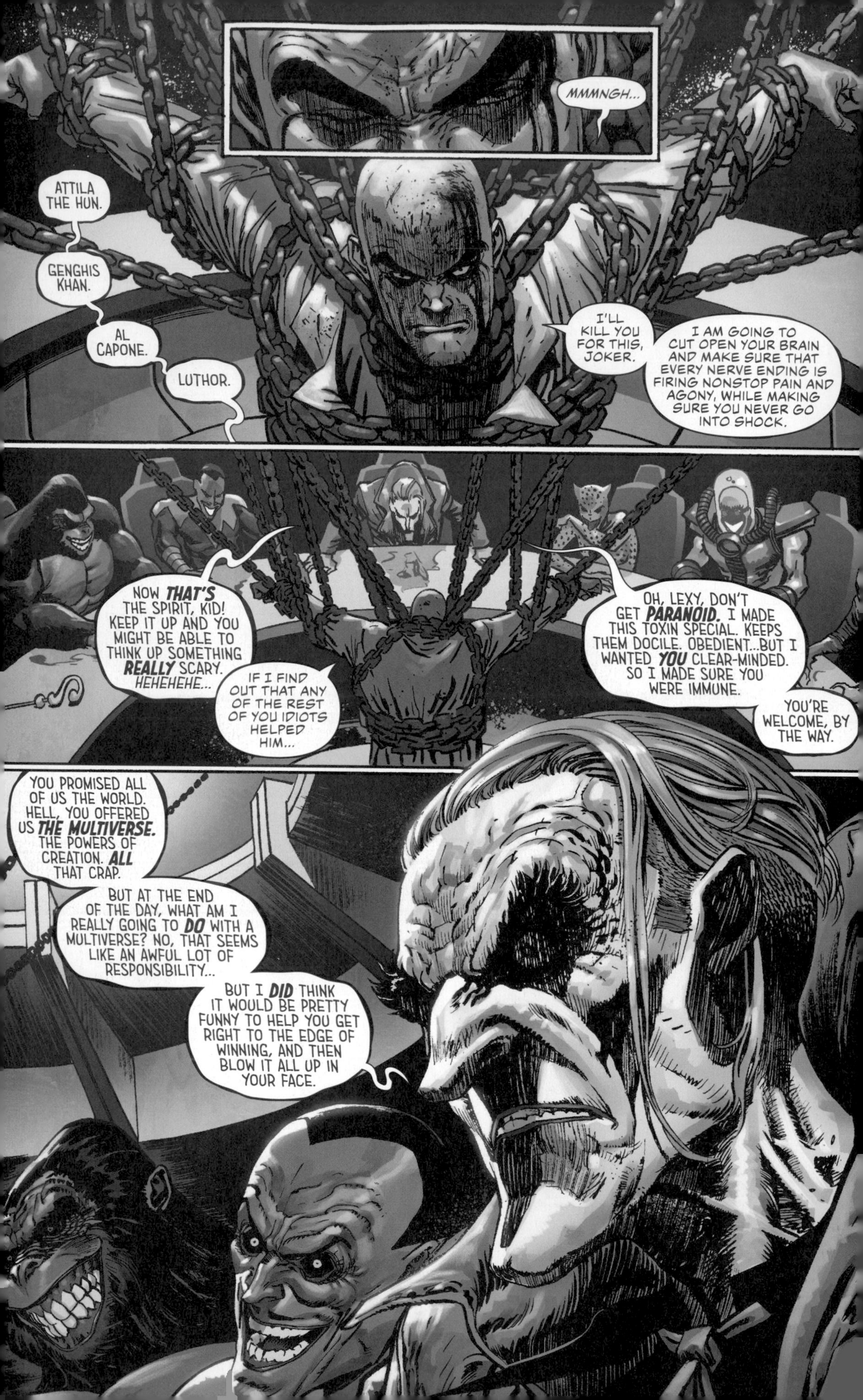

MMMNGH...
ATTILA THE HUN.
GENGHIS KHAN.
AL CAPONE.
LUTHOR.
I'LL KILL YOU FOR THIS, JOKER.
I AM GOING TO CUT OPEN YOUR BRAIN AND MAKE SURE THAT EVERY NERVE ENDING IS FIRING NONSTOP PAIN AND AGONY, WHILE MAKING SURE YOU NEVER GO INTO SHOCK.
NOW **THAT'S** THE SPIRIT, KID! KEEP IT UP AND YOU MIGHT BE ABLE TO THINK UP SOMETHING **REALLY** SCARY. HEHEHEHE...
IF I FIND OUT THAT ANY OF THE REST OF YOU IDIOTS HELPED HIM...
OH, LEXY, DON'T GET **PARANOID.** I MADE THIS TOXIN SPECIAL. KEEPS THEM DOCILE. OBEDIENT...BUT I WANTED **YOU** CLEAR-MINDED. SO I MADE SURE YOU WERE IMMUNE.
YOU'RE WELCOME, BY THE WAY.
YOU PROMISED ALL OF US THE WORLD. HELL, YOU OFFERED US **THE MULTIVERSE.** THE POWERS OF CREATION. **ALL** THAT CRAP.
BUT AT THE END OF THE DAY, WHAT AM I REALLY GOING TO **DO** WITH A MULTIVERSE? NO, THAT SEEMS LIKE AN AWFUL LOT OF RESPONSIBILITY...
BUT I **DID** THINK IT WOULD BE PRETTY FUNNY TO HELP YOU GET RIGHT TO THE EDGE OF WINNING, AND THEN BLOW IT ALL UP IN YOUR FACE.

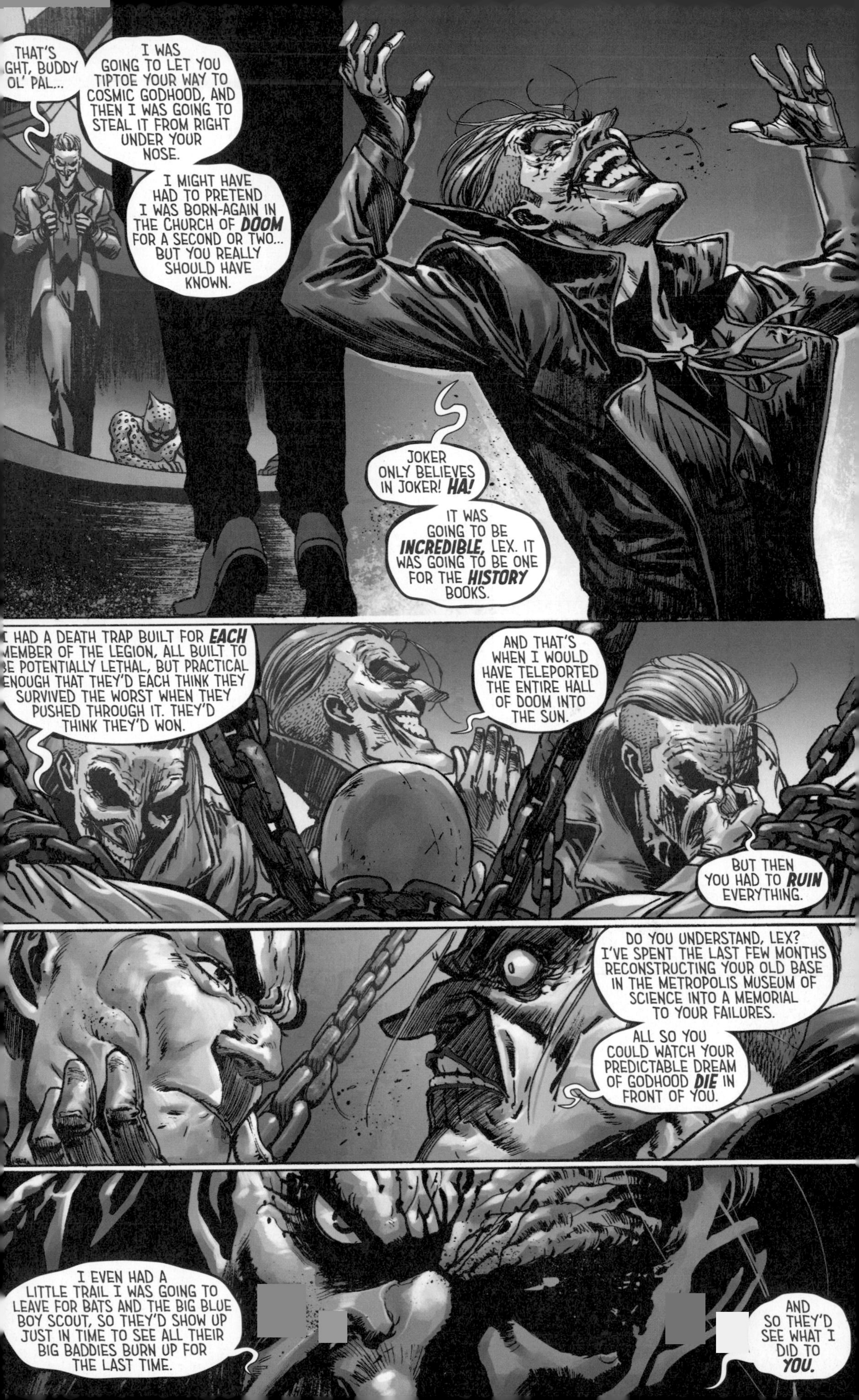
THAT'S GHT, BUDDY OL' PAL...
I WAS GOING TO LET YOU TIPTOE YOUR WAY TO COSMIC GODHOOD, AND THEN I WAS GOING TO STEAL IT FROM RIGHT UNDER YOUR NOSE.
I MIGHT HAVE HAD TO PRETEND I WAS BORN-AGAIN IN THE CHURCH OF **DOOM** FOR A SECOND OR TWO... BUT YOU REALLY SHOULD HAVE KNOWN.
JOKER ONLY BELIEVES IN JOKER! **HA!**
IT WAS GOING TO BE **INCREDIBLE,** LEX. IT WAS GOING TO BE ONE FOR THE **HISTORY** BOOKS.
I HAD A DEATH TRAP BUILT FOR **EACH** MEMBER OF THE LEGION, ALL BUILT TO BE POTENTIALLY LETHAL, BUT PRACTICAL ENOUGH THAT THEY'D EACH THINK THEY SURVIVED THE WORST WHEN THEY PUSHED THROUGH IT. THEY'D THINK THEY'D WON.
AND THAT'S WHEN I WOULD HAVE TELEPORTED THE ENTIRE HALL OF DOOM INTO THE SUN.
BUT THEN YOU HAD TO **RUIN** EVERYTHING.
DO YOU UNDERSTAND, LEX? I'VE SPENT THE LAST FEW MONTHS RECONSTRUCTING YOUR OLD BASE IN THE METROPOLIS MUSEUM OF SCIENCE INTO A MEMORIAL TO YOUR FAILURES.
ALL SO YOU COULD WATCH YOUR PREDICTABLE DREAM OF GODHOOD **DIE** IN FRONT OF YOU.
I EVEN HAD A LITTLE TRAIL I WAS GOING TO LEAVE FOR BATS AND THE BIG BLUE BOY SCOUT, SO THEY'D SHOW UP JUST IN TIME TO SEE ALL THEIR BIG BADDIES BURN UP FOR THE LAST TIME.
AND SO THEY'D SEE WHAT I DID TO **YOU.**

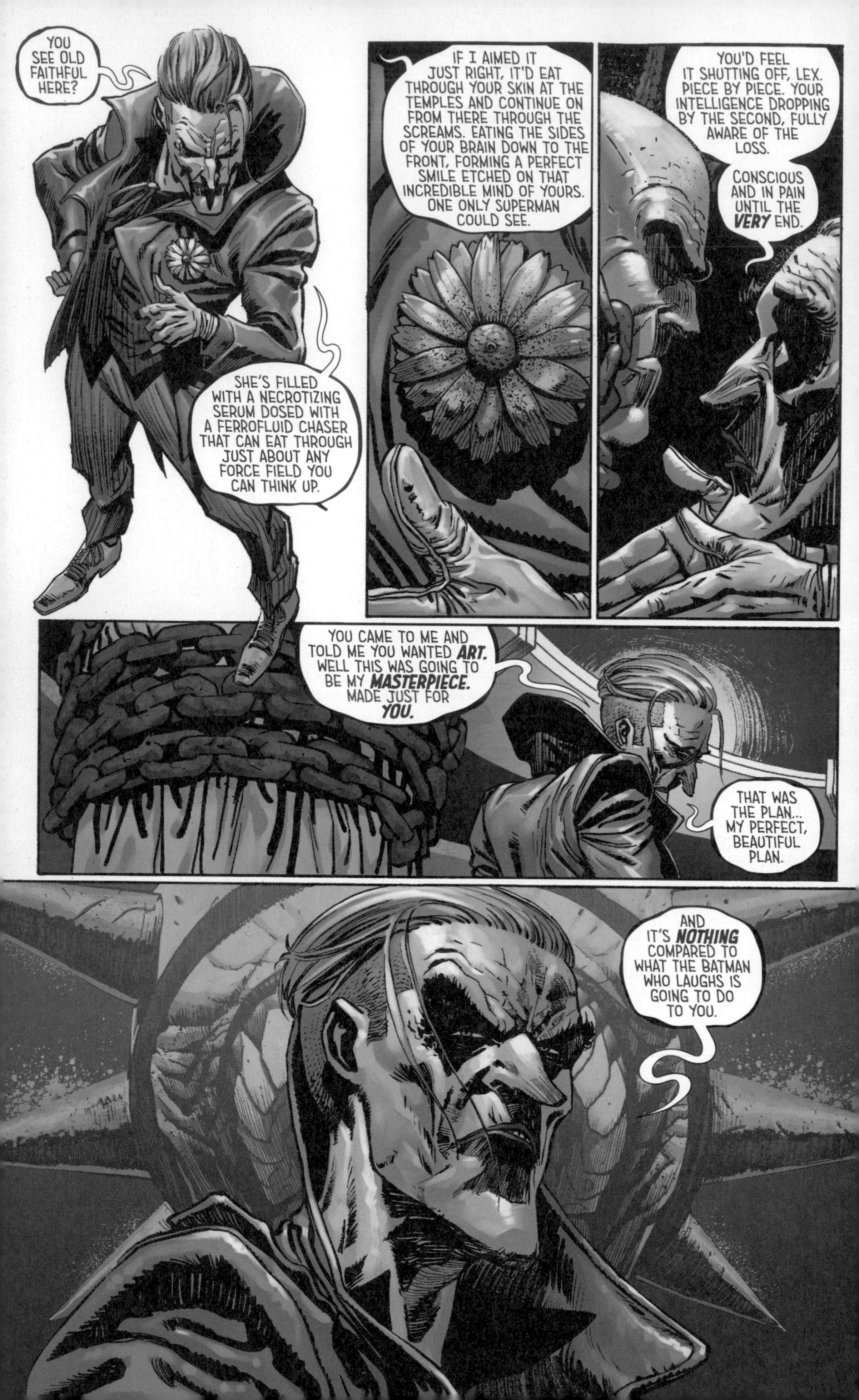
YOU SEE OLD FAITHFUL HERE?
SHE'S FILLED WITH A NECROTIZING SERUM DOSED WITH A FERROFLUID CHASER THAT CAN EAT THROUGH JUST ABOUT ANY FORCE FIELD YOU CAN THINK UP.
IF I AIMED IT JUST RIGHT, IT'D EAT THROUGH YOUR SKIN AT THE TEMPLES AND CONTINUE ON FROM THERE THROUGH THE SCREAMS. EATING THE SIDES OF YOUR BRAIN DOWN TO THE FRONT, FORMING A PERFECT SMILE ETCHED ON THAT INCREDIBLE MIND OF YOURS. ONE ONLY SUPERMAN COULD SEE.
YOU'D FEEL IT SHUTTING OFF, LEX. PIECE BY PIECE. YOUR INTELLIGENCE DROPPING BY THE SECOND, FULLY AWARE OF THE LOSS.
CONSCIOUS AND IN PAIN UNTIL THE ***VERY*** END.
YOU CAME TO ME AND TOLD ME YOU WANTED ***ART.*** WELL THIS WAS GOING TO BE MY ***MASTERPIECE.*** MADE JUST FOR ***YOU.***
THAT WAS THE PLAN... MY PERFECT, BEAUTIFUL PLAN.
AND IT'S ***NOTHING*** COMPARED TO WHAT THE BATMAN WHO LAUGHS IS GOING TO DO TO YOU.

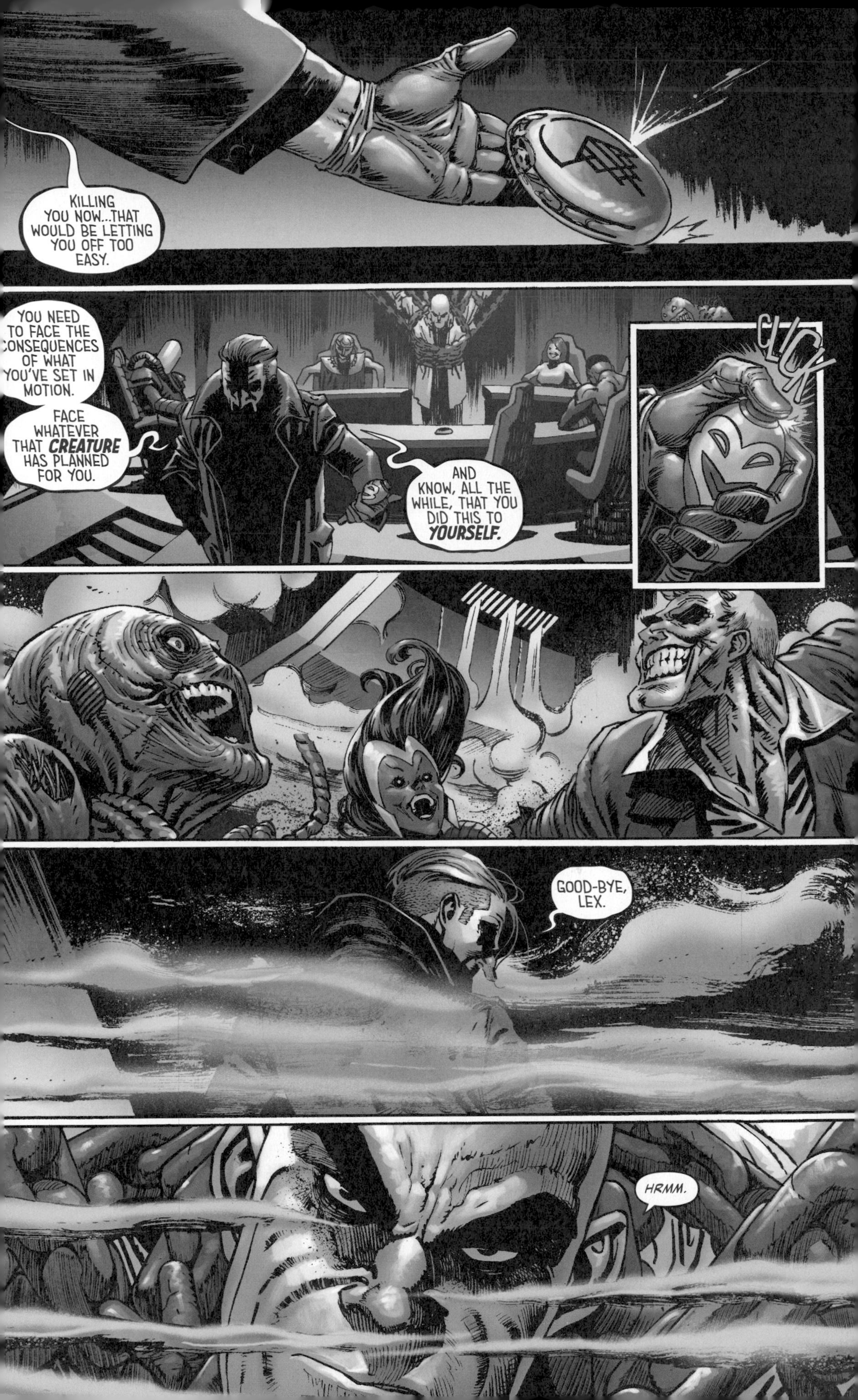
KILLING YOU NOW...THAT WOULD BE LETTING YOU OFF TOO EASY.
YOU NEED TO FACE THE CONSEQUENCES OF WHAT YOU'VE SET IN MOTION.
FACE WHATEVER THAT CREATURE HAS PLANNED FOR YOU.
AND KNOW, ALL THE WHILE, THAT YOU DID THIS TO YOURSELF.
CLICK
GOOD-BYE, LEX.
HRMM.

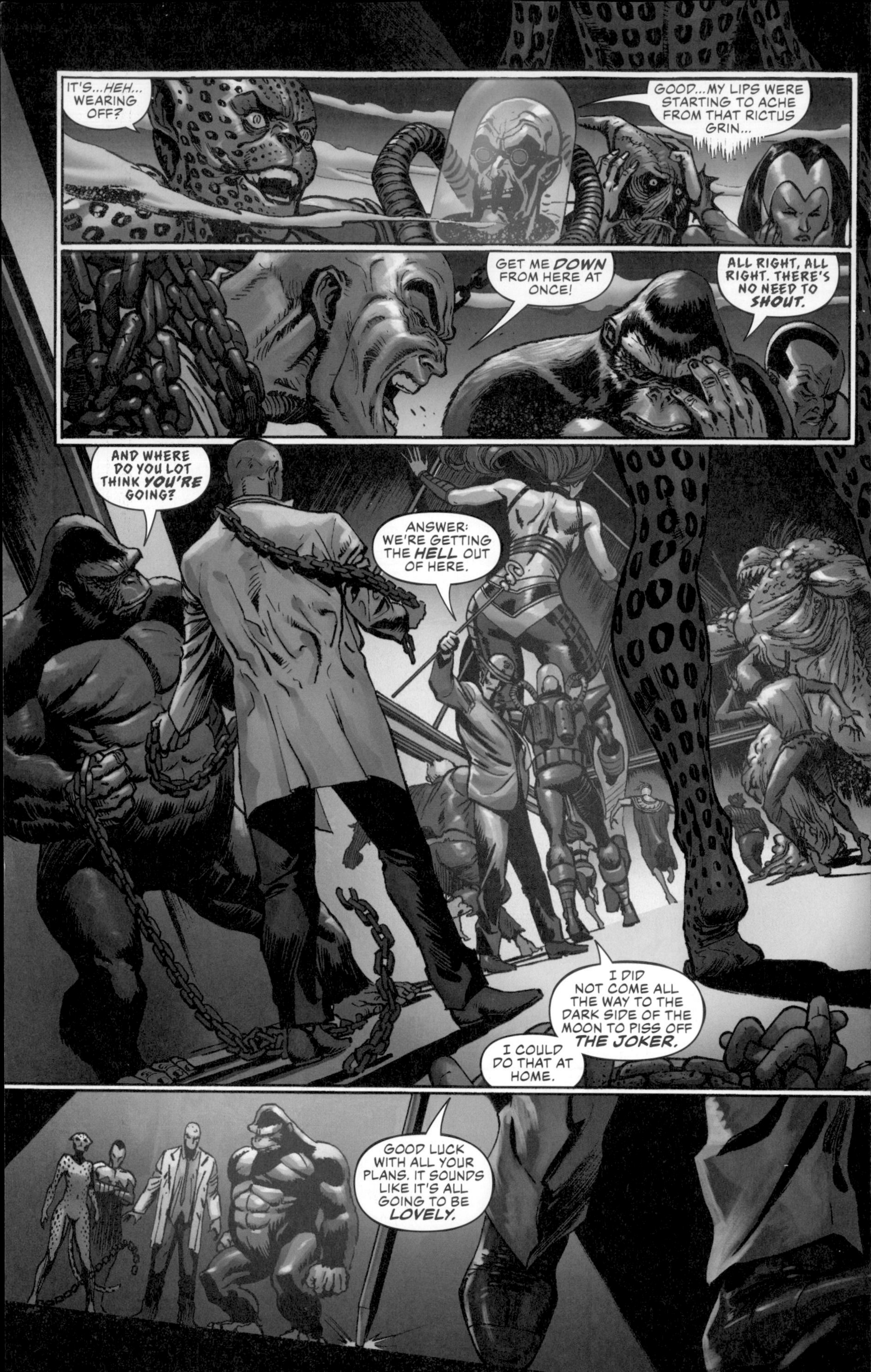

IT'S...HEH... WEARING OFF?
GOOD...MY LIPS WERE STARTING TO ACHE FROM THAT RICTUS GRIN...
GET ME DOWN FROM HERE AT ONCE!
ALL RIGHT, ALL RIGHT. THERE'S NO NEED TO SHOUT.
AND WHERE DO YOU LOT THINK YOU'RE GOING?
ANSWER: WE'RE GETTING THE HELL OUT OF HERE.
I DID NOT COME ALL THE WAY TO THE DARK SIDE OF THE MOON TO PISS OFF THE JOKER.
I COULD DO THAT AT HOME.
GOOD LUCK WITH ALL YOUR PLANS. IT SOUNDS LIKE IT'S ALL GOING TO BE LOVELY.

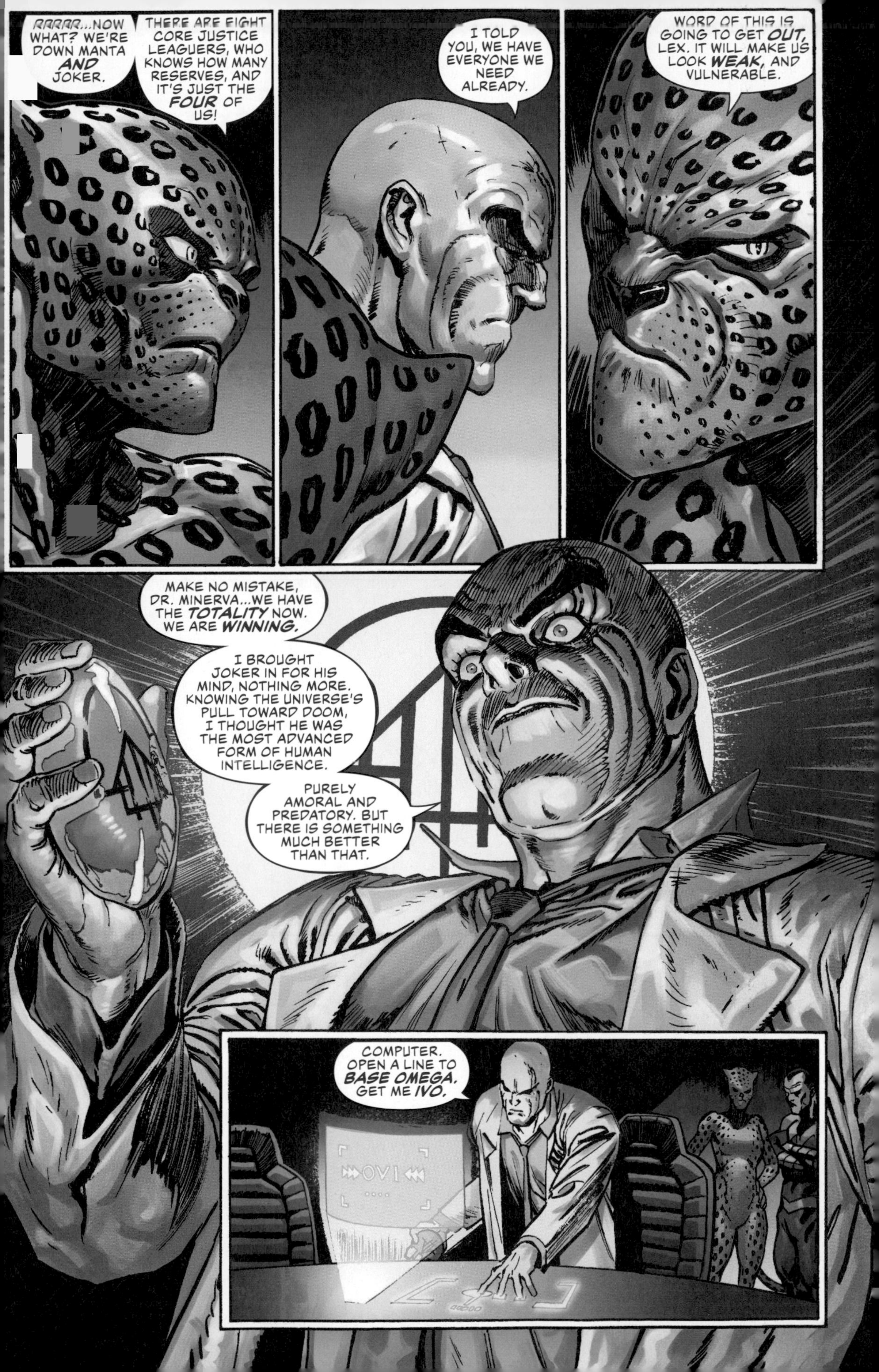

RRRRR...NOW WHAT? WE'RE DOWN MANTA AND JOKER.
THERE ARE EIGHT CORE JUSTICE LEAGUERS, WHO KNOWS HOW MANY RESERVES, AND IT'S JUST THE FOUR OF US!
I TOLD YOU, WE HAVE EVERYONE WE NEED ALREADY.
WORD OF THIS IS GOING TO GET OUT, LEX. IT WILL MAKE US LOOK WEAK, AND VULNERABLE.
MAKE NO MISTAKE, DR. MINERVA...WE HAVE THE TOTALITY NOW. WE ARE WINNING.
I BROUGHT JOKER IN FOR HIS MIND, NOTHING MORE. KNOWING THE UNIVERSE'S PULL TOWARD DOOM, I THOUGHT HE WAS THE MOST ADVANCED FORM OF HUMAN INTELLIGENCE.
PURELY AMORAL AND PREDATORY. BUT THERE IS SOMETHING MUCH BETTER THAN THAT.
COMPUTER. OPEN A LINE TO BASE OMEGA. GET ME IVO.
OVI

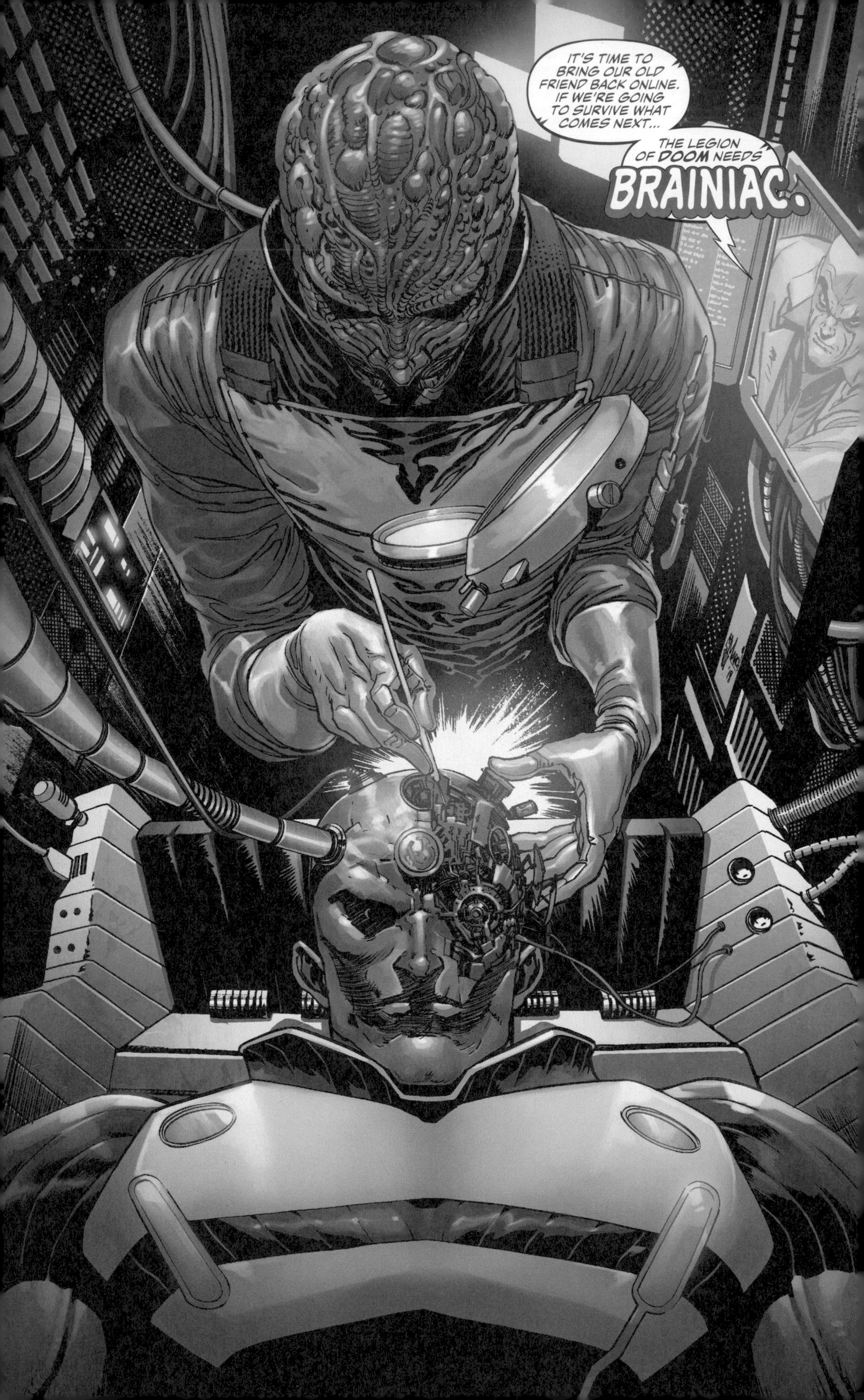
IT'S TIME TO BRING OUR OLD FRIEND BACK ONLINE. IF WE'RE GOING TO SURVIVE WHAT COMES NEXT...
THE LEGION OF DOOM NEEDS BRAINIAC.

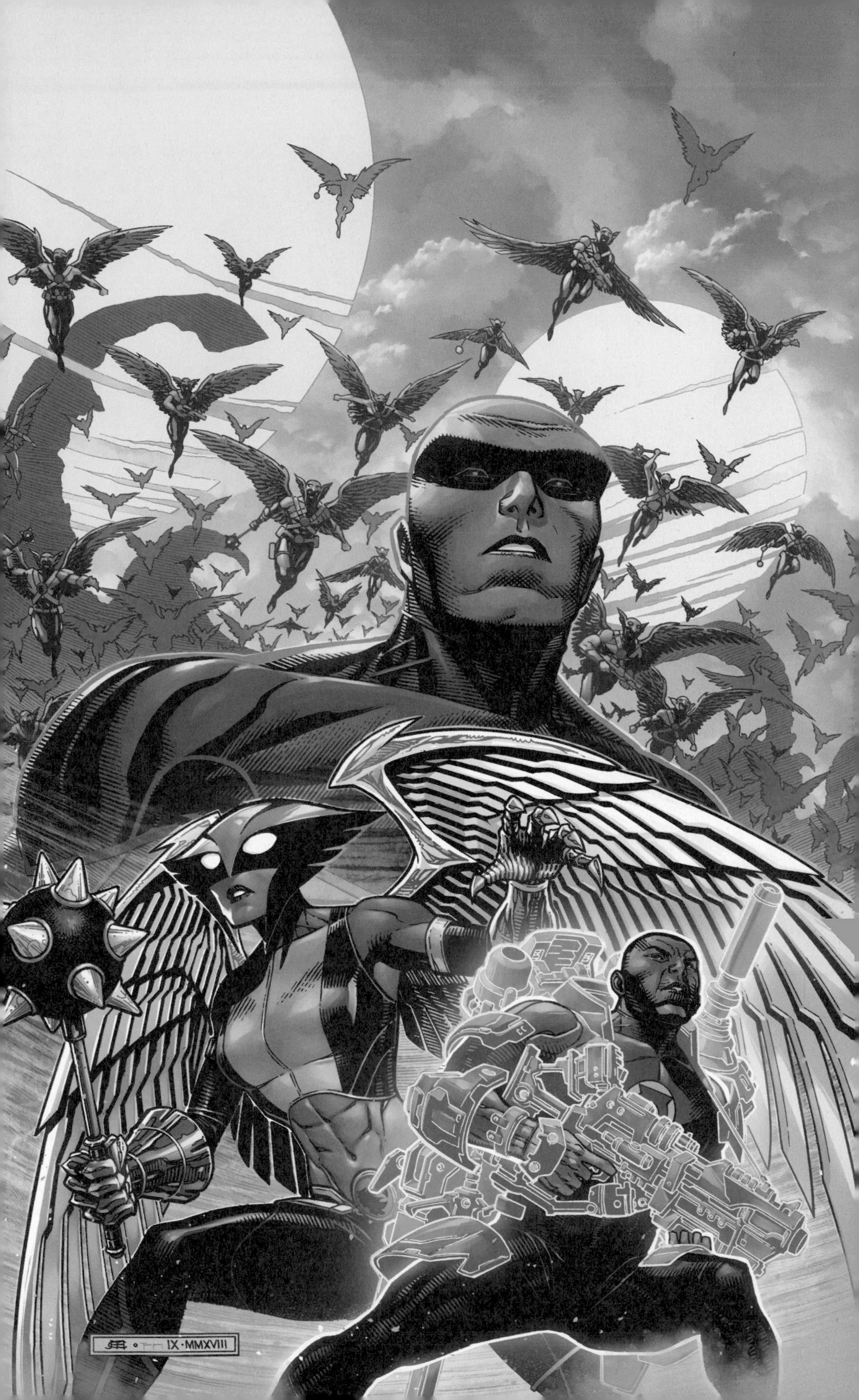
IX · MMXVIII

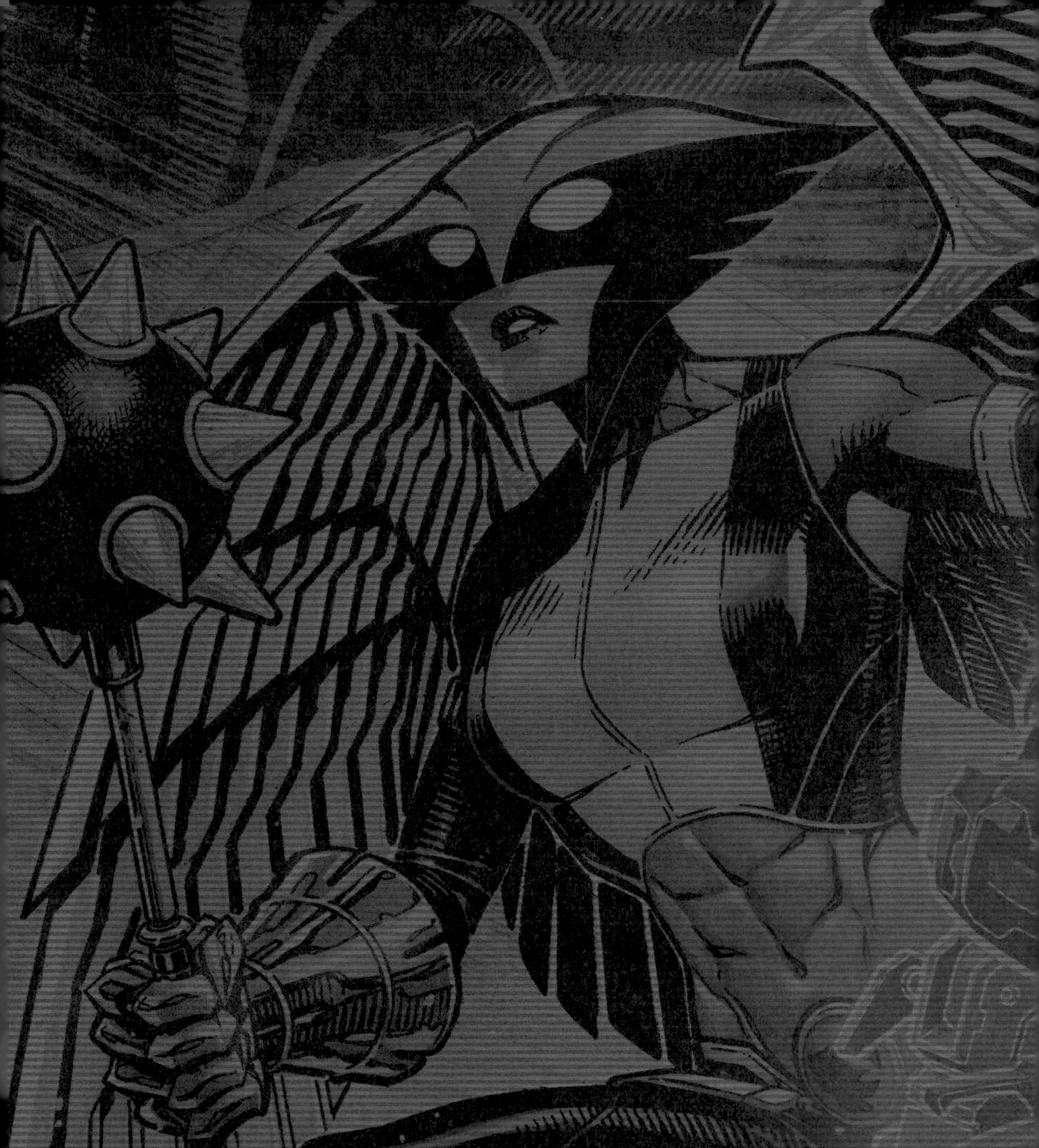

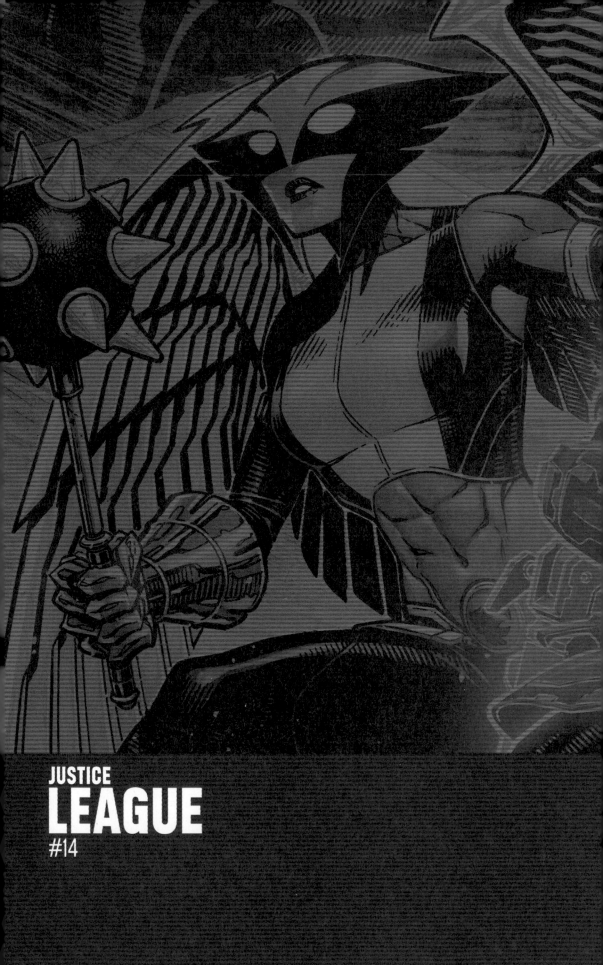

JUSTICE
LEAGUE
#14

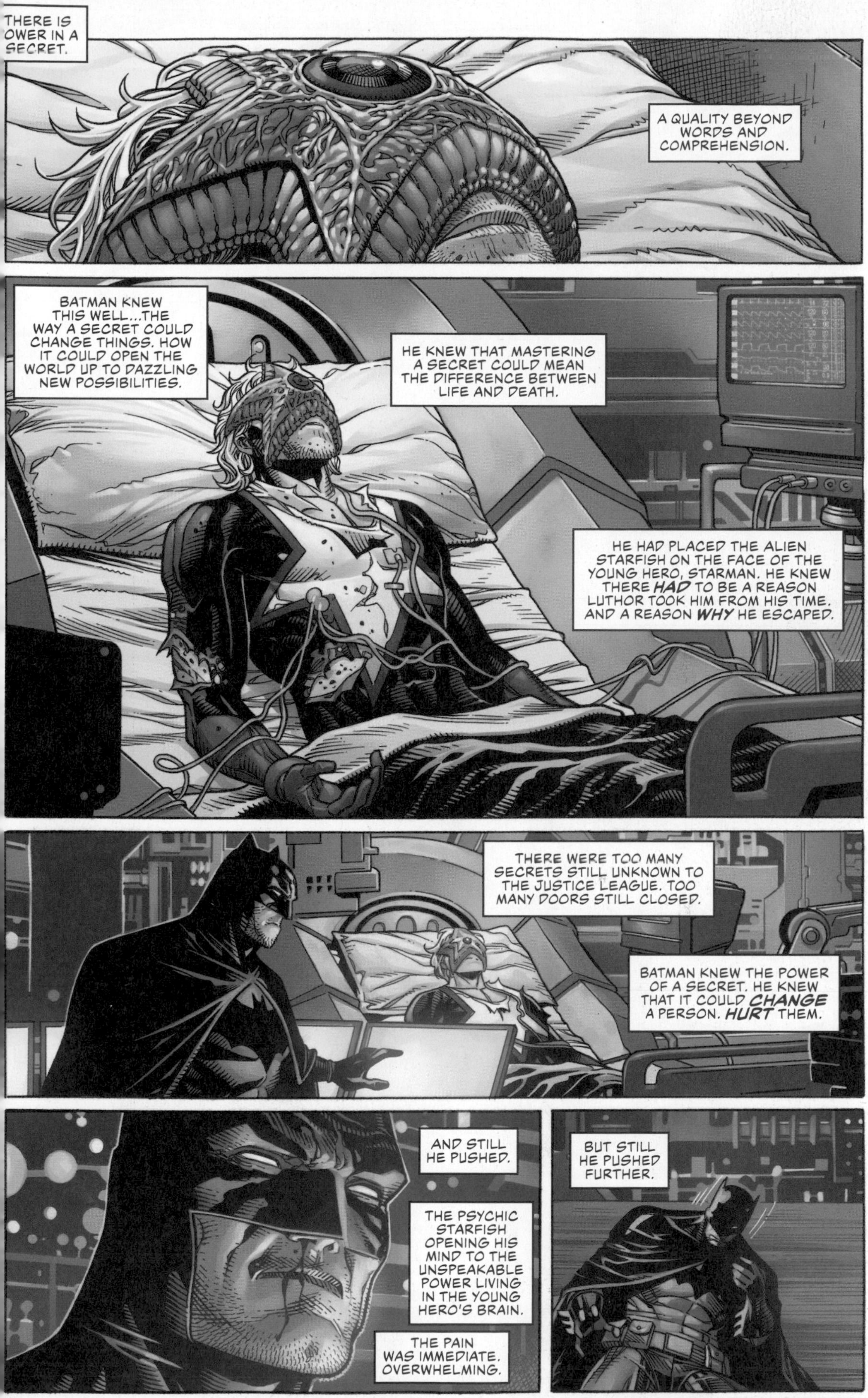

THERE IS OWER IN A SECRET.
A QUALITY BEYOND WORDS AND COMPREHENSION.
BATMAN KNEW THIS WELL...THE WAY A SECRET COULD CHANGE THINGS. HOW IT COULD OPEN THE WORLD UP TO DAZZLING NEW POSSIBILITIES.
HE KNEW THAT MASTERING A SECRET COULD MEAN THE DIFFERENCE BETWEEN LIFE AND DEATH.
HE HAD PLACED THE ALIEN STARFISH ON THE FACE OF THE YOUNG HERO, STARMAN. HE KNEW THERE HAD TO BE A REASON LUTHOR TOOK HIM FROM HIS TIME. AND A REASON WHY HE ESCAPED.
THERE WERE TOO MANY SECRETS STILL UNKNOWN TO THE JUSTICE LEAGUE. TOO MANY DOORS STILL CLOSED.
BATMAN KNEW THE POWER OF A SECRET. HE KNEW THAT IT COULD CHANGE A PERSON. HURT THEM.
AND STILL HE PUSHED.
THE PSYCHIC STARFISH OPENING HIS MIND TO THE UNSPEAKABLE POWER LIVING IN THE YOUNG HERO'S BRAIN.
THE PAIN WAS IMMEDIATE. OVERWHELMING.
BUT STILL HE PUSHED FURTHER.

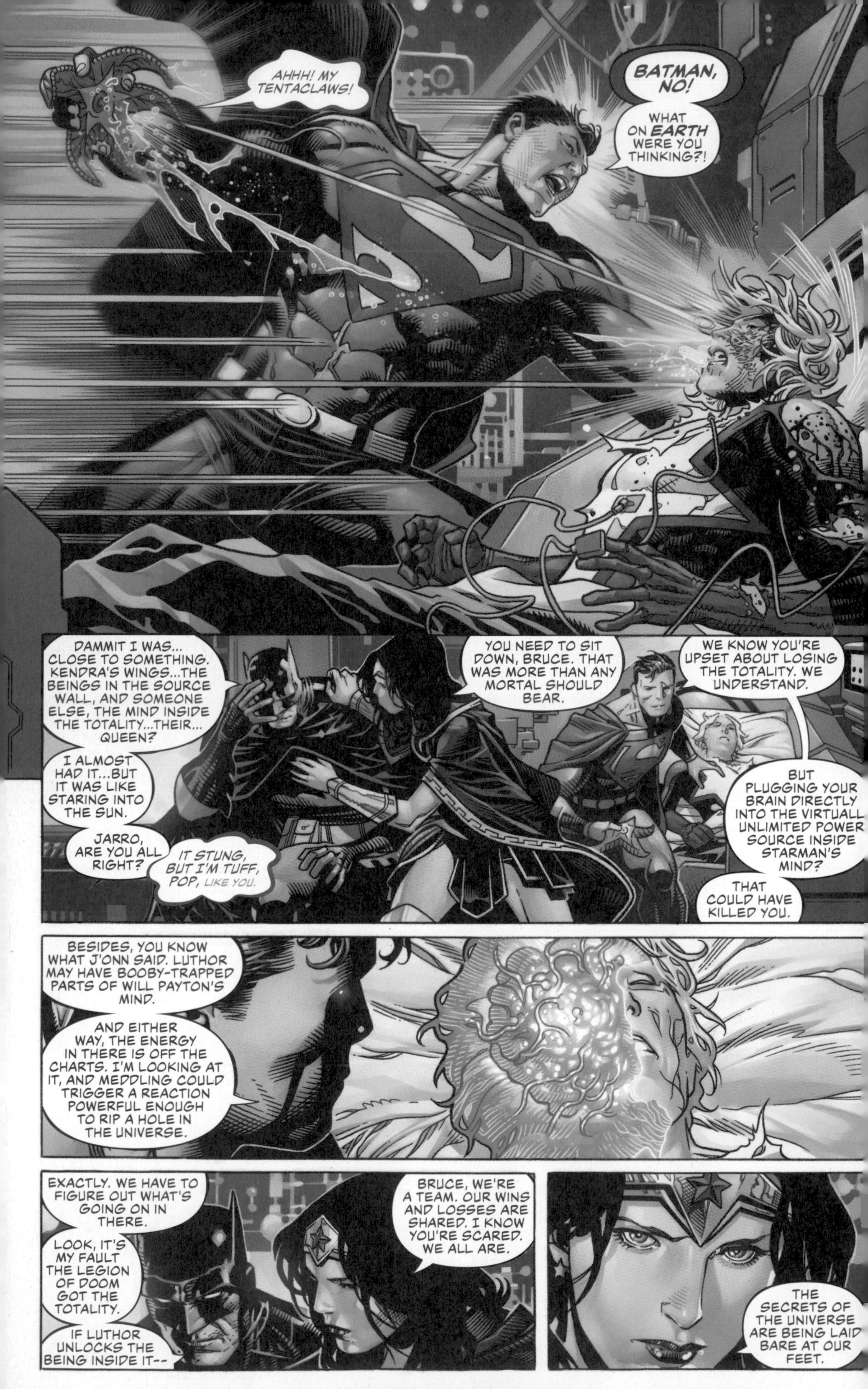
AHHH! MY TENTACLAWS!
BATMAN, NO!
WHAT ON EARTH WERE YOU THINKING?!
DAMMIT I WAS... CLOSE TO SOMETHING. KENDRA'S WINGS...THE BEINGS IN THE SOURCE WALL, AND SOMEONE ELSE, THE MIND INSIDE THE TOTALITY...THEIR... QUEEN?
I ALMOST HAD IT...BUT IT WAS LIKE STARING INTO THE SUN.
JARRO, ARE YOU ALL RIGHT?
IT STUNG, BUT I'M TUFF, POP, LIKE YOU.
YOU NEED TO SIT DOWN, BRUCE. THAT WAS MORE THAN ANY MORTAL SHOULD BEAR.
WE KNOW YOU'RE UPSET ABOUT LOSING THE TOTALITY. WE UNDERSTAND.
BUT PLUGGING YOUR BRAIN DIRECTLY INTO THE VIRTUALL UNLIMITED POWER SOURCE INSIDE STARMAN'S MIND?
THAT COULD HAVE KILLED YOU.
BESIDES, YOU KNOW WHAT J'ONN SAID. LUTHOR MAY HAVE BOOBY-TRAPPED PARTS OF WILL PAYTON'S MIND.
AND EITHER WAY, THE ENERGY IN THERE IS OFF THE CHARTS. I'M LOOKING AT IT, AND MEDDLING COULD TRIGGER A REACTION POWERFUL ENOUGH TO RIP A HOLE IN THE UNIVERSE.
EXACTLY. WE HAVE TO FIGURE OUT WHAT'S GOING ON IN THERE.
LOOK, IT'S MY FAULT THE LEGION OF DOOM GOT THE TOTALITY.
IF LUTHOR UNLOCKS THE BEING INSIDE IT--
BRUCE, WE'RE A TEAM. OUR WINS AND LOSSES ARE SHARED. I KNOW YOU'RE SCARED. WE ALL ARE.
THE SECRETS OF THE UNIVERSE ARE BEING LAID BARE AT OUR FEET.

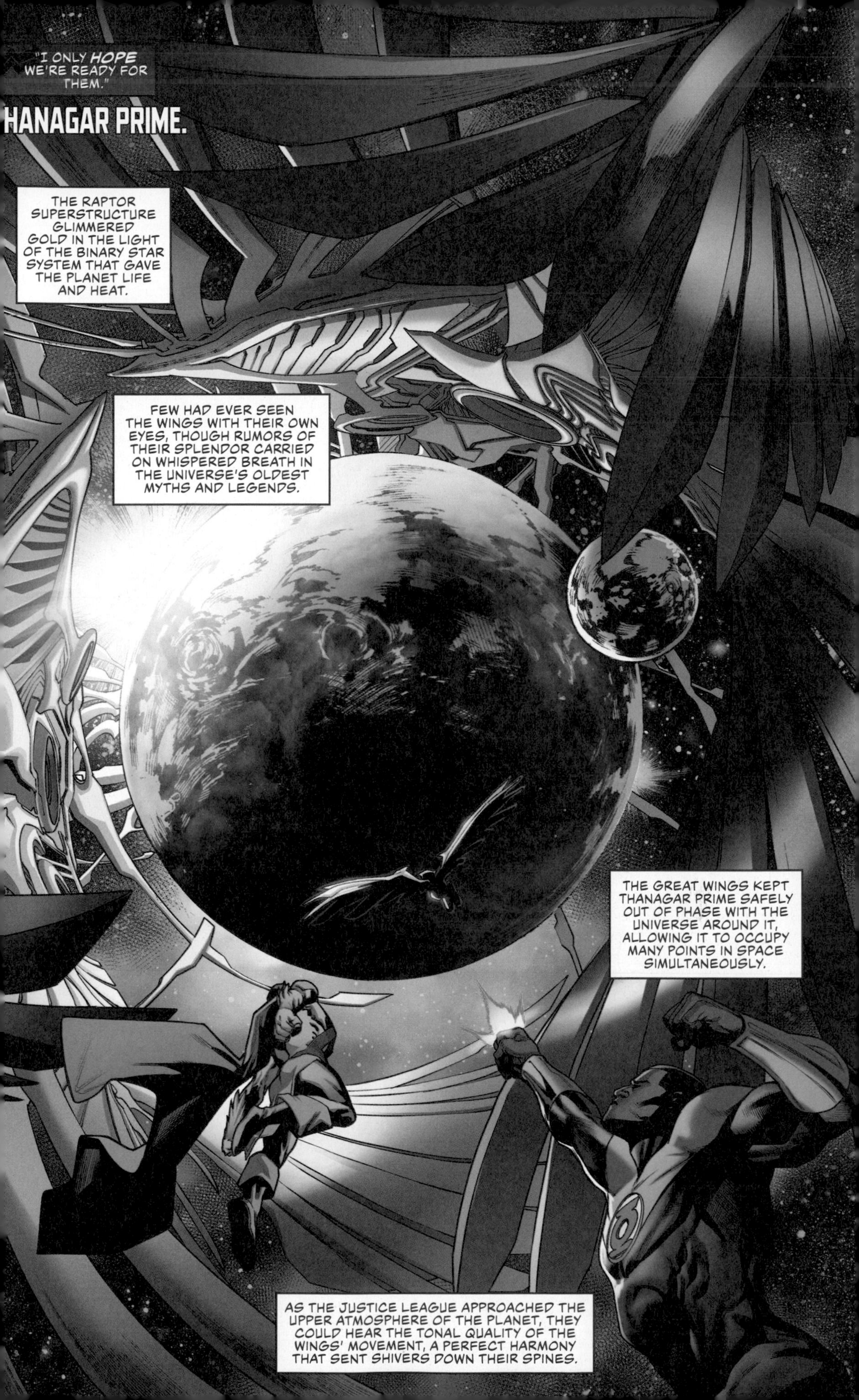
"I ONLY HOPE WE'RE READY FOR THEM."
HANAGAR PRIME.
THE RAPTOR SUPERSTRUCTURE GLIMMERED GOLD IN THE LIGHT OF THE BINARY STAR SYSTEM THAT GAVE THE PLANET LIFE AND HEAT.
FEW HAD EVER SEEN THE WINGS WITH THEIR OWN EYES, THOUGH RUMORS OF THEIR SPLENDOR CARRIED ON WHISPERED BREATH IN THE UNIVERSE'S OLDEST MYTHS AND LEGENDS.
THE GREAT WINGS KEPT THANAGAR PRIME SAFELY OUT OF PHASE WITH THE UNIVERSE AROUND IT, ALLOWING IT TO OCCUPY MANY POINTS IN SPACE SIMULTANEOUSLY.
AS THE JUSTICE LEAGUE APPROACHED THE UPPER ATMOSPHERE OF THE PLANET, THEY COULD HEAR THE TONAL QUALITY OF THE WINGS' MOVEMENT, A PERFECT HARMONY THAT SENT SHIVERS DOWN THEIR SPINES.

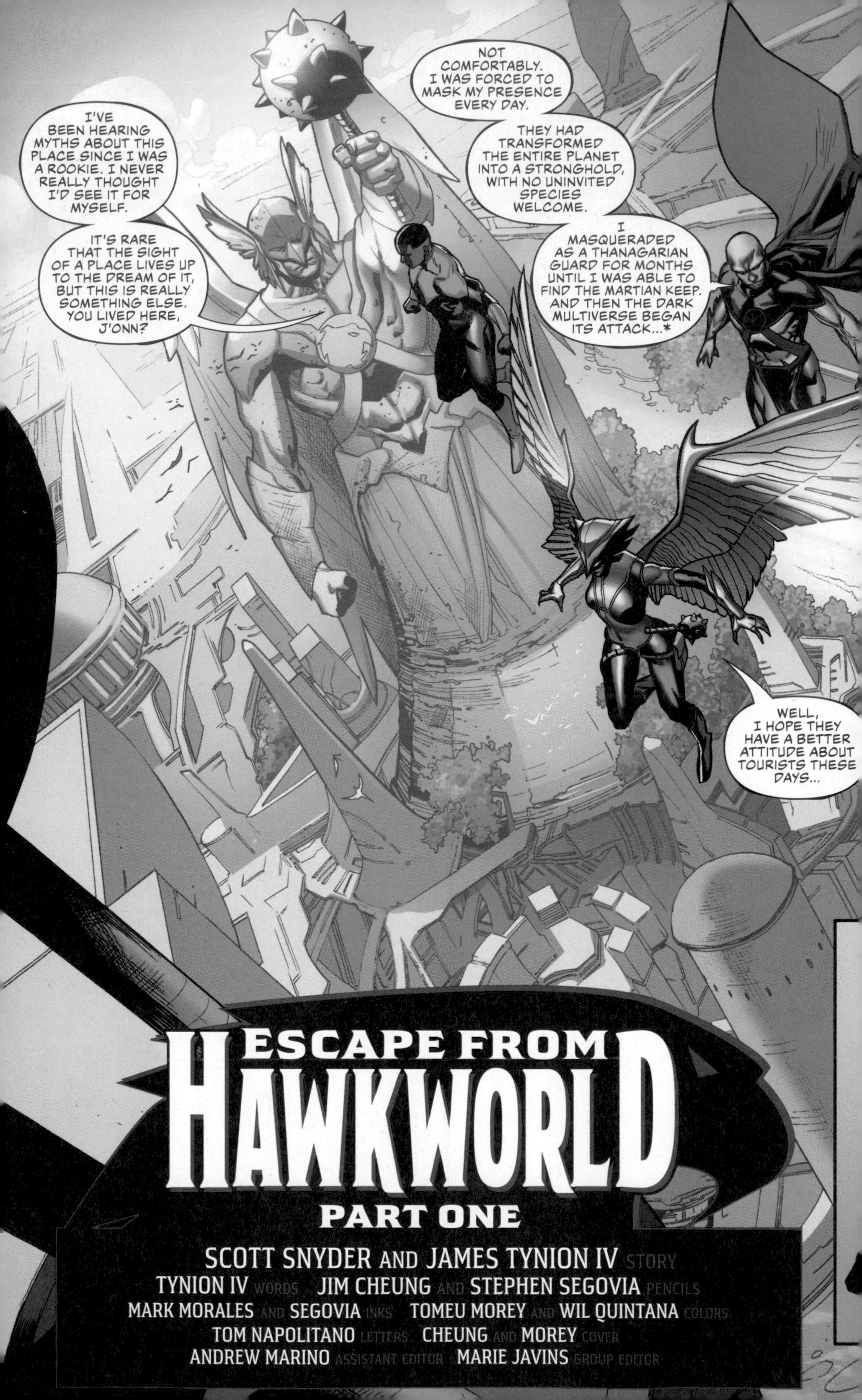
I'VE BEEN HEARING MYTHS ABOUT THIS PLACE SINCE I WAS A ROOKIE. I NEVER REALLY THOUGHT I'D SEE IT FOR MYSELF.
IT'S RARE THAT THE SIGHT OF A PLACE LIVES UP TO THE DREAM OF IT, BUT THIS IS REALLY SOMETHING ELSE. YOU LIVED HERE, J'ONN?
NOT COMFORTABLY. I WAS FORCED TO MASK MY PRESENCE EVERY DAY.
THEY HAD TRANSFORMED THE ENTIRE PLANET INTO A STRONGHOLD, WITH NO UNINVITED SPECIES WELCOME.
I MASQUERADED AS A THANAGARIAN GUARD FOR MONTHS UNTIL I WAS ABLE TO FIND THE MARTIAN KEEP. AND THEN THE DARK MULTIVERSE BEGAN ITS ATTACK...*
WELL, I HOPE THEY HAVE A BETTER ATTITUDE ABOUT TOURISTS THESE DAYS...
ESCAPE FROM
HAWKWORLD
PART ONE
SCOTT SNYDER AND JAMES TYNION IV STORY
TYNION IV WORDS JIM CHEUNG AND STEPHEN SEGOVIA PENCILS
MARK MORALES AND SEGOVIA INKS TOMEU MOREY AND WIL QUINTANA COLORS
TOM NAPOLITANO LETTERS CHEUNG AND MOREY COVER
ANDREW MARINO ASSISTANT EDITOR MARIE JAVINS GROUP EDITOR

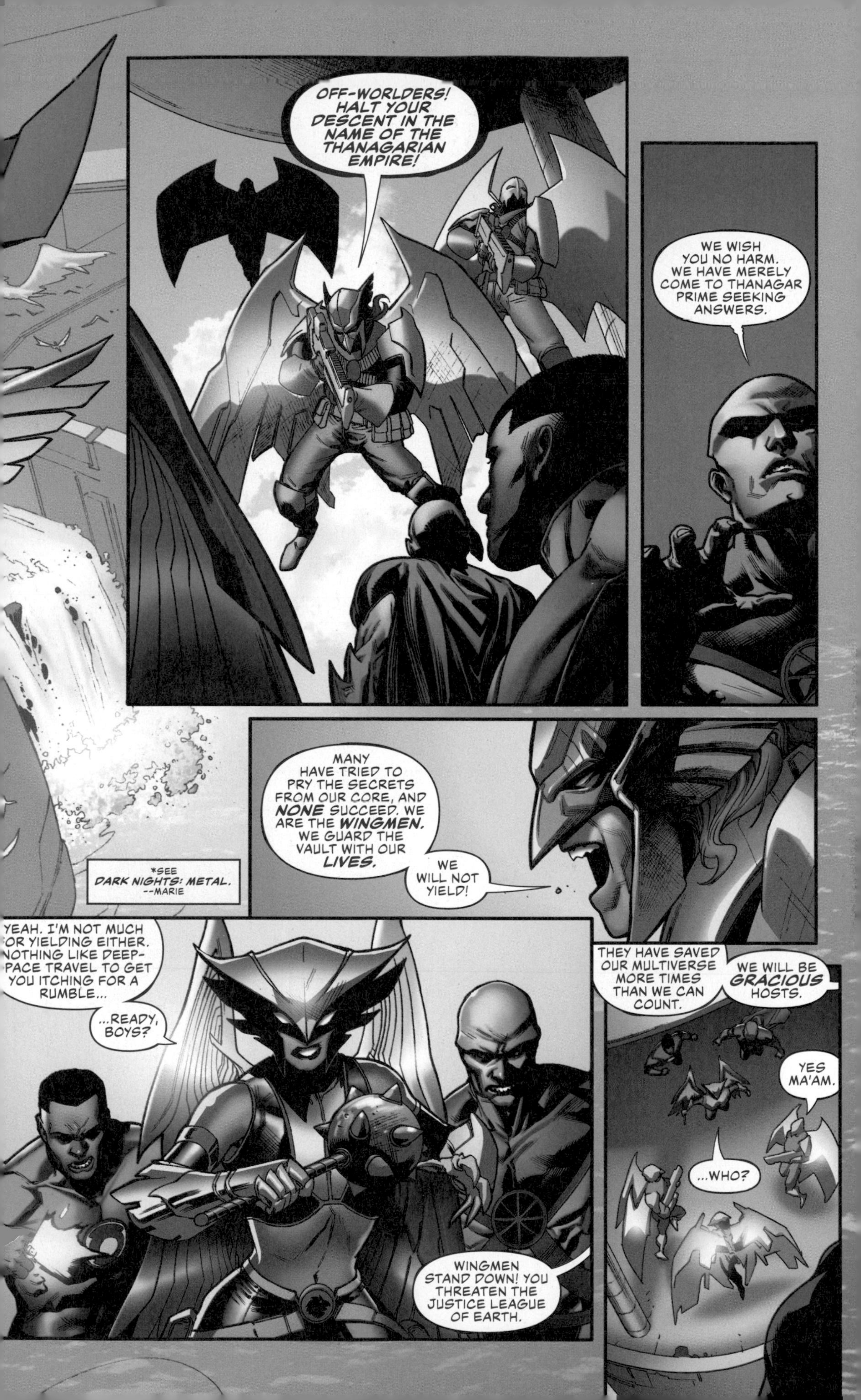
OFF-WORLDERS! HALT YOUR DESCENT IN THE NAME OF THE THANAGARIAN EMPIRE!
WE WISH YOU NO HARM. WE HAVE MERELY COME TO THANAGAR PRIME SEEKING ANSWERS.
MANY HAVE TRIED TO PRY THE SECRETS FROM OUR CORE, AND NONE SUCCEED. WE ARE THE WINGMEN. WE GUARD THE VAULT WITH OUR LIVES.
WE WILL NOT YIELD!
*SEE DARK NIGHTS: METAL. --MARIE
YEAH. I'M NOT MUCH FOR YIELDING EITHER. NOTHING LIKE DEEP-SPACE TRAVEL TO GET YOU ITCHING FOR A RUMBLE...
...READY, BOYS?
WINGMEN STAND DOWN! YOU THREATEN THE JUSTICE LEAGUE OF EARTH.
THEY HAVE SAVED OUR MULTIVERSE MORE TIMES THAN WE CAN COUNT.
WE WILL BE GRACIOUS HOSTS.
YES MA'AM.
...WHO?

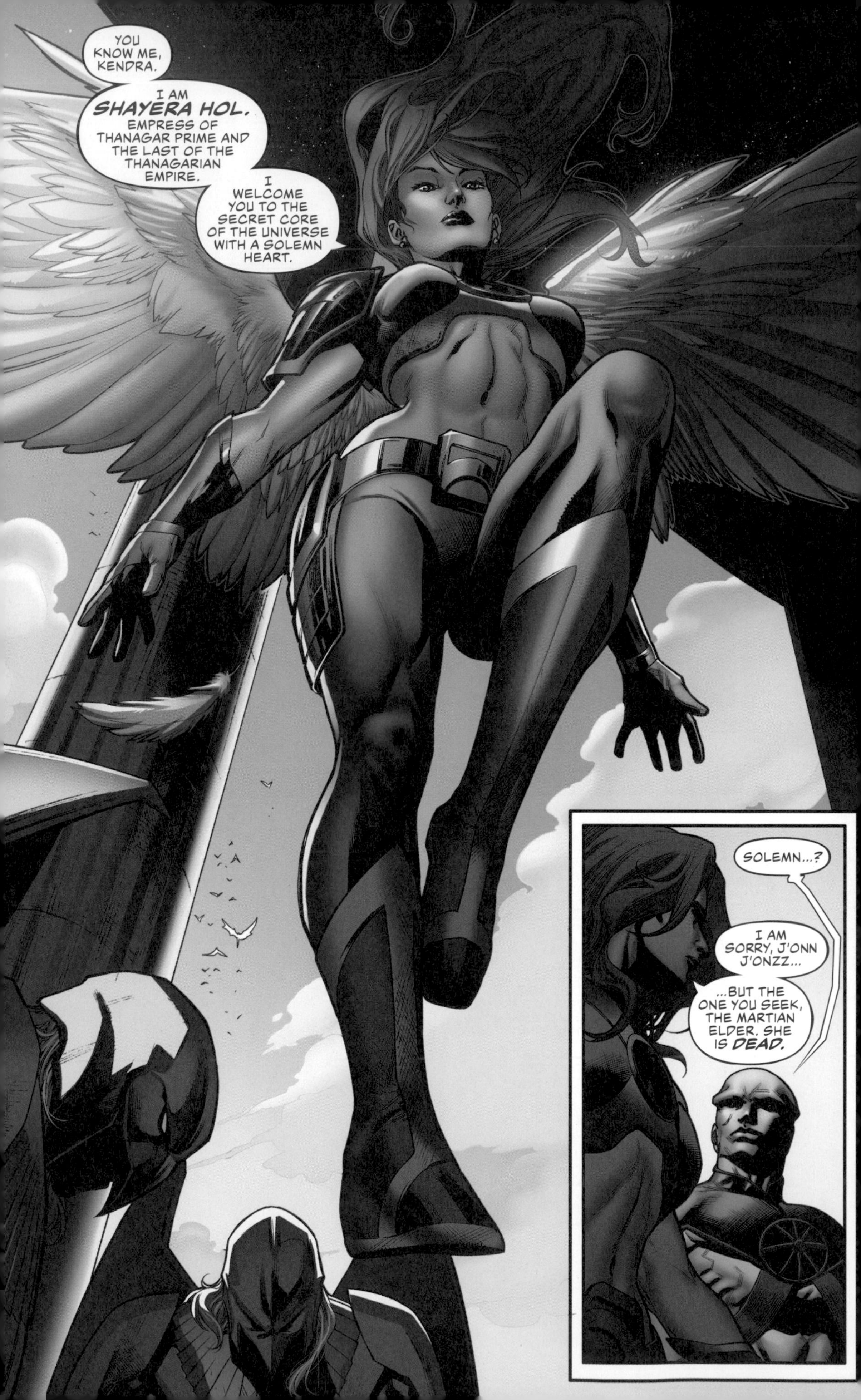
YOU KNOW ME, KENDRA.
I AM SHAYERA HOL. EMPRESS OF THANAGAR PRIME AND THE LAST OF THE THANAGARIAN EMPIRE.
I WELCOME YOU TO THE SECRET CORE OF THE UNIVERSE WITH A SOLEMN HEART.
SOLEMN...?
I AM SORRY, J'ONN J'ONZZ...
...BUT THE ONE YOU SEEK, THE MARTIAN ELDER. SHE IS DEAD.

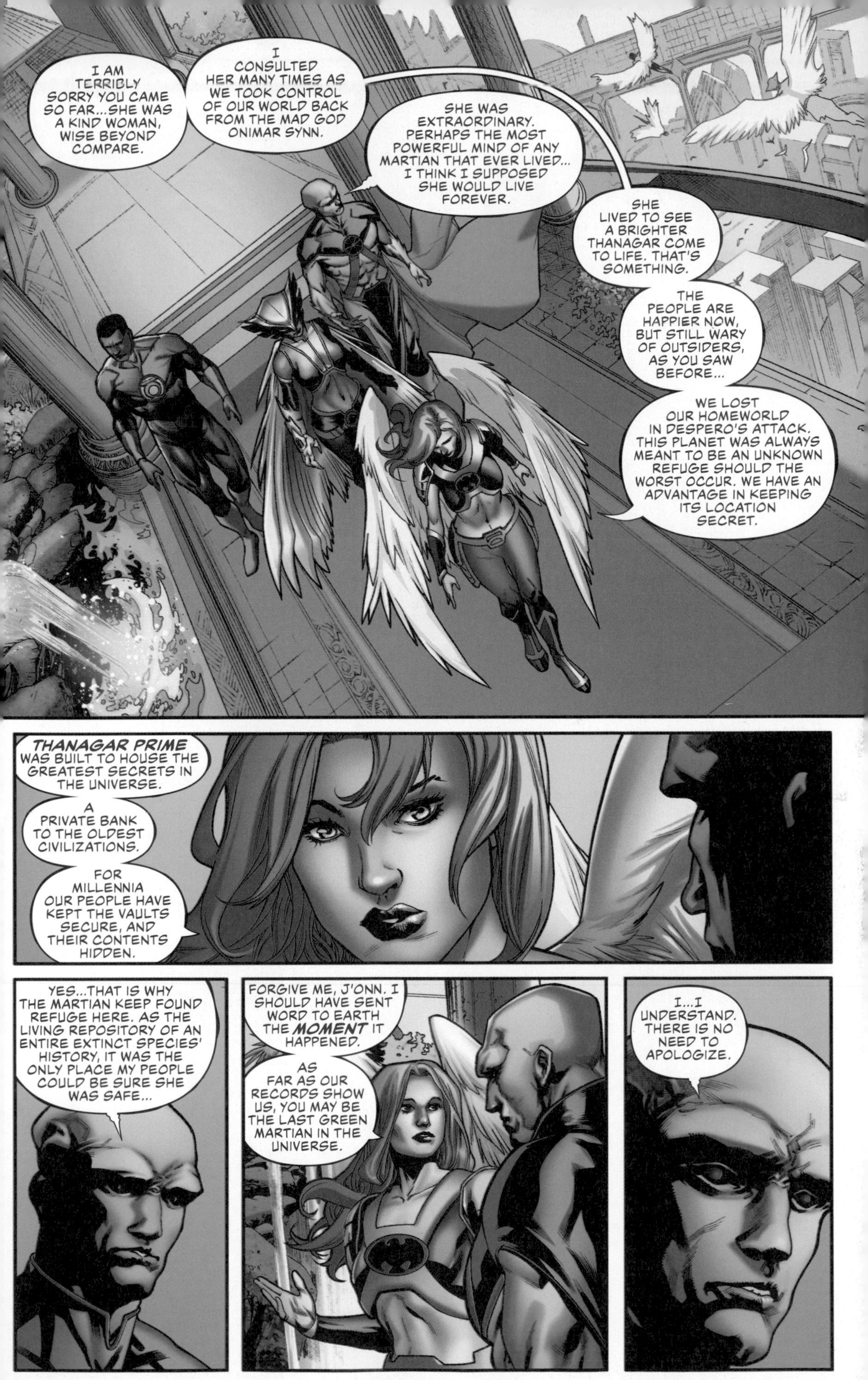
I AM TERRIBLY SORRY YOU CAME SO FAR...SHE WAS A KIND WOMAN, WISE BEYOND COMPARE.
I CONSULTED HER MANY TIMES AS WE TOOK CONTROL OF OUR WORLD BACK FROM THE MAD GOD ONIMAR SYNN.
SHE WAS EXTRAORDINARY. PERHAPS THE MOST POWERFUL MIND OF ANY MARTIAN THAT EVER LIVED... I THINK I SUPPOSED SHE WOULD LIVE FOREVER.
SHE LIVED TO SEE A BRIGHTER THANAGAR COME TO LIFE. THAT'S SOMETHING.
THE PEOPLE ARE HAPPIER NOW, BUT STILL WARY OF OUTSIDERS, AS YOU SAW BEFORE...
WE LOST OUR HOMEWORLD IN DESPERO'S ATTACK. THIS PLANET WAS ALWAYS MEANT TO BE AN UNKNOWN REFUGE SHOULD THE WORST OCCUR. WE HAVE AN ADVANTAGE IN KEEPING ITS LOCATION SECRET.
THANAGAR PRIME WAS BUILT TO HOUSE THE GREATEST SECRETS IN THE UNIVERSE.
A PRIVATE BANK TO THE OLDEST CIVILIZATIONS.
FOR MILLENNIA OUR PEOPLE HAVE KEPT THE VAULTS SECURE, AND THEIR CONTENTS HIDDEN.
YES...THAT IS WHY THE MARTIAN KEEP FOUND REFUGE HERE. AS THE LIVING REPOSITORY OF AN ENTIRE EXTINCT SPECIES' HISTORY, IT WAS THE ONLY PLACE MY PEOPLE COULD BE SURE SHE WAS SAFE...
FORGIVE ME, J'ONN. I SHOULD HAVE SENT WORD TO EARTH THE *MOMENT* IT HAPPENED.
AS FAR AS OUR RECORDS SHOW US, YOU MAY BE THE LAST GREEN MARTIAN IN THE UNIVERSE.
I...I UNDERSTAND. THERE IS NO NEED TO APOLOGIZE.

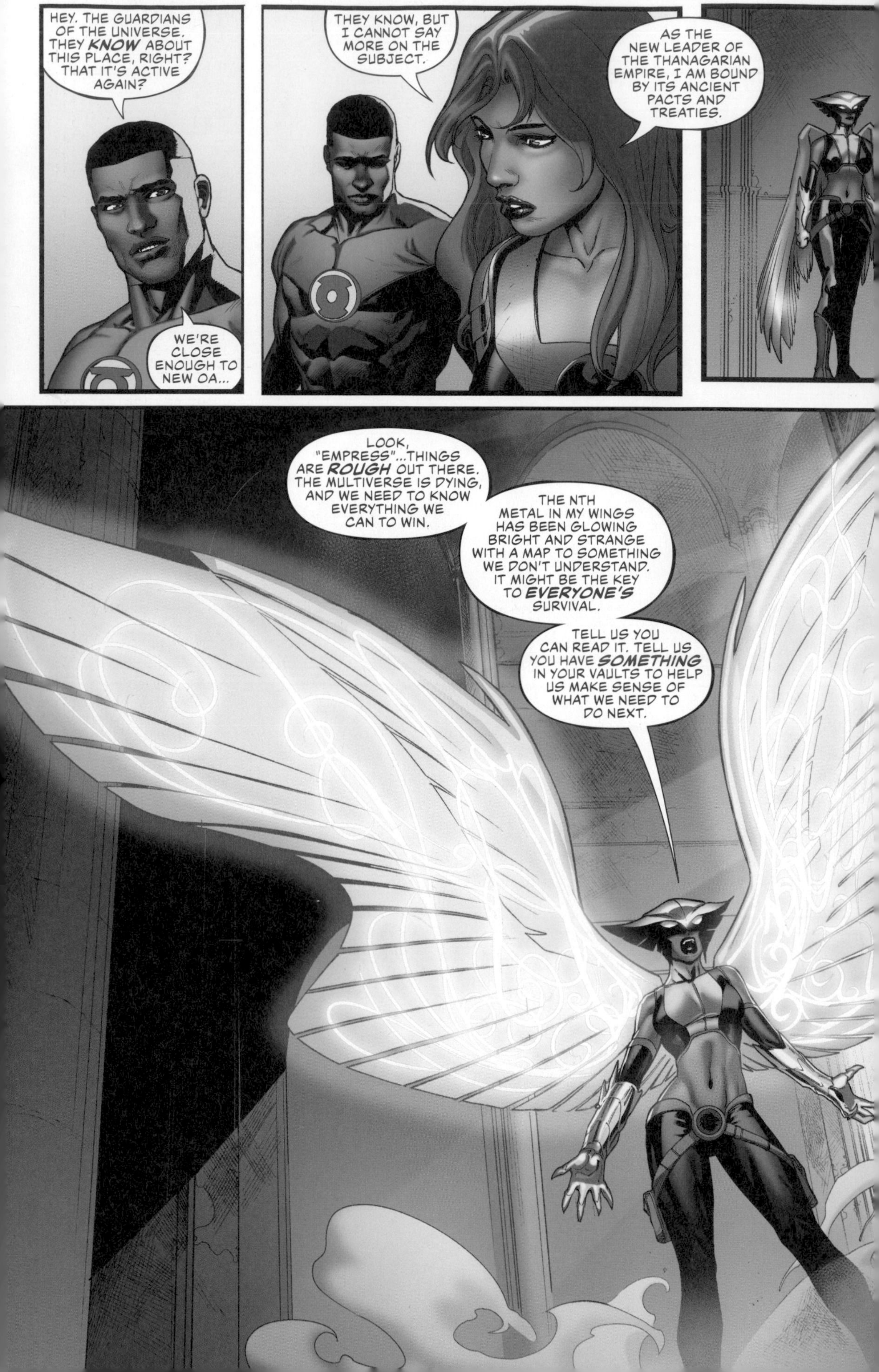
HEY. THE GUARDIANS OF THE UNIVERSE. THEY **KNOW** ABOUT THIS PLACE, RIGHT? THAT IT'S ACTIVE AGAIN?
WE'RE CLOSE ENOUGH TO NEW OA...
THEY KNOW, BUT I CANNOT SAY MORE ON THE SUBJECT.
AS THE NEW LEADER OF THE THANAGARIAN EMPIRE, I AM BOUND BY ITS ANCIENT PACTS AND TREATIES.
LOOK, "EMPRESS"...THINGS ARE **ROUGH** OUT THERE. THE MULTIVERSE IS DYING, AND WE NEED TO KNOW EVERYTHING WE CAN TO WIN.
THE NTH METAL IN MY WINGS HAS BEEN GLOWING BRIGHT AND STRANGE WITH A MAP TO SOMETHING WE DON'T UNDERSTAND. IT MIGHT BE THE KEY TO **EVERYONE'S** SURVIVAL.
TELL US YOU CAN READ IT. TELL US YOU HAVE **SOMETHING** IN YOUR VAULTS TO HELP US MAKE SENSE OF WHAT WE NEED TO DO NEXT.

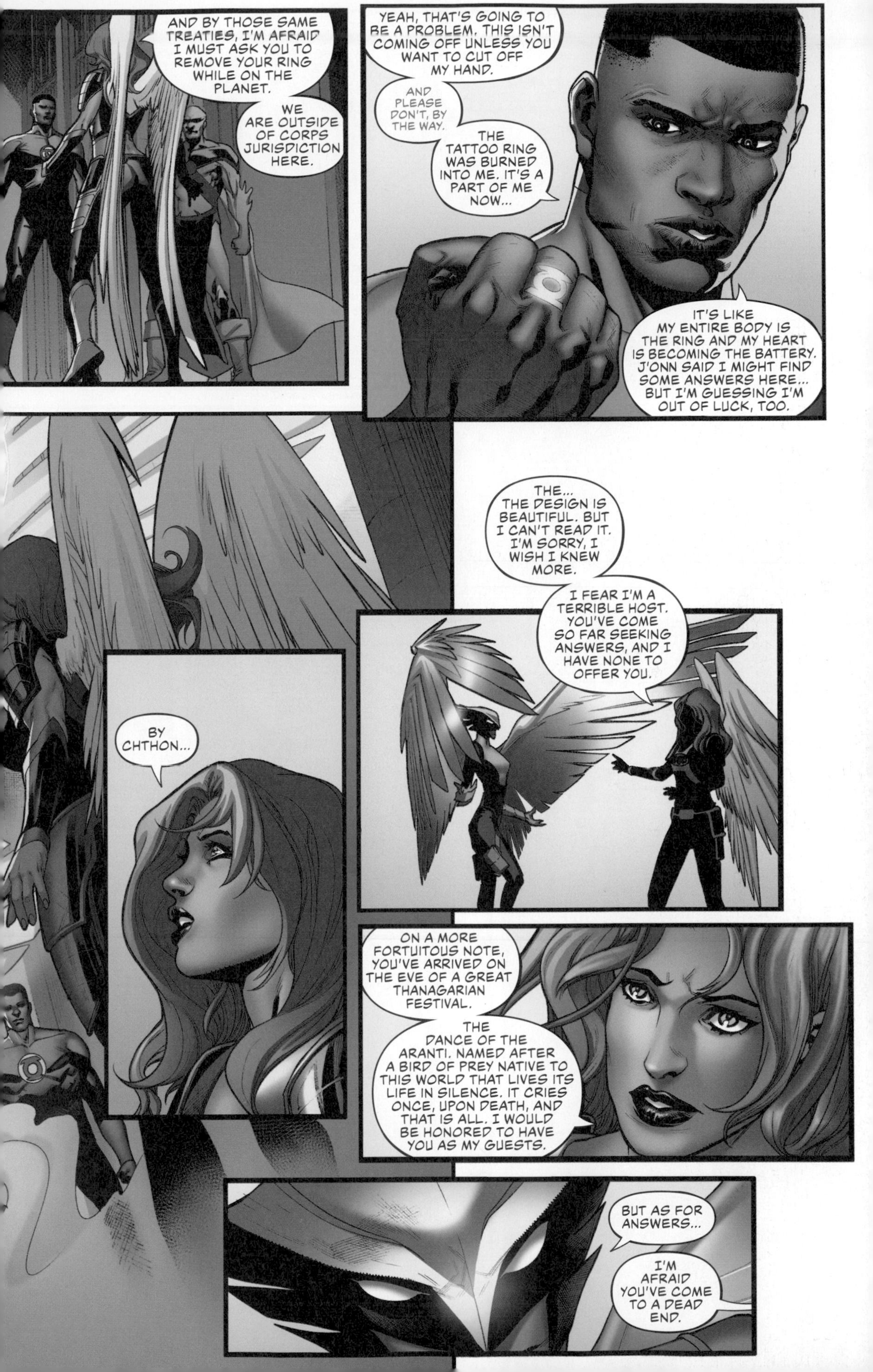
AND BY THOSE SAME TREATIES, I'M AFRAID I MUST ASK YOU TO REMOVE YOUR RING WHILE ON THE PLANET.
WE ARE OUTSIDE OF CORPS JURISDICTION HERE.
YEAH, THAT'S GOING TO BE A PROBLEM. THIS ISN'T COMING OFF UNLESS YOU WANT TO CUT OFF MY HAND.
AND PLEASE DON'T, BY THE WAY.
THE TATTOO RING WAS BURNED INTO ME. IT'S A PART OF ME NOW...
IT'S LIKE MY ENTIRE BODY IS THE RING AND MY HEART IS BECOMING THE BATTERY. J'ONN SAID I MIGHT FIND SOME ANSWERS HERE... BUT I'M GUESSING I'M OUT OF LUCK, TOO.
BY CHTHON...
THE... THE DESIGN IS BEAUTIFUL. BUT I CAN'T READ IT. I'M SORRY, I WISH I KNEW MORE.
I FEAR I'M A TERRIBLE HOST. YOU'VE COME SO FAR SEEKING ANSWERS, AND I HAVE NONE TO OFFER YOU.
ON A MORE FORTUITOUS NOTE, YOU'VE ARRIVED ON THE EVE OF A GREAT THANAGARIAN FESTIVAL.
THE DANCE OF THE ARANTI. NAMED AFTER A BIRD OF PREY NATIVE TO THIS WORLD THAT LIVES ITS LIFE IN SILENCE. IT CRIES ONCE, UPON DEATH, AND THAT IS ALL. I WOULD BE HONORED TO HAVE YOU AS MY GUESTS.
BUT AS FOR ANSWERS...
I'M AFRAID YOU'VE COME TO A DEAD END.

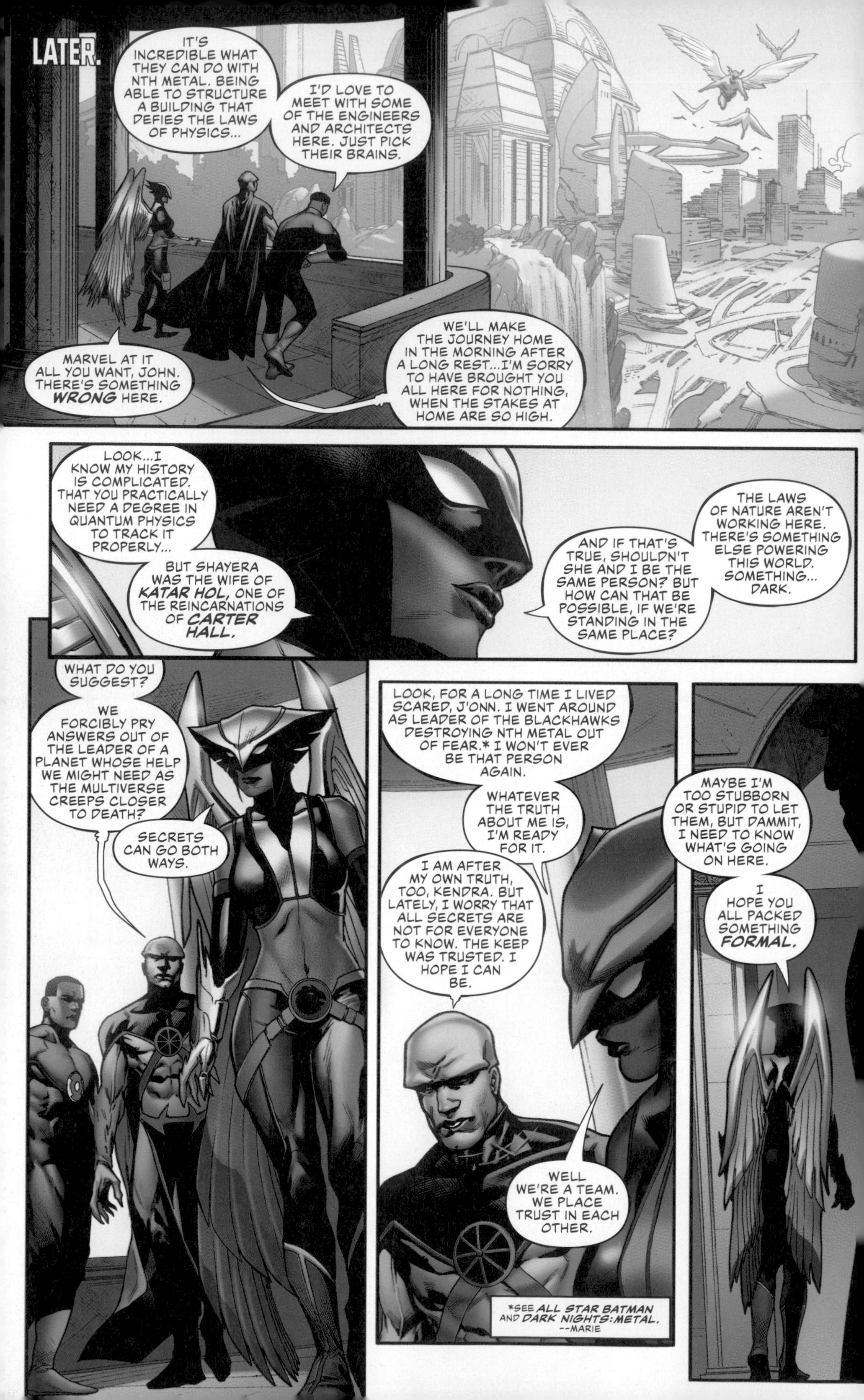

LATER.
IT'S INCREDIBLE WHAT THEY CAN DO WITH NTH METAL. BEING ABLE TO STRUCTURE A BUILDING THAT DEFIES THE LAWS OF PHYSICS...
I'D LOVE TO MEET WITH SOME OF THE ENGINEERS AND ARCHITECTS HERE. JUST PICK THEIR BRAINS.
MARVEL AT IT ALL YOU WANT, JOHN. THERE'S SOMETHING WRONG HERE.
WE'LL MAKE THE JOURNEY HOME IN THE MORNING AFTER A LONG REST...I'M SORRY TO HAVE BROUGHT YOU ALL HERE FOR NOTHING, WHEN THE STAKES AT HOME ARE SO HIGH.
LOOK...I KNOW MY HISTORY IS COMPLICATED. THAT YOU PRACTICALLY NEED A DEGREE IN QUANTUM PHYSICS TO TRACK IT PROPERLY...
BUT SHAYERA WAS THE WIFE OF KATAR HOL, ONE OF THE REINCARNATIONS OF CARTER HALL.
AND IF THAT'S TRUE, SHOULDN'T SHE AND I BE THE SAME PERSON? BUT HOW CAN THAT BE POSSIBLE, IF WE'RE STANDING IN THE SAME PLACE?
THE LAWS OF NATURE AREN'T WORKING HERE. THERE'S SOMETHING ELSE POWERING THIS WORLD. SOMETHING... DARK.
WHAT DO YOU SUGGEST?
WE FORCIBLY PRY ANSWERS OUT OF THE LEADER OF A PLANET WHOSE HELP WE MIGHT NEED AS THE MULTIVERSE CREEPS CLOSER TO DEATH?
SECRETS CAN GO BOTH WAYS.
LOOK, FOR A LONG TIME I LIVED SCARED, J'ONN. I WENT AROUND AS LEADER OF THE BLACKHAWKS DESTROYING NTH METAL OUT OF FEAR.* I WON'T EVER BE THAT PERSON AGAIN.
WHATEVER THE TRUTH ABOUT ME IS, I'M READY FOR IT.
I AM AFTER MY OWN TRUTH, TOO, KENDRA. BUT LATELY, I WORRY THAT ALL SECRETS ARE NOT FOR EVERYONE TO KNOW. THE KEEP WAS TRUSTED. I HOPE I CAN BE.
WELL WE'RE A TEAM. WE PLACE TRUST IN EACH OTHER.
*SEE ALL STAR BATMAN AND DARK NIGHTS: METAL. --MARIE
MAYBE I'M TOO STUBBORN OR STUPID TO LET THEM, BUT DAMMIT, I NEED TO KNOW WHAT'S GOING ON HERE.
I HOPE YOU ALL PACKED SOMETHING FORMAL.

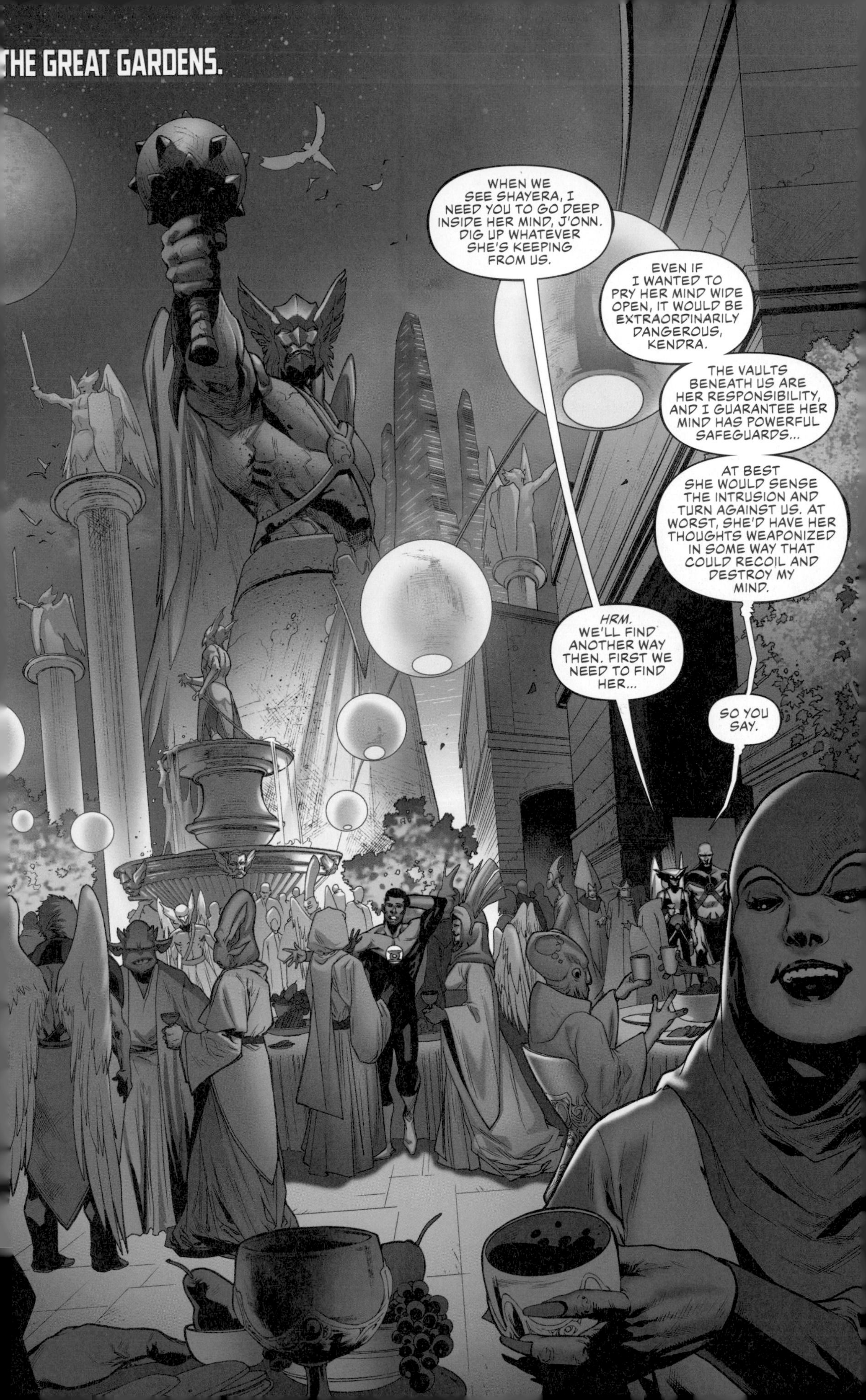
THE GREAT GARDENS.
WHEN WE SEE SHAYERA, I NEED YOU TO GO DEEP INSIDE HER MIND, J'ONN. DIG UP WHATEVER SHE'S KEEPING FROM US.
EVEN IF I WANTED TO PRY HER MIND WIDE OPEN, IT WOULD BE EXTRAORDINARILY DANGEROUS, KENDRA.
THE VAULTS BENEATH US ARE HER RESPONSIBILITY, AND I GUARANTEE HER MIND HAS POWERFUL SAFEGUARDS...
AT BEST SHE WOULD SENSE THE INTRUSION AND TURN AGAINST US. AT WORST, SHE'D HAVE HER THOUGHTS WEAPONIZED IN SOME WAY THAT COULD RECOIL AND DESTROY MY MIND.
HRM. WE'LL FIND ANOTHER WAY THEN. FIRST WE NEED TO FIND HER...
SO YOU SAY.

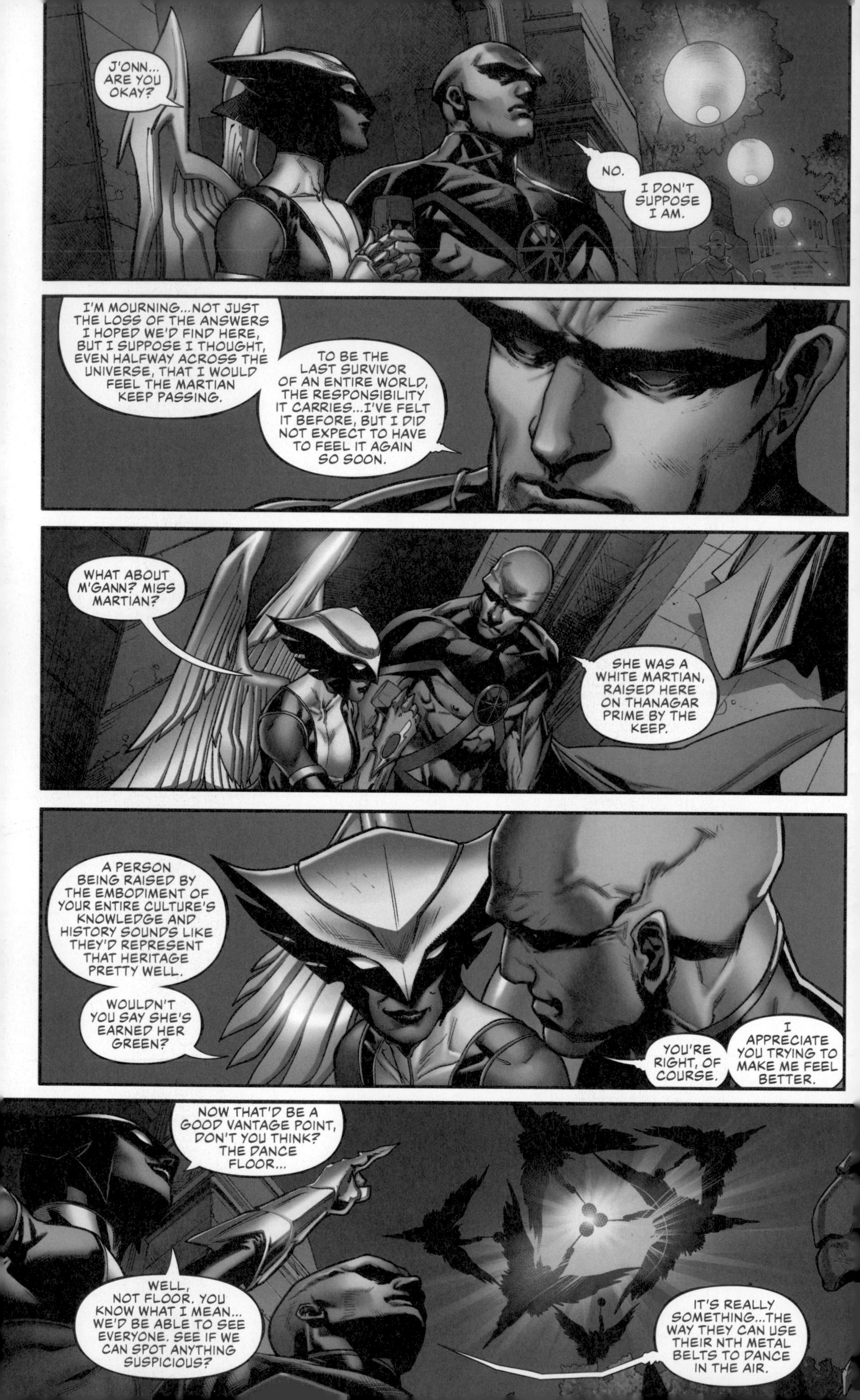
J'ONN... ARE YOU OKAY?
NO.
I DON'T SUPPOSE I AM.
I'M MOURNING...NOT JUST THE LOSS OF THE ANSWERS I HOPED WE'D FIND HERE, BUT I SUPPOSE I THOUGHT, EVEN HALFWAY ACROSS THE UNIVERSE, THAT I WOULD FEEL THE MARTIAN KEEP PASSING.
TO BE THE LAST SURVIVOR OF AN ENTIRE WORLD, THE RESPONSIBILITY IT CARRIES...I'VE FELT IT BEFORE, BUT I DID NOT EXPECT TO HAVE TO FEEL IT AGAIN SO SOON.
WHAT ABOUT M'GANN? MISS MARTIAN?
SHE WAS A WHITE MARTIAN, RAISED HERE ON THANAGAR PRIME BY THE KEEP.
A PERSON BEING RAISED BY THE EMBODIMENT OF YOUR ENTIRE CULTURE'S KNOWLEDGE AND HISTORY SOUNDS LIKE THEY'D REPRESENT THAT HERITAGE PRETTY WELL.
WOULDN'T YOU SAY SHE'S EARNED HER GREEN?
YOU'RE RIGHT, OF COURSE.
I APPRECIATE YOU TRYING TO MAKE ME FEEL BETTER.
NOW THAT'D BE A GOOD VANTAGE POINT, DON'T YOU THINK? THE DANCE FLOOR...
WELL, NOT FLOOR. YOU KNOW WHAT I MEAN... WE'D BE ABLE TO SEE EVERYONE. SEE IF WE CAN SPOT ANYTHING SUSPICIOUS?
IT'S REALLY SOMETHING...THE WAY THEY CAN USE THEIR NTH METAL BELTS TO DANCE IN THE AIR.

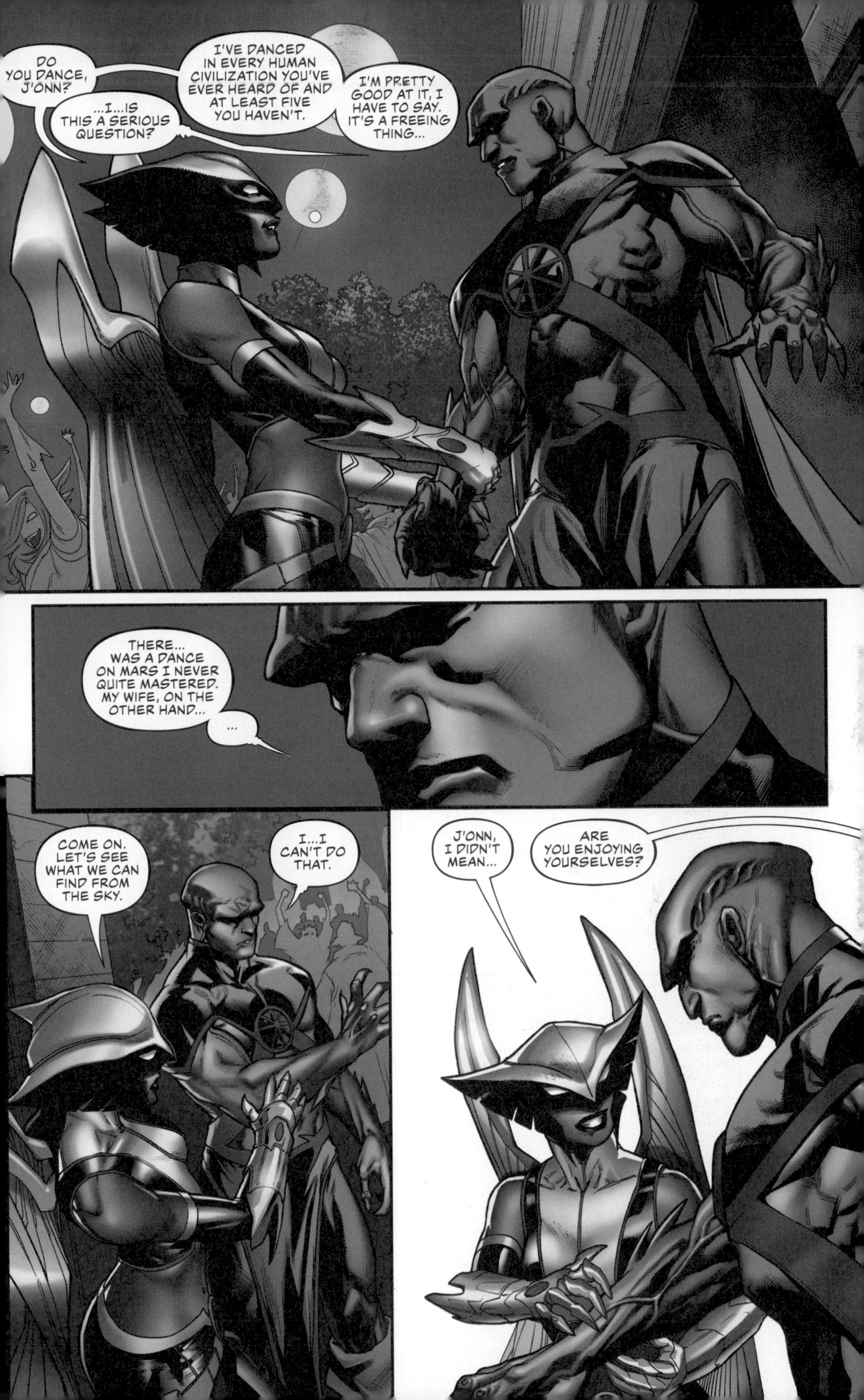
DO YOU DANCE, J'ONN?
...I...IS THIS A SERIOUS QUESTION?
I'VE DANCED IN EVERY HUMAN CIVILIZATION YOU'VE EVER HEARD OF AND AT LEAST FIVE YOU HAVEN'T.
I'M PRETTY GOOD AT IT, I HAVE TO SAY. IT'S A FREEING THING...
THERE... WAS A DANCE ON MARS I NEVER QUITE MASTERED. MY WIFE, ON THE OTHER HAND...
...
COME ON. LET'S SEE WHAT WE CAN FIND FROM THE SKY.
I...I CAN'T DO THAT.
J'ONN, I DIDN'T MEAN...
ARE YOU ENJOYING YOURSELVES?

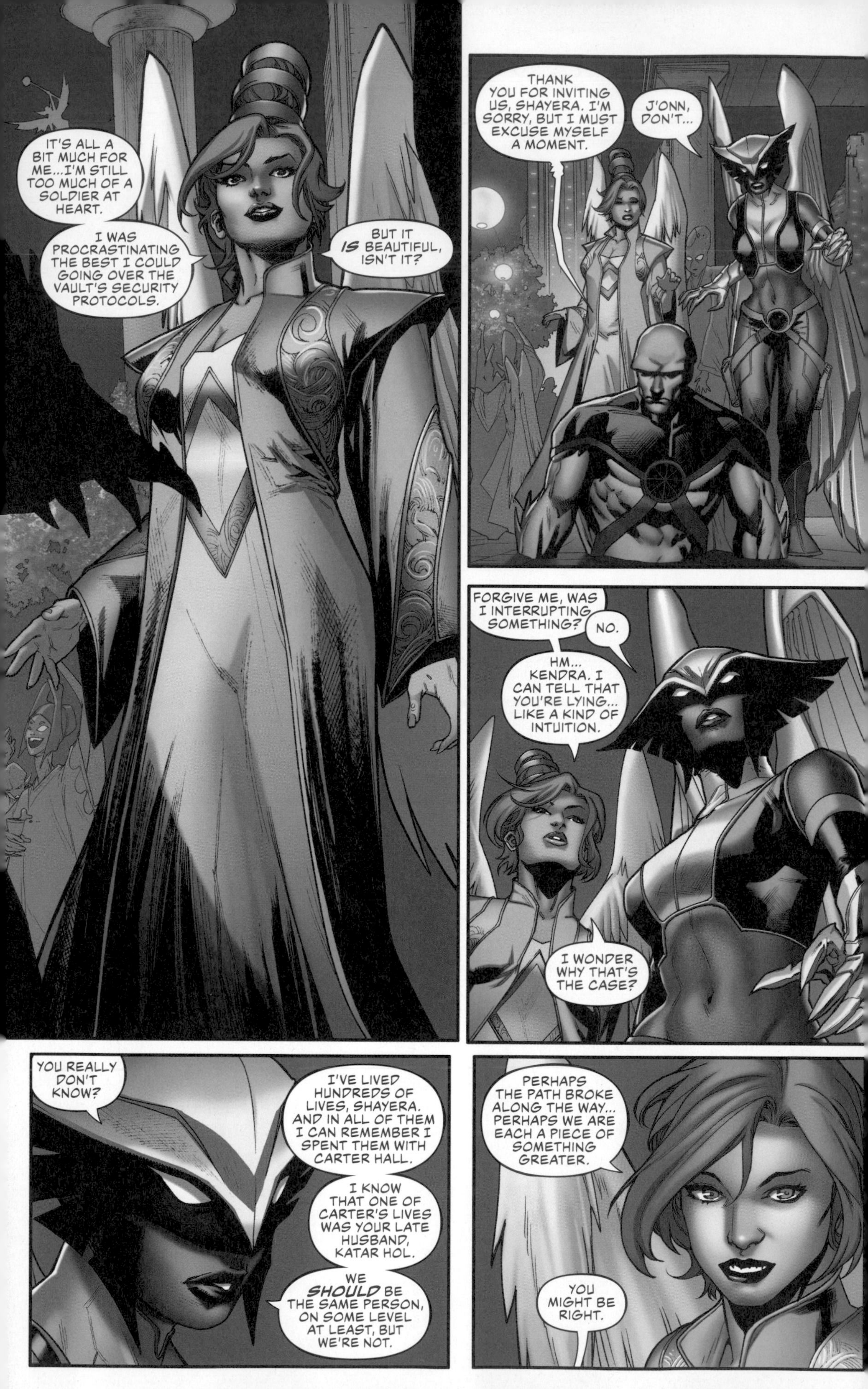
IT'S ALL A BIT MUCH FOR ME...I'M STILL TOO MUCH OF A SOLDIER AT HEART.
I WAS PROCRASTINATING THE BEST I COULD GOING OVER THE VAULT'S SECURITY PROTOCOLS.
BUT IT *IS* BEAUTIFUL, ISN'T IT?
THANK YOU FOR INVITING US, SHAYERA. I'M SORRY, BUT I MUST EXCUSE MYSELF A MOMENT.
J'ONN, DON'T...
FORGIVE ME, WAS I INTERRUPTING SOMETHING?
NO.
HM... KENDRA. I CAN TELL THAT YOU'RE LYING... LIKE A KIND OF INTUITION.
I WONDER WHY THAT'S THE CASE?
YOU REALLY DON'T KNOW?
I'VE LIVED HUNDREDS OF LIVES, SHAYERA. AND IN ALL OF THEM I CAN REMEMBER I SPENT THEM WITH CARTER HALL.
I KNOW THAT ONE OF CARTER'S LIVES WAS YOUR LATE HUSBAND, KATAR HOL.
WE *SHOULD* BE THE SAME PERSON, ON SOME LEVEL AT LEAST, BUT WE'RE NOT.
PERHAPS THE PATH BROKE ALONG THE WAY... PERHAPS WE ARE EACH A PIECE OF SOMETHING GREATER.
YOU MIGHT BE RIGHT.

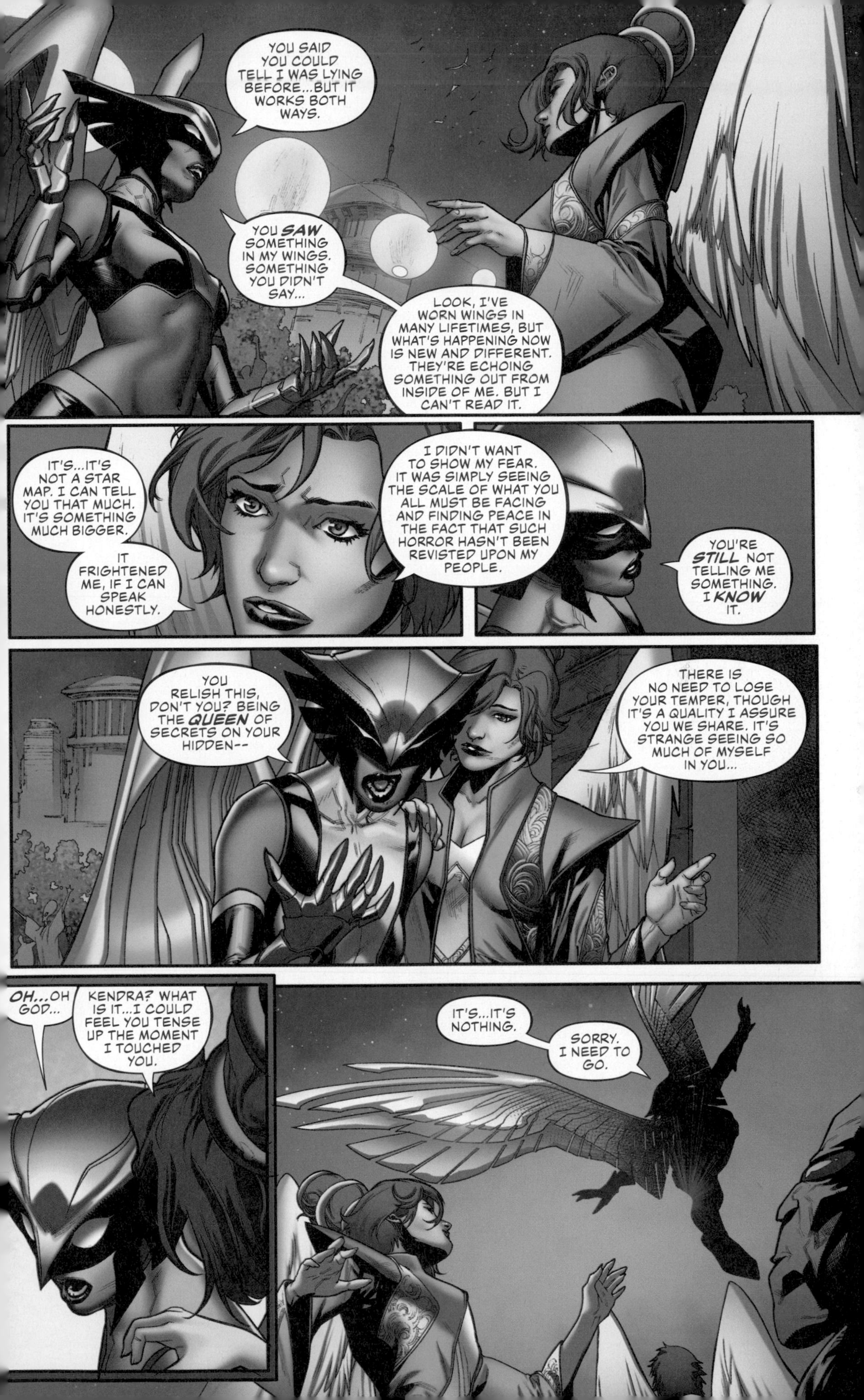
YOU SAID YOU COULD TELL I WAS LYING BEFORE...BUT IT WORKS BOTH WAYS.
YOU SAW SOMETHING IN MY WINGS. SOMETHING YOU DIDN'T SAY...
LOOK, I'VE WORN WINGS IN MANY LIFETIMES, BUT WHAT'S HAPPENING NOW IS NEW AND DIFFERENT. THEY'RE ECHOING SOMETHING OUT FROM INSIDE OF ME. BUT I CAN'T READ IT.
IT'S...IT'S NOT A STAR MAP. I CAN TELL YOU THAT MUCH. IT'S SOMETHING MUCH BIGGER.
IT FRIGHTENED ME, IF I CAN SPEAK HONESTLY.
I DIDN'T WANT TO SHOW MY FEAR. IT WAS SIMPLY SEEING THE SCALE OF WHAT YOU ALL MUST BE FACING AND FINDING PEACE IN THE FACT THAT SUCH HORROR HASN'T BEEN REVISTED UPON MY PEOPLE.
YOU'RE STILL NOT TELLING ME SOMETHING. I KNOW IT.
YOU RELISH THIS, DON'T YOU? BEING THE QUEEN OF SECRETS ON YOUR HIDDEN--
THERE IS NO NEED TO LOSE YOUR TEMPER, THOUGH IT'S A QUALITY I ASSURE YOU WE SHARE. IT'S STRANGE SEEING SO MUCH OF MYSELF IN YOU...
OH...OH GOD...
KENDRA? WHAT IS IT...I COULD FEEL YOU TENSE UP THE MOMENT I TOUCHED YOU.
IT'S...IT'S NOTHING.
SORRY. I NEED TO GO.

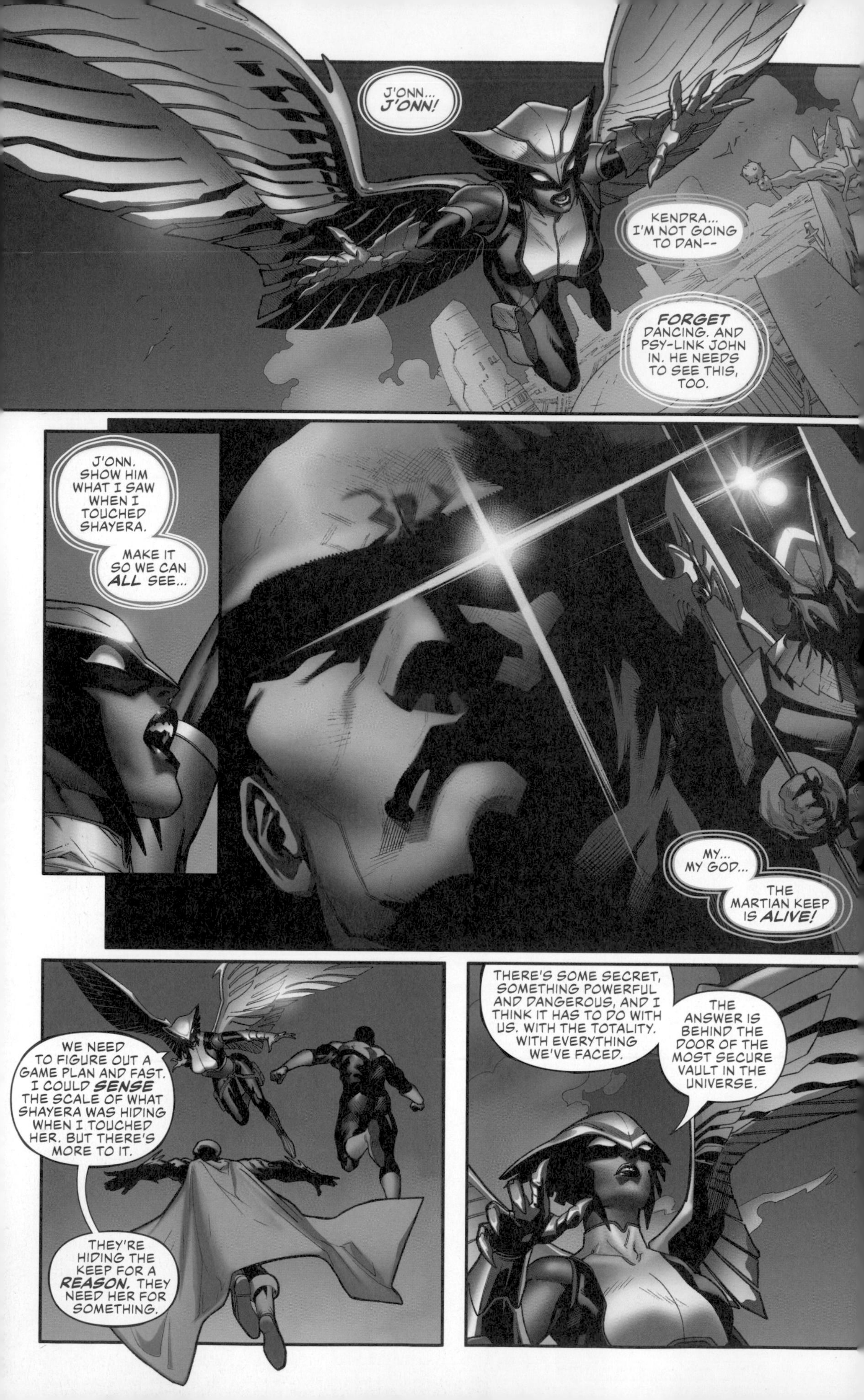
J'ONN... J'ONN!
KENDRA... I'M NOT GOING TO DAN--
FORGET DANCING. AND PSY-LINK JOHN IN. HE NEEDS TO SEE THIS, TOO.
J'ONN. SHOW HIM WHAT I SAW WHEN I TOUCHED SHAYERA.
MAKE IT SO WE CAN ALL SEE...
MY... MY GOD...
THE MARTIAN KEEP IS ALIVE!
WE NEED TO FIGURE OUT A GAME PLAN AND FAST. I COULD SENSE THE SCALE OF WHAT SHAYERA WAS HIDING WHEN I TOUCHED HER. BUT THERE'S MORE TO IT.
THEY'RE HIDING THE KEEP FOR A REASON. THEY NEED HER FOR SOMETHING.
THERE'S SOME SECRET, SOMETHING POWERFUL AND DANGEROUS, AND I THINK IT HAS TO DO WITH US. WITH THE TOTALITY. WITH EVERYTHING WE'VE FACED.
THE ANSWER IS BEHIND THE DOOR OF THE MOST SECURE VAULT IN THE UNIVERSE.

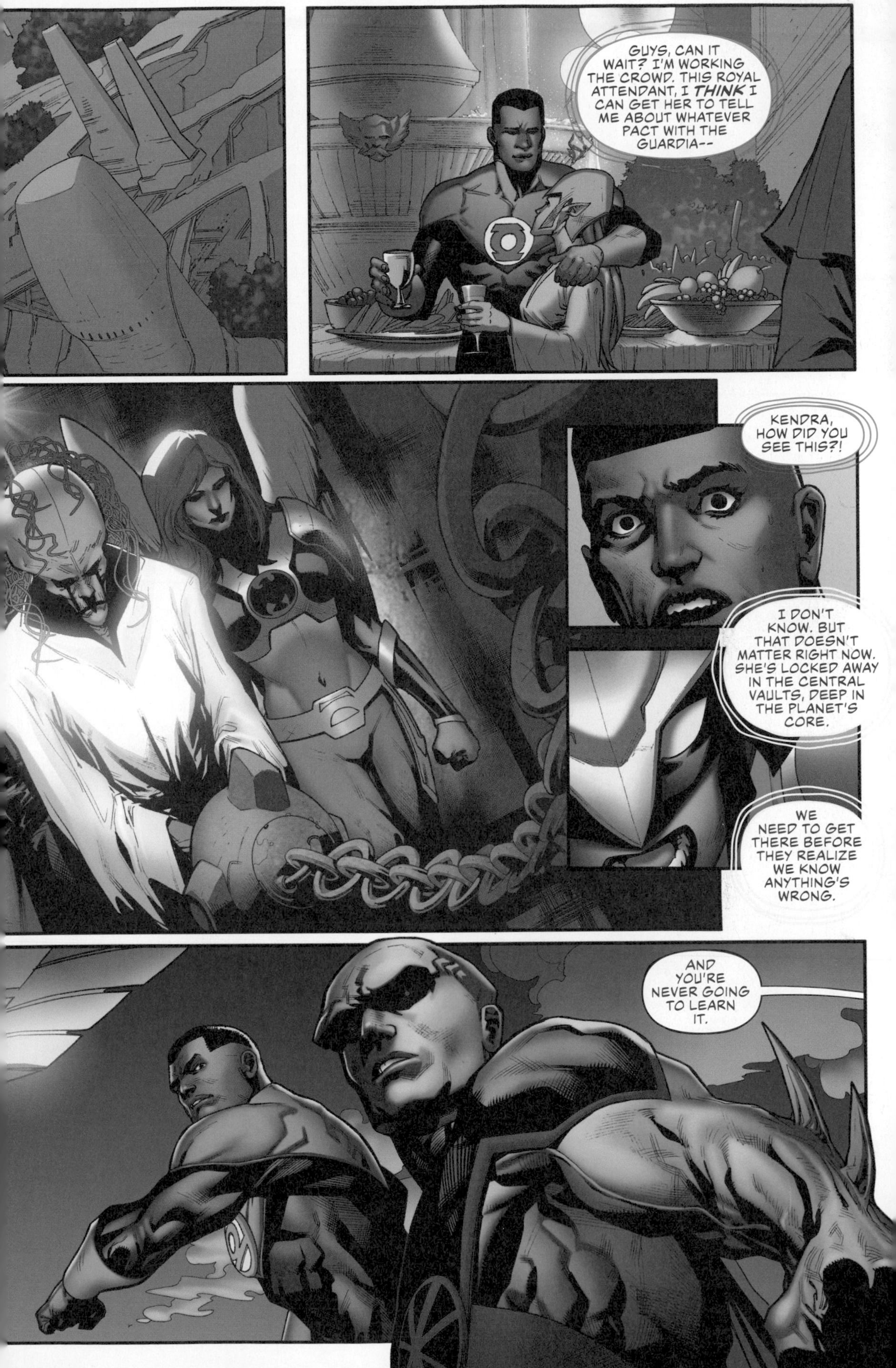
GUYS, CAN IT WAIT? I'M WORKING THE CROWD. THIS ROYAL ATTENDANT, I *THINK* I CAN GET HER TO TELL ME ABOUT WHATEVER PACT WITH THE GUARDIA--
KENDRA, HOW DID YOU SEE THIS?!
I DON'T KNOW. BUT THAT DOESN'T MATTER RIGHT NOW. SHE'S LOCKED AWAY IN THE CENTRAL VAULTS, DEEP IN THE PLANET'S CORE.
WE NEED TO GET THERE BEFORE THEY REALIZE WE KNOW ANYTHING'S WRONG.
AND YOU'RE NEVER GOING TO LEARN IT.

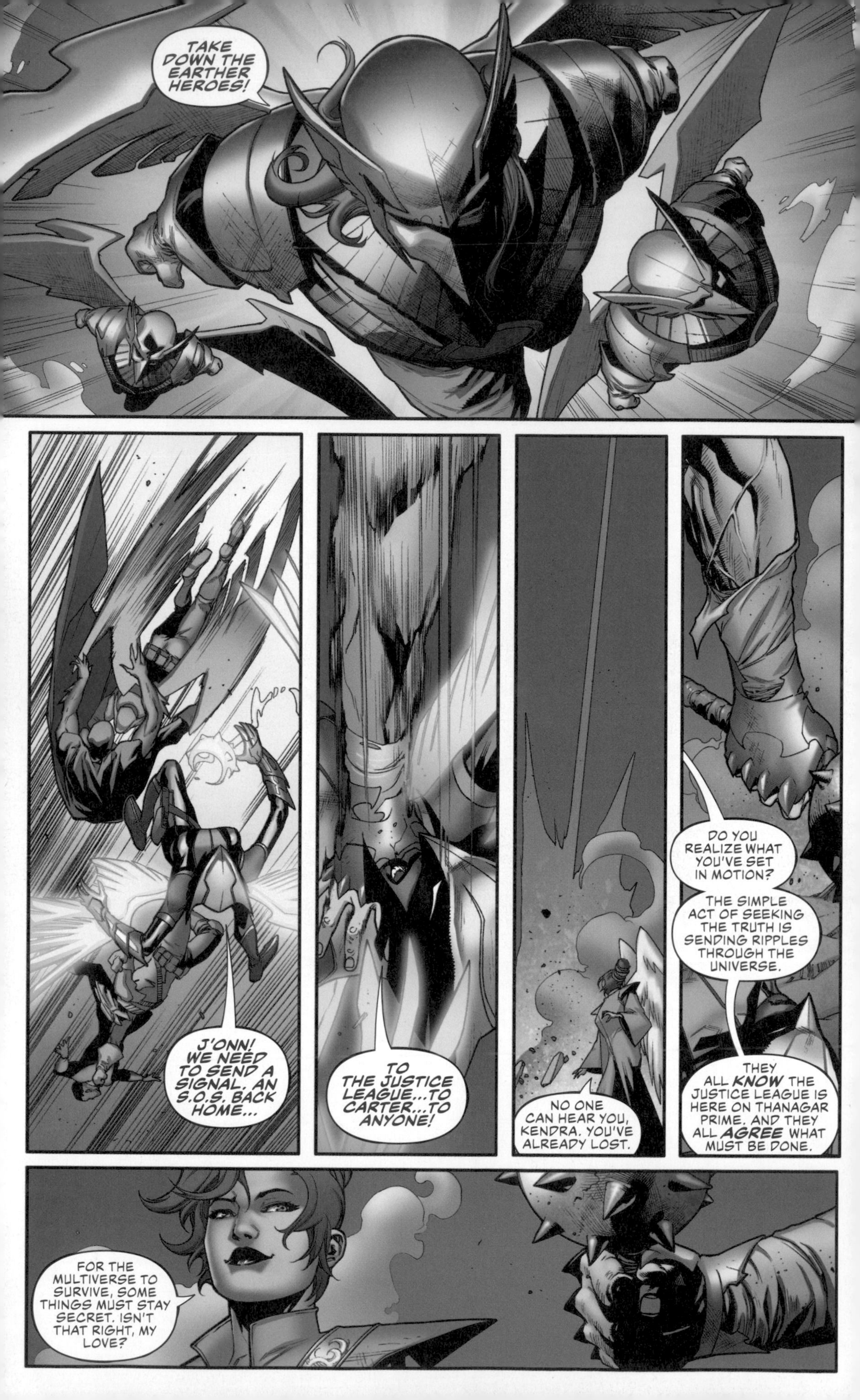
TAKE DOWN THE EARTHER HEROES!
J'ONN! WE NEED TO SEND A SIGNAL. AN S.O.S. BACK HOME...
TO THE JUSTICE LEAGUE...TO CARTER...TO ANYONE!
NO ONE CAN HEAR YOU, KENDRA. YOU'VE ALREADY LOST.
DO YOU REALIZE WHAT YOU'VE SET IN MOTION?
THE SIMPLE ACT OF SEEKING THE TRUTH IS SENDING RIPPLES THROUGH THE UNIVERSE.
THEY ALL KNOW THE JUSTICE LEAGUE IS HERE ON THANAGAR PRIME. AND THEY ALL AGREE WHAT MUST BE DONE.
FOR THE MULTIVERSE TO SURVIVE, SOME THINGS MUST STAY SECRET. ISN'T THAT RIGHT, MY LOVE?

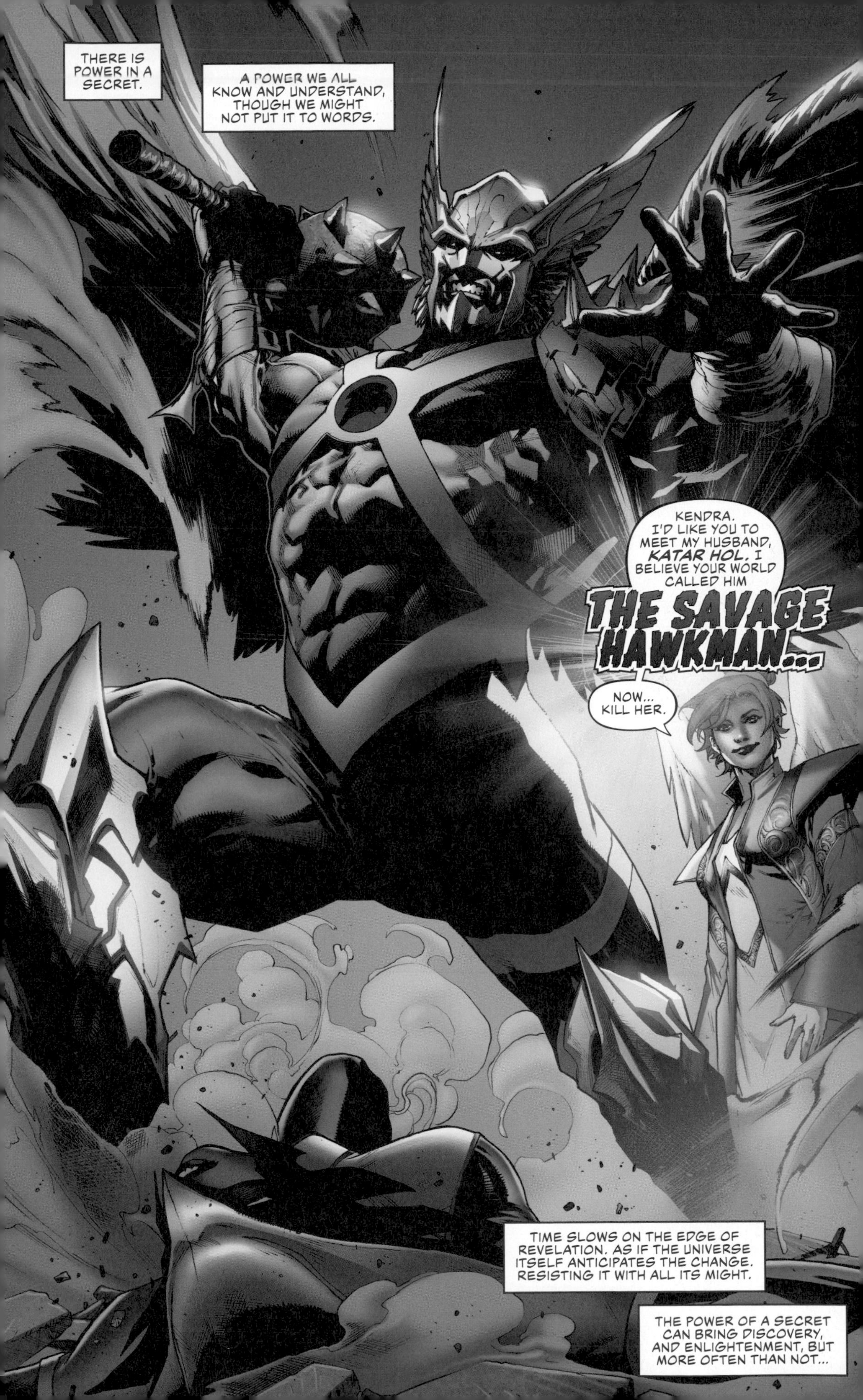
THERE IS POWER IN A SECRET.
A POWER WE ALL KNOW AND UNDERSTAND, THOUGH WE MIGHT NOT PUT IT TO WORDS.
KENDRA. I'D LIKE YOU TO MEET MY HUSBAND, KATAR HOL. I BELIEVE YOUR WORLD CALLED HIM THE SAVAGE HAWKMAN...
NOW... KILL HER.
TIME SLOWS ON THE EDGE OF REVELATION. AS IF THE UNIVERSE ITSELF ANTICIPATES THE CHANGE. RESISTING IT WITH ALL ITS MIGHT.
THE POWER OF A SECRET CAN BRING DISCOVERY, AND ENLIGHTENMENT, BUT MORE OFTEN THAN NOT...

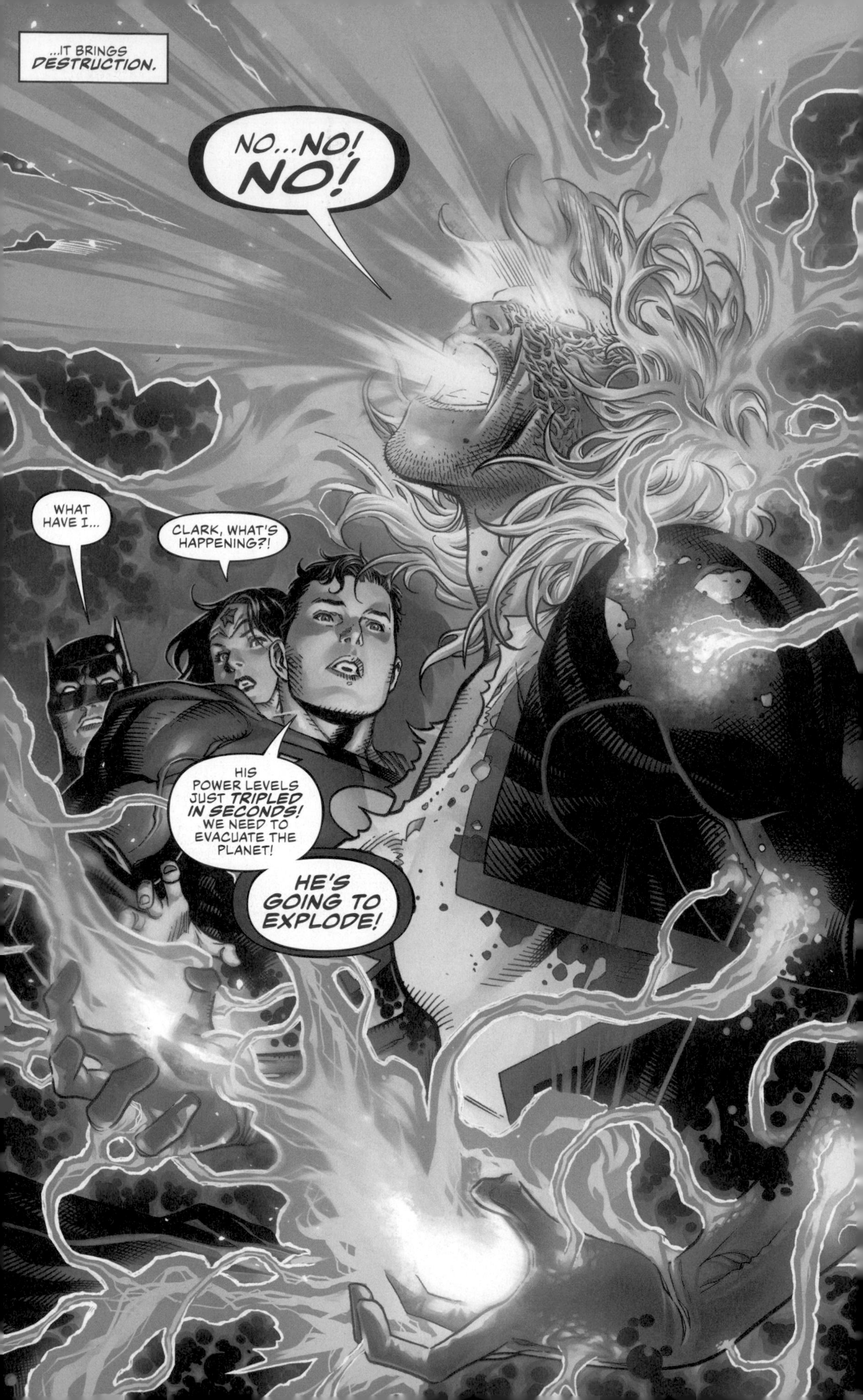
...IT BRINGS DESTRUCTION.
NO...NO! NO!
WHAT HAVE I...
CLARK, WHAT'S HAPPENING?!
HIS POWER LEVELS JUST TRIPLED IN SECONDS! WE NEED TO EVACUATE THE PLANET!
HE'S GOING TO EXPLODE!

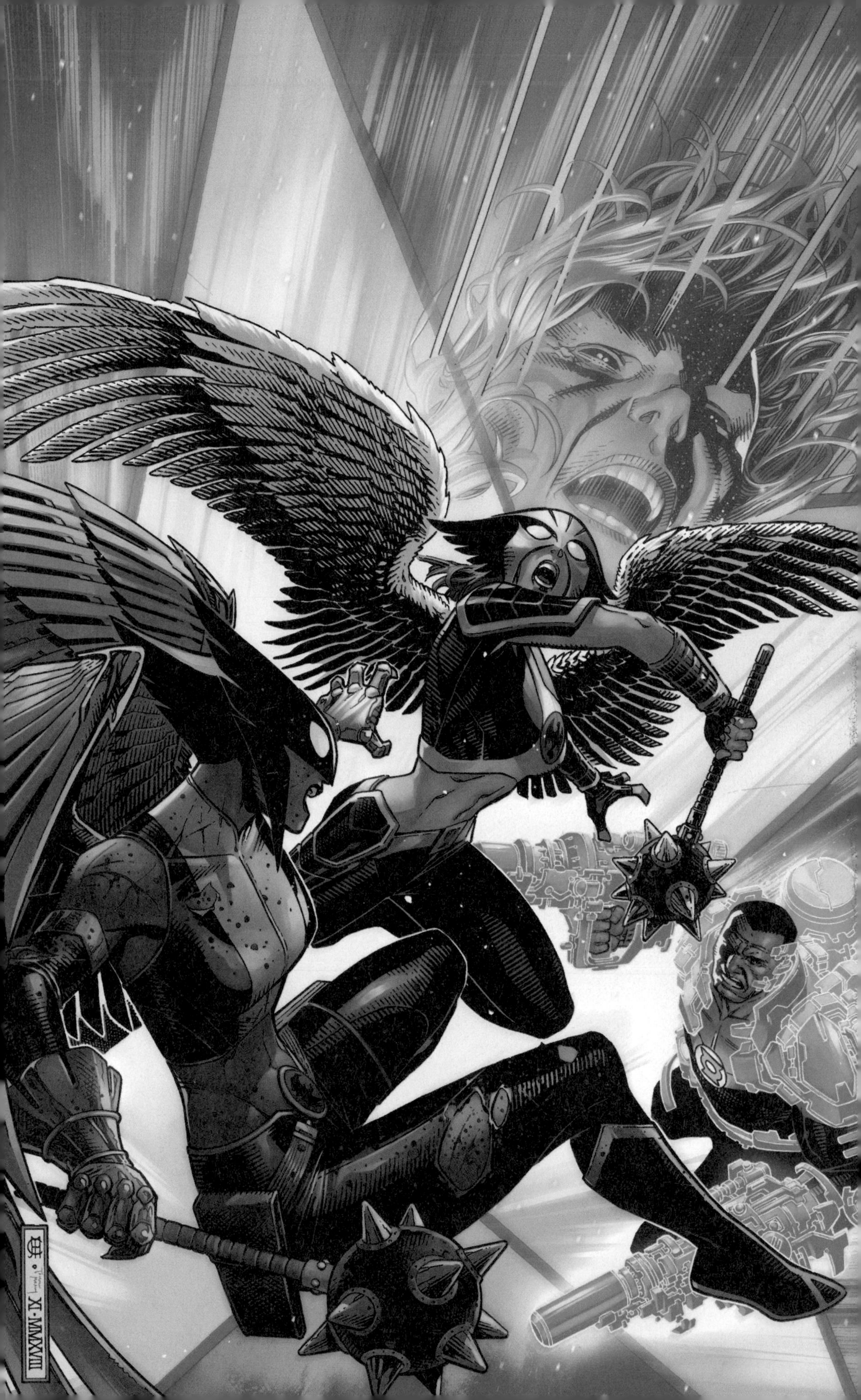
XI·MMXVIII

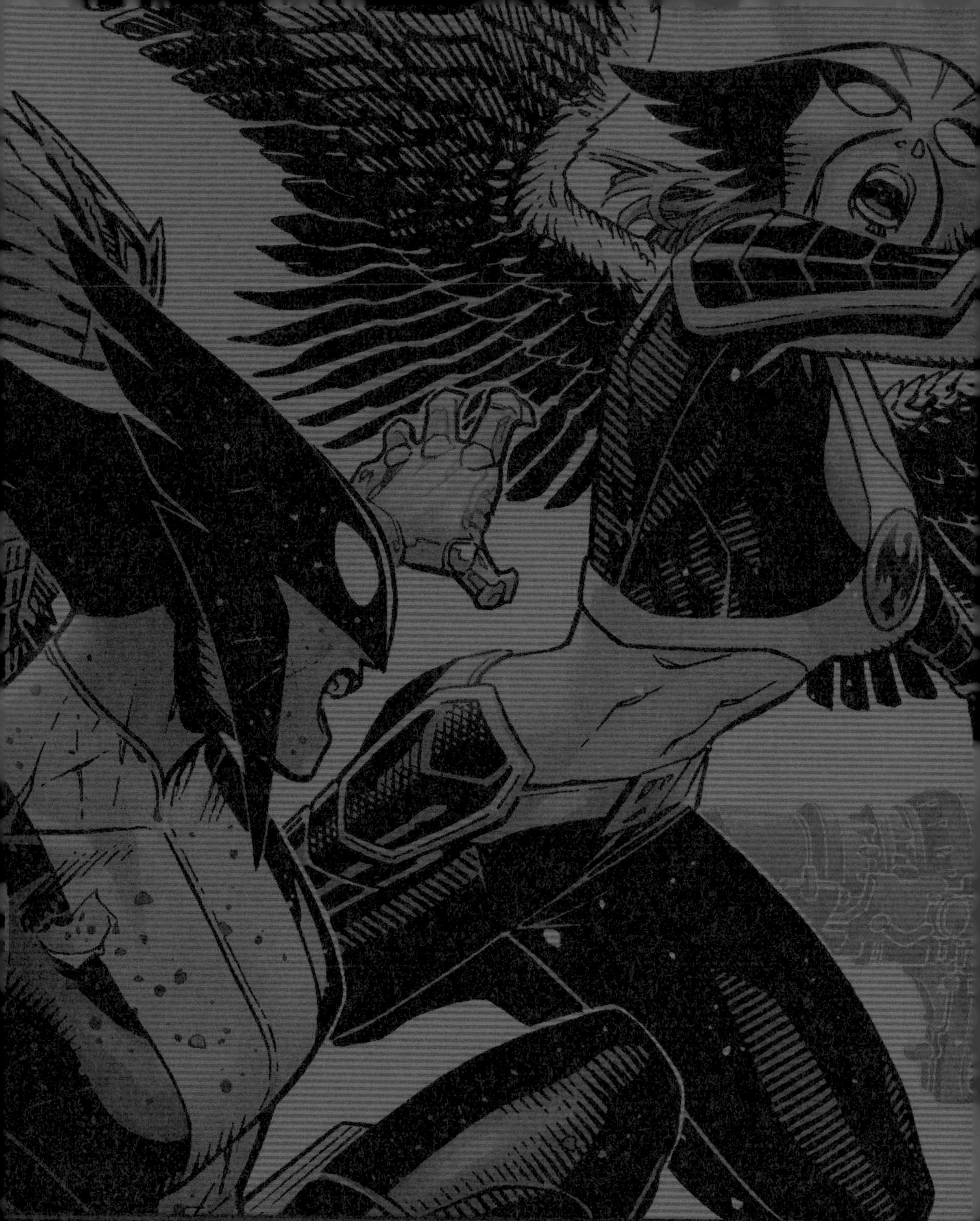

JUSTICE
LEAGUE
#15

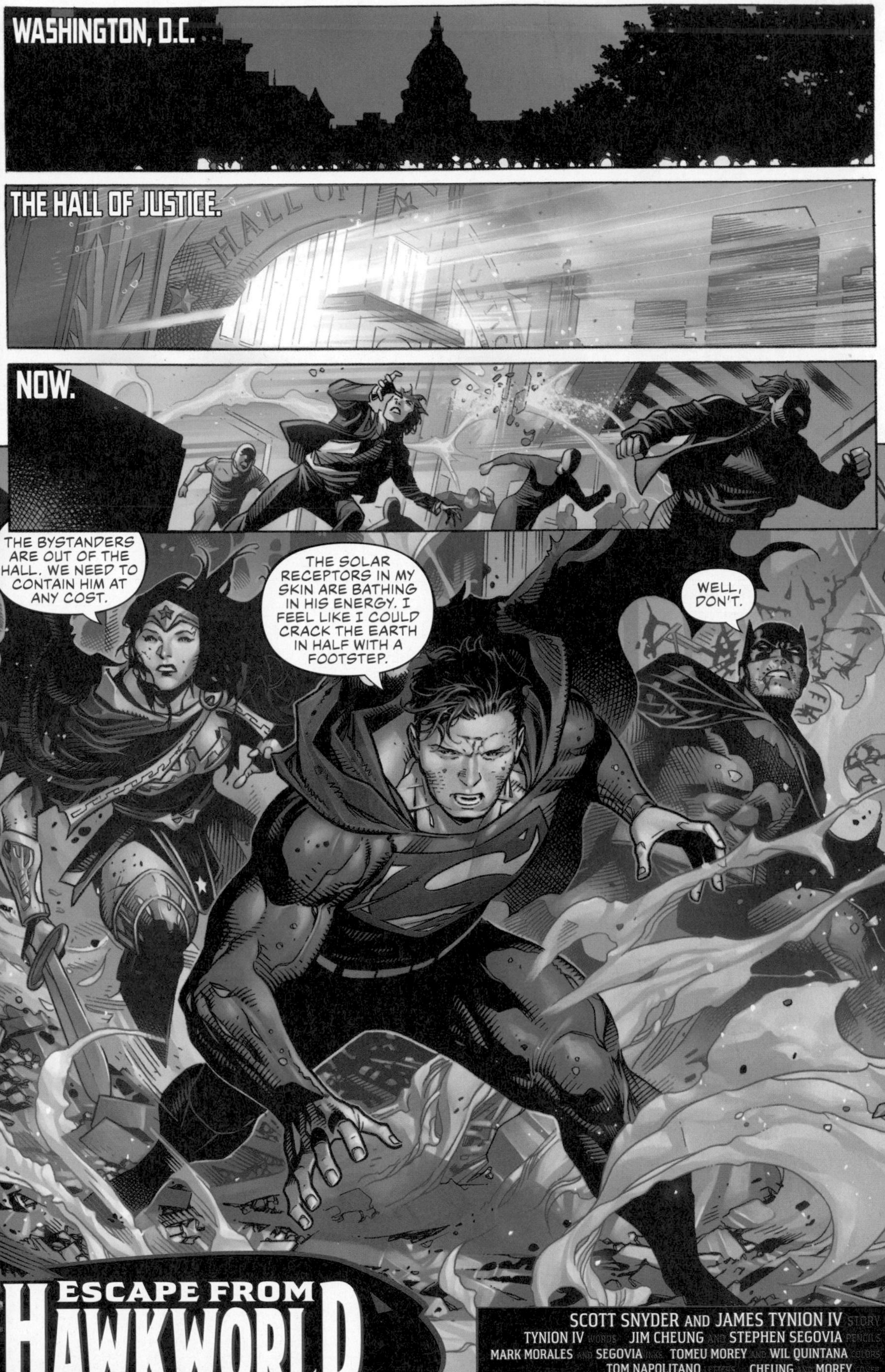
WASHINGTON, D.C.
THE HALL OF JUSTICE.
NOW.
THE BYSTANDERS ARE OUT OF THE HALL. WE NEED TO CONTAIN HIM AT ANY COST.
THE SOLAR RECEPTORS IN MY SKIN ARE BATHING IN HIS ENERGY. I FEEL LIKE I COULD CRACK THE EARTH IN HALF WITH A FOOTSTEP.
WELL, DON'T.
ESCAPE FROM HAWKWORLD PART TWO
SCOTT SNYDER AND JAMES TYNION IV STORY
TYNION IV WORDS JIM CHEUNG AND STEPHEN SEGOVIA PENCILS
MARK MORALES AND SEGOVIA INKS TOMEU MOREY AND WIL QUINTANA COLORS
TOM NAPOLITANO LETTERS CHEUNG AND MOREY COVER
ANDREW MARINO ASSISTANT EDITOR MARIE JAVINS GROUP EDITOR

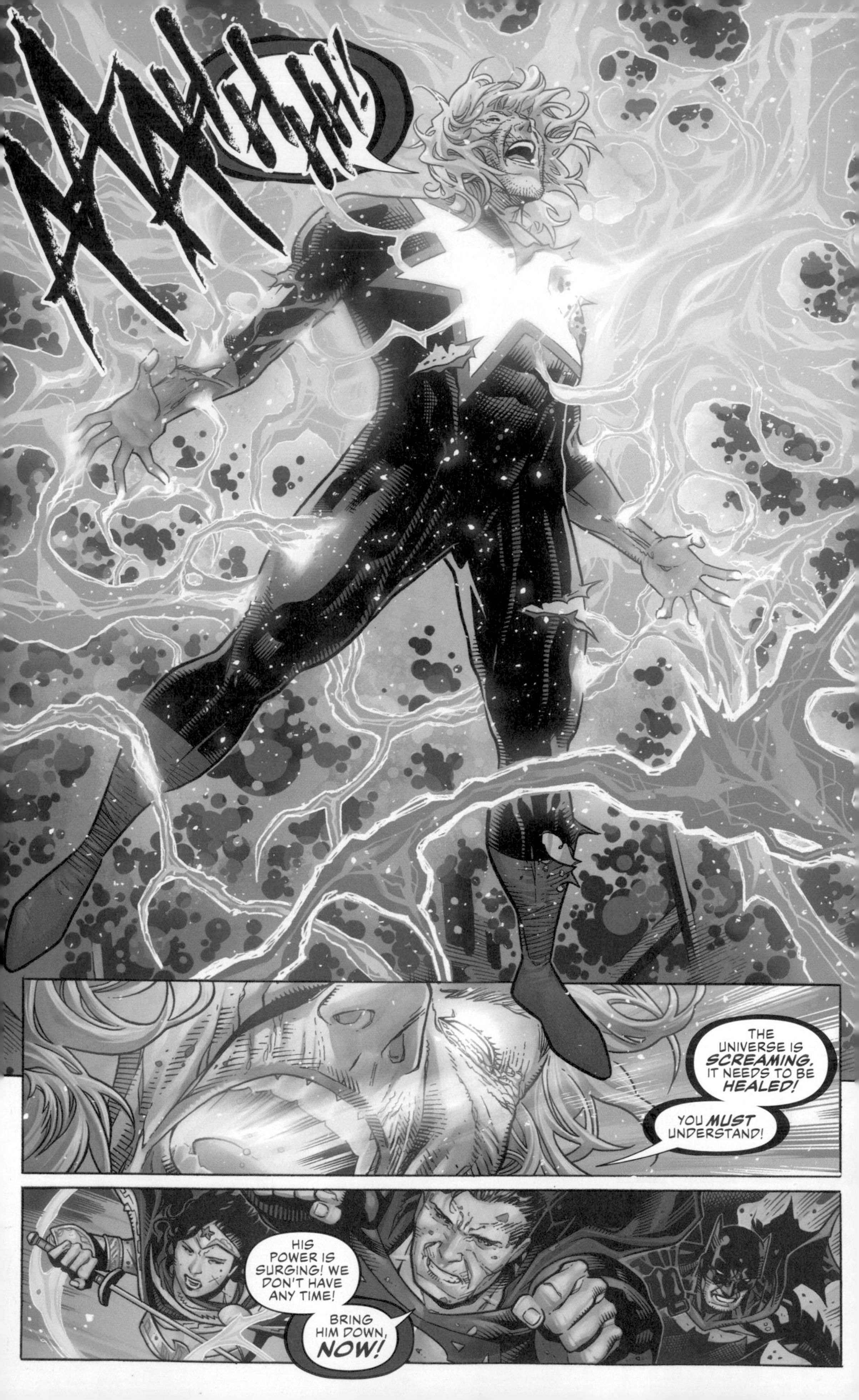
THE UNIVERSE IS SCREAMING. IT NEEDS TO BE HEALED!
YOU MUST UNDERSTAND!
HIS POWER IS SURGING! WE DON'T HAVE ANY TIME!
BRING HIM DOWN, NOW!

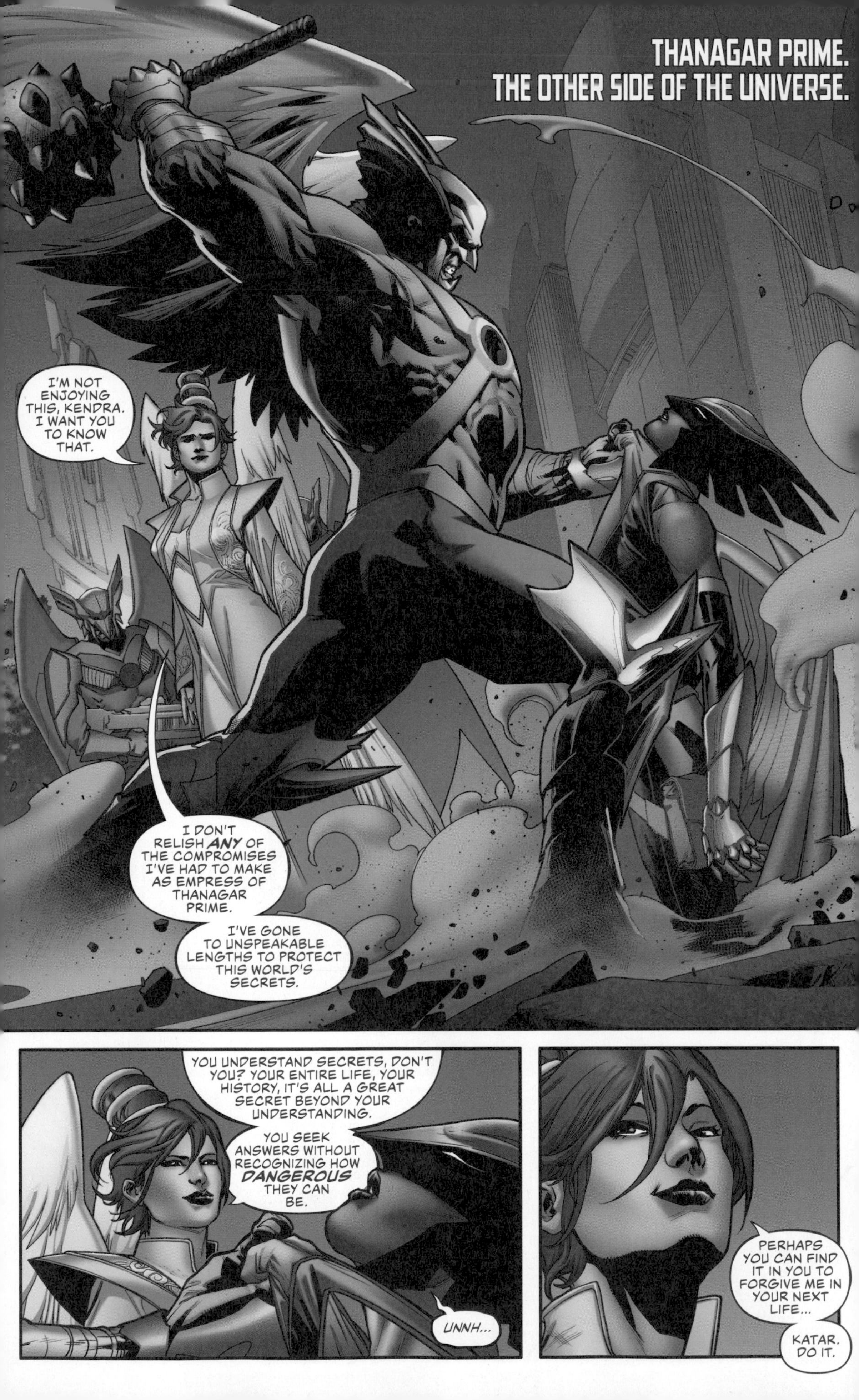
THANAGAR PRIME.
THE OTHER SIDE OF THE UNIVERSE.
I'M NOT ENJOYING THIS, KENDRA. I WANT YOU TO KNOW THAT.
I DON'T RELISH ANY OF THE COMPROMISES I'VE HAD TO MAKE AS EMPRESS OF THANAGAR PRIME.
I'VE GONE TO UNSPEAKABLE LENGTHS TO PROTECT THIS WORLD'S SECRETS.
YOU UNDERSTAND SECRETS, DON'T YOU? YOUR ENTIRE LIFE, YOUR HISTORY, IT'S ALL A GREAT SECRET BEYOND YOUR UNDERSTANDING.
YOU SEEK ANSWERS WITHOUT RECOGNIZING HOW DANGEROUS THEY CAN BE.
UNNH...
PERHAPS YOU CAN FIND IT IN YOU TO FORGIVE ME IN YOUR NEXT LIFE...
KATAR. DO IT.

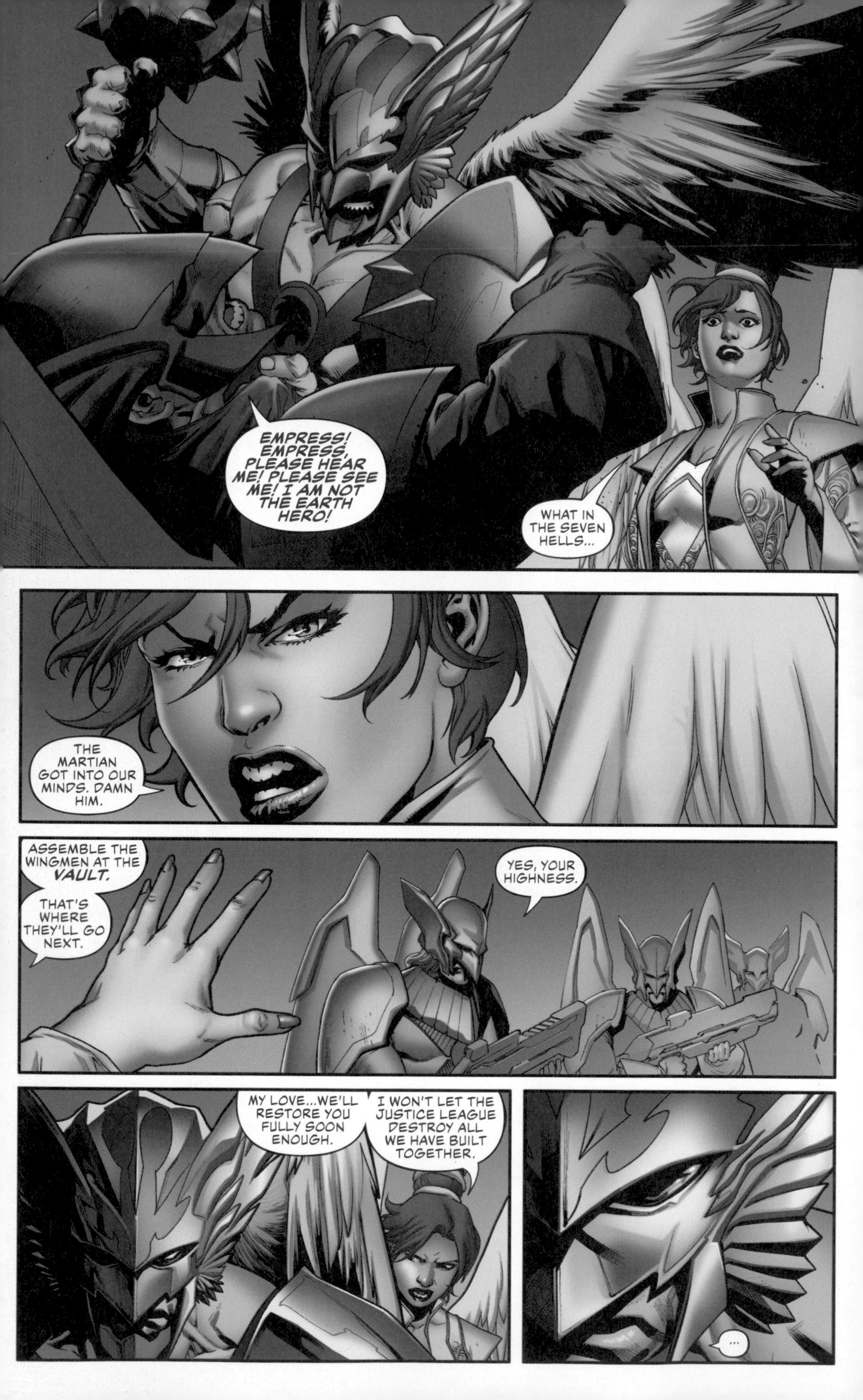
EMPRESS! EMPRESS, PLEASE HEAR ME! PLEASE SEE ME! I AM NOT THE EARTH HERO!
WHAT IN THE SEVEN HELLS...
THE MARTIAN GOT INTO OUR MINDS. DAMN HIM.
ASSEMBLE THE WINGMEN AT THE VAULT.
THAT'S WHERE THEY'LL GO NEXT.
YES, YOUR HIGHNESS.
MY LOVE...WE'LL RESTORE YOU FULLY SOON ENOUGH.
I WON'T LET THE JUSTICE LEAGUE DESTROY ALL WE HAVE BUILT TOGETHER.
...

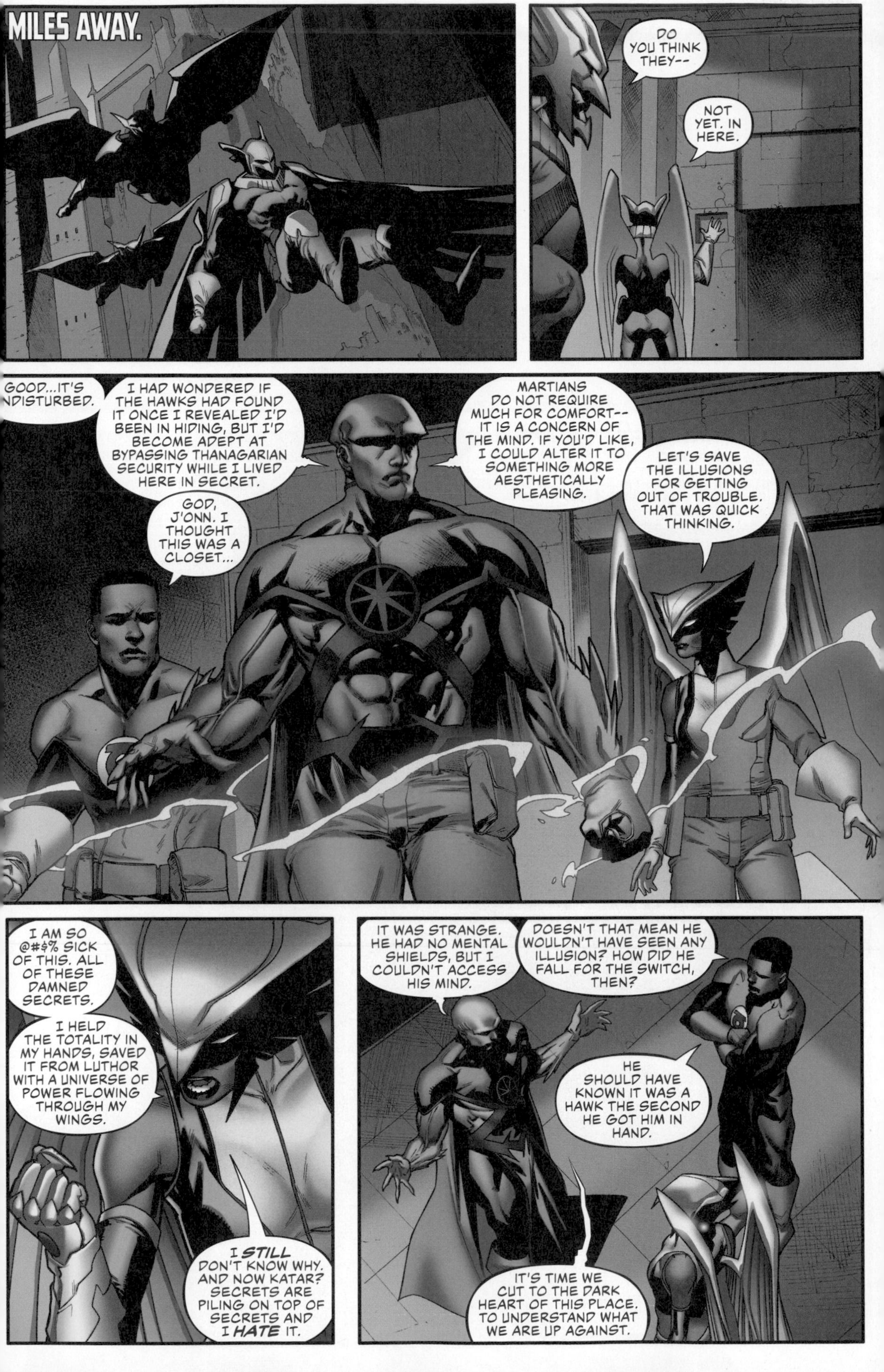
MILES AWAY.
DO YOU THINK THEY--
NOT YET. IN HERE.
GOOD...IT'S UNDISTURBED.
I HAD WONDERED IF THE HAWKS HAD FOUND IT ONCE I REVEALED I'D BEEN IN HIDING, BUT I'D BECOME ADEPT AT BYPASSING THANAGARIAN SECURITY WHILE I LIVED HERE IN SECRET.
GOD, J'ONN. I THOUGHT THIS WAS A CLOSET...
MARTIANS DO NOT REQUIRE MUCH FOR COMFORT-- IT IS A CONCERN OF THE MIND. IF YOU'D LIKE, I COULD ALTER IT TO SOMETHING MORE AESTHETICALLY PLEASING.
LET'S SAVE THE ILLUSIONS FOR GETTING OUT OF TROUBLE. THAT WAS QUICK THINKING.
I AM SO @#$% SICK OF THIS. ALL OF THESE DAMNED SECRETS.
I HELD THE TOTALITY IN MY HANDS, SAVED IT FROM LUTHOR WITH A UNIVERSE OF POWER FLOWING THROUGH MY WINGS.
I STILL DON'T KNOW WHY. AND NOW KATAR? SECRETS ARE PILING ON TOP OF SECRETS AND I HATE IT.
IT WAS STRANGE. HE HAD NO MENTAL SHIELDS, BUT I COULDN'T ACCESS HIS MIND.
DOESN'T THAT MEAN HE WOULDN'T HAVE SEEN ANY ILLUSION? HOW DID HE FALL FOR THE SWITCH, THEN?
HE SHOULD HAVE KNOWN IT WAS A HAWK THE SECOND HE GOT HIM IN HAND.
IT'S TIME WE CUT TO THE DARK HEART OF THIS PLACE. TO UNDERSTAND WHAT WE ARE UP AGAINST.

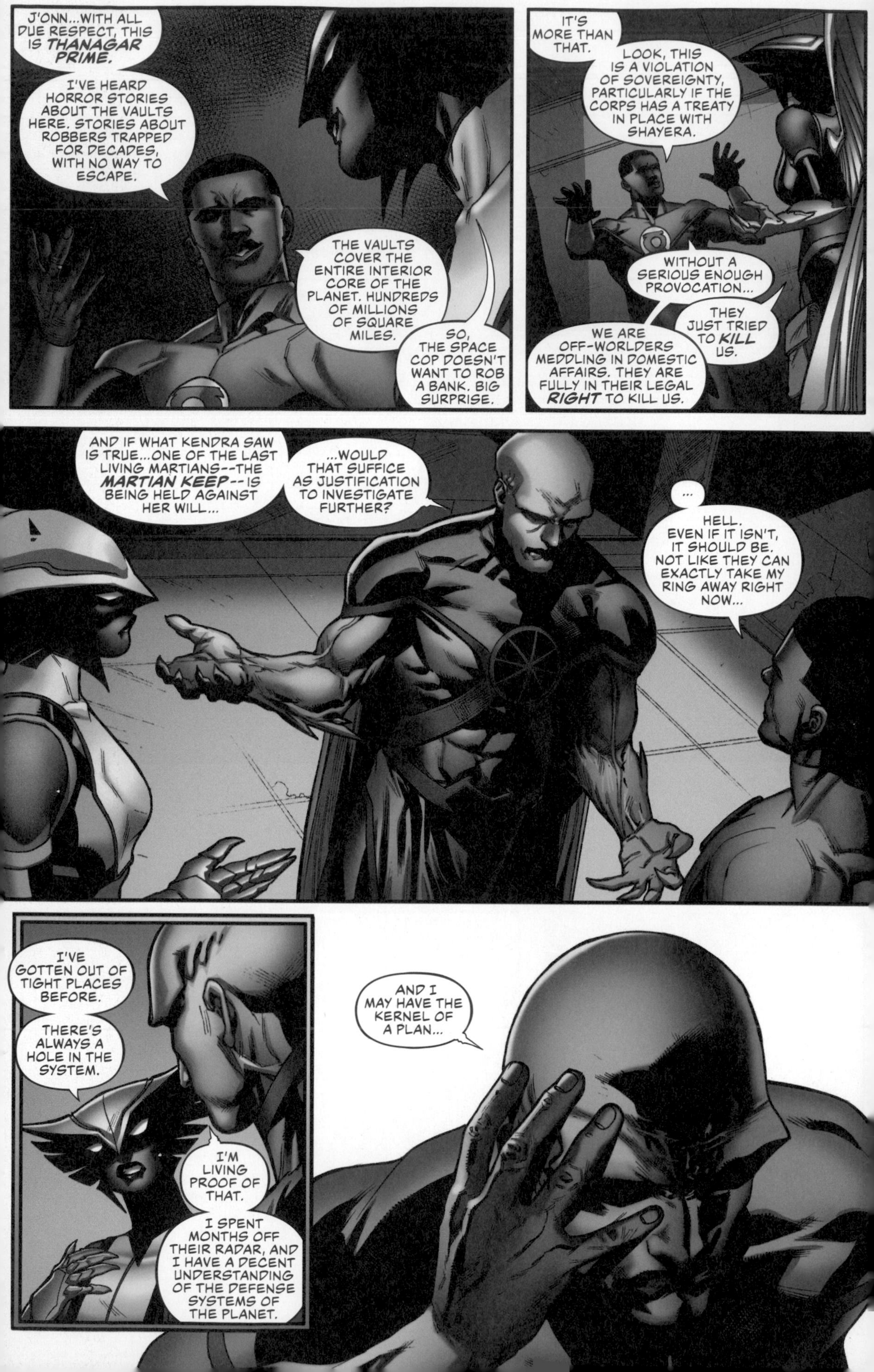
J'ONN...WITH ALL DUE RESPECT, THIS IS THANAGAR PRIME.
I'VE HEARD HORROR STORIES ABOUT THE VAULTS HERE. STORIES ABOUT ROBBERS TRAPPED FOR DECADES, WITH NO WAY TO ESCAPE.
THE VAULTS COVER THE ENTIRE INTERIOR CORE OF THE PLANET. HUNDREDS OF MILLIONS OF SQUARE MILES.
SO, THE SPACE COP DOESN'T WANT TO ROB A BANK. BIG SURPRISE.
IT'S MORE THAN THAT.
LOOK, THIS IS A VIOLATION OF SOVEREIGNTY, PARTICULARLY IF THE CORPS HAS A TREATY IN PLACE WITH SHAYERA.
WITHOUT A SERIOUS ENOUGH PROVOCATION...
WE ARE OFF-WORLDERS MEDDLING IN DOMESTIC AFFAIRS. THEY ARE FULLY IN THEIR LEGAL RIGHT TO KILL US.
THEY JUST TRIED TO KILL US.
AND IF WHAT KENDRA SAW IS TRUE...ONE OF THE LAST LIVING MARTIANS--THE MARTIAN KEEP--IS BEING HELD AGAINST HER WILL...
...WOULD THAT SUFFICE AS JUSTIFICATION TO INVESTIGATE FURTHER?
...
HELL. EVEN IF IT ISN'T, IT SHOULD BE. NOT LIKE THEY CAN EXACTLY TAKE MY RING AWAY RIGHT NOW...
I'VE GOTTEN OUT OF TIGHT PLACES BEFORE.
THERE'S ALWAYS A HOLE IN THE SYSTEM.
I'M LIVING PROOF OF THAT.
I SPENT MONTHS OFF THEIR RADAR, AND I HAVE A DECENT UNDERSTANDING OF THE DEFENSE SYSTEMS OF THE PLANET.
AND I MAY HAVE THE KERNEL OF A PLAN...

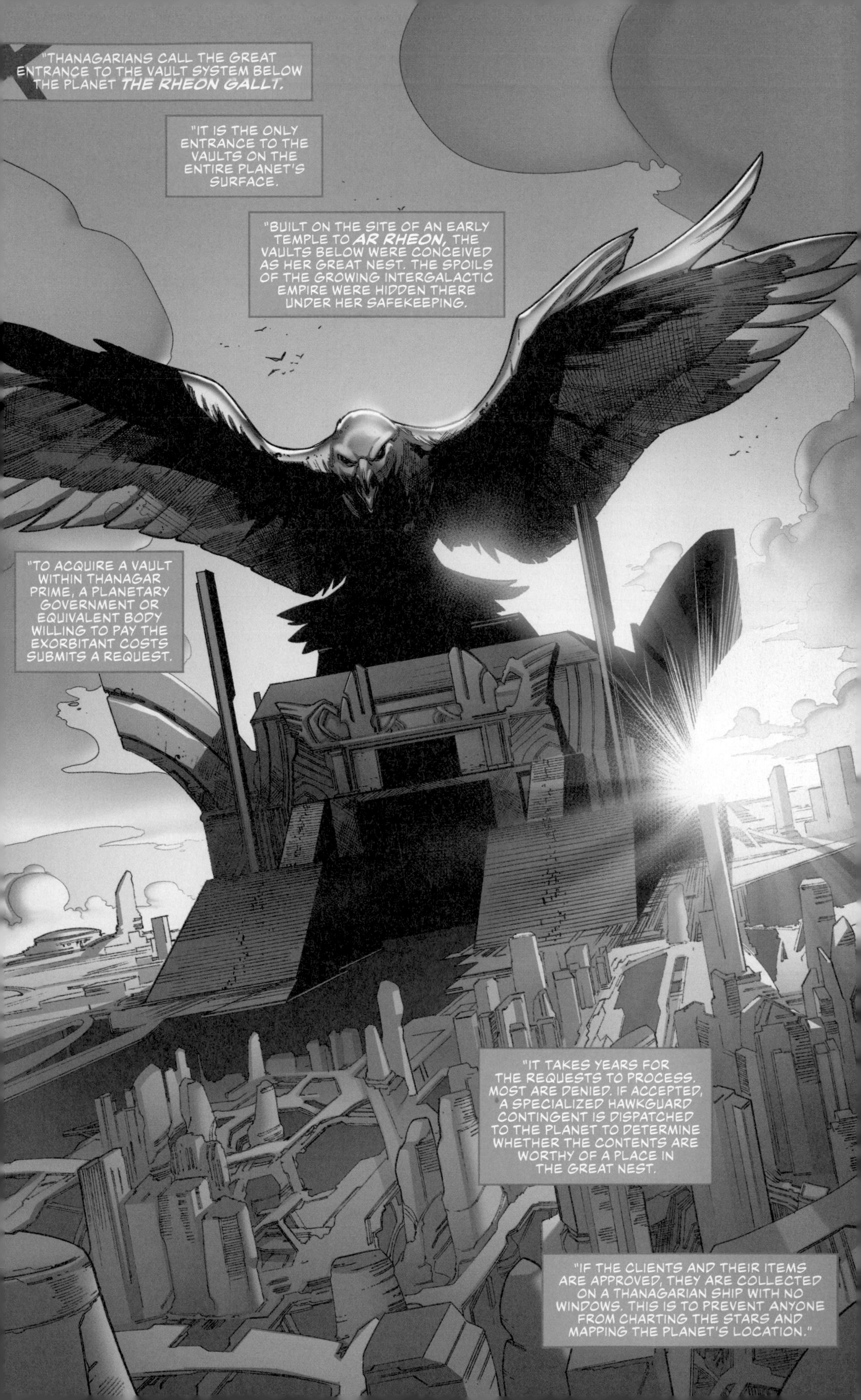
"THANAGARIANS CALL THE GREAT ENTRANCE TO THE VAULT SYSTEM BELOW THE PLANET *THE RHEON GALLT.*
"IT IS THE ONLY ENTRANCE TO THE VAULTS ON THE ENTIRE PLANET'S SURFACE.
"BUILT ON THE SITE OF AN EARLY TEMPLE TO *AR RHEON,* THE VAULTS BELOW WERE CONCEIVED AS HER GREAT NEST. THE SPOILS OF THE GROWING INTERGALACTIC EMPIRE WERE HIDDEN THERE UNDER HER SAFEKEEPING.
"TO ACQUIRE A VAULT WITHIN THANAGAR PRIME, A PLANETARY GOVERNMENT OR EQUIVALENT BODY WILLING TO PAY THE EXORBITANT COSTS SUBMITS A REQUEST.
"IT TAKES YEARS FOR THE REQUESTS TO PROCESS. MOST ARE DENIED. IF ACCEPTED, A SPECIALIZED HAWKGUARD CONTINGENT IS DISPATCHED TO THE PLANET TO DETERMINE WHETHER THE CONTENTS ARE WORTHY OF A PLACE IN THE GREAT NEST.
"IF THE CLIENTS AND THEIR ITEMS ARE APPROVED, THEY ARE COLLECTED ON A THANAGARIAN SHIP WITH NO WINDOWS. THIS IS TO PREVENT ANYONE FROM CHARTING THE STARS AND MAPPING THE PLANET'S LOCATION."

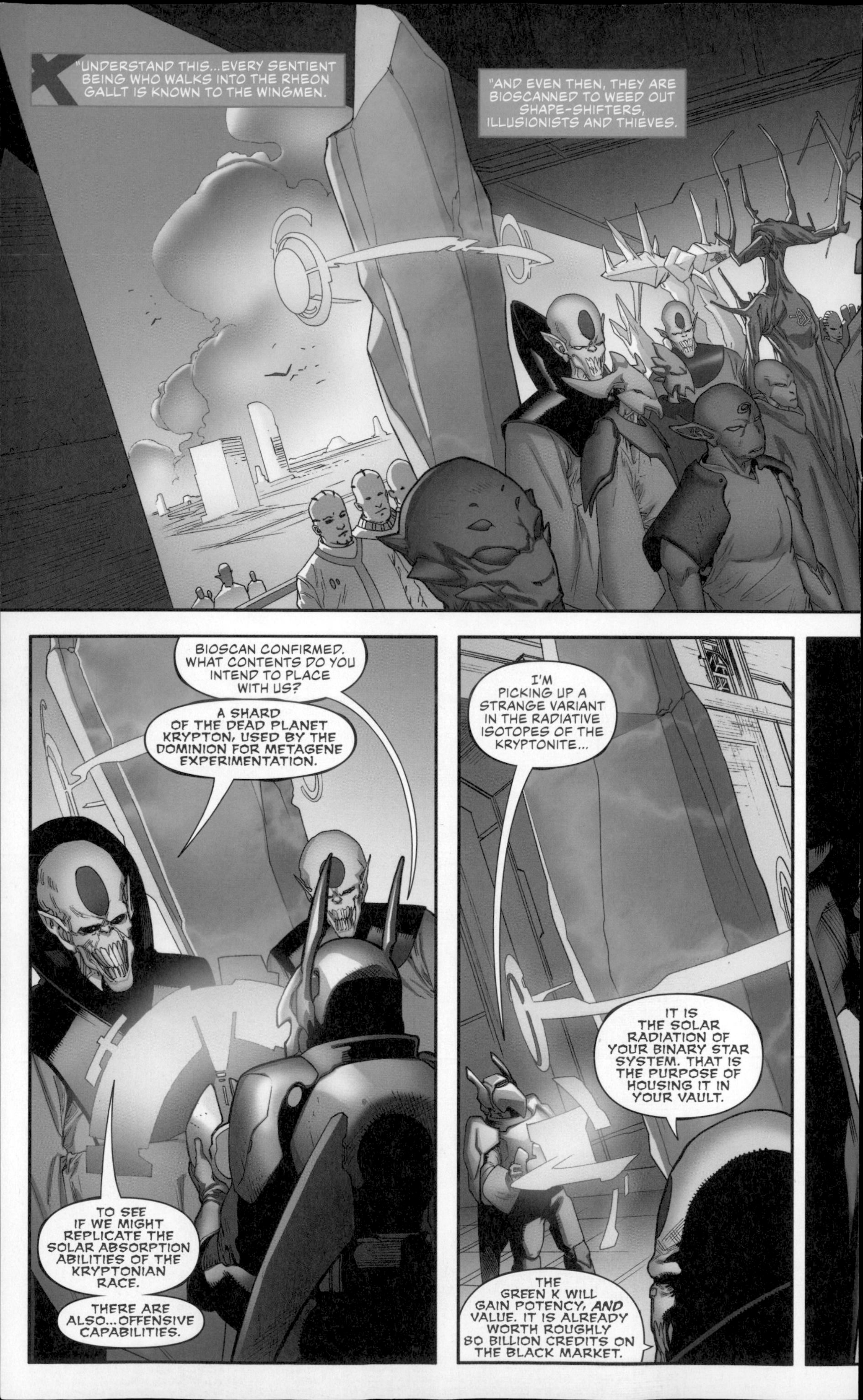
"UNDERSTAND THIS...EVERY SENTIENT BEING WHO WALKS INTO THE RHEON GALLT IS KNOWN TO THE WINGMEN.
"AND EVEN THEN, THEY ARE BIOSCANNED TO WEED OUT SHAPE-SHIFTERS, ILLUSIONISTS AND THIEVES.
BIOSCAN CONFIRMED. WHAT CONTENTS DO YOU INTEND TO PLACE WITH US?
A SHARD OF THE DEAD PLANET KRYPTON, USED BY THE DOMINION FOR METAGENE EXPERIMENTATION.
TO SEE IF WE MIGHT REPLICATE THE SOLAR ABSORPTION ABILITIES OF THE KRYPTONIAN RACE.
THERE ARE ALSO...OFFENSIVE CAPABILITIES.
I'M PICKING UP A STRANGE VARIANT IN THE RADIATIVE ISOTOPES OF THE KRYPTONITE...
IT IS THE SOLAR RADIATION OF YOUR BINARY STAR SYSTEM. THAT IS THE PURPOSE OF HOUSING IT IN YOUR VAULT.
THE GREEN K WILL GAIN POTENCY, AND VALUE. IT IS ALREADY WORTH ROUGHLY 80 BILLION CREDITS ON THE BLACK MARKET.

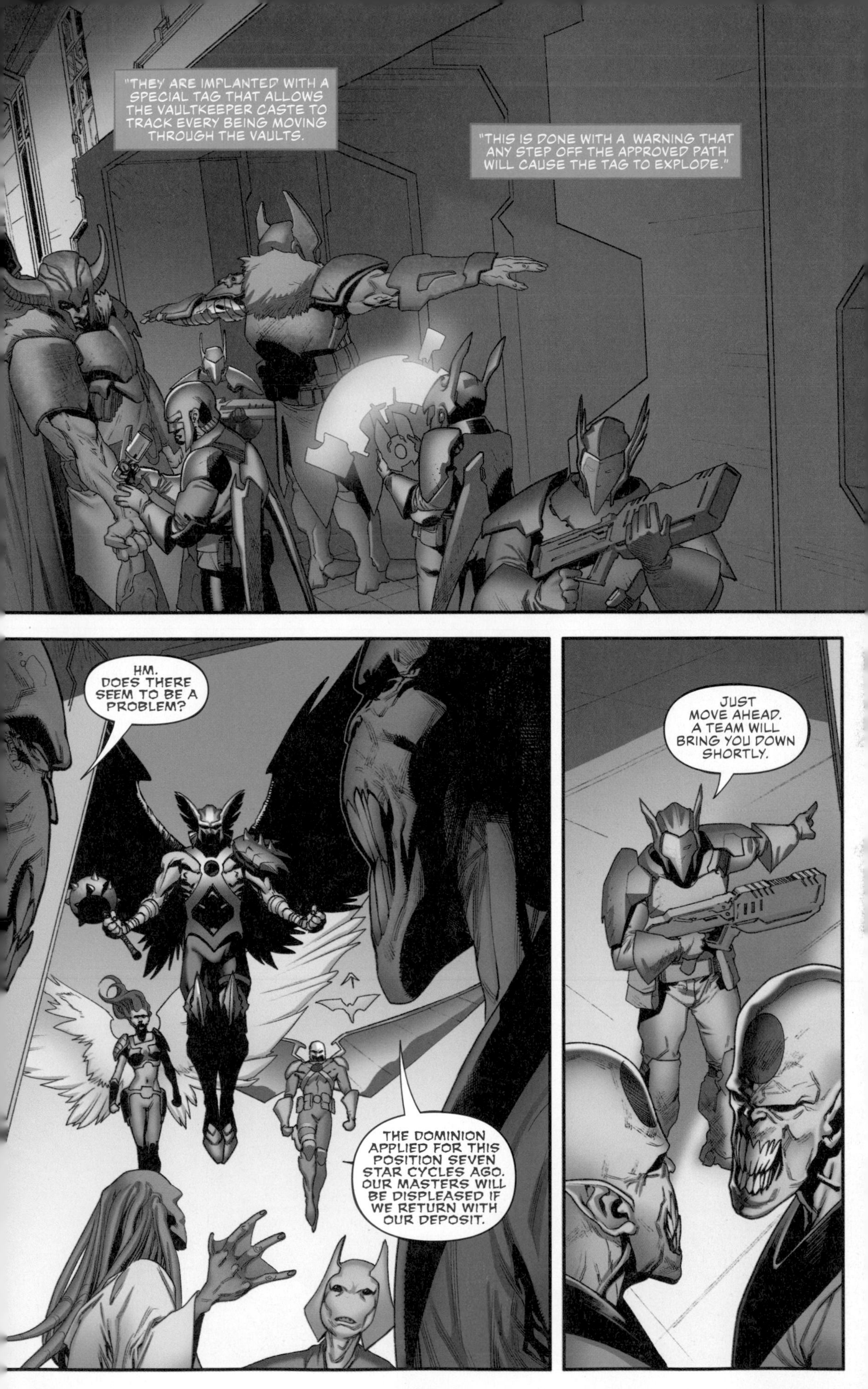
"THEY ARE IMPLANTED WITH A SPECIAL TAG THAT ALLOWS THE VAULTKEEPER CASTE TO TRACK EVERY BEING MOVING THROUGH THE VAULTS.
"THIS IS DONE WITH A WARNING THAT ANY STEP OFF THE APPROVED PATH WILL CAUSE THE TAG TO EXPLODE."
HM. DOES THERE SEEM TO BE A PROBLEM?
THE DOMINION APPLIED FOR THIS POSITION SEVEN STAR CYCLES AGO. OUR MASTERS WILL BE DISPLEASED IF WE RETURN WITH OUR DEPOSIT.
JUST MOVE AHEAD. A TEAM WILL BRING YOU DOWN SHORTLY.

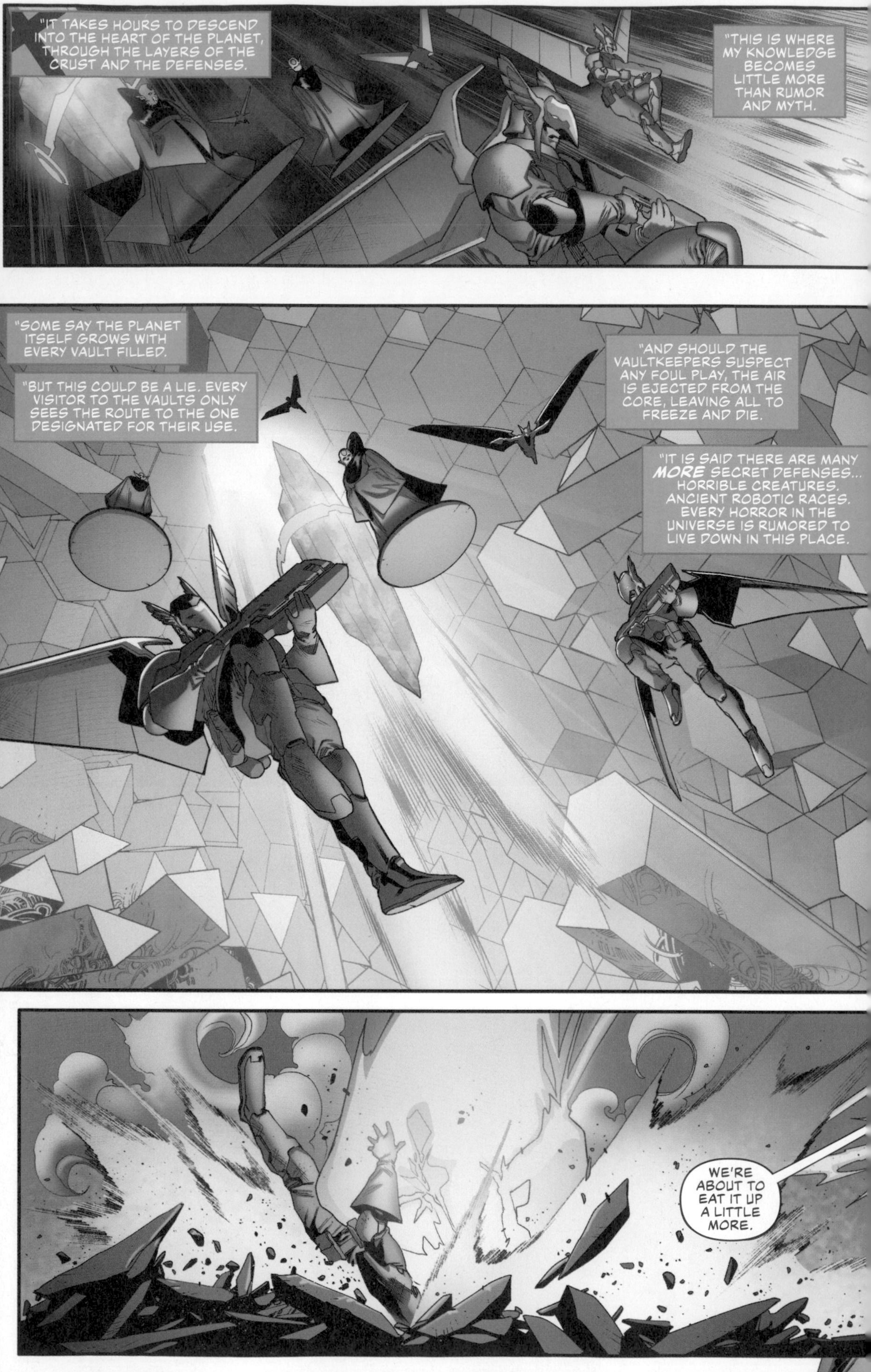
"IT TAKES HOURS TO DESCEND INTO THE HEART OF THE PLANET, THROUGH THE LAYERS OF THE CRUST AND THE DEFENSES.
"THIS IS WHERE MY KNOWLEDGE BECOMES LITTLE MORE THAN RUMOR AND MYTH.
"SOME SAY THE PLANET ITSELF GROWS WITH EVERY VAULT FILLED.
"BUT THIS COULD BE A LIE. EVERY VISITOR TO THE VAULTS ONLY SEES THE ROUTE TO THE ONE DESIGNATED FOR THEIR USE.
"AND SHOULD THE VAULTKEEPERS SUSPECT ANY FOUL PLAY, THE AIR IS EJECTED FROM THE CORE, LEAVING ALL TO FREEZE AND DIE.
"IT IS SAID THERE ARE MANY MORE SECRET DEFENSES... HORRIBLE CREATURES. ANCIENT ROBOTIC RACES. EVERY HORROR IN THE UNIVERSE IS RUMORED TO LIVE DOWN IN THIS PLACE.
WE'RE ABOUT TO EAT IT UP A LITTLE MORE.

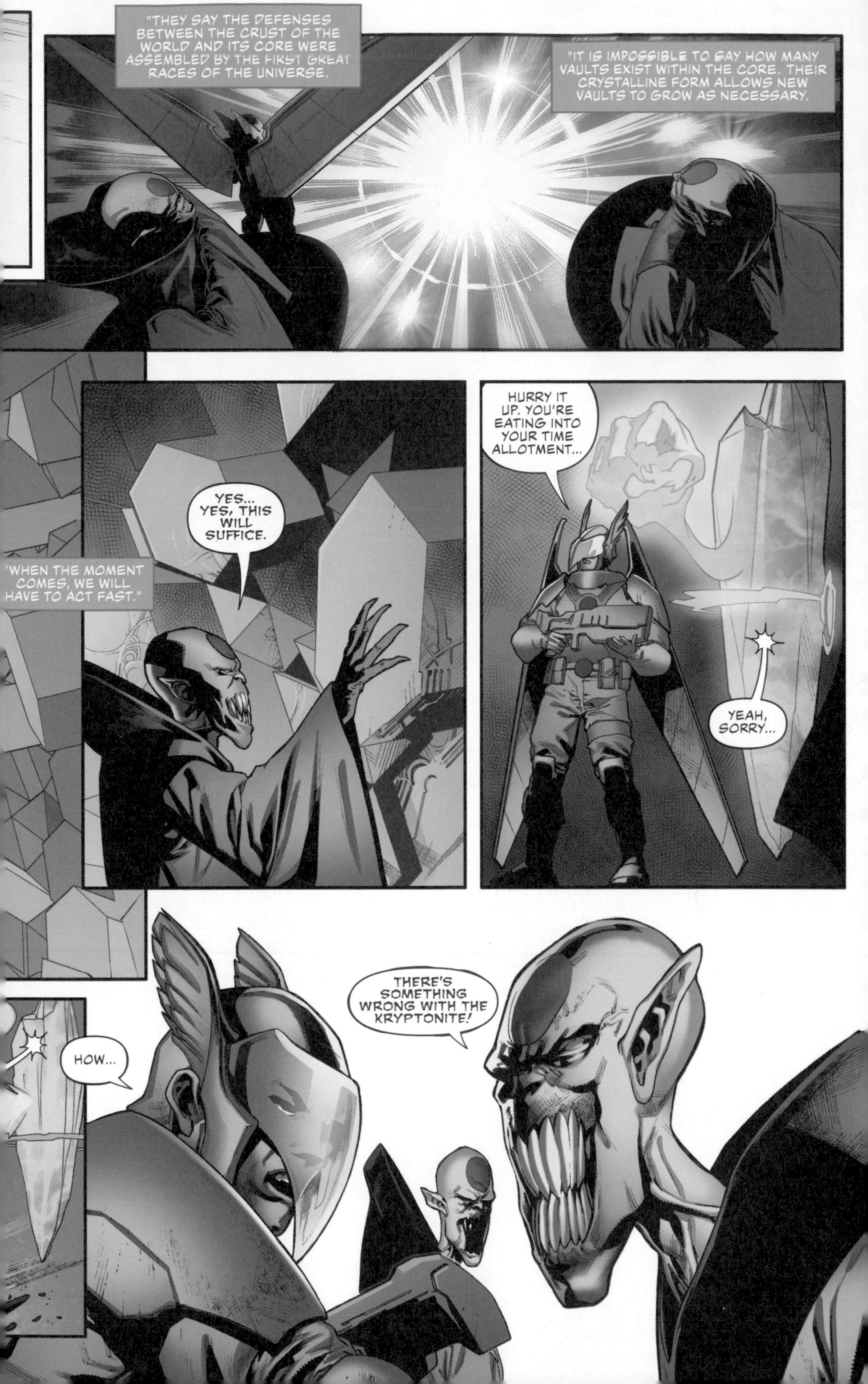
"THEY SAY THE DEFENSES BETWEEN THE CRUST OF THE WORLD AND ITS CORE WERE ASSEMBLED BY THE FIRST GREAT RACES OF THE UNIVERSE.
"IT IS IMPOSSIBLE TO SAY HOW MANY VAULTS EXIST WITHIN THE CORE. THEIR CRYSTALLINE FORM ALLOWS NEW VAULTS TO GROW AS NECESSARY.
"WHEN THE MOMENT COMES, WE WILL HAVE TO ACT FAST."
YES... YES, THIS WILL SUFFICE.
HURRY IT UP. YOU'RE EATING INTO YOUR TIME ALLOTMENT...
YEAH, SORRY...
HOW...
THERE'S SOMETHING WRONG WITH THE KRYPTONITE!

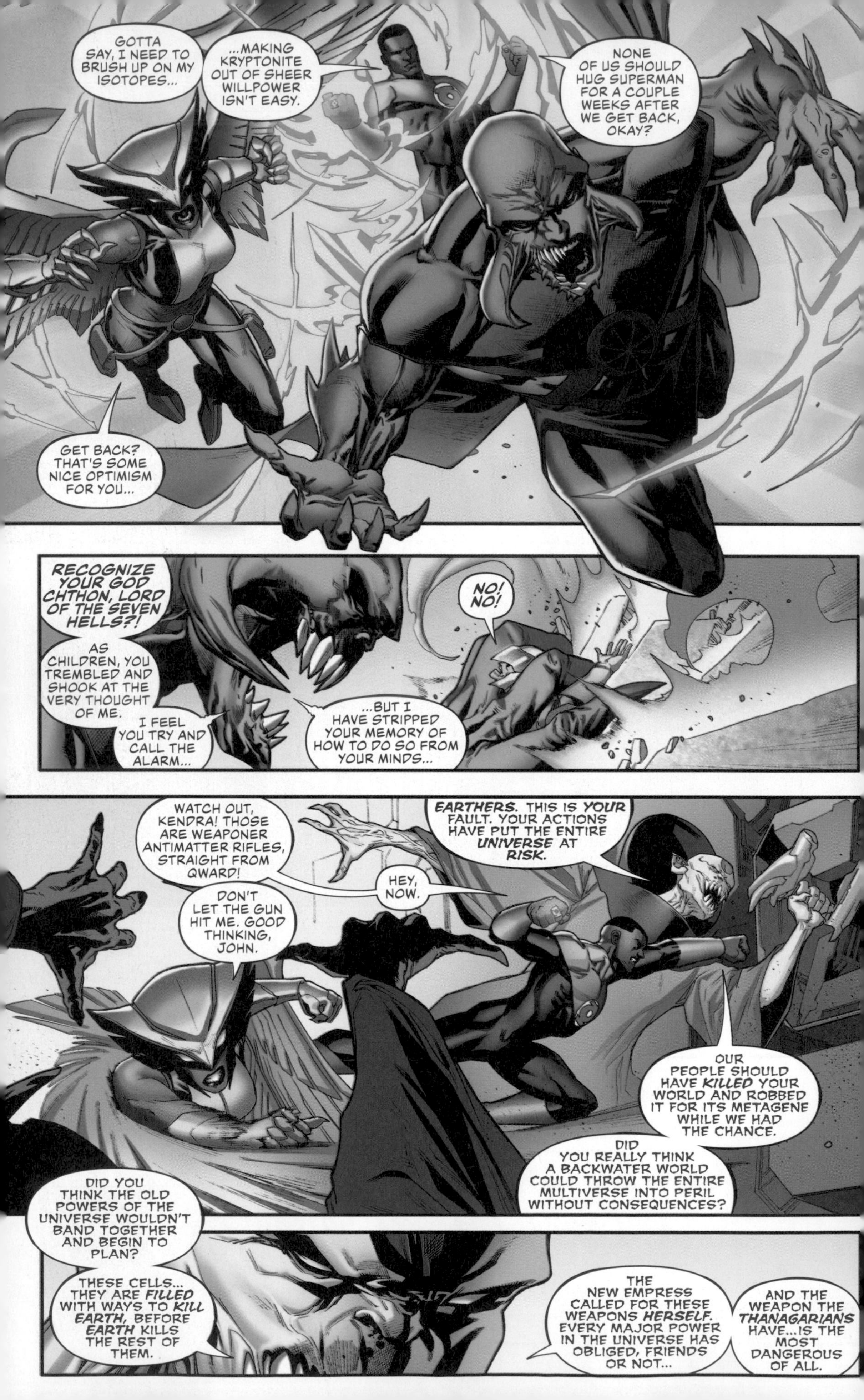

GOTTA SAY, I NEED TO BRUSH UP ON MY ISOTOPES...
...MAKING KRYPTONITE OUT OF SHEER WILLPOWER ISN'T EASY.
NONE OF US SHOULD HUG SUPERMAN FOR A COUPLE WEEKS AFTER WE GET BACK, OKAY?
GET BACK? THAT'S SOME NICE OPTIMISM FOR YOU...
RECOGNIZE YOUR GOD CHTHON, LORD OF THE SEVEN HELLS?!
AS CHILDREN, YOU TREMBLED AND SHOOK AT THE VERY THOUGHT OF ME.
NO! NO!
I FEEL YOU TRY AND CALL THE ALARM...
...BUT I HAVE STRIPPED YOUR MEMORY OF HOW TO DO SO FROM YOUR MINDS...
WATCH OUT, KENDRA! THOSE ARE WEAPONER ANTIMATTER RIFLES, STRAIGHT FROM QWARD!
EARTHERS. THIS IS YOUR FAULT. YOUR ACTIONS HAVE PUT THE ENTIRE UNIVERSE AT RISK.
HEY, NOW.
DON'T LET THE GUN HIT ME. GOOD THINKING, JOHN.
OUR PEOPLE SHOULD HAVE KILLED YOUR WORLD AND ROBBED IT FOR ITS METAGENE WHILE WE HAD THE CHANCE.
DID YOU REALLY THINK A BACKWATER WORLD COULD THROW THE ENTIRE MULTIVERSE INTO PERIL WITHOUT CONSEQUENCES?
DID YOU THINK THE OLD POWERS OF THE UNIVERSE WOULDN'T BAND TOGETHER AND BEGIN TO PLAN?
THESE CELLS... THEY ARE FILLED WITH WAYS TO KILL EARTH, BEFORE EARTH KILLS THE REST OF THEM.
THE NEW EMPRESS CALLED FOR THESE WEAPONS HERSELF. EVERY MAJOR POWER IN THE UNIVERSE HAS OBLIGED, FRIENDS OR NOT...
AND THE WEAPON THE THANAGARIANS HAVE...IS THE MOST DANGEROUS OF ALL.

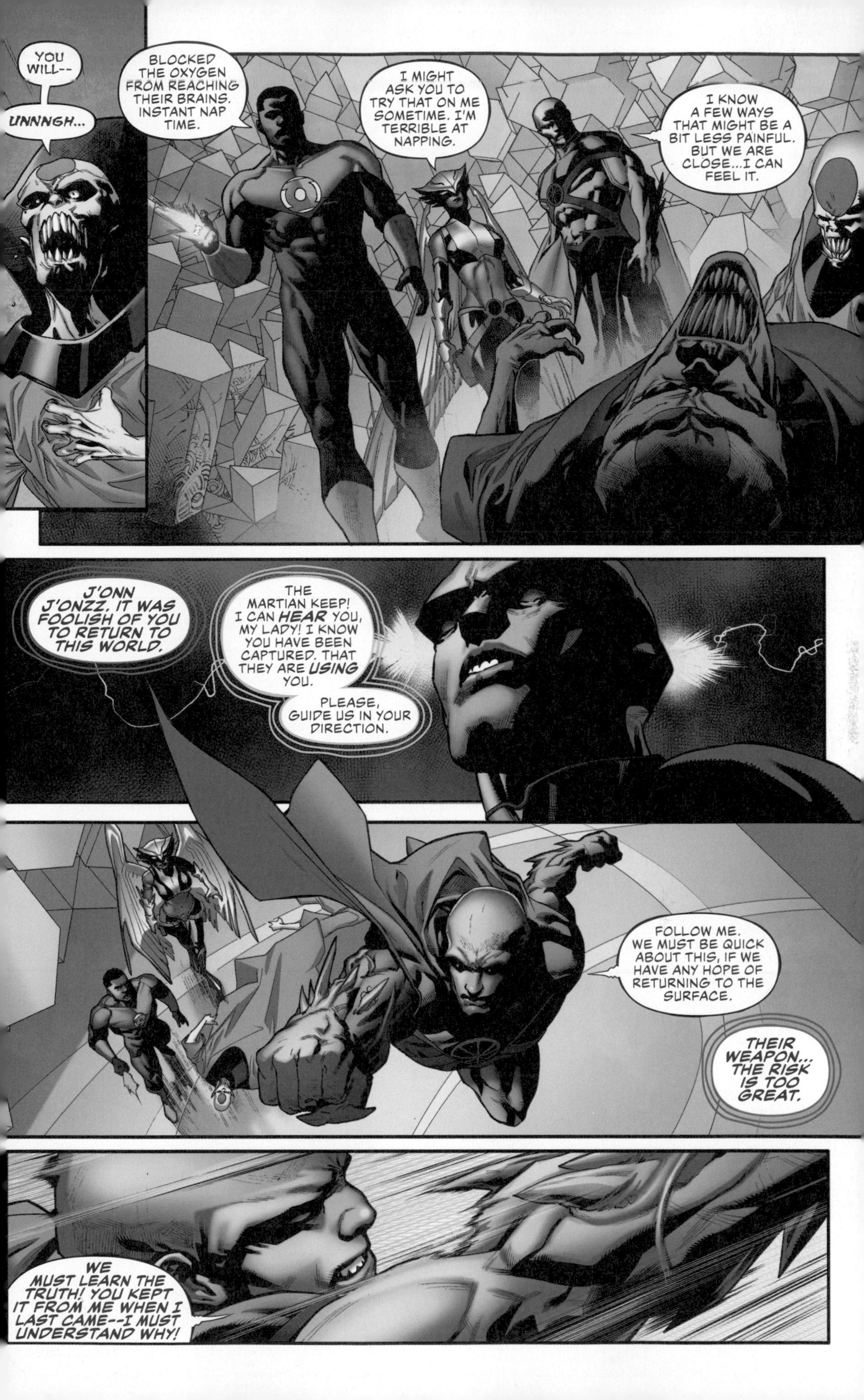
YOU WILL--
UNNNGH...
BLOCKED THE OXYGEN FROM REACHING THEIR BRAINS. INSTANT NAP TIME.
I MIGHT ASK YOU TO TRY THAT ON ME SOMETIME. I'M TERRIBLE AT NAPPING.
I KNOW A FEW WAYS THAT MIGHT BE A BIT LESS PAINFUL. BUT WE ARE CLOSE...I CAN FEEL IT.
J'ONN J'ONZZ. IT WAS FOOLISH OF YOU TO RETURN TO THIS WORLD.
THE MARTIAN KEEP! I CAN HEAR YOU, MY LADY! I KNOW YOU HAVE BEEN CAPTURED. THAT THEY ARE USING YOU.
PLEASE, GUIDE US IN YOUR DIRECTION.
FOLLOW ME. WE MUST BE QUICK ABOUT THIS, IF WE HAVE ANY HOPE OF RETURNING TO THE SURFACE.
THEIR WEAPON... THE RISK IS TOO GREAT.
WE MUST LEARN THE TRUTH! YOU KEPT IT FROM ME WHEN I LAST CAME--I MUST UNDERSTAND WHY!

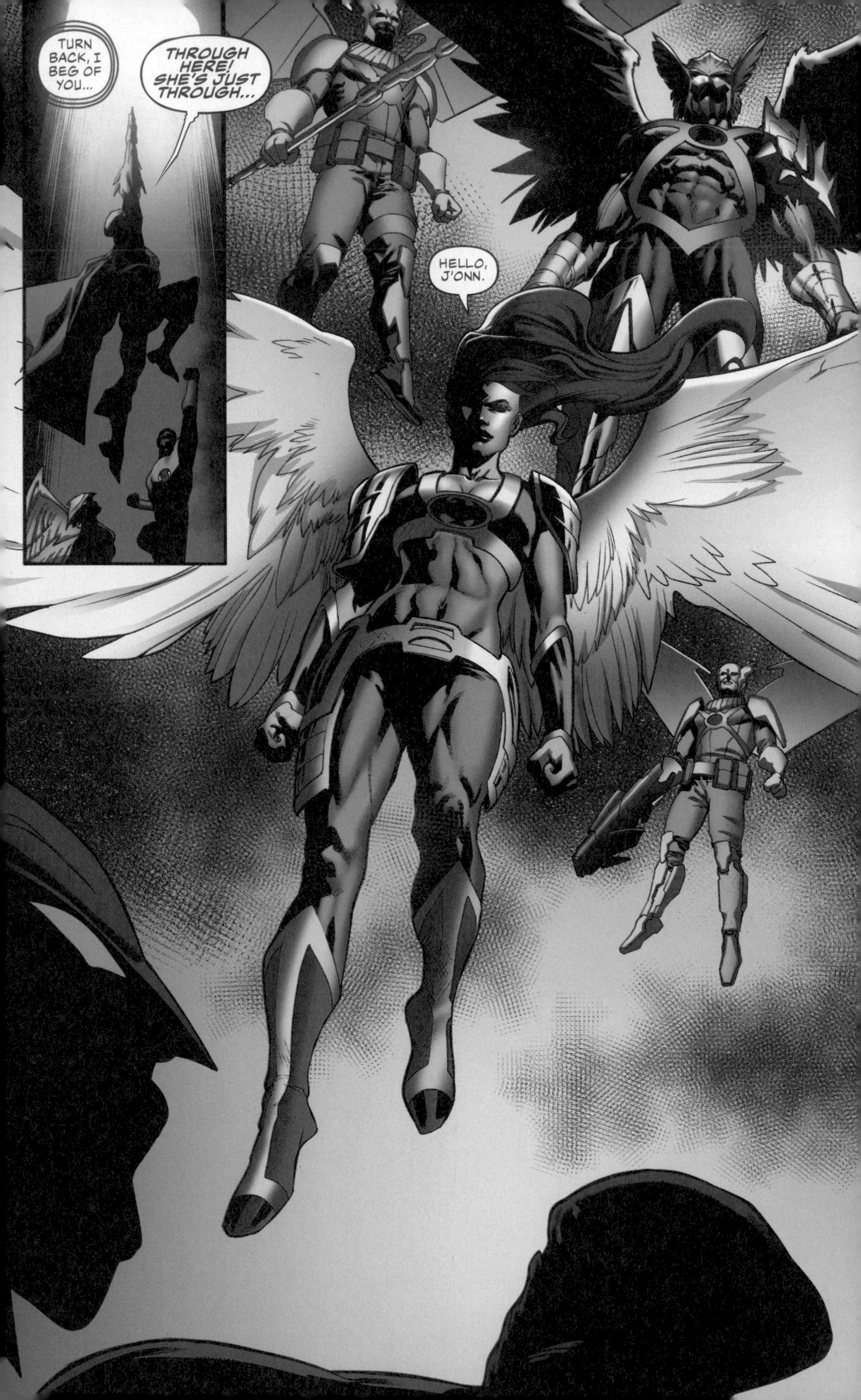

TURN BACK, I BEG OF YOU...
THROUGH HERE! SHE'S JUST THROUGH...
HELLO, J'ONN.

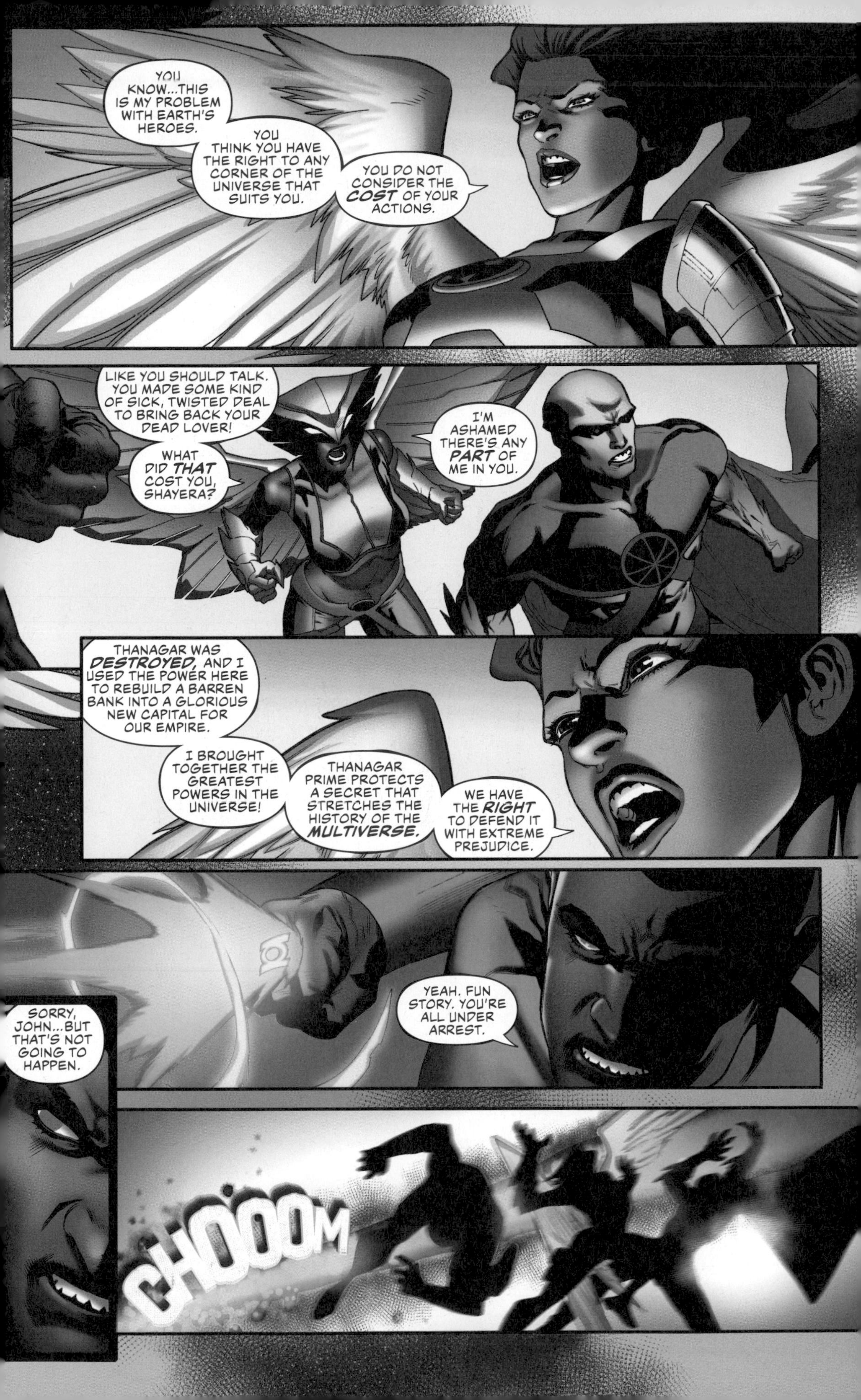
YOU KNOW...THIS IS MY PROBLEM WITH EARTH'S HEROES.
YOU THINK YOU HAVE THE RIGHT TO ANY CORNER OF THE UNIVERSE THAT SUITS YOU.
YOU DO NOT CONSIDER THE COST OF YOUR ACTIONS.
LIKE YOU SHOULD TALK. YOU MADE SOME KIND OF SICK, TWISTED DEAL TO BRING BACK YOUR DEAD LOVER!
WHAT DID THAT COST YOU, SHAYERA?
I'M ASHAMED THERE'S ANY PART OF ME IN YOU.
THANAGAR WAS DESTROYED, AND I USED THE POWER HERE TO REBUILD A BARREN BANK INTO A GLORIOUS NEW CAPITAL FOR OUR EMPIRE.
I BROUGHT TOGETHER THE GREATEST POWERS IN THE UNIVERSE!
THANAGAR PRIME PROTECTS A SECRET THAT STRETCHES THE HISTORY OF THE MULTIVERSE.
WE HAVE THE RIGHT TO DEFEND IT WITH EXTREME PREJUDICE.
YEAH. FUN STORY. YOU'RE ALL UNDER ARREST.
SORRY, JOHN...BUT THAT'S NOT GOING TO HAPPEN.
CHOOOM

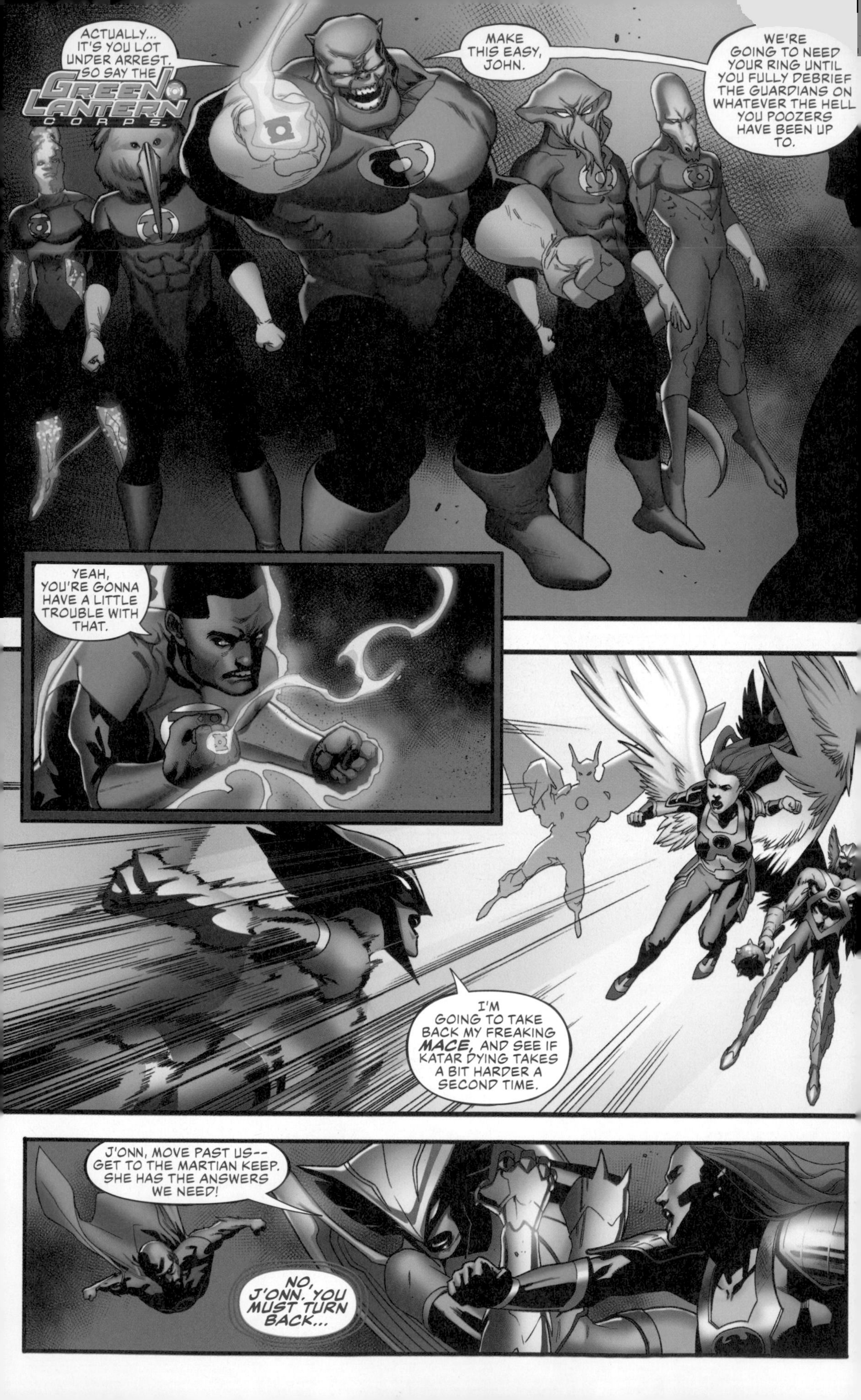
ACTUALLY... IT'S YOU LOT UNDER ARREST. SO SAY THE
GREEN LANTERN CORPS.
MAKE THIS EASY, JOHN.
WE'RE GOING TO NEED YOUR RING UNTIL YOU FULLY DEBRIEF THE GUARDIANS ON WHATEVER THE HELL YOU POOZERS HAVE BEEN UP TO.
YEAH, YOU'RE GONNA HAVE A LITTLE TROUBLE WITH THAT.
I'M GOING TO TAKE BACK MY FREAKING MACE, AND SEE IF KATAR DYING TAKES A BIT HARDER A SECOND TIME.
J'ONN, MOVE PAST US-- GET TO THE MARTIAN KEEP. SHE HAS THE ANSWERS WE NEED!
NO, J'ONN. YOU MUST TURN BACK...

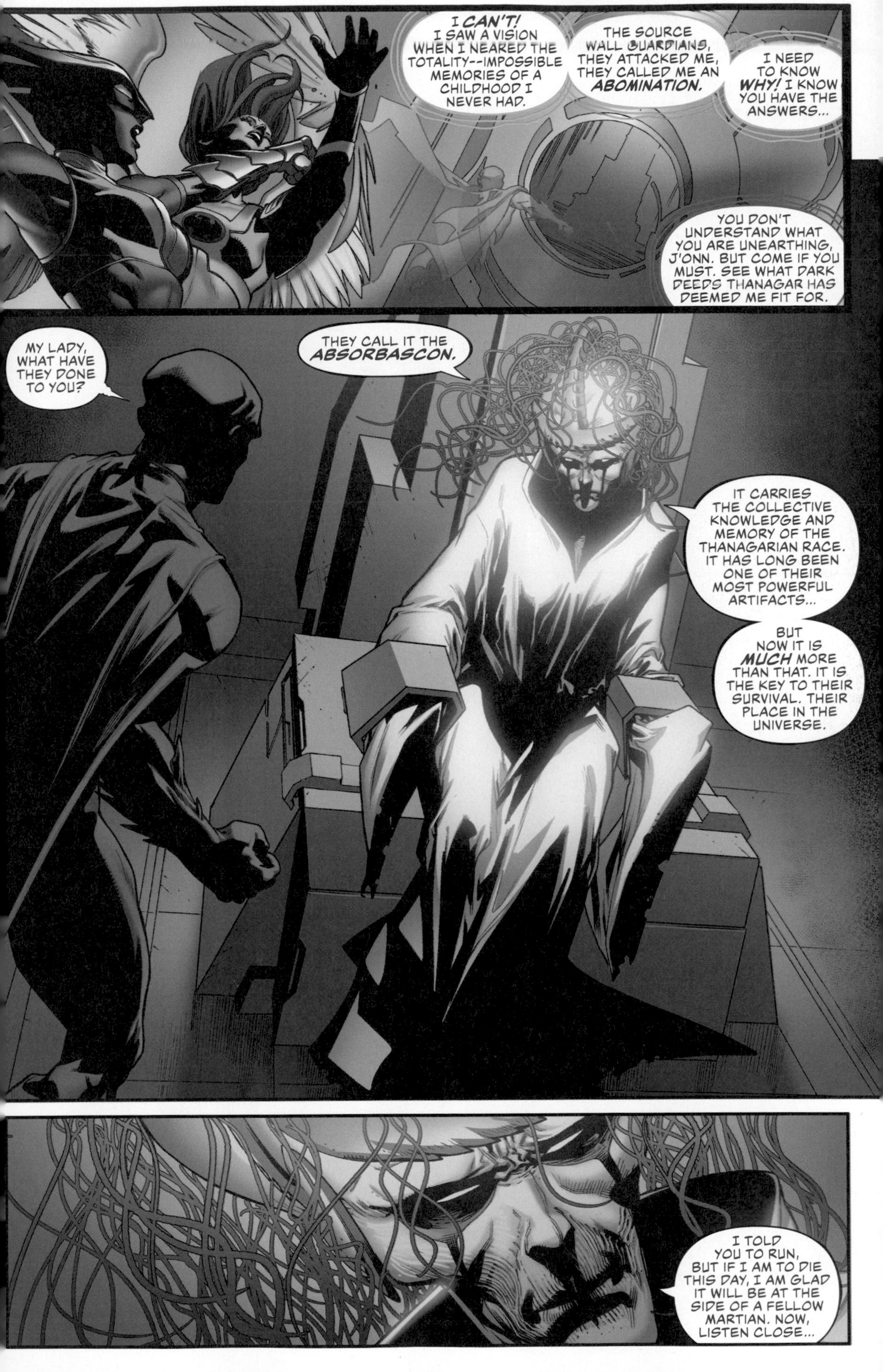
I CAN'T! I SAW A VISION WHEN I NEARED THE TOTALITY--IMPOSSIBLE MEMORIES OF A CHILDHOOD I NEVER HAD.
THE SOURCE WALL GUARDIANS, THEY ATTACKED ME, THEY CALLED ME AN ABOMINATION.
I NEED TO KNOW WHY! I KNOW YOU HAVE THE ANSWERS...
YOU DON'T UNDERSTAND WHAT YOU ARE UNEARTHING, J'ONN. BUT COME IF YOU MUST. SEE WHAT DARK DEEDS THANAGAR HAS DEEMED ME FIT FOR.
MY LADY, WHAT HAVE THEY DONE TO YOU?
THEY CALL IT THE ABSORBASCON.
IT CARRIES THE COLLECTIVE KNOWLEDGE AND MEMORY OF THE THANAGARIAN RACE. IT HAS LONG BEEN ONE OF THEIR MOST POWERFUL ARTIFACTS...
BUT NOW IT IS MUCH MORE THAN THAT. IT IS THE KEY TO THEIR SURVIVAL. THEIR PLACE IN THE UNIVERSE.
I TOLD YOU TO RUN, BUT IF I AM TO DIE THIS DAY, I AM GLAD IT WILL BE AT THE SIDE OF A FELLOW MARTIAN. NOW, LISTEN CLOSE...

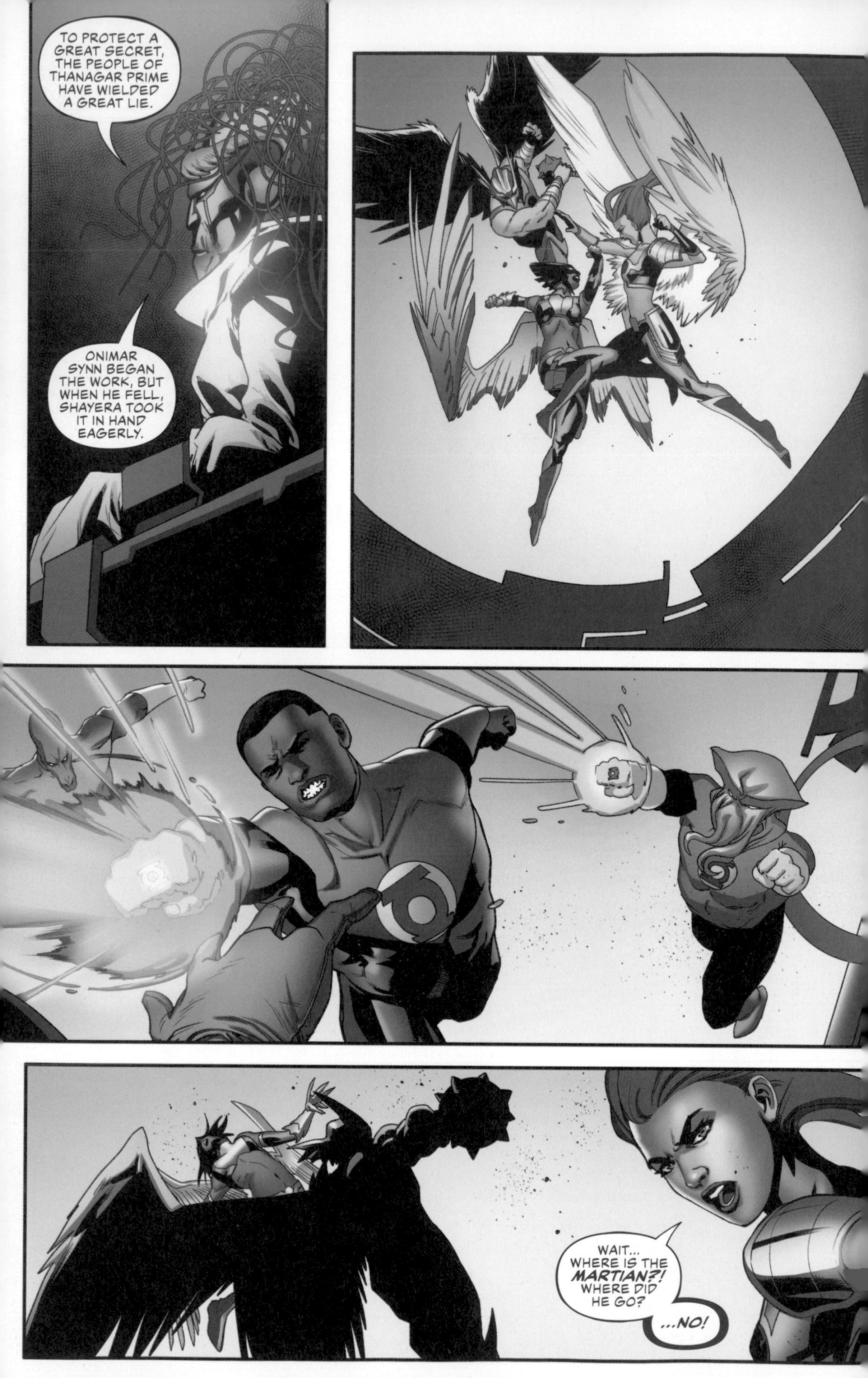
TO PROTECT A GREAT SECRET, THE PEOPLE OF THANAGAR PRIME HAVE WIELDED A GREAT LIE.
ONIMAR SYNN BEGAN THE WORK, BUT WHEN HE FELL, SHAYERA TOOK IT IN HAND EAGERLY.
WAIT... WHERE IS THE *MARTIAN?!* WHERE DID HE GO?
...NO!

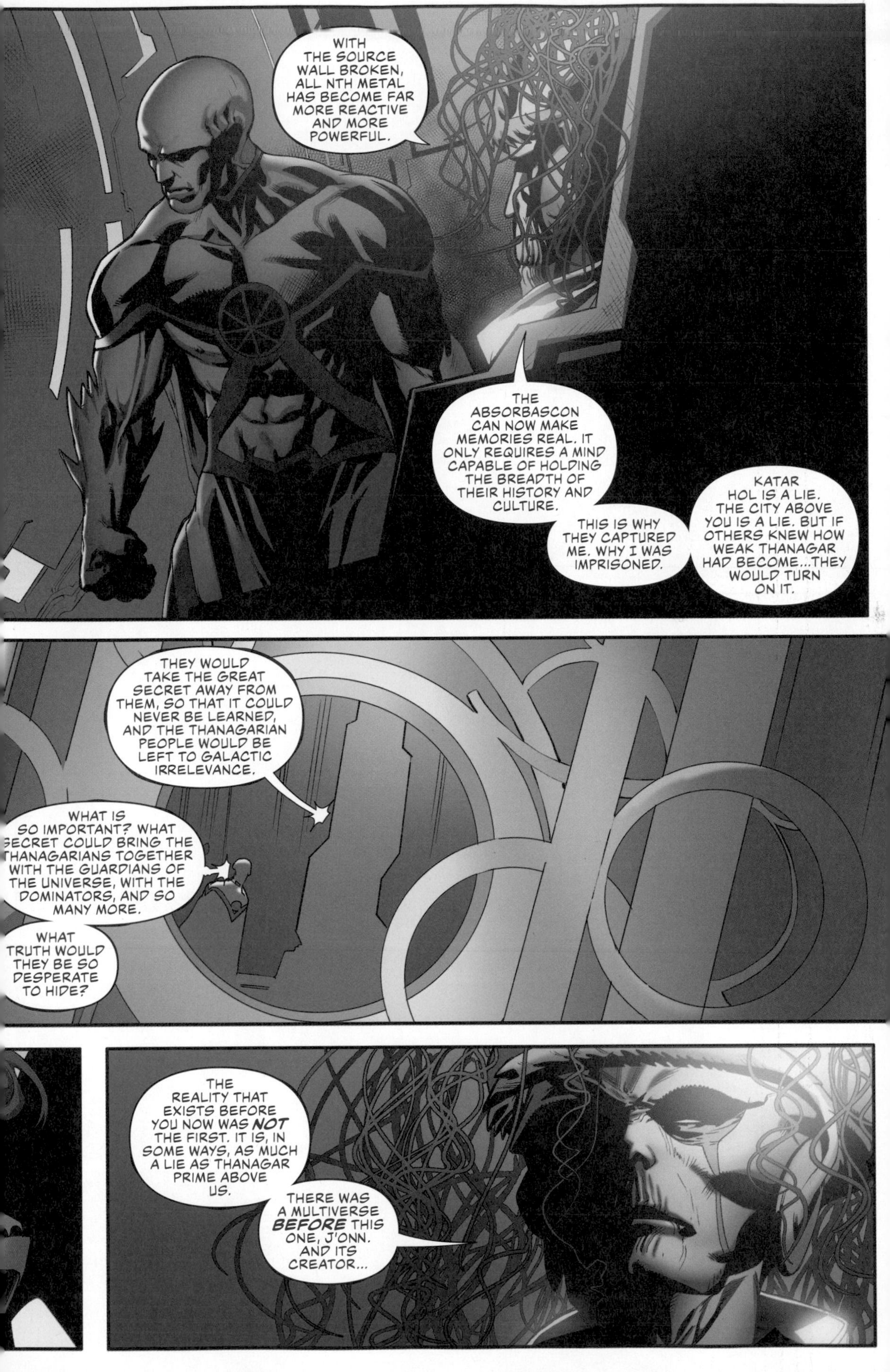
WITH THE SOURCE WALL BROKEN, ALL NTH METAL HAS BECOME FAR MORE REACTIVE AND MORE POWERFUL.
THE ABSORBASCON CAN NOW MAKE MEMORIES REAL. IT ONLY REQUIRES A MIND CAPABLE OF HOLDING THE BREADTH OF THEIR HISTORY AND CULTURE.
THIS IS WHY THEY CAPTURED ME. WHY I WAS IMPRISONED.
KATAR HOL IS A LIE. THE CITY ABOVE YOU IS A LIE. BUT IF OTHERS KNEW HOW WEAK THANAGAR HAD BECOME...THEY WOULD TURN ON IT.
THEY WOULD TAKE THE GREAT SECRET AWAY FROM THEM, SO THAT IT COULD NEVER BE LEARNED, AND THE THANAGARIAN PEOPLE WOULD BE LEFT TO GALACTIC IRRELEVANCE.
WHAT IS SO IMPORTANT? WHAT SECRET COULD BRING THE THANAGARIANS TOGETHER WITH THE GUARDIANS OF THE UNIVERSE, WITH THE DOMINATORS, AND SO MANY MORE.
WHAT TRUTH WOULD THEY BE SO DESPERATE TO HIDE?
THE REALITY THAT EXISTS BEFORE YOU NOW WAS ***NOT*** THE FIRST. IT IS, IN SOME WAYS, AS MUCH A LIE AS THANAGAR PRIME ABOVE US.
THERE WAS A MULTIVERSE ***BEFORE*** THIS ONE, J'ONN. AND ITS CREATOR...

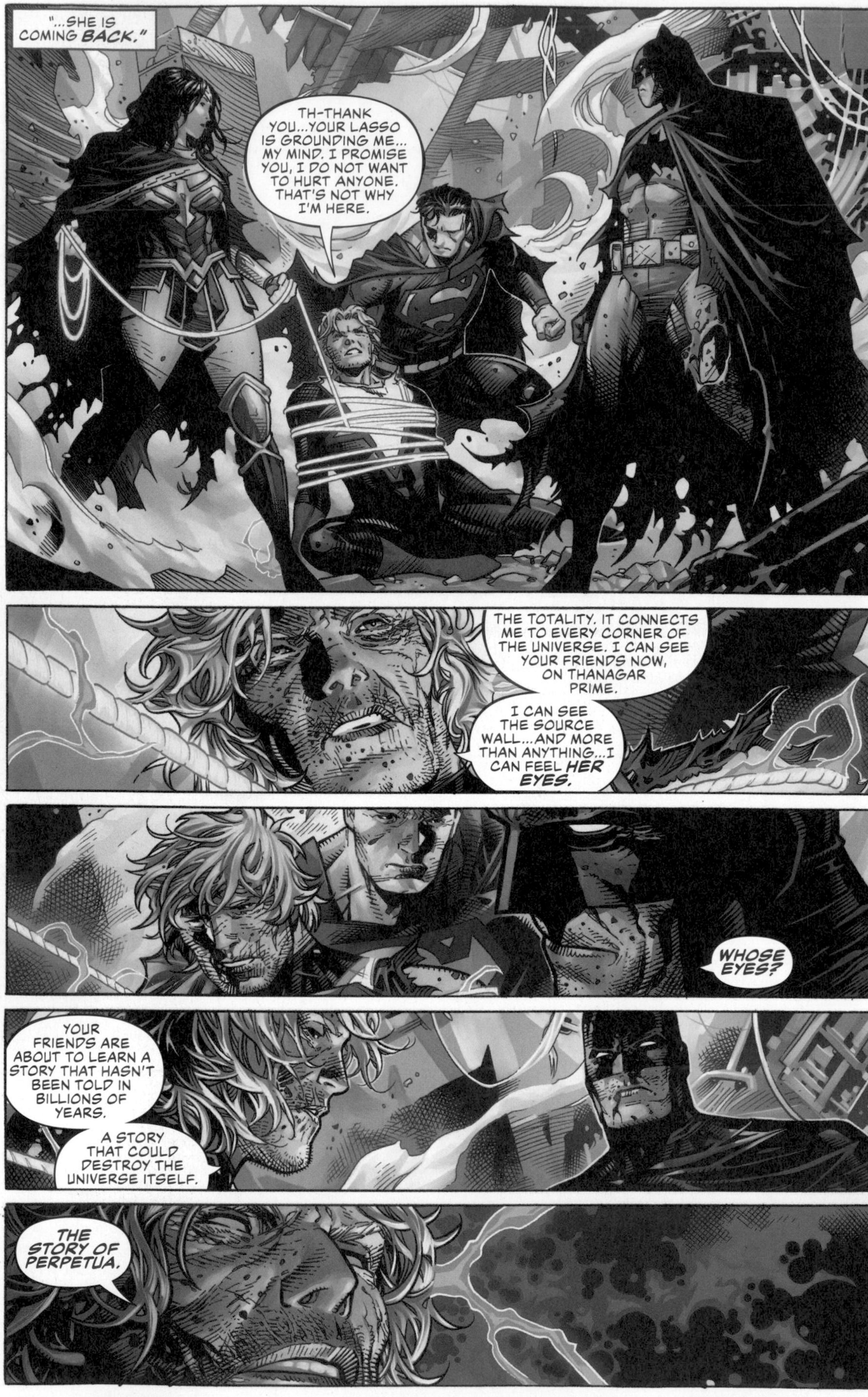
"...SHE IS COMING BACK."
TH-THANK YOU...YOUR LASSO IS GROUNDING ME... MY MIND. I PROMISE YOU, I DO NOT WANT TO HURT ANYONE. THAT'S NOT WHY I'M HERE.
THE TOTALITY. IT CONNECTS ME TO EVERY CORNER OF THE UNIVERSE. I CAN SEE YOUR FRIENDS NOW, ON THANAGAR PRIME.
I CAN SEE THE SOURCE WALL...AND MORE THAN ANYTHING...I CAN FEEL HER EYES.
WHOSE EYES?
YOUR FRIENDS ARE ABOUT TO LEARN A STORY THAT HASN'T BEEN TOLD IN BILLIONS OF YEARS.
A STORY THAT COULD DESTROY THE UNIVERSE ITSELF.
THE STORY OF PERPETUA.

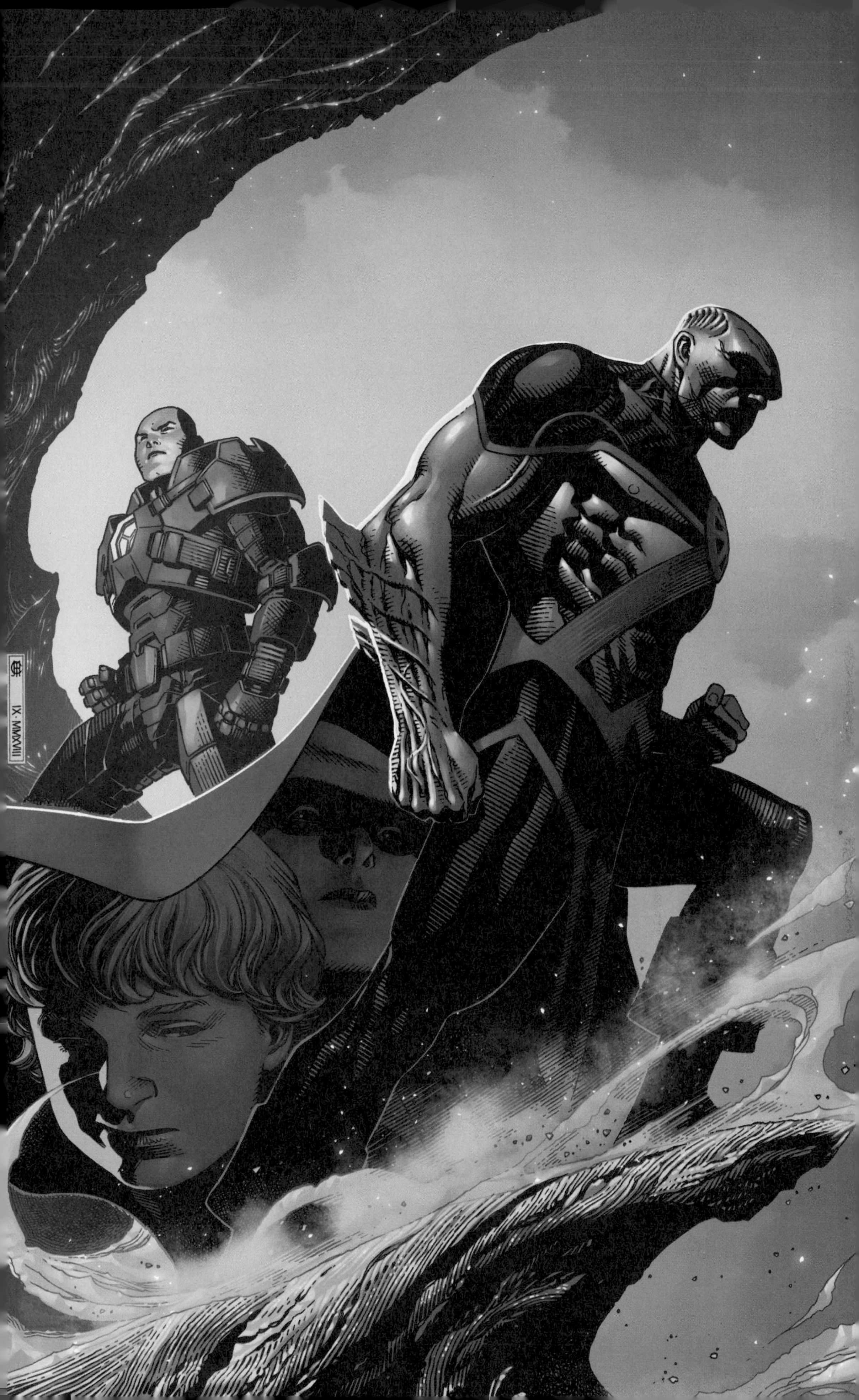
IX · MMXVIII

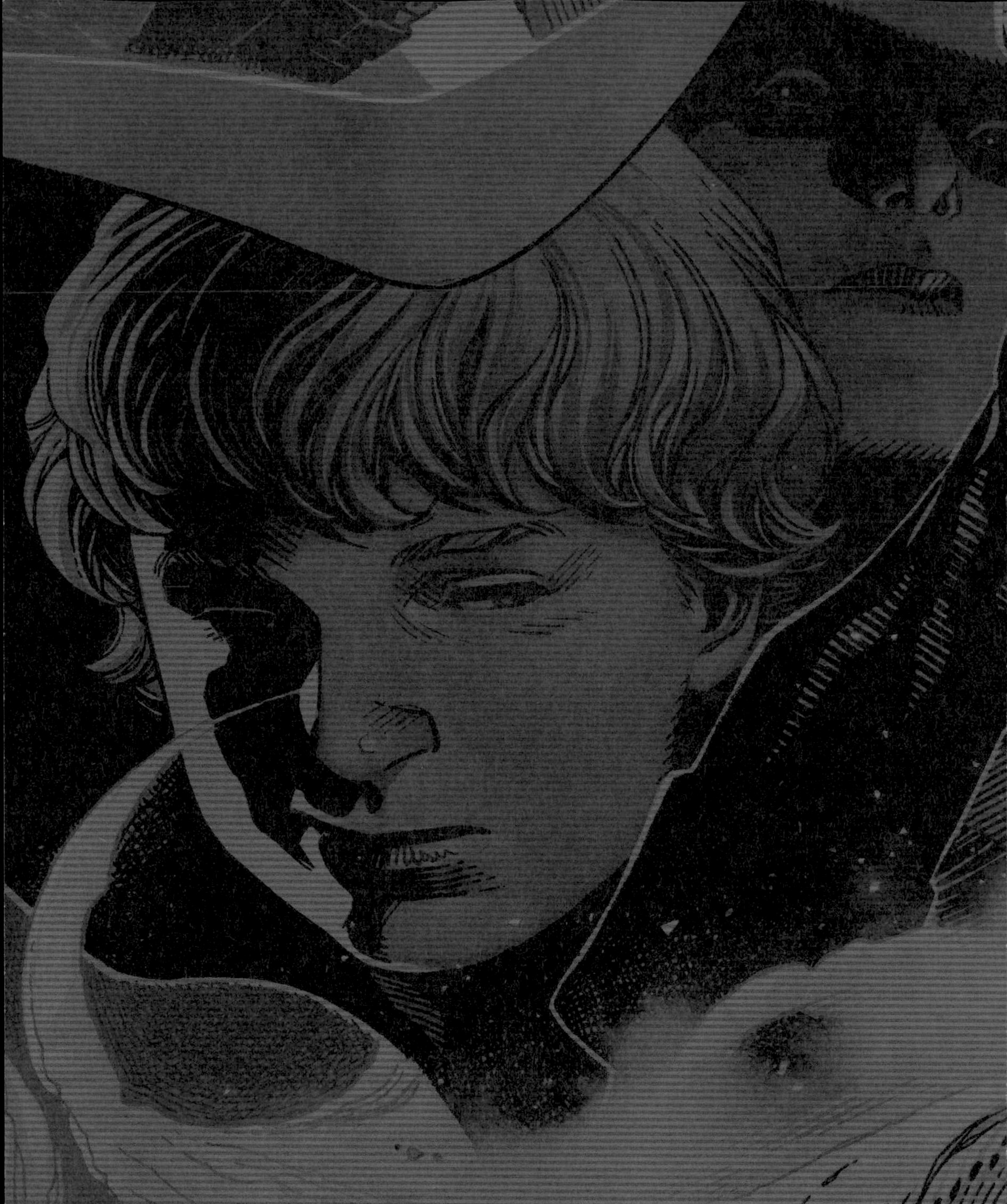

JUSTICE
LEAGUE
#16

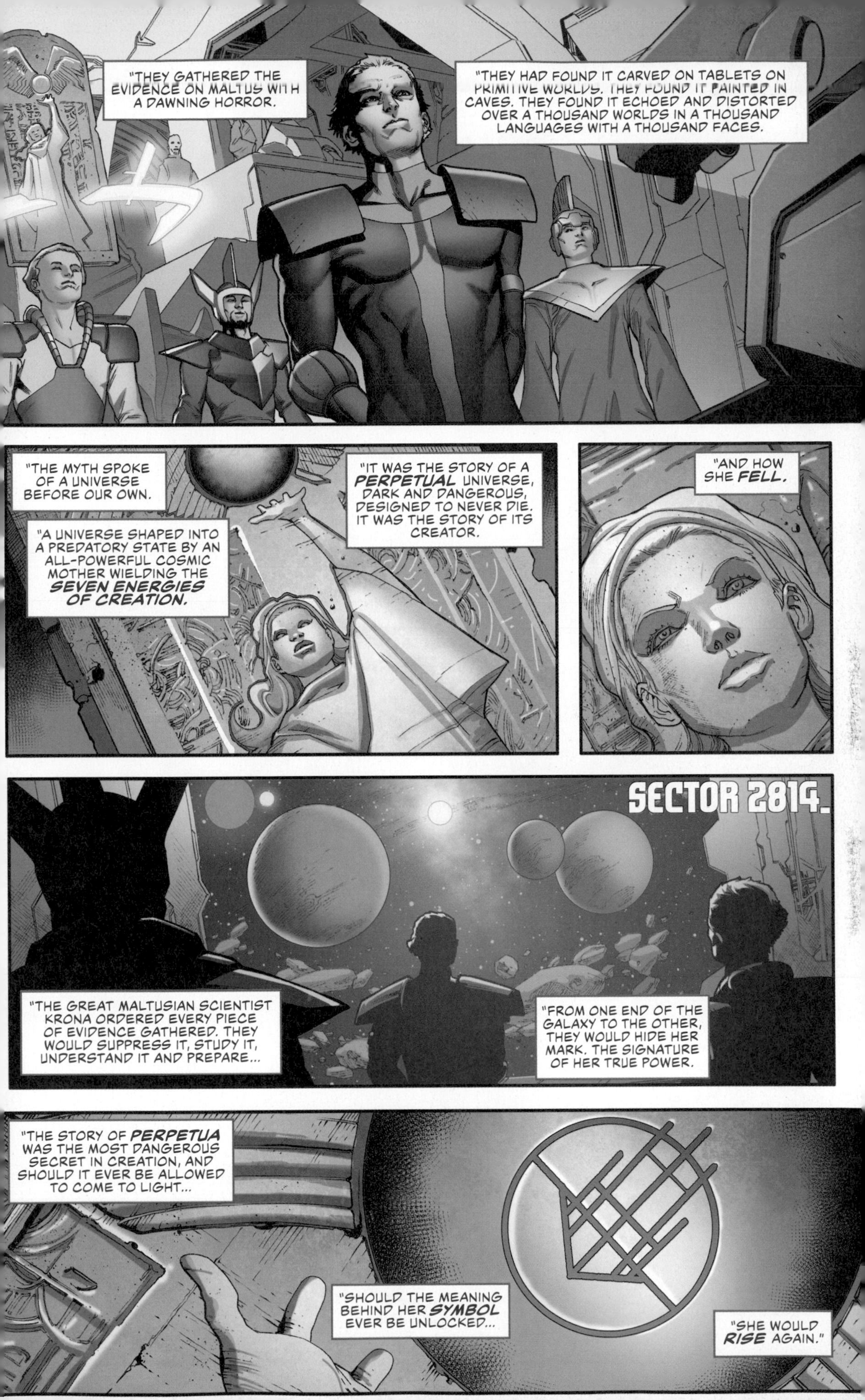
"THEY GATHERED THE EVIDENCE ON MALTUS WITH A DAWNING HORROR.
"THEY HAD FOUND IT CARVED ON TABLETS ON PRIMITIVE WORLDS. THEY FOUND IT PAINTED IN CAVES. THEY FOUND IT ECHOED AND DISTORTED OVER A THOUSAND WORLDS IN A THOUSAND LANGUAGES WITH A THOUSAND FACES.
"THE MYTH SPOKE OF A UNIVERSE BEFORE OUR OWN.
"A UNIVERSE SHAPED INTO A PREDATORY STATE BY AN ALL-POWERFUL COSMIC MOTHER WIELDING THE ***SEVEN ENERGIES OF CREATION.***
"IT WAS THE STORY OF A ***PERPETUAL*** UNIVERSE, DARK AND DANGEROUS, DESIGNED TO NEVER DIE. IT WAS THE STORY OF ITS CREATOR.
"AND HOW SHE ***FELL.***
SECTOR 2814.
"THE GREAT MALTUSIAN SCIENTIST KRONA ORDERED EVERY PIECE OF EVIDENCE GATHERED. THEY WOULD SUPPRESS IT, STUDY IT, UNDERSTAND IT AND PREPARE...
"FROM ONE END OF THE GALAXY TO THE OTHER, THEY WOULD HIDE HER MARK. THE SIGNATURE OF HER TRUE POWER.
"THE STORY OF ***PERPETUA*** WAS THE MOST DANGEROUS SECRET IN CREATION, AND SHOULD IT EVER BE ALLOWED TO COME TO LIGHT...
"SHOULD THE MEANING BEHIND HER ***SYMBOL*** EVER BE UNLOCKED...
"SHE WOULD ***RISE*** AGAIN."

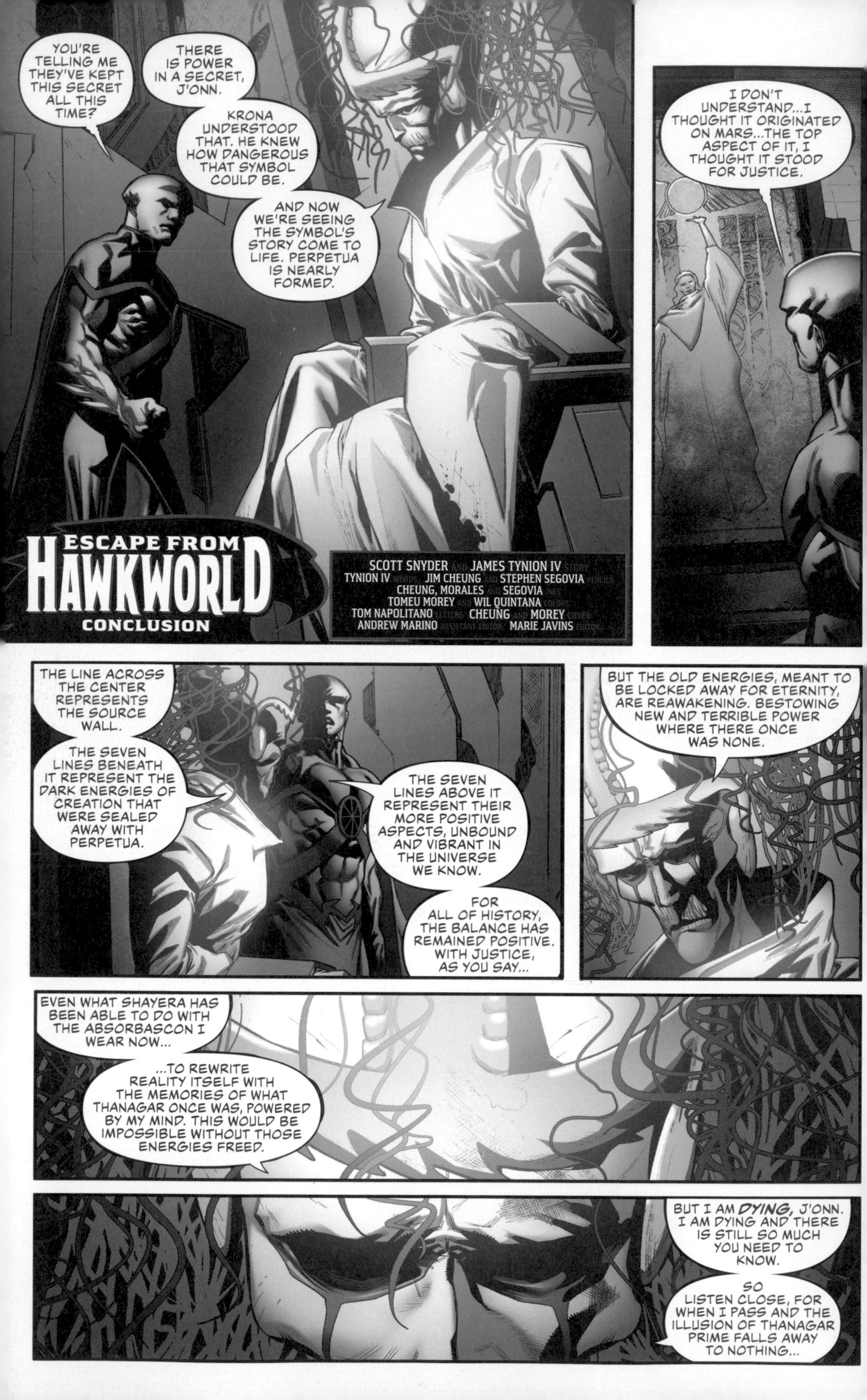
YOU'RE TELLING ME THEY'VE KEPT THIS SECRET ALL THIS TIME?
THERE IS POWER IN A SECRET, J'ONN.
KRONA UNDERSTOOD THAT. HE KNEW HOW DANGEROUS THAT SYMBOL COULD BE.
AND NOW WE'RE SEEING THE SYMBOL'S STORY COME TO LIFE. PERPETUA IS NEARLY FORMED.
ESCAPE FROM HAWKWORLD CONCLUSION
SCOTT SNYDER AND JAMES TYNION IV STORY
TYNION IV WORDS JIM CHEUNG AND STEPHEN SEGOVIA PENCILS
CHEUNG, MORALES AND SEGOVIA INKS
TOMEU MOREY AND WIL QUINTANA COLORS
TOM NAPOLITANO LETTERS CHEUNG AND MOREY COVER
ANDREW MARINO ASSISTANT EDITOR MARIE JAVINS EDITOR
I DON'T UNDERSTAND...I THOUGHT IT ORIGINATED ON MARS...THE TOP ASPECT OF IT, I THOUGHT IT STOOD FOR JUSTICE.
THE LINE ACROSS THE CENTER REPRESENTS THE SOURCE WALL.
THE SEVEN LINES BENEATH IT REPRESENT THE DARK ENERGIES OF CREATION THAT WERE SEALED AWAY WITH PERPETUA.
THE SEVEN LINES ABOVE IT REPRESENT THEIR MORE POSITIVE ASPECTS, UNBOUND AND VIBRANT IN THE UNIVERSE WE KNOW.
FOR ALL OF HISTORY, THE BALANCE HAS REMAINED POSITIVE. WITH JUSTICE, AS YOU SAY...
BUT THE OLD ENERGIES, MEANT TO BE LOCKED AWAY FOR ETERNITY, ARE REAWAKENING. BESTOWING NEW AND TERRIBLE POWER WHERE THERE ONCE WAS NONE.
EVEN WHAT SHAYERA HAS BEEN ABLE TO DO WITH THE ABSORBASCON I WEAR NOW...
...TO REWRITE REALITY ITSELF WITH THE MEMORIES OF WHAT THANAGAR ONCE WAS, POWERED BY MY MIND. THIS WOULD BE IMPOSSIBLE WITHOUT THOSE ENERGIES FREED.
BUT I AM DYING, J'ONN. I AM DYING AND THERE IS STILL SO MUCH YOU NEED TO KNOW.
SO LISTEN CLOSE, FOR WHEN I PASS AND THE ILLUSION OF THANAGAR PRIME FALLS AWAY TO NOTHING...

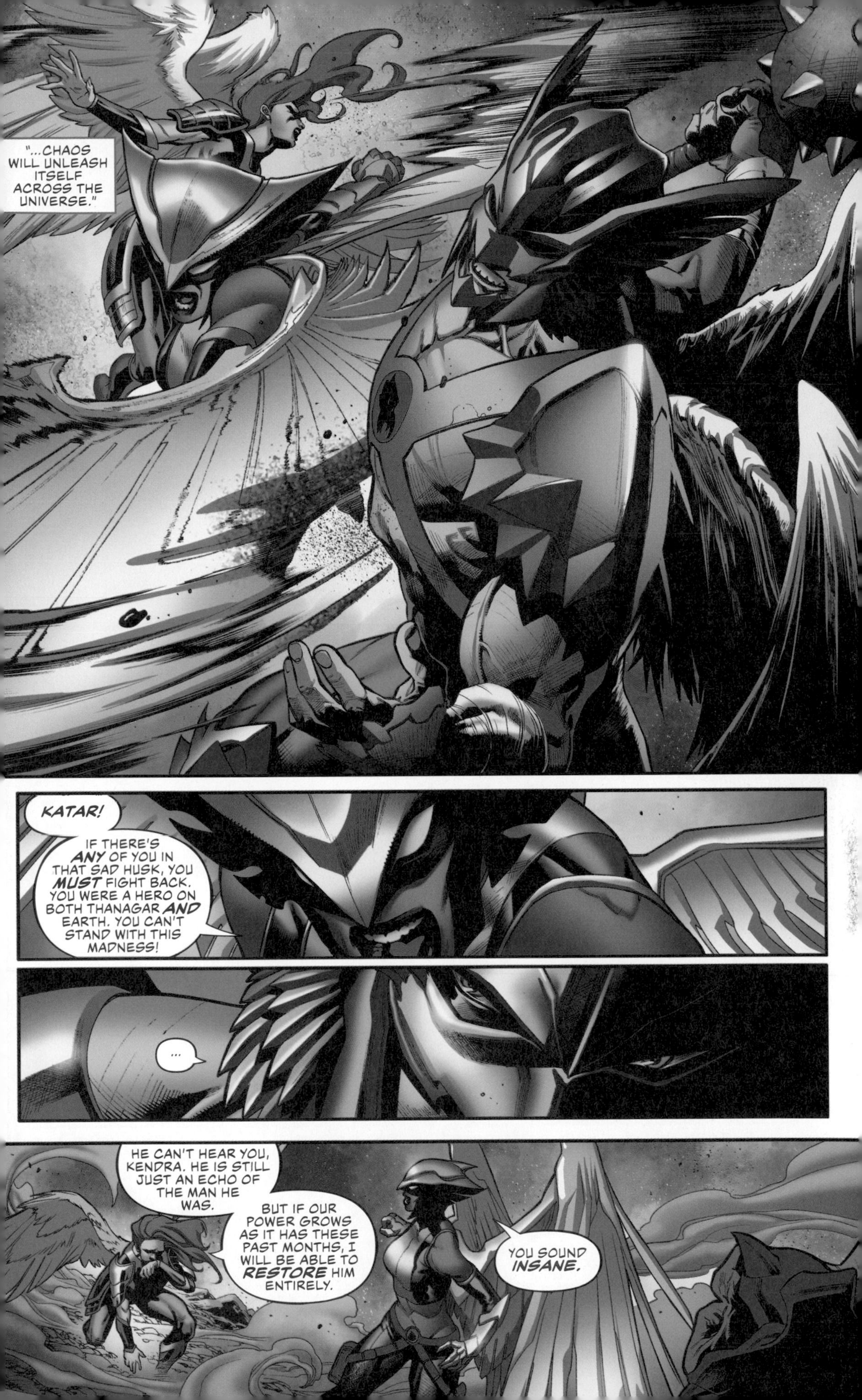
"...CHAOS WILL UNLEASH ITSELF ACROSS THE UNIVERSE."
KATAR!
IF THERE'S ANY OF YOU IN THAT SAD HUSK, YOU MUST FIGHT BACK. YOU WERE A HERO ON BOTH THANAGAR AND EARTH. YOU CAN'T STAND WITH THIS MADNESS!
...
HE CAN'T HEAR YOU, KENDRA. HE IS STILL JUST AN ECHO OF THE MAN HE WAS.
BUT IF OUR POWER GROWS AS IT HAS THESE PAST MONTHS, I WILL BE ABLE TO RESTORE HIM ENTIRELY.
YOU SOUND INSANE.

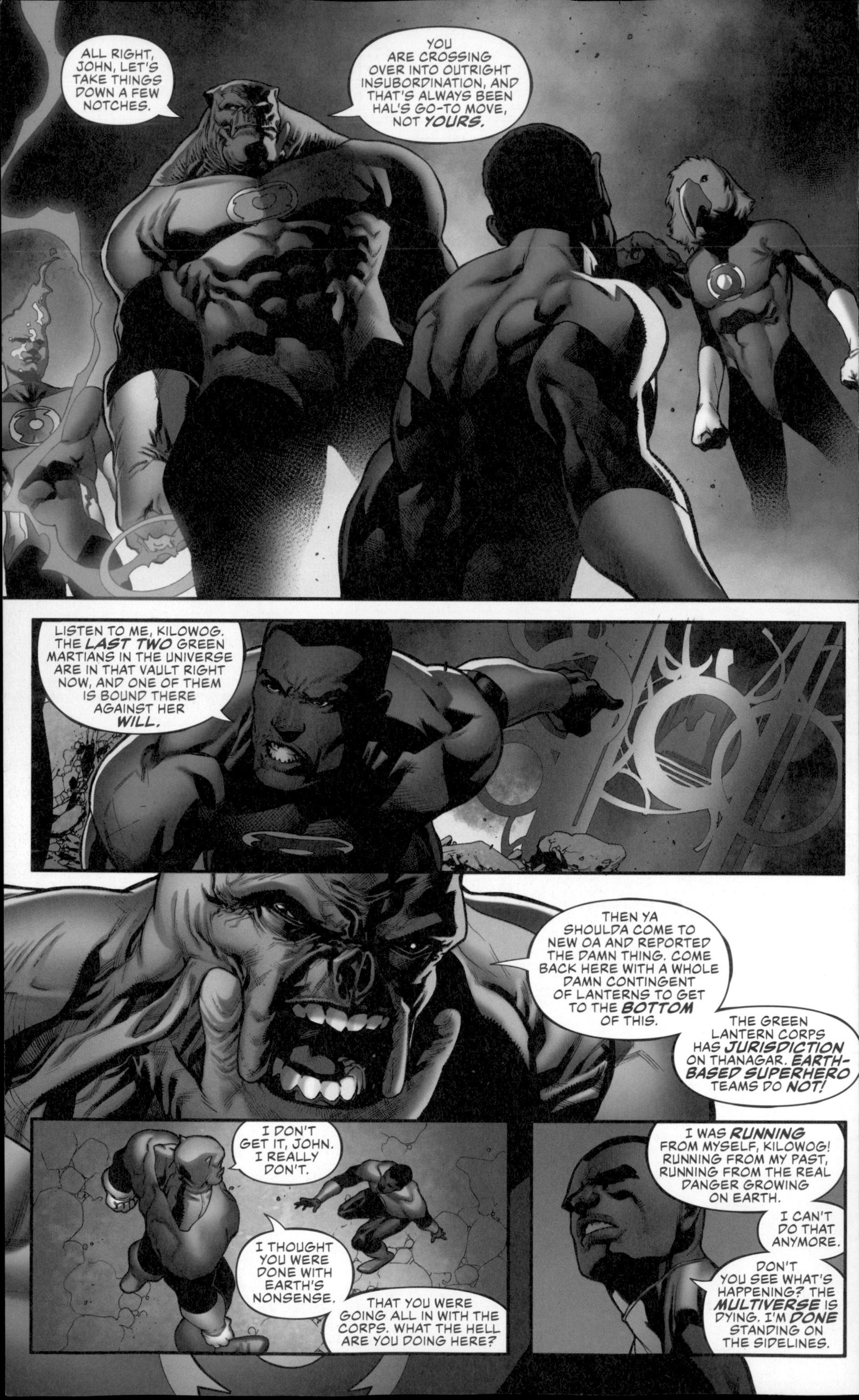
ALL RIGHT, JOHN, LET'S TAKE THINGS DOWN A FEW NOTCHES.
YOU ARE CROSSING OVER INTO OUTRIGHT INSUBORDINATION, AND THAT'S ALWAYS BEEN HAL'S GO-TO MOVE, NOT *YOURS.*
LISTEN TO ME, KILOWOG. THE *LAST TWO* GREEN MARTIANS IN THE UNIVERSE ARE IN THAT VAULT RIGHT NOW, AND ONE OF THEM IS BOUND THERE AGAINST HER *WILL.*
THEN YA SHOULDA COME TO NEW OA AND REPORTED THE DAMN THING. COME BACK HERE WITH A WHOLE DAMN CONTINGENT OF LANTERNS TO GET TO THE *BOTTOM* OF THIS.
THE GREEN LANTERN CORPS HAS *JURISDICTION* ON THANAGAR. *EARTH-BASED SUPERHERO* TEAMS DO *NOT!*
I DON'T GET IT, JOHN. I REALLY DON'T.
I THOUGHT YOU WERE DONE WITH EARTH'S NONSENSE.
THAT YOU WERE GOING ALL IN WITH THE CORPS. WHAT THE HELL ARE YOU DOING HERE?
I WAS *RUNNING* FROM MYSELF, KILOWOG! RUNNING FROM MY PAST, RUNNING FROM THE REAL DANGER GROWING ON EARTH.
I CAN'T DO THAT ANYMORE.
DON'T YOU SEE WHAT'S HAPPENING? THE *MULTIVERSE* IS DYING. I'M *DONE* STANDING ON THE SIDELINES.

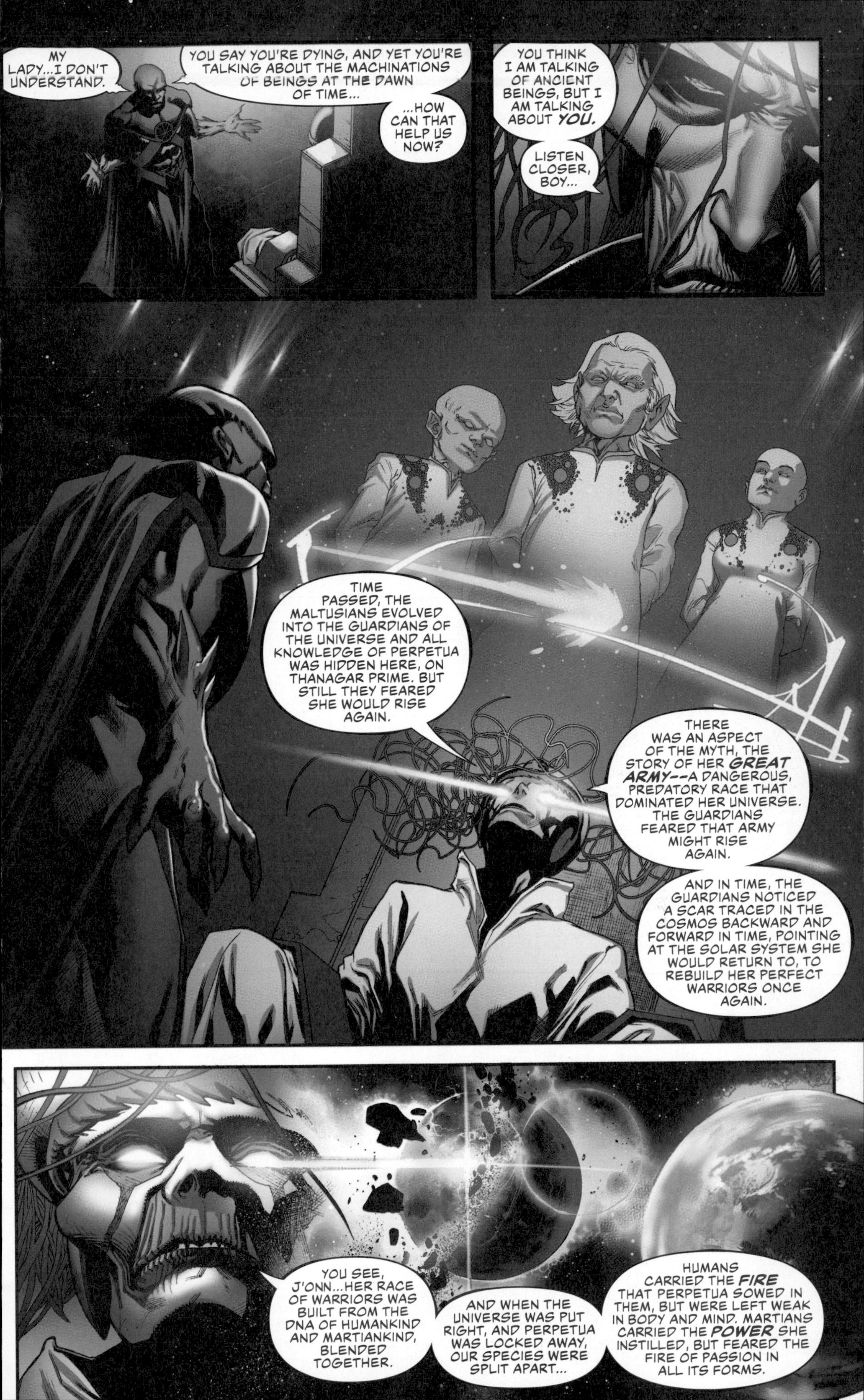
MY LADY...I DON'T UNDERSTAND.
YOU SAY YOU'RE DYING, AND YET YOU'RE TALKING ABOUT THE MACHINATIONS OF BEINGS AT THE DAWN OF TIME...
...HOW CAN THAT HELP US NOW?
YOU THINK I AM TALKING OF ANCIENT BEINGS, BUT I AM TALKING ABOUT YOU.
LISTEN CLOSER, BOY...
TIME PASSED, THE MALTUSIANS EVOLVED INTO THE GUARDIANS OF THE UNIVERSE AND ALL KNOWLEDGE OF PERPETUA WAS HIDDEN HERE, ON THANAGAR PRIME. BUT STILL THEY FEARED SHE WOULD RISE AGAIN.
THERE WAS AN ASPECT OF THE MYTH, THE STORY OF HER GREAT ARMY--A DANGEROUS, PREDATORY RACE THAT DOMINATED HER UNIVERSE. THE GUARDIANS FEARED THAT ARMY MIGHT RISE AGAIN.
AND IN TIME, THE GUARDIANS NOTICED A SCAR TRACED IN THE COSMOS BACKWARD AND FORWARD IN TIME, POINTING AT THE SOLAR SYSTEM SHE WOULD RETURN TO, TO REBUILD HER PERFECT WARRIORS ONCE AGAIN.
YOU SEE, J'ONN...HER RACE OF WARRIORS WAS BUILT FROM THE DNA OF HUMANKIND AND MARTIANKIND, BLENDED TOGETHER.
AND WHEN THE UNIVERSE WAS PUT RIGHT, AND PERPETUA WAS LOCKED AWAY, OUR SPECIES WERE SPLIT APART...
HUMANS CARRIED THE FIRE THAT PERPETUA SOWED IN THEM, BUT WERE LEFT WEAK IN BODY AND MIND. MARTIANS CARRIED THE POWER SHE INSTILLED, BUT FEARED THE FIRE OF PASSION IN ALL ITS FORMS.

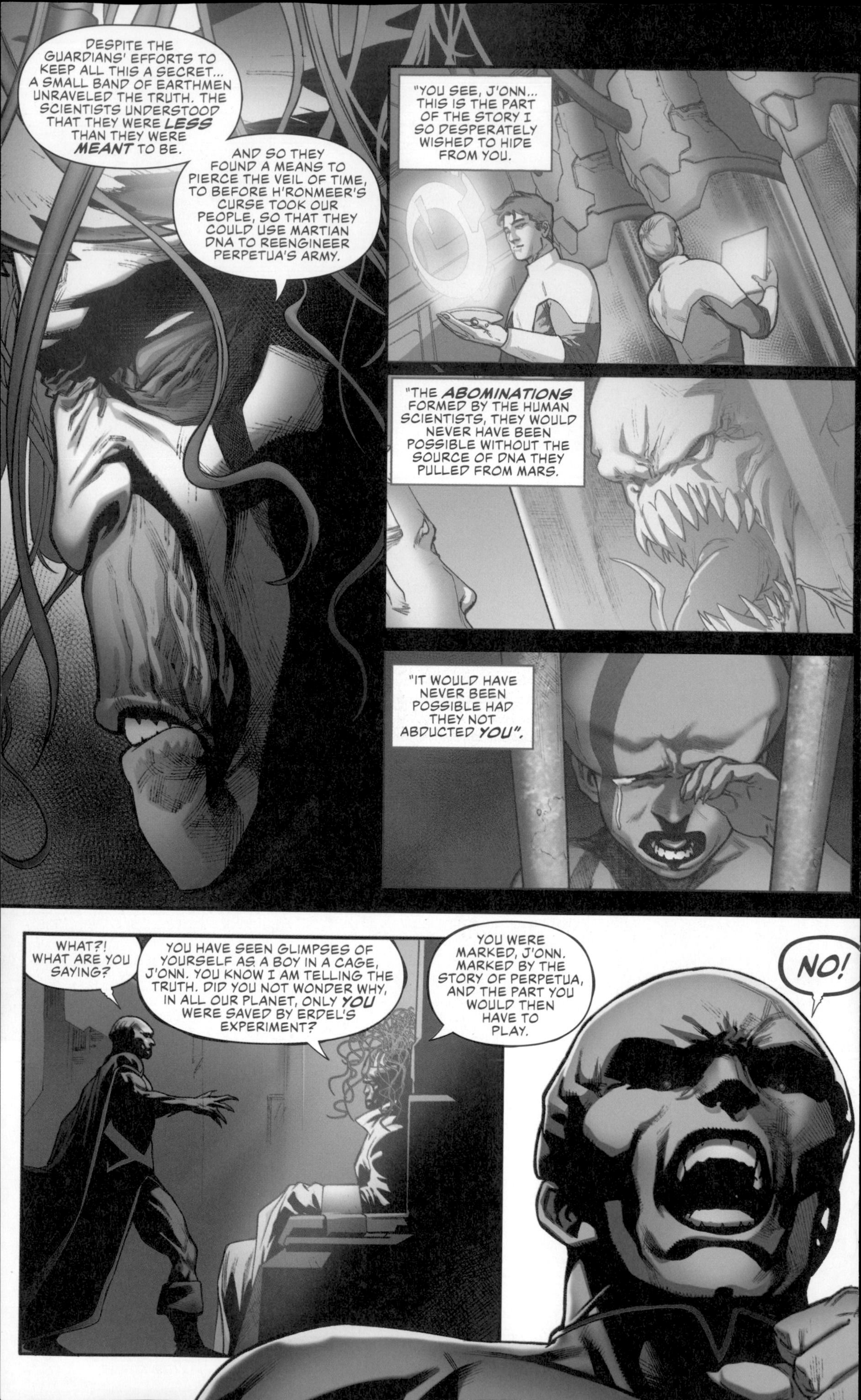

DESPITE THE GUARDIANS' EFFORTS TO KEEP ALL THIS A SECRET... A SMALL BAND OF EARTHMEN UNRAVELED THE TRUTH. THE SCIENTISTS UNDERSTOOD THAT THEY WERE LESS THAN THEY WERE MEANT TO BE.
AND SO THEY FOUND A MEANS TO PIERCE THE VEIL OF TIME, TO BEFORE H'RONMEER'S CURSE TOOK OUR PEOPLE, SO THAT THEY COULD USE MARTIAN DNA TO REENGINEER PERPETUA'S ARMY.
"YOU SEE, J'ONN... THIS IS THE PART OF THE STORY I SO DESPERATELY WISHED TO HIDE FROM YOU.
"THE ABOMINATIONS FORMED BY THE HUMAN SCIENTISTS, THEY WOULD NEVER HAVE BEEN POSSIBLE WITHOUT THE SOURCE OF DNA THEY PULLED FROM MARS.
"IT WOULD HAVE NEVER BEEN POSSIBLE HAD THEY NOT ABDUCTED YOU".
WHAT?! WHAT ARE YOU SAYING?
YOU HAVE SEEN GLIMPSES OF YOURSELF AS A BOY IN A CAGE, J'ONN. YOU KNOW I AM TELLING THE TRUTH. DID YOU NOT WONDER WHY, IN ALL OUR PLANET, ONLY YOU WERE SAVED BY ERDEL'S EXPERIMENT?
YOU WERE MARKED, J'ONN. MARKED BY THE STORY OF PERPETUA, AND THE PART YOU WOULD THEN HAVE TO PLAY.
NO!

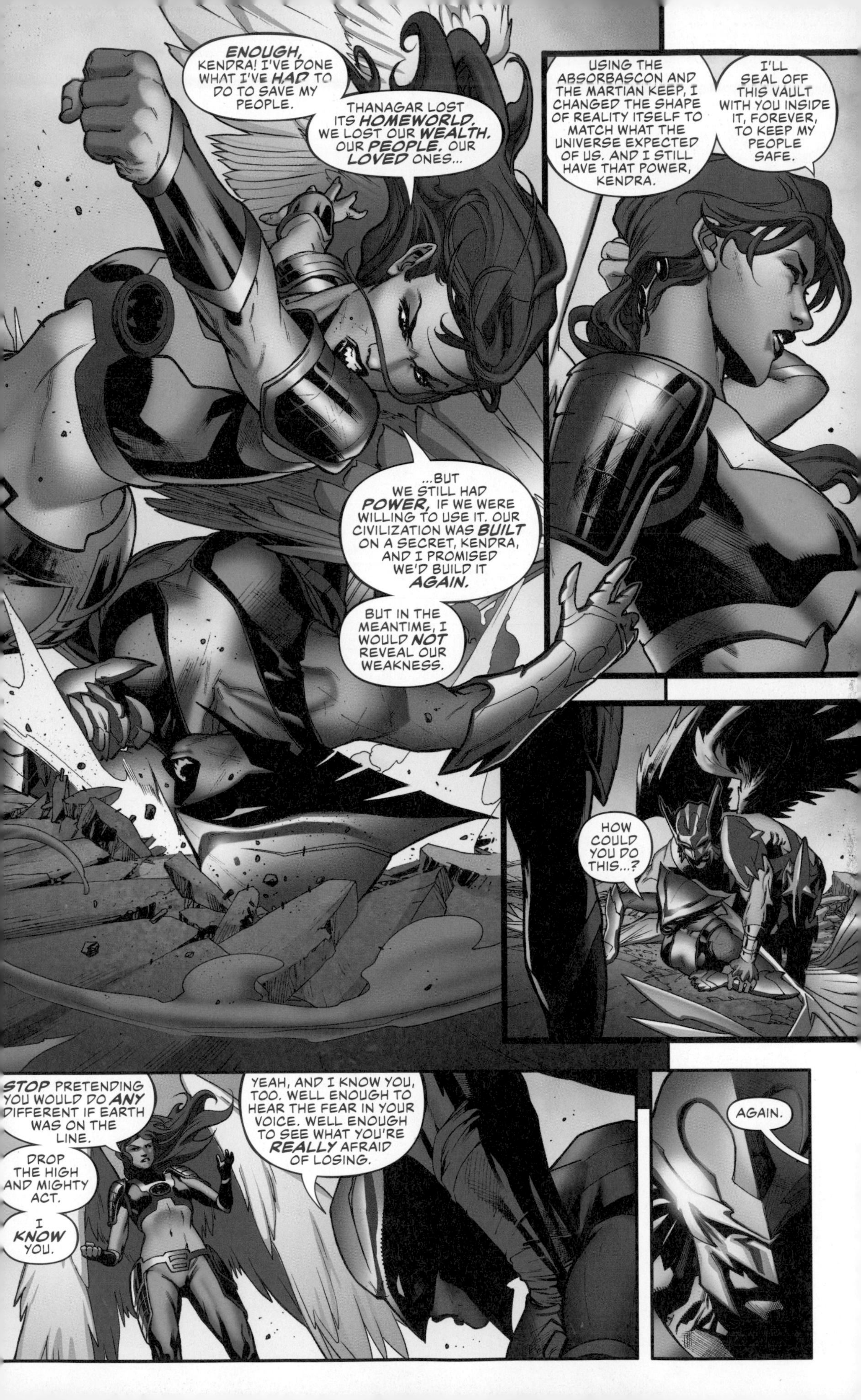
ENOUGH, KENDRA! I'VE DONE WHAT I'VE HAD TO DO TO SAVE MY PEOPLE.
THANAGAR LOST ITS HOMEWORLD. WE LOST OUR WEALTH. OUR PEOPLE. OUR LOVED ONES...
...BUT WE STILL HAD POWER, IF WE WERE WILLING TO USE IT. OUR CIVILIZATION WAS BUILT ON A SECRET, KENDRA, AND I PROMISED WE'D BUILD IT AGAIN.
BUT IN THE MEANTIME, I WOULD NOT REVEAL OUR WEAKNESS.
USING THE ABSORBASCON AND THE MARTIAN KEEP, I CHANGED THE SHAPE OF REALITY ITSELF TO MATCH WHAT THE UNIVERSE EXPECTED OF US. AND I STILL HAVE THAT POWER, KENDRA.
I'LL SEAL OFF THIS VAULT WITH YOU INSIDE IT, FOREVER, TO KEEP MY PEOPLE SAFE.
HOW COULD YOU DO THIS...?
STOP PRETENDING YOU WOULD DO ANY DIFFERENT IF EARTH WAS ON THE LINE.
DROP THE HIGH AND MIGHTY ACT.
I KNOW YOU.
YEAH, AND I KNOW YOU, TOO. WELL ENOUGH TO HEAR THE FEAR IN YOUR VOICE. WELL ENOUGH TO SEE WHAT YOU'RE REALLY AFRAID OF LOSING.
AGAIN.

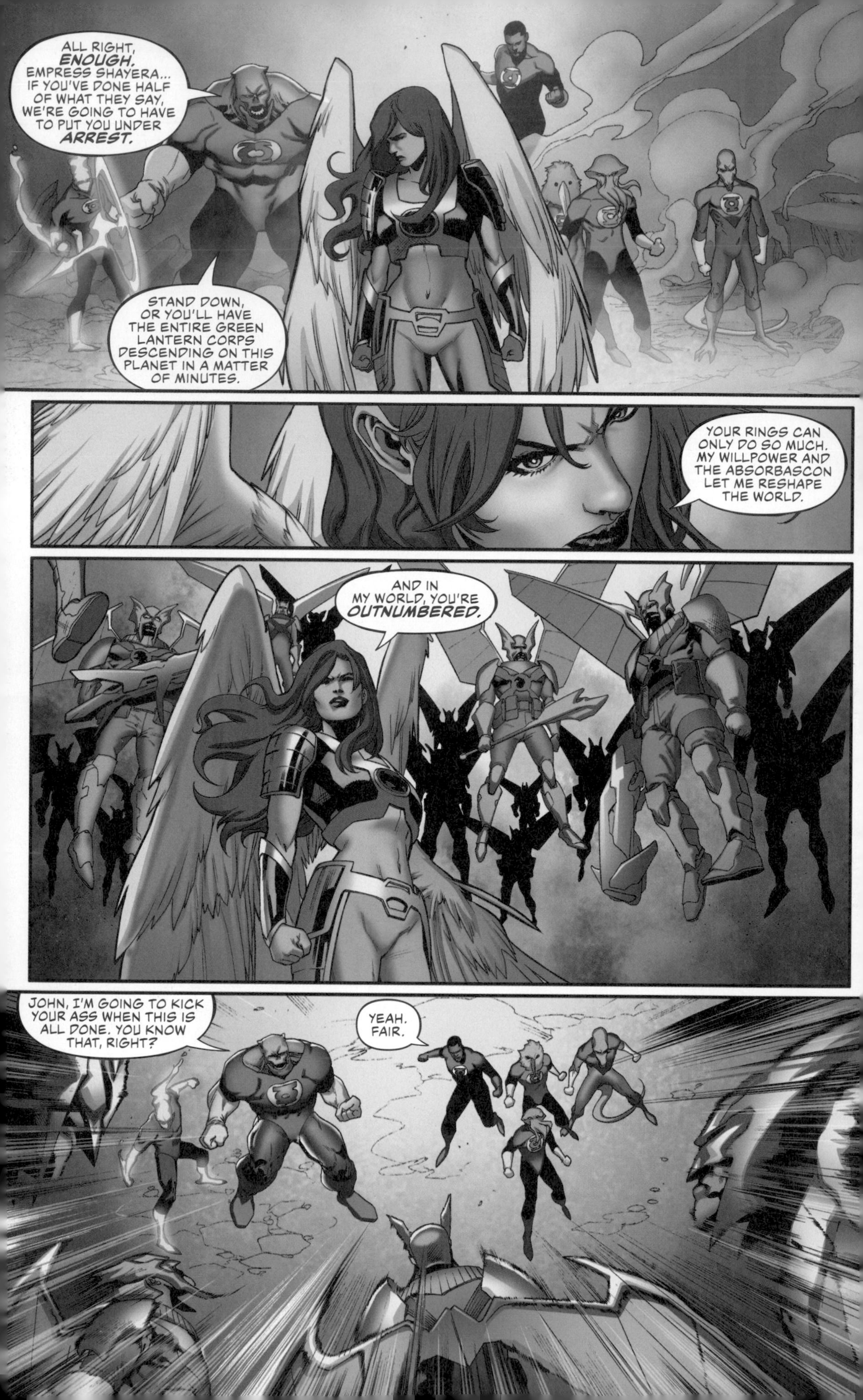
ALL RIGHT, ENOUGH. EMPRESS SHAYERA... IF YOU'VE DONE HALF OF WHAT THEY SAY, WE'RE GOING TO HAVE TO PUT YOU UNDER ARREST.
STAND DOWN, OR YOU'LL HAVE THE ENTIRE GREEN LANTERN CORPS DESCENDING ON THIS PLANET IN A MATTER OF MINUTES.
YOUR RINGS CAN ONLY DO SO MUCH. MY WILLPOWER AND THE ABSORBASCON LET ME RESHAPE THE WORLD.
AND IN MY WORLD, YOU'RE OUTNUMBERED.
JOHN, I'M GOING TO KICK YOUR ASS WHEN THIS IS ALL DONE. YOU KNOW THAT, RIGHT?
YEAH. FAIR.

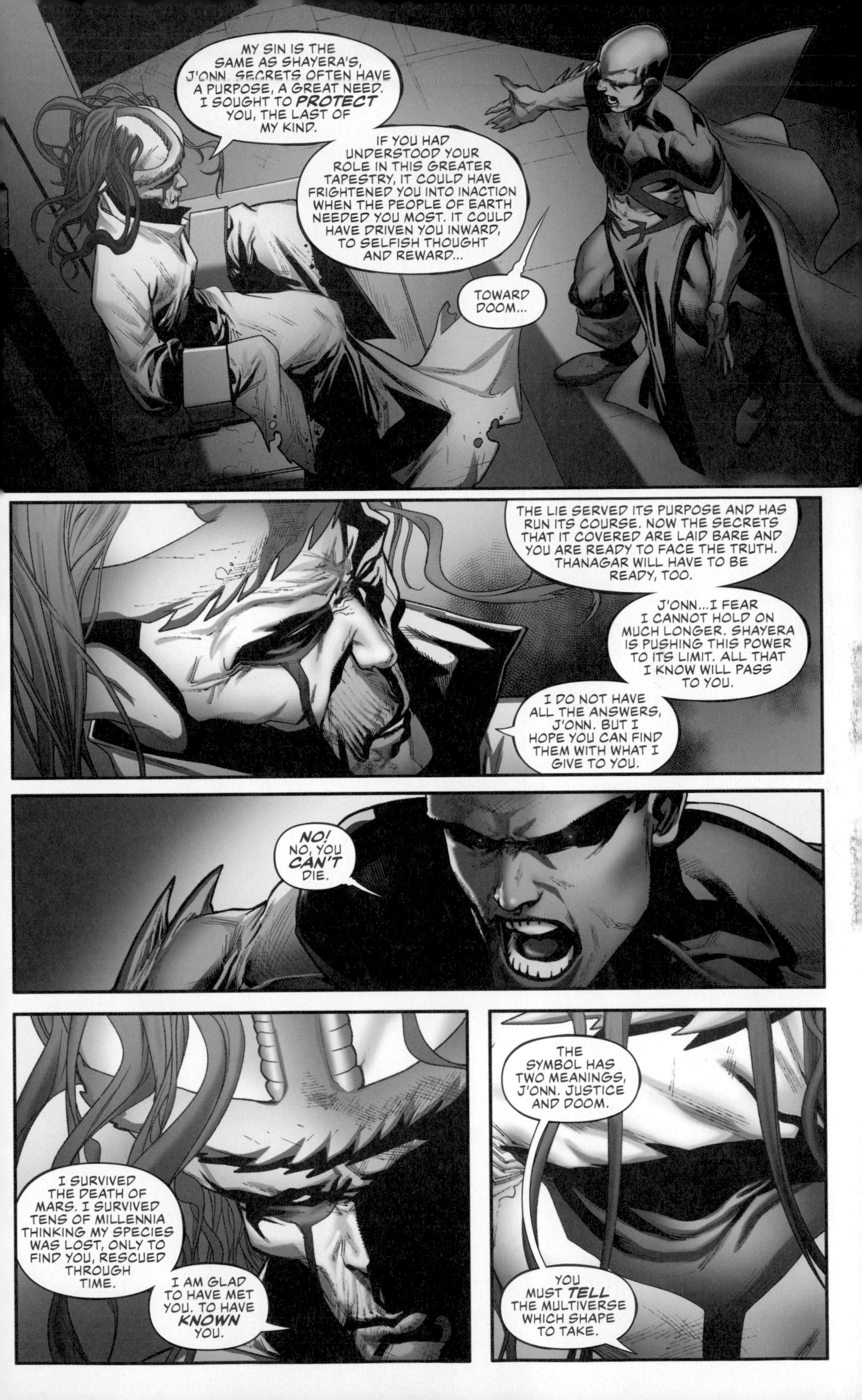
MY SIN IS THE SAME AS SHAYERA'S, J'ONN. SECRETS OFTEN HAVE A PURPOSE, A GREAT NEED. I SOUGHT TO *PROTECT* YOU, THE LAST OF MY KIND.
IF YOU HAD UNDERSTOOD YOUR ROLE IN THIS GREATER TAPESTRY, IT COULD HAVE FRIGHTENED YOU INTO INACTION WHEN THE PEOPLE OF EARTH NEEDED YOU MOST. IT COULD HAVE DRIVEN YOU INWARD, TO SELFISH THOUGHT AND REWARD...
TOWARD DOOM...
THE LIE SERVED ITS PURPOSE AND HAS RUN ITS COURSE. NOW THE SECRETS THAT IT COVERED ARE LAID BARE AND YOU ARE READY TO FACE THE TRUTH. THANAGAR WILL HAVE TO BE READY, TOO.
J'ONN...I FEAR I CANNOT HOLD ON MUCH LONGER. SHAYERA IS PUSHING THIS POWER TO ITS LIMIT. ALL THAT I KNOW WILL PASS TO YOU.
I DO NOT HAVE ALL THE ANSWERS, J'ONN. BUT I HOPE YOU CAN FIND THEM WITH WHAT I GIVE TO YOU.
NO! NO, YOU *CAN'T* DIE.
I SURVIVED THE DEATH OF MARS. I SURVIVED TENS OF MILLENNIA THINKING MY SPECIES WAS LOST, ONLY TO FIND YOU, RESCUED THROUGH TIME.
I AM GLAD TO HAVE MET YOU. TO HAVE *KNOWN* YOU.
THE SYMBOL HAS TWO MEANINGS, J'ONN. JUSTICE AND DOOM.
YOU MUST *TELL* THE MULTIVERSE WHICH SHAPE TO TAKE.

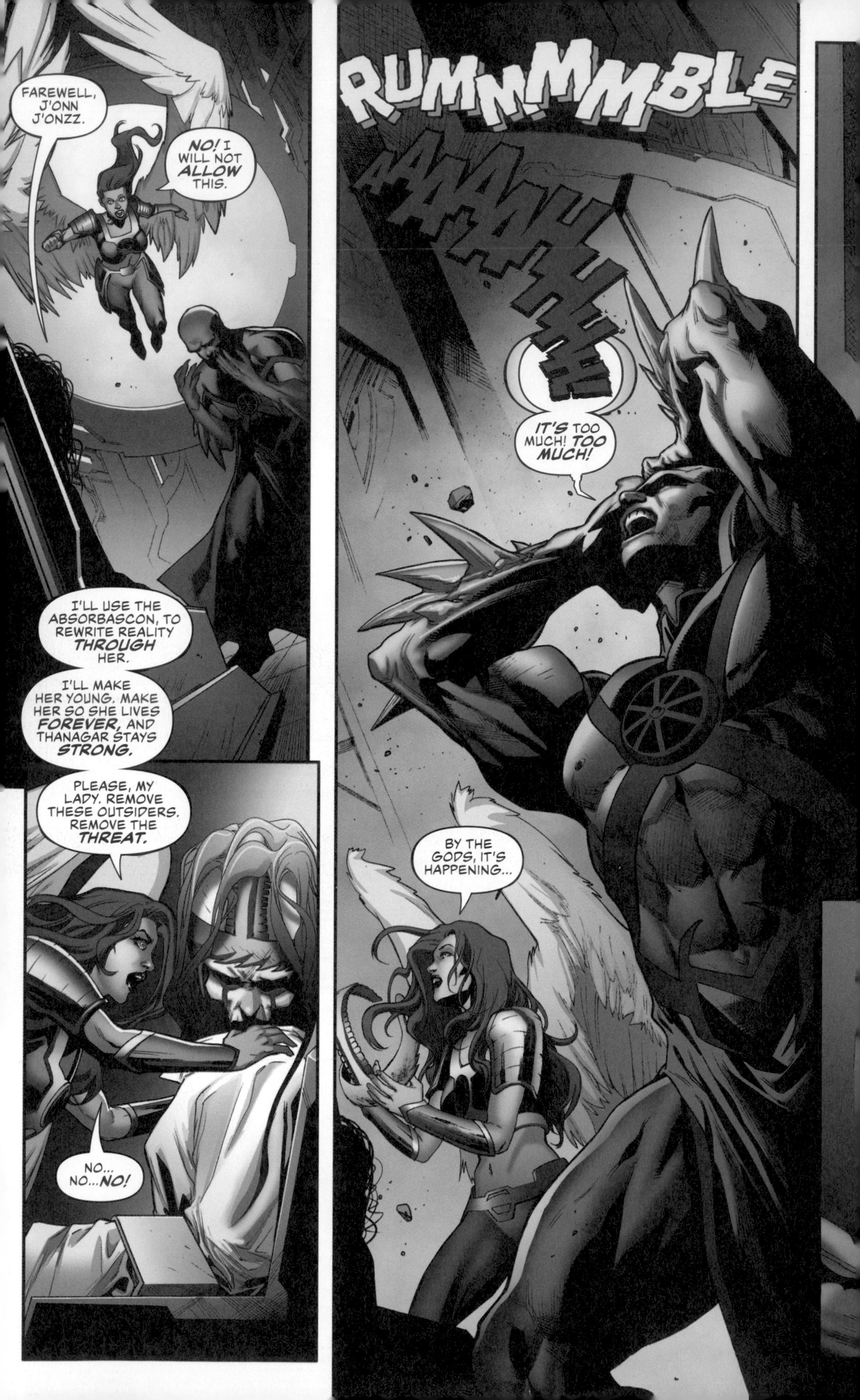
FAREWELL, J'ONN J'ONZZ.
NO! I WILL NOT ALLOW THIS.
I'LL USE THE ABSORBASCON, TO REWRITE REALITY THROUGH HER.
I'LL MAKE HER YOUNG. MAKE HER SO SHE LIVES FOREVER, AND THANAGAR STAYS STRONG.
PLEASE, MY LADY. REMOVE THESE OUTSIDERS. REMOVE THE THREAT.
NO... NO...NO!
RUMMMMMBLE
AAAAAUUGHH!
IT'S TOO MUCH! TOO MUCH!
BY THE GODS, IT'S HAPPENING...

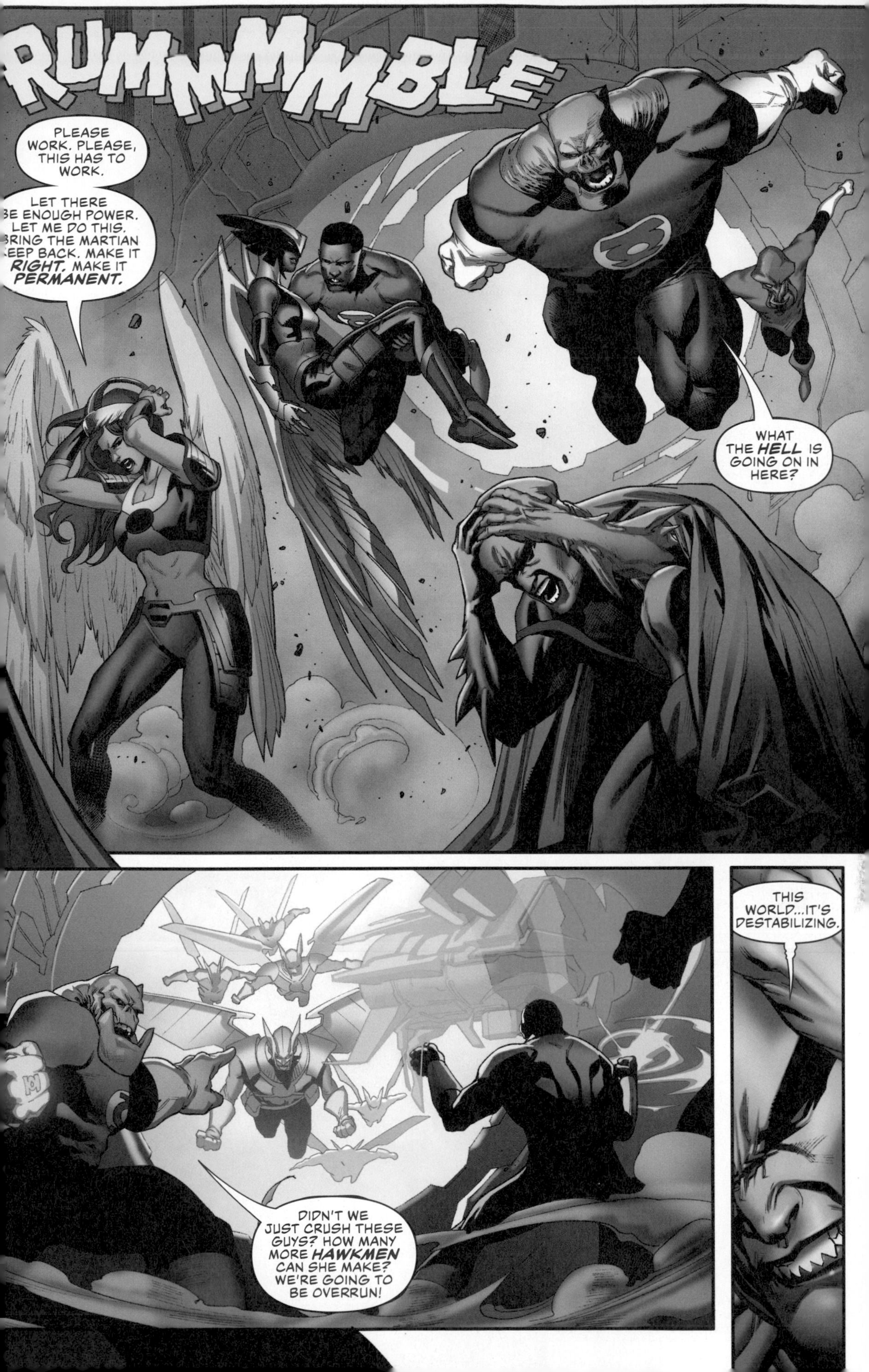
RUMMMMBLE
PLEASE WORK. PLEASE, THIS HAS TO WORK.
LET THERE BE ENOUGH POWER. LET ME DO THIS. BRING THE MARTIAN KEEP BACK. MAKE IT RIGHT. MAKE IT PERMANENT.
WHAT THE HELL IS GOING ON IN HERE?
DIDN'T WE JUST CRUSH THESE GUYS? HOW MANY MORE HAWKMEN CAN SHE MAKE? WE'RE GOING TO BE OVERRUN!
THIS WORLD...IT'S DESTABILIZING.

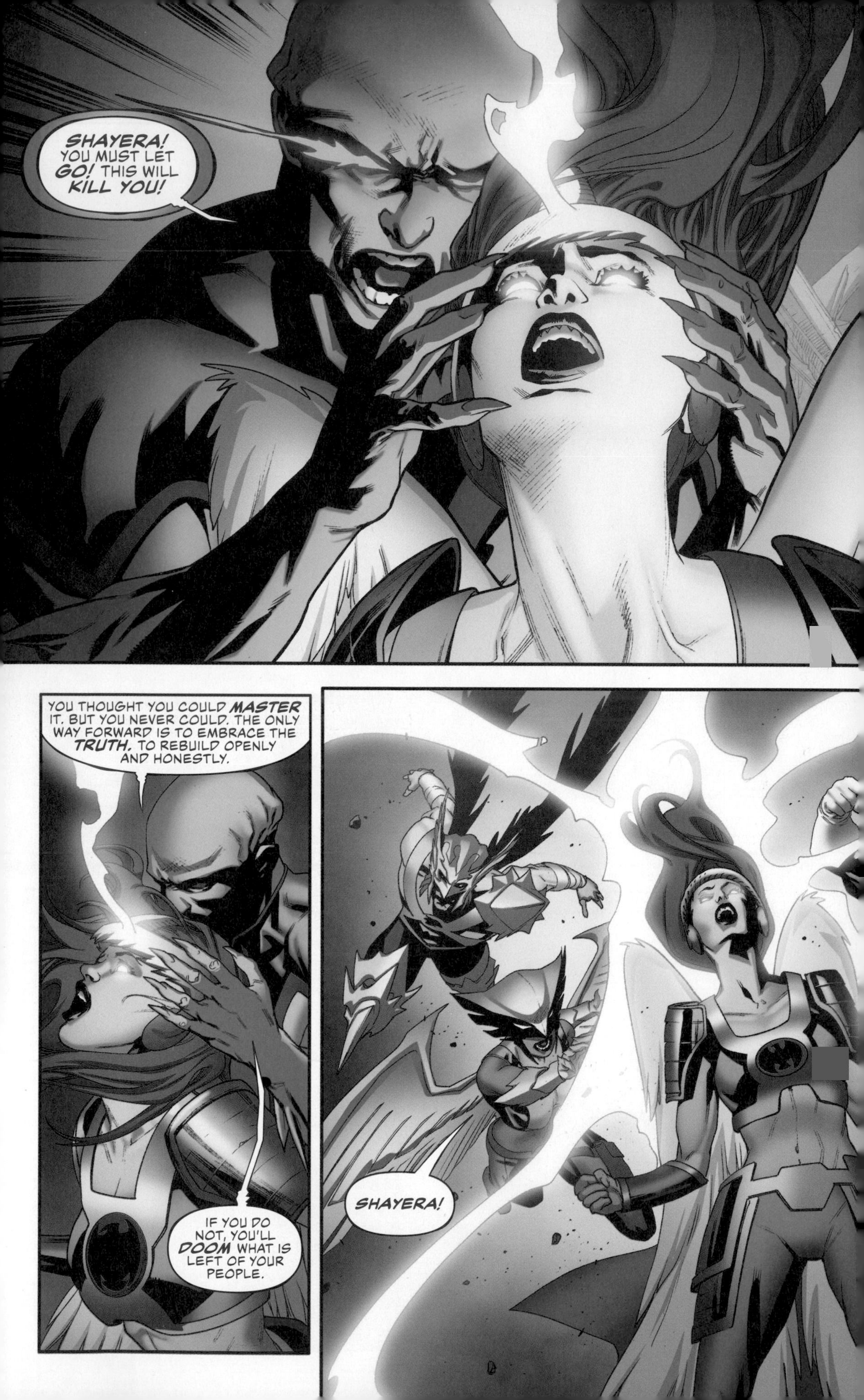
SHAYERA! YOU MUST LET GO! THIS WILL KILL YOU!
YOU THOUGHT YOU COULD MASTER IT. BUT YOU NEVER COULD. THE ONLY WAY FORWARD IS TO EMBRACE THE TRUTH. TO REBUILD OPENLY AND HONESTLY.
IF YOU DO NOT, YOU'LL DOOM WHAT IS LEFT OF YOUR PEOPLE.
SHAYERA!

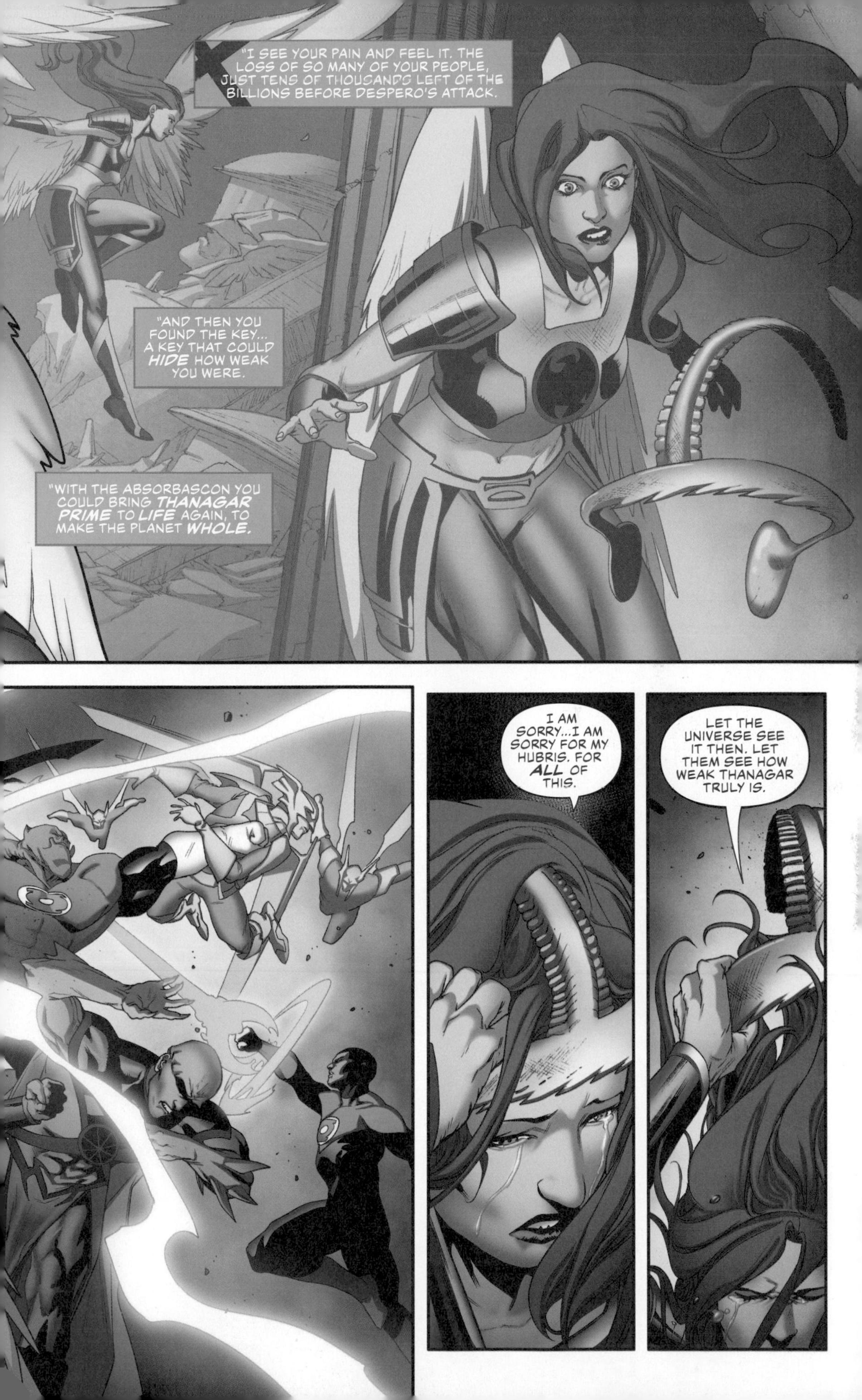
"I SEE YOUR PAIN AND FEEL IT. THE LOSS OF SO MANY OF YOUR PEOPLE, JUST TENS OF THOUSANDS LEFT OF THE BILLIONS BEFORE DESPERO'S ATTACK.
"AND THEN YOU FOUND THE KEY... A KEY THAT COULD HIDE HOW WEAK YOU WERE.
"WITH THE ABSORBASCON YOU COULD BRING THANAGAR PRIME TO LIFE AGAIN, TO MAKE THE PLANET WHOLE.
I AM SORRY...I AM SORRY FOR MY HUBRIS. FOR ALL OF THIS.
LET THE UNIVERSE SEE IT THEN. LET THEM SEE HOW WEAK THANAGAR TRULY IS.

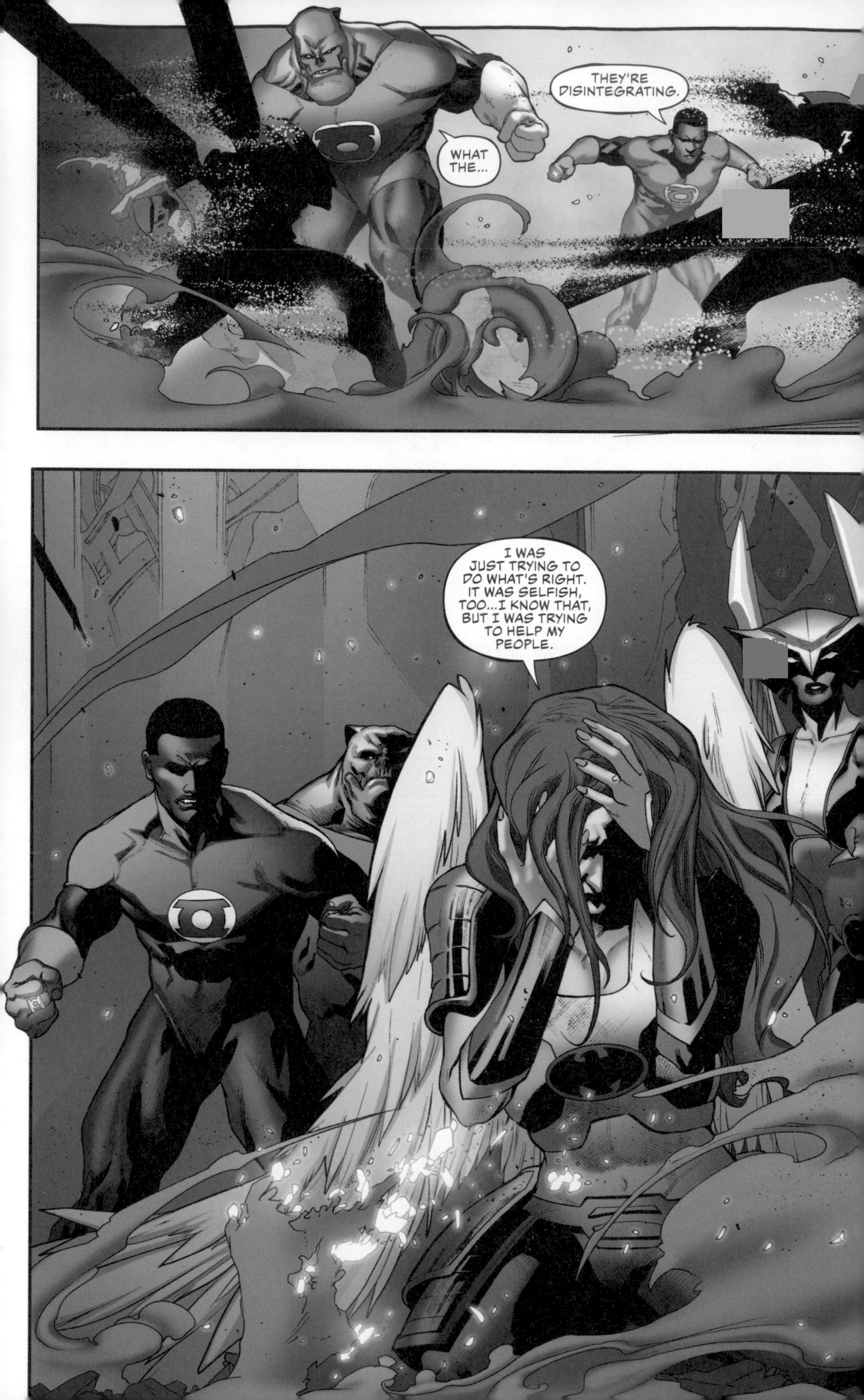
WHAT THE...
THEY'RE DISINTEGRATING.
I WAS JUST TRYING TO DO WHAT'S RIGHT. IT WAS SELFISH, TOO...I KNOW THAT, BUT I WAS TRYING TO HELP MY PEOPLE.

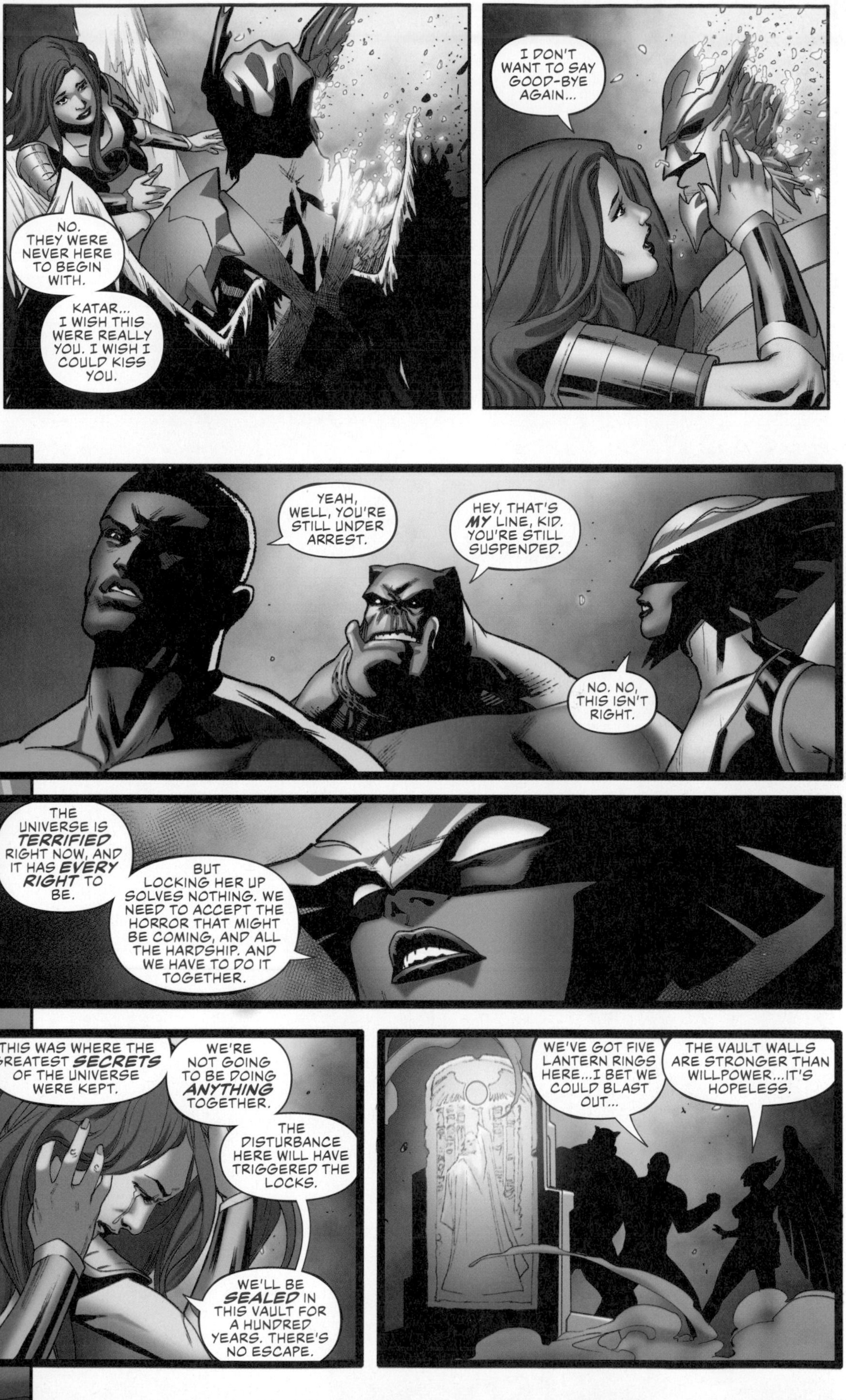
NO. THEY WERE NEVER HERE TO BEGIN WITH.
KATAR... I WISH THIS WERE REALLY YOU. I WISH I COULD KISS YOU.
I DON'T WANT TO SAY GOOD-BYE AGAIN...
YEAH, WELL, YOU'RE STILL UNDER ARREST.
HEY, THAT'S MY LINE, KID. YOU'RE STILL SUSPENDED.
NO. NO, THIS ISN'T RIGHT.
THE UNIVERSE IS TERRIFIED RIGHT NOW, AND IT HAS EVERY RIGHT TO BE.
BUT LOCKING HER UP SOLVES NOTHING. WE NEED TO ACCEPT THE HORROR THAT MIGHT BE COMING, AND ALL THE HARDSHIP. AND WE HAVE TO DO IT TOGETHER.
THIS WAS WHERE THE GREATEST SECRETS OF THE UNIVERSE WERE KEPT.
WE'RE NOT GOING TO BE DOING ANYTHING TOGETHER.
THE DISTURBANCE HERE WILL HAVE TRIGGERED THE LOCKS.
WE'LL BE SEALED IN THIS VAULT FOR A HUNDRED YEARS. THERE'S NO ESCAPE.
WE'VE GOT FIVE LANTERN RINGS HERE...I BET WE COULD BLAST OUT...
THE VAULT WALLS ARE STRONGER THAN WILLPOWER...IT'S HOPELESS.

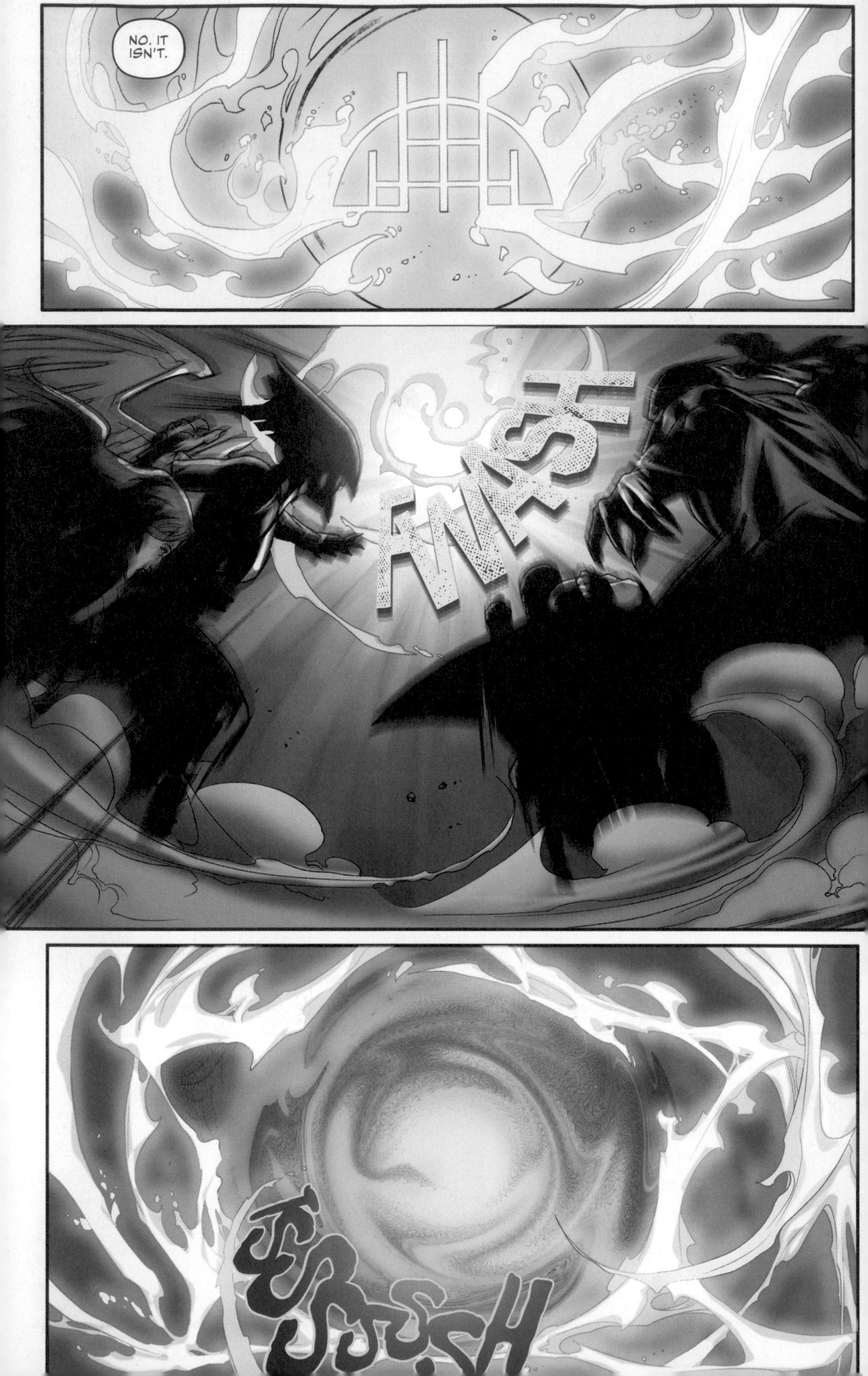
NO. IT ISN'T.
FWASH

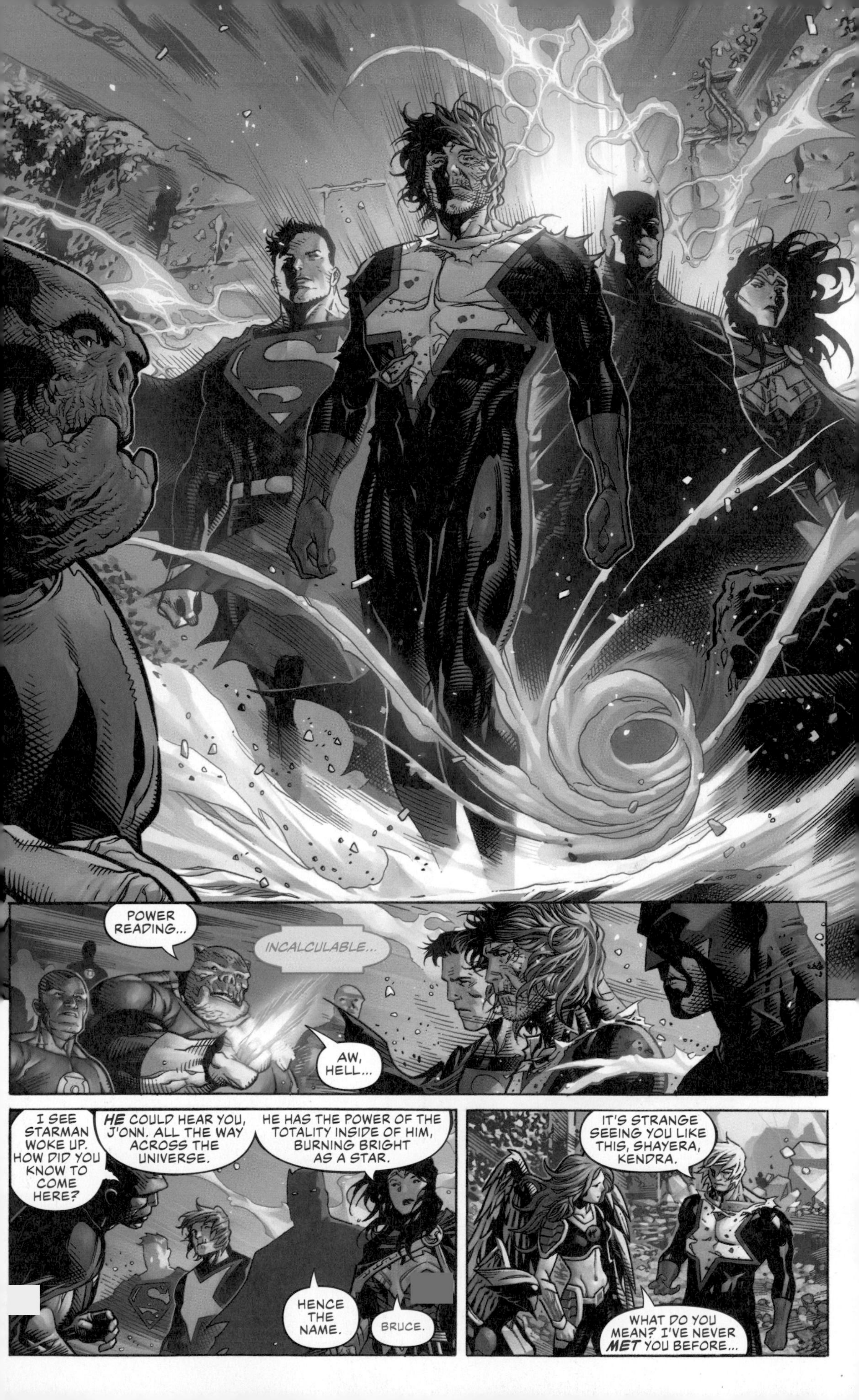
POWER READING...
INCALCULABLE...
AW, HELL...
I SEE STARMAN WOKE UP. HOW DID YOU KNOW TO COME HERE?
HE COULD HEAR YOU, J'ONN. ALL THE WAY ACROSS THE UNIVERSE.
HE HAS THE POWER OF THE TOTALITY INSIDE OF HIM, BURNING BRIGHT AS A STAR.
HENCE THE NAME.
BRUCE.
IT'S STRANGE SEEING YOU LIKE THIS, SHAYERA, KENDRA.
WHAT DO YOU MEAN? I'VE NEVER **MET** YOU BEFORE...

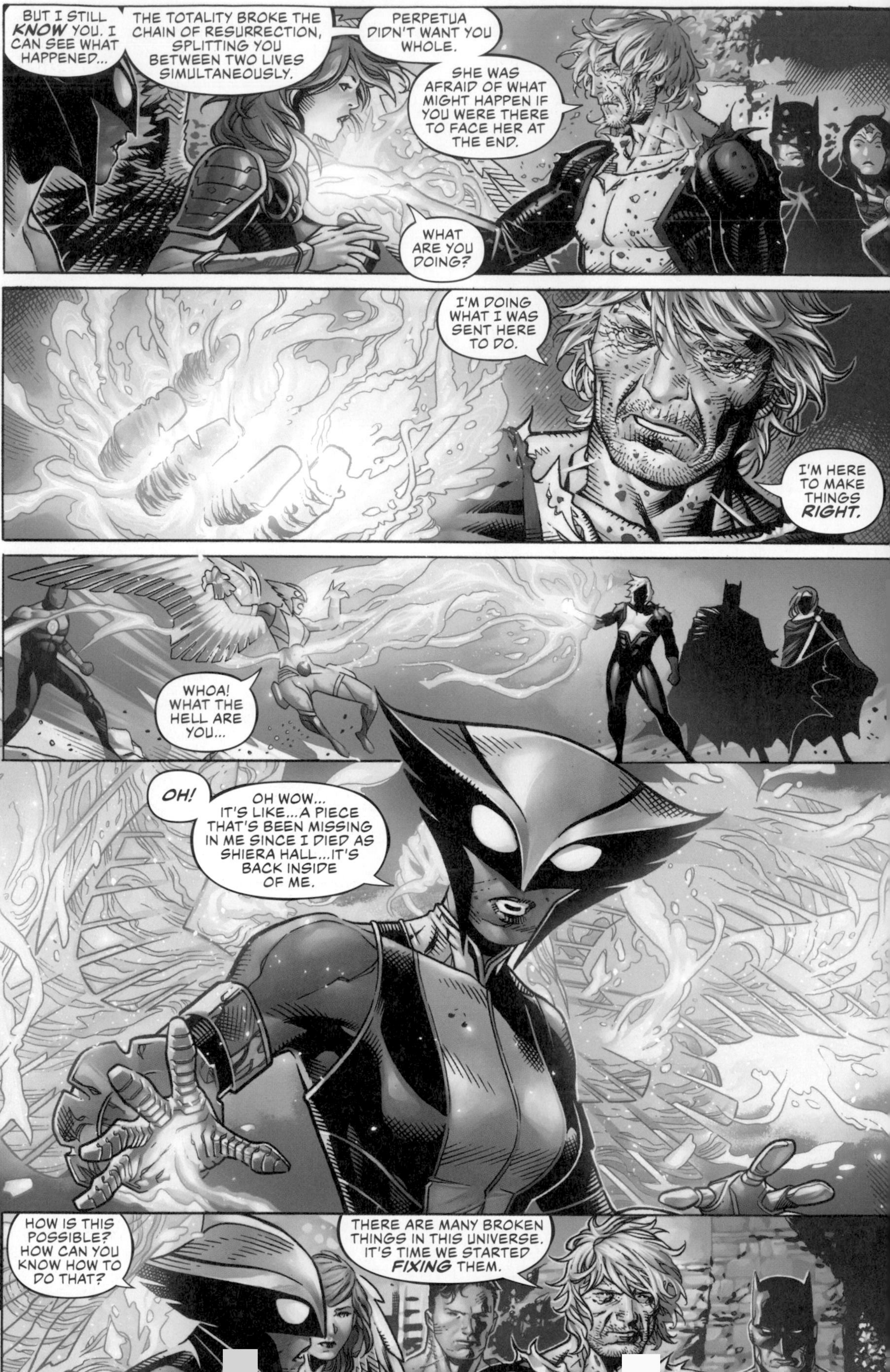
BUT I STILL KNOW YOU. I CAN SEE WHAT HAPPENED...
THE TOTALITY BROKE THE CHAIN OF RESURRECTION, SPLITTING YOU BETWEEN TWO LIVES SIMULTANEOUSLY.
PERPETUA DIDN'T WANT YOU WHOLE.
SHE WAS AFRAID OF WHAT MIGHT HAPPEN IF YOU WERE THERE TO FACE HER AT THE END.
WHAT ARE YOU DOING?
I'M DOING WHAT I WAS SENT HERE TO DO.
I'M HERE TO MAKE THINGS RIGHT.
WHOA! WHAT THE HELL ARE YOU...
OH!
OH WOW... IT'S LIKE...A PIECE THAT'S BEEN MISSING IN ME SINCE I DIED AS SHIERA HALL...IT'S BACK INSIDE OF ME.
HOW IS THIS POSSIBLE? HOW CAN YOU KNOW HOW TO DO THAT?
THERE ARE MANY BROKEN THINGS IN THIS UNIVERSE. IT'S TIME WE STARTED FIXING THEM.

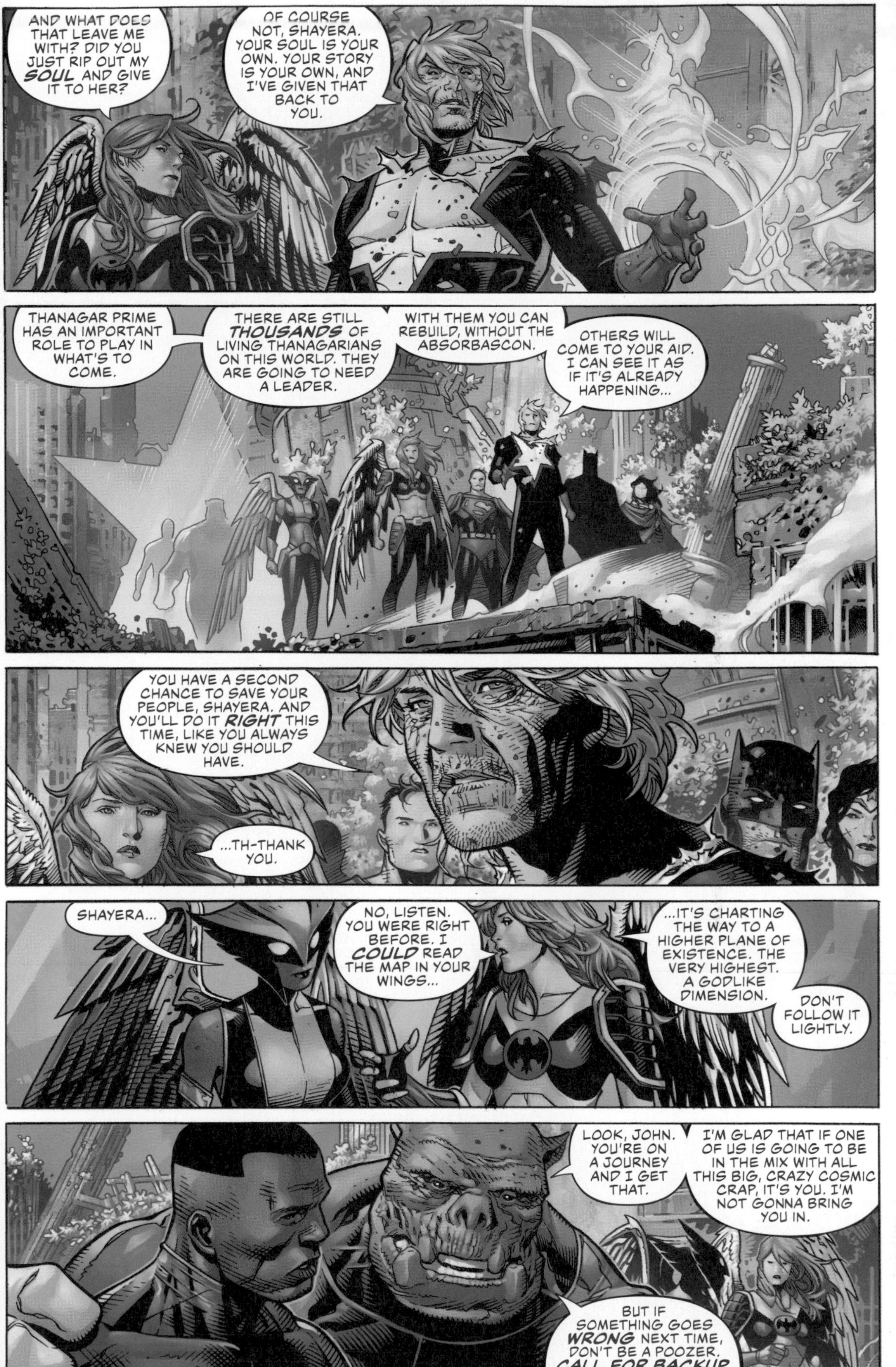
AND WHAT DOES THAT LEAVE ME WITH? DID YOU JUST RIP OUT MY SOUL AND GIVE IT TO HER?
OF COURSE NOT, SHAYERA. YOUR SOUL IS YOUR OWN. YOUR STORY IS YOUR OWN, AND I'VE GIVEN THAT BACK TO YOU.
THANAGAR PRIME HAS AN IMPORTANT ROLE TO PLAY IN WHAT'S TO COME.
THERE ARE STILL THOUSANDS OF LIVING THANAGARIANS ON THIS WORLD. THEY ARE GOING TO NEED A LEADER.
WITH THEM YOU CAN REBUILD, WITHOUT THE ABSORBASCON.
OTHERS WILL COME TO YOUR AID. I CAN SEE IT AS IF IT'S ALREADY HAPPENING...
YOU HAVE A SECOND CHANCE TO SAVE YOUR PEOPLE, SHAYERA. AND YOU'LL DO IT RIGHT THIS TIME, LIKE YOU ALWAYS KNEW YOU SHOULD HAVE.
...TH-THANK YOU.
SHAYERA...
NO, LISTEN. YOU WERE RIGHT BEFORE. I COULD READ THE MAP IN YOUR WINGS...
...IT'S CHARTING THE WAY TO A HIGHER PLANE OF EXISTENCE. THE VERY HIGHEST. A GODLIKE DIMENSION.
DON'T FOLLOW IT LIGHTLY.
LOOK, JOHN. YOU'RE ON A JOURNEY AND I GET THAT.
I'M GLAD THAT IF ONE OF US IS GOING TO BE IN THE MIX WITH ALL THIS BIG, CRAZY COSMIC CRAP, IT'S YOU. I'M NOT GONNA BRING YOU IN.
BUT IF SOMETHING GOES WRONG NEXT TIME, DON'T BE A POOZER. CALL FOR BACKUP.

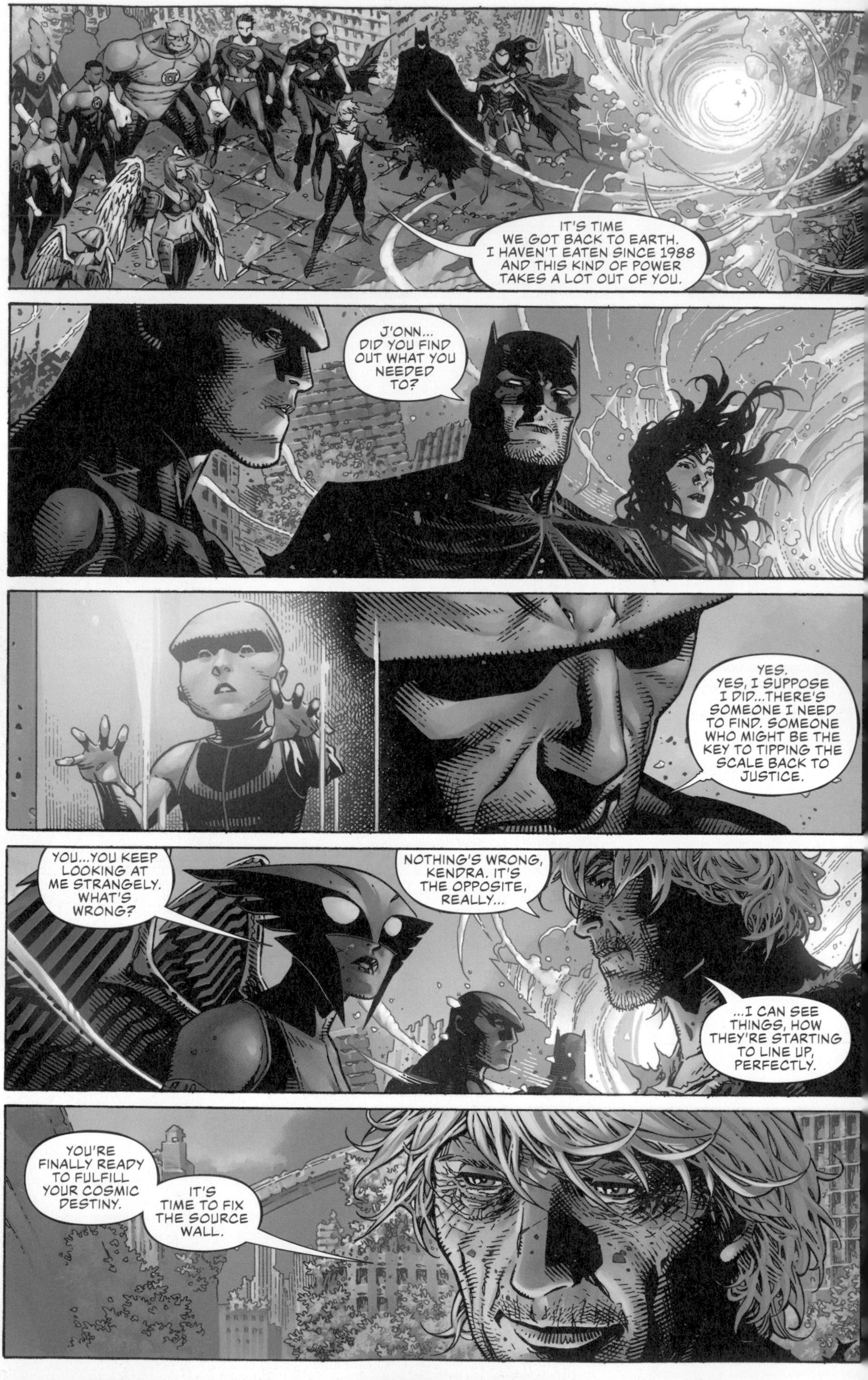
IT'S TIME WE GOT BACK TO EARTH. I HAVEN'T EATEN SINCE 1988 AND THIS KIND OF POWER TAKES A LOT OUT OF YOU.
J'ONN... DID YOU FIND OUT WHAT YOU NEEDED TO?
YES. YES, I SUPPOSE I DID...THERE'S SOMEONE I NEED TO FIND. SOMEONE WHO MIGHT BE THE KEY TO TIPPING THE SCALE BACK TO JUSTICE.
YOU...YOU KEEP LOOKING AT ME STRANGELY. WHAT'S WRONG?
NOTHING'S WRONG, KENDRA. IT'S THE OPPOSITE, REALLY...
...I CAN SEE THINGS, HOW THEY'RE STARTING TO LINE UP, PERFECTLY.
YOU'RE FINALLY READY TO FULFILL YOUR COSMIC DESTINY.
IT'S TIME TO FIX THE SOURCE WALL.

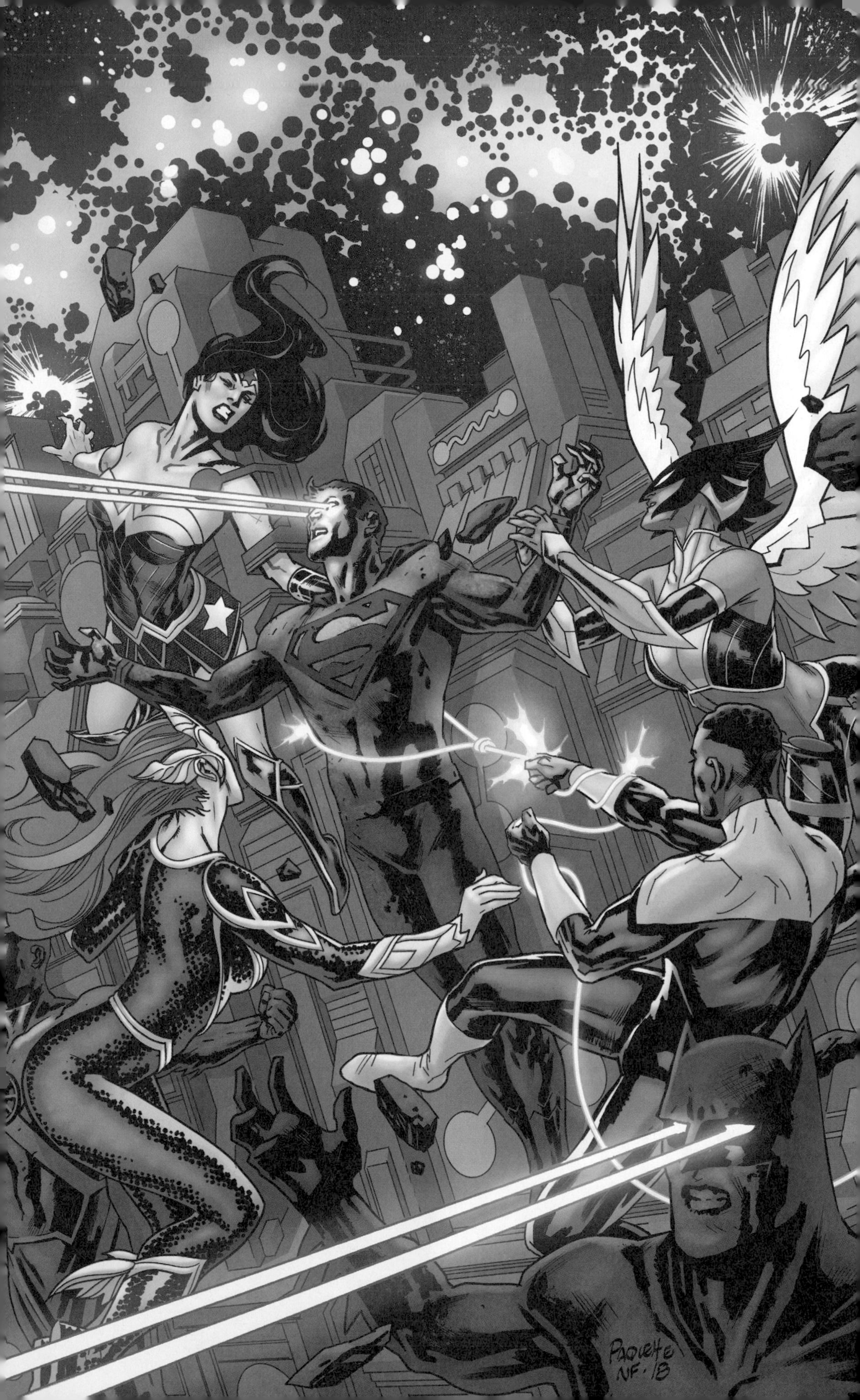
PAQUETTE
NF·18

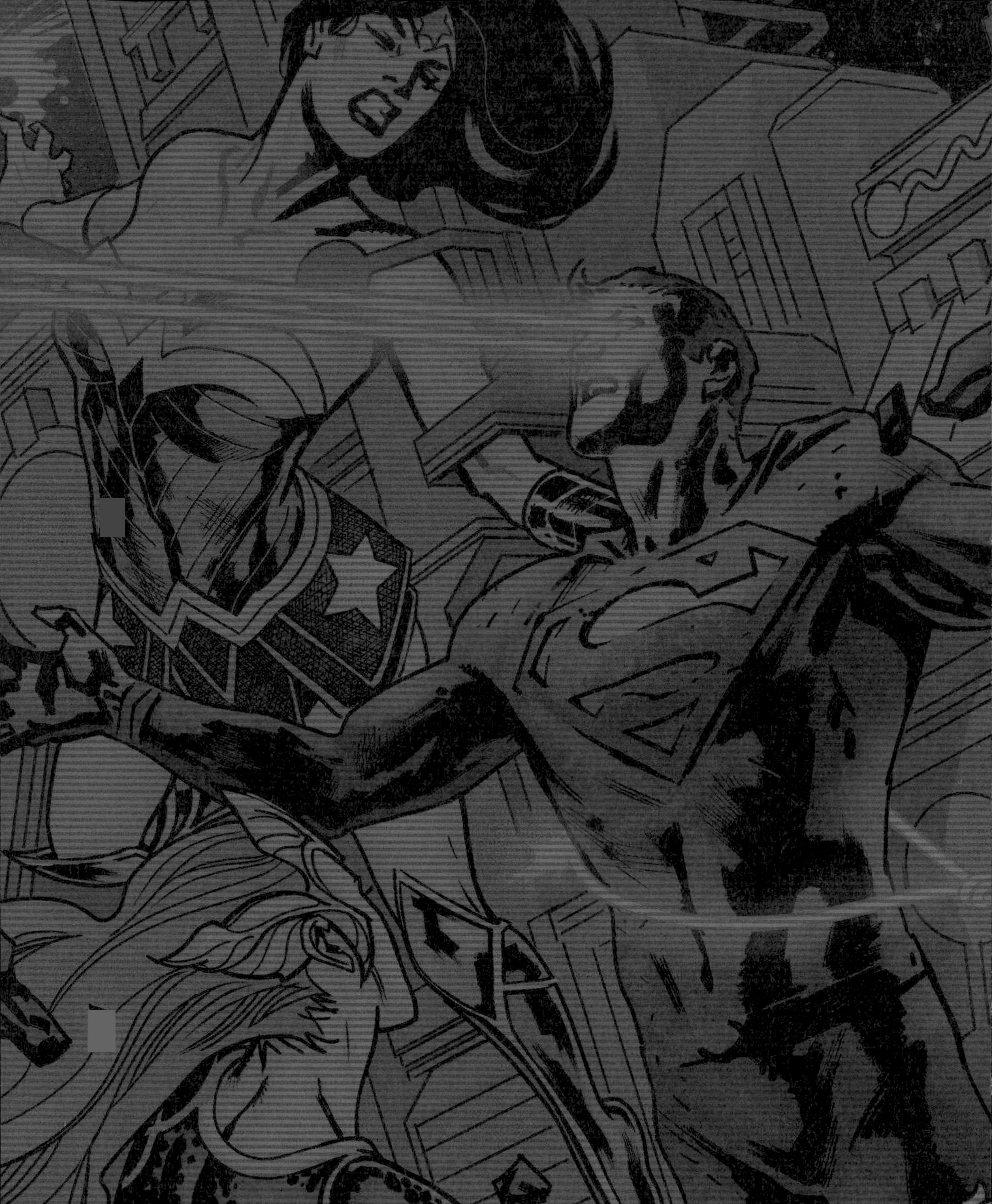

JUSTICE
LEAGUE
ANNUAL #1

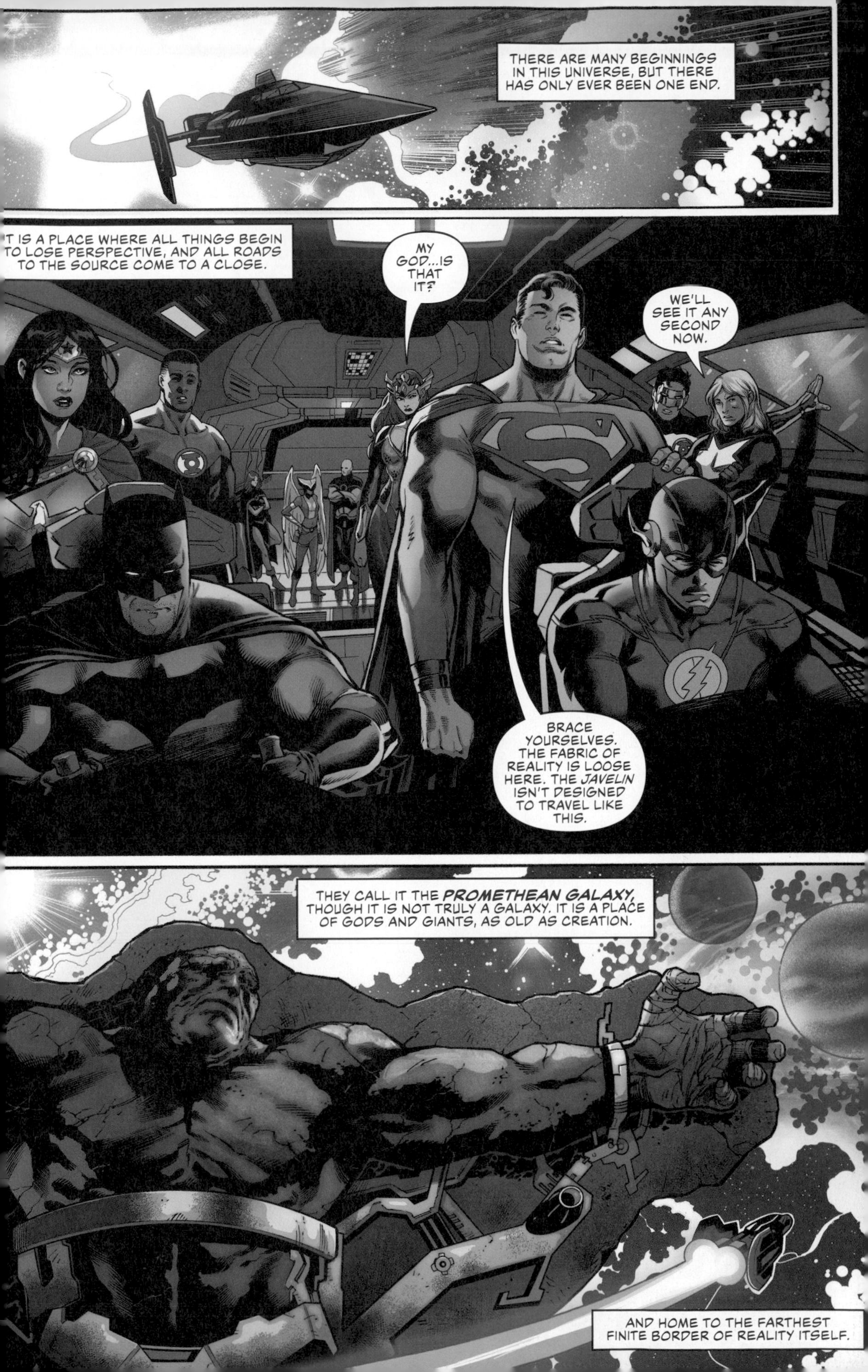
THERE ARE MANY BEGINNINGS IN THIS UNIVERSE, BUT THERE HAS ONLY EVER BEEN ONE END.
IT IS A PLACE WHERE ALL THINGS BEGIN TO LOSE PERSPECTIVE, AND ALL ROADS TO THE SOURCE COME TO A CLOSE.
MY GOD...IS THAT IT?
WE'LL SEE IT ANY SECOND NOW.
BRACE YOURSELVES. THE FABRIC OF REALITY IS LOOSE HERE. THE *JAVELIN* ISN'T DESIGNED TO TRAVEL LIKE THIS.
THEY CALL IT THE ***PROMETHEAN GALAXY,*** THOUGH IT IS NOT TRULY A GALAXY. IT IS A PLACE OF GODS AND GIANTS, AS OLD AS CREATION.
AND HOME TO THE FARTHEST FINITE BORDER OF REALITY ITSELF.

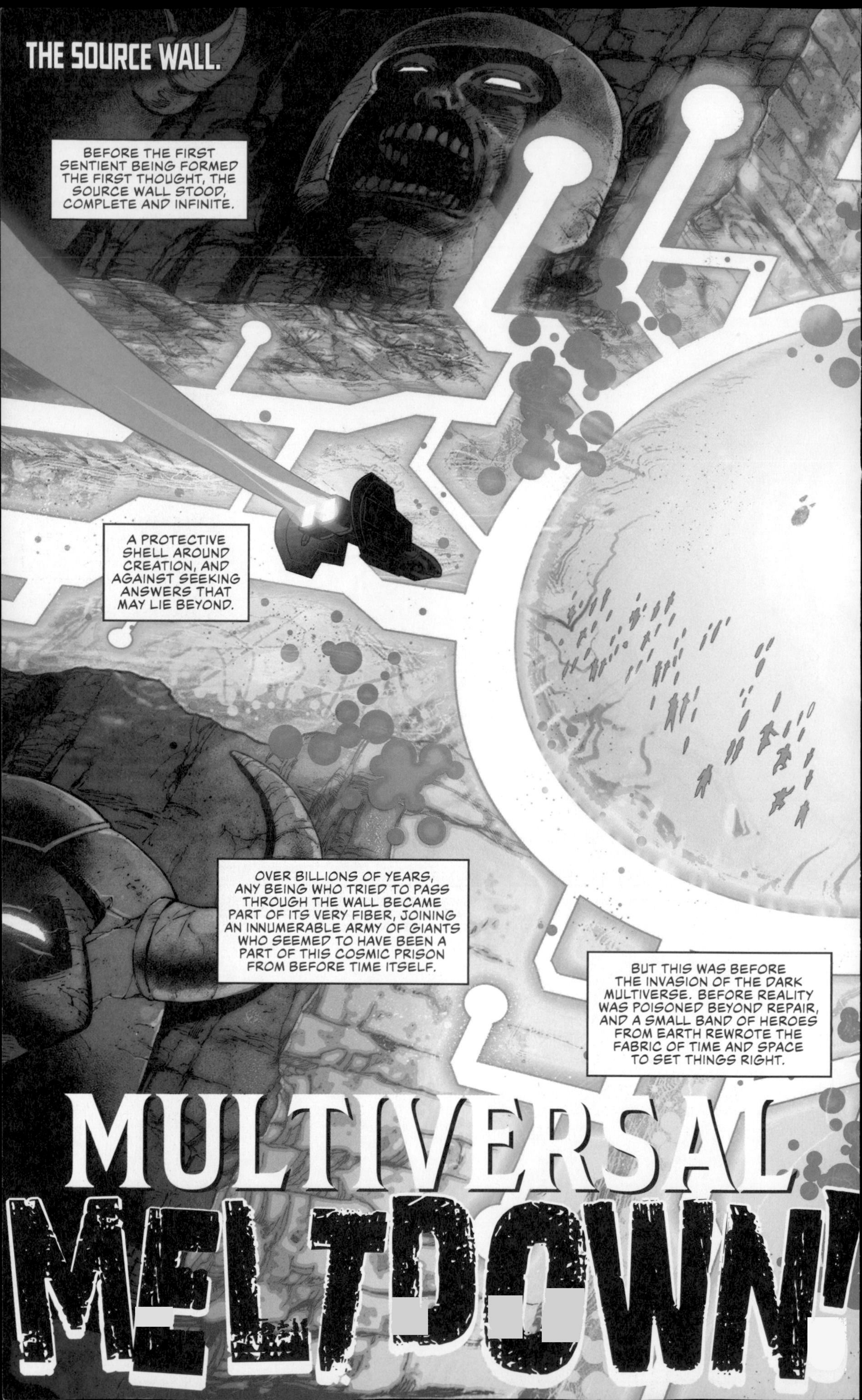
THE SOURCE WALL.
BEFORE THE FIRST SENTIENT BEING FORMED THE FIRST THOUGHT, THE SOURCE WALL STOOD, COMPLETE AND INFINITE.
A PROTECTIVE SHELL AROUND CREATION, AND AGAINST SEEKING ANSWERS THAT MAY LIE BEYOND.
OVER BILLIONS OF YEARS, ANY BEING WHO TRIED TO PASS THROUGH THE WALL BECAME PART OF ITS VERY FIBER, JOINING AN INNUMERABLE ARMY OF GIANTS WHO SEEMED TO HAVE BEEN A PART OF THIS COSMIC PRISON FROM BEFORE TIME ITSELF.
BUT THIS WAS BEFORE THE INVASION OF THE DARK MULTIVERSE. BEFORE REALITY WAS POISONED BEYOND REPAIR, AND A SMALL BAND OF HEROES FROM EARTH REWROTE THE FABRIC OF TIME AND SPACE TO SET THINGS RIGHT.
MULTIVERSAL
MELTDOWN!

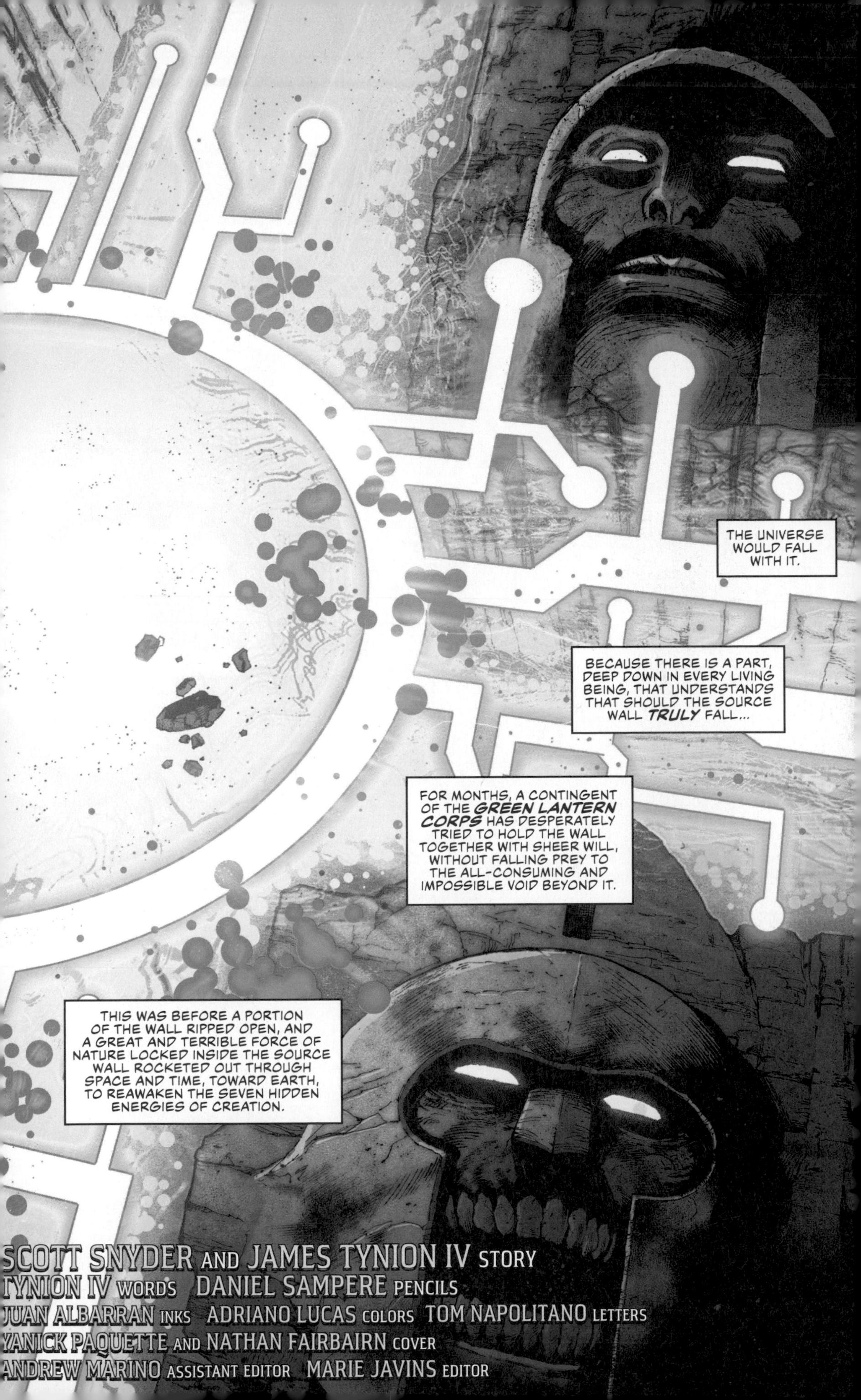

THE UNIVERSE WOULD FALL WITH IT.
BECAUSE THERE IS A PART, DEEP DOWN IN EVERY LIVING BEING, THAT UNDERSTANDS THAT SHOULD THE SOURCE WALL *TRULY* FALL...
FOR MONTHS, A CONTINGENT OF THE *GREEN LANTERN CORPS* HAS DESPERATELY TRIED TO HOLD THE WALL TOGETHER WITH SHEER WILL, WITHOUT FALLING PREY TO THE ALL-CONSUMING AND IMPOSSIBLE VOID BEYOND IT.
THIS WAS BEFORE A PORTION OF THE WALL RIPPED OPEN, AND A GREAT AND TERRIBLE FORCE OF NATURE LOCKED INSIDE THE SOURCE WALL ROCKETED OUT THROUGH SPACE AND TIME, TOWARD EARTH, TO REAWAKEN THE SEVEN HIDDEN ENERGIES OF CREATION.
SCOTT SNYDER AND JAMES TYNION IV STORY
TYNION IV WORDS DANIEL SAMPERE PENCILS
JUAN ALBARRAN INKS ADRIANO LUCAS COLORS TOM NAPOLITANO LETTERS
YANICK PAQUETTE AND NATHAN FAIRBAIRN COVER
ANDREW MARINO ASSISTANT EDITOR MARIE JAVINS EDITOR

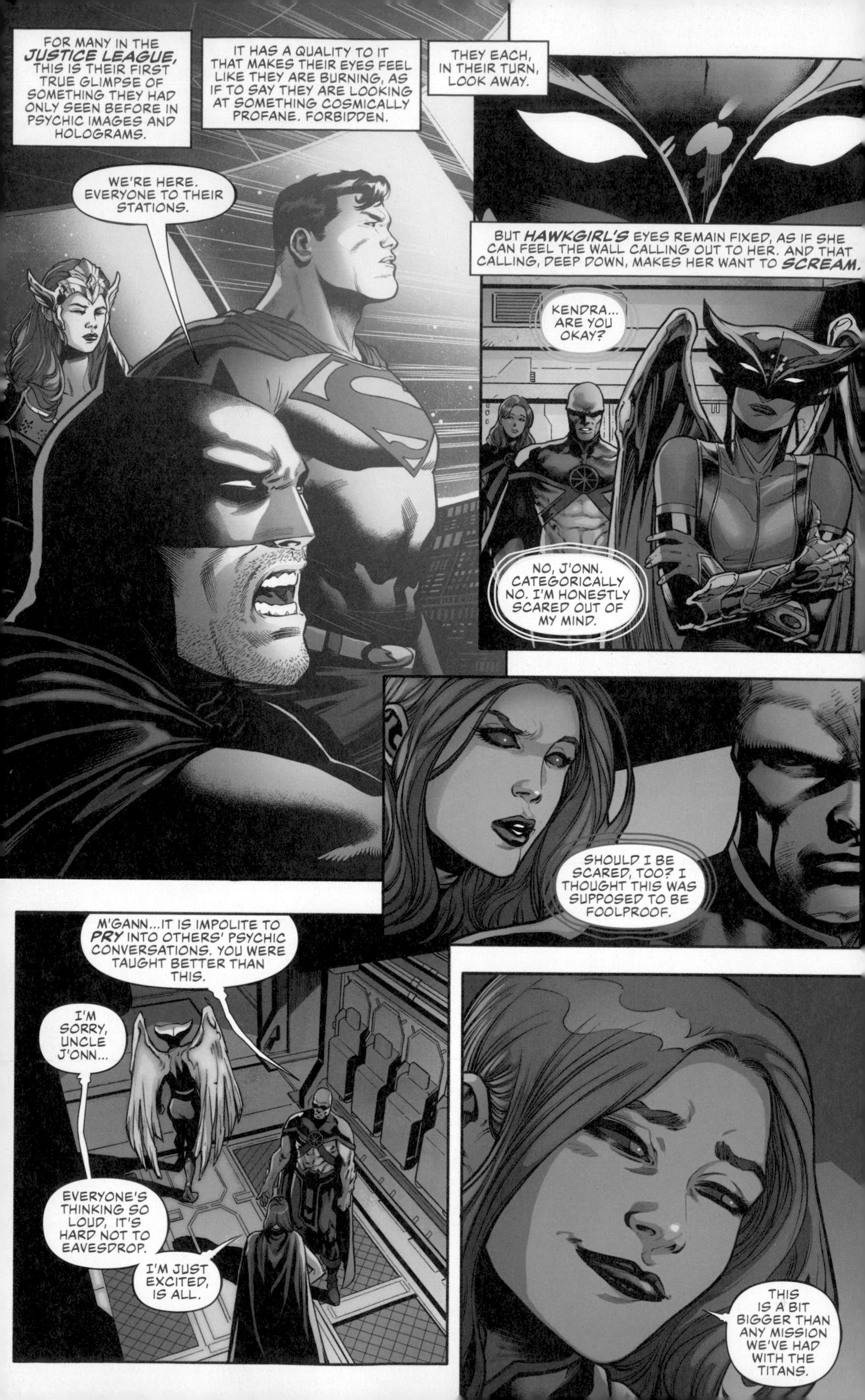
FOR MANY IN THE JUSTICE LEAGUE, THIS IS THEIR FIRST TRUE GLIMPSE OF SOMETHING THEY HAD ONLY SEEN BEFORE IN PSYCHIC IMAGES AND HOLOGRAMS.
IT HAS A QUALITY TO IT THAT MAKES THEIR EYES FEEL LIKE THEY ARE BURNING, AS IF TO SAY THEY ARE LOOKING AT SOMETHING COSMICALLY PROFANE. FORBIDDEN.
THEY EACH, IN THEIR TURN, LOOK AWAY.
WE'RE HERE. EVERYONE TO THEIR STATIONS.
BUT HAWKGIRL'S EYES REMAIN FIXED, AS IF SHE CAN FEEL THE WALL CALLING OUT TO HER. AND THAT CALLING, DEEP DOWN, MAKES HER WANT TO SCREAM.
KENDRA... ARE YOU OKAY?
NO, J'ONN. CATEGORICALLY NO. I'M HONESTLY SCARED OUT OF MY MIND.
SHOULD I BE SCARED, TOO? I THOUGHT THIS WAS SUPPOSED TO BE FOOLPROOF.
M'GANN...IT IS IMPOLITE TO PRY INTO OTHERS' PSYCHIC CONVERSATIONS. YOU WERE TAUGHT BETTER THAN THIS.
I'M SORRY, UNCLE J'ONN...
EVERYONE'S THINKING SO LOUD, IT'S HARD NOT TO EAVESDROP.
I'M JUST EXCITED, IS ALL.
THIS IS A BIT BIGGER THAN ANY MISSION WE'VE HAD WITH THE TITANS.

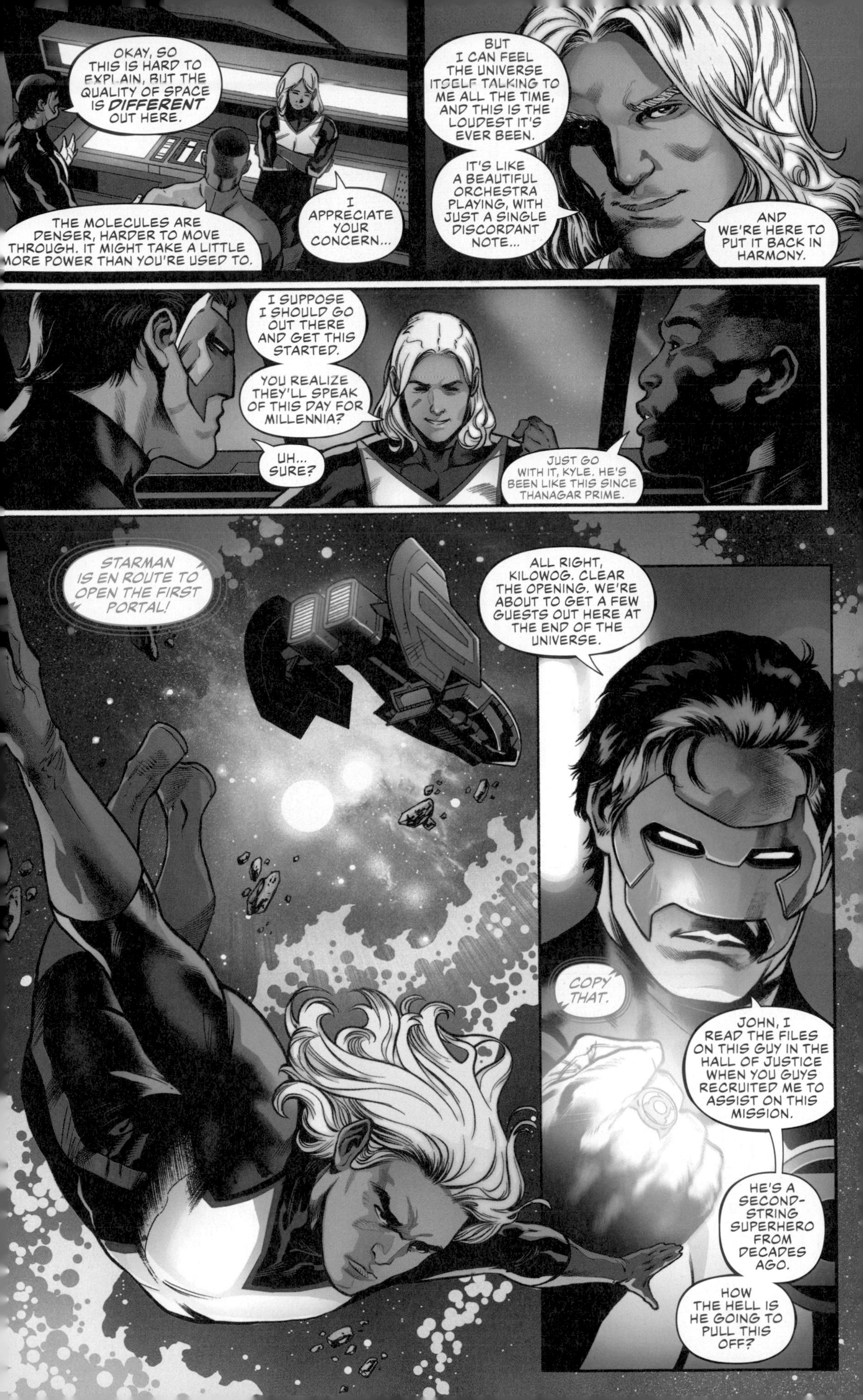

OKAY, SO THIS IS HARD TO EXPLAIN, BUT THE QUALITY OF SPACE IS ***DIFFERENT*** OUT HERE.
THE MOLECULES ARE DENSER, HARDER TO MOVE THROUGH. IT MIGHT TAKE A LITTLE MORE POWER THAN YOU'RE USED TO.
I APPRECIATE YOUR CONCERN...
BUT I CAN FEEL THE UNIVERSE ITSELF TALKING TO ME ALL THE TIME, AND THIS IS THE LOUDEST IT'S EVER BEEN.
IT'S LIKE A BEAUTIFUL ORCHESTRA PLAYING, WITH JUST A SINGLE DISCORDANT NOTE...
AND WE'RE HERE TO PUT IT BACK IN HARMONY.
I SUPPOSE I SHOULD GO OUT THERE AND GET THIS STARTED.
YOU REALIZE THEY'LL SPEAK OF THIS DAY FOR MILLENNIA?
UH... SURE?
JUST GO WITH IT, KYLE. HE'S BEEN LIKE THIS SINCE THANAGAR PRIME.
STARMAN IS EN ROUTE TO OPEN THE FIRST PORTAL!
ALL RIGHT, KILOWOG. CLEAR THE OPENING. WE'RE ABOUT TO GET A FEW GUESTS OUT HERE AT THE END OF THE UNIVERSE.
COPY THAT.
JOHN, I READ THE FILES ON THIS GUY IN THE HALL OF JUSTICE WHEN YOU GUYS RECRUITED ME TO ASSIST ON THIS MISSION.
HE'S A SECOND-STRING SUPERHERO FROM DECADES AGO.
HOW THE HELL IS HE GOING TO PULL THIS OFF?

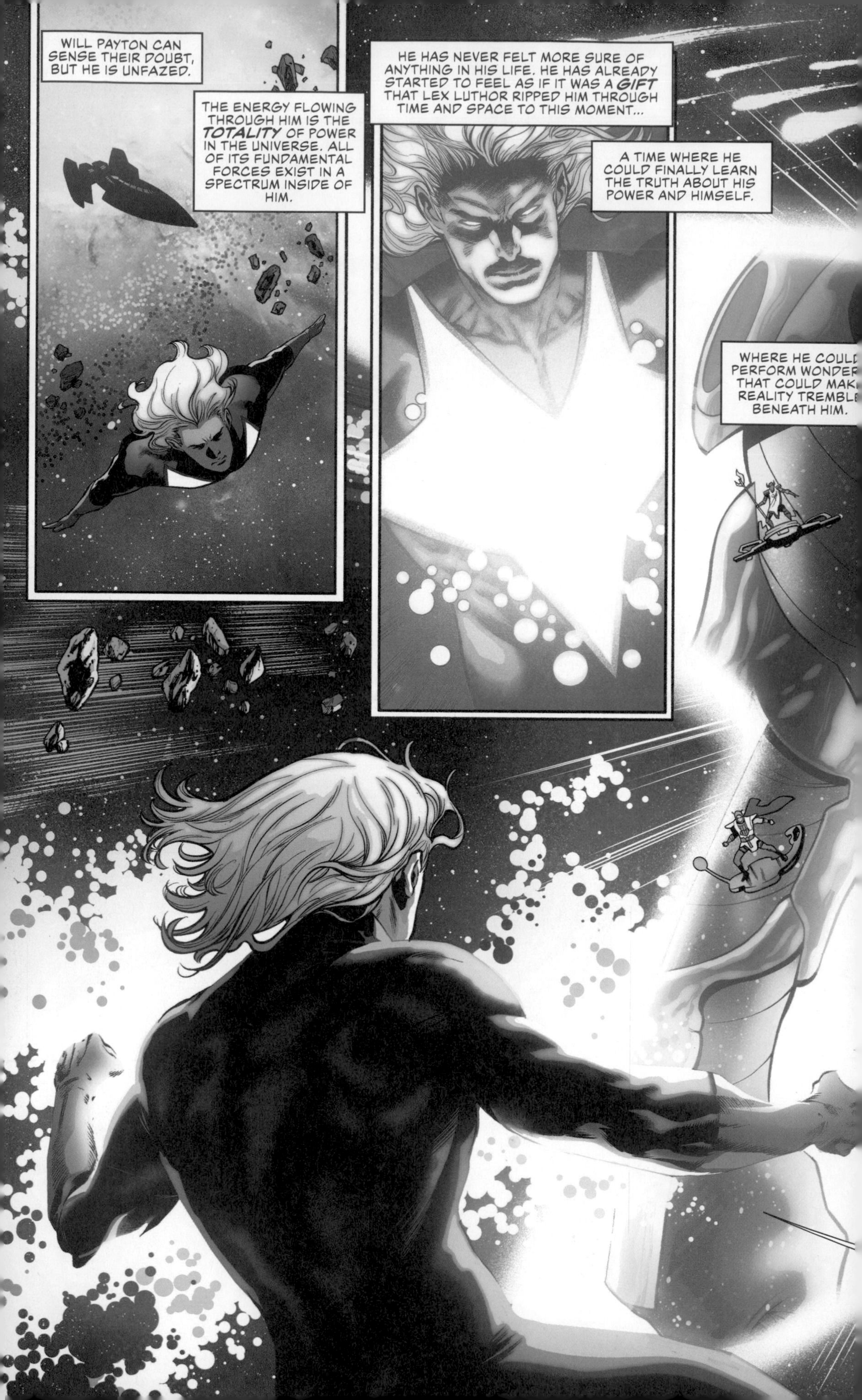
WILL PAYTON CAN SENSE THEIR DOUBT, BUT HE IS UNFAZED.
THE ENERGY FLOWING THROUGH HIM IS THE TOTALITY OF POWER IN THE UNIVERSE. ALL OF ITS FUNDAMENTAL FORCES EXIST IN A SPECTRUM INSIDE OF HIM.
HE HAS NEVER FELT MORE SURE OF ANYTHING IN HIS LIFE. HE HAS ALREADY STARTED TO FEEL AS IF IT WAS A GIFT THAT LEX LUTHOR RIPPED HIM THROUGH TIME AND SPACE TO THIS MOMENT...
A TIME WHERE HE COULD FINALLY LEARN THE TRUTH ABOUT HIS POWER AND HIMSELF.
WHERE HE COUL PERFORM WONDER THAT COULD MAK REALITY TREMBL BENEATH HIM.

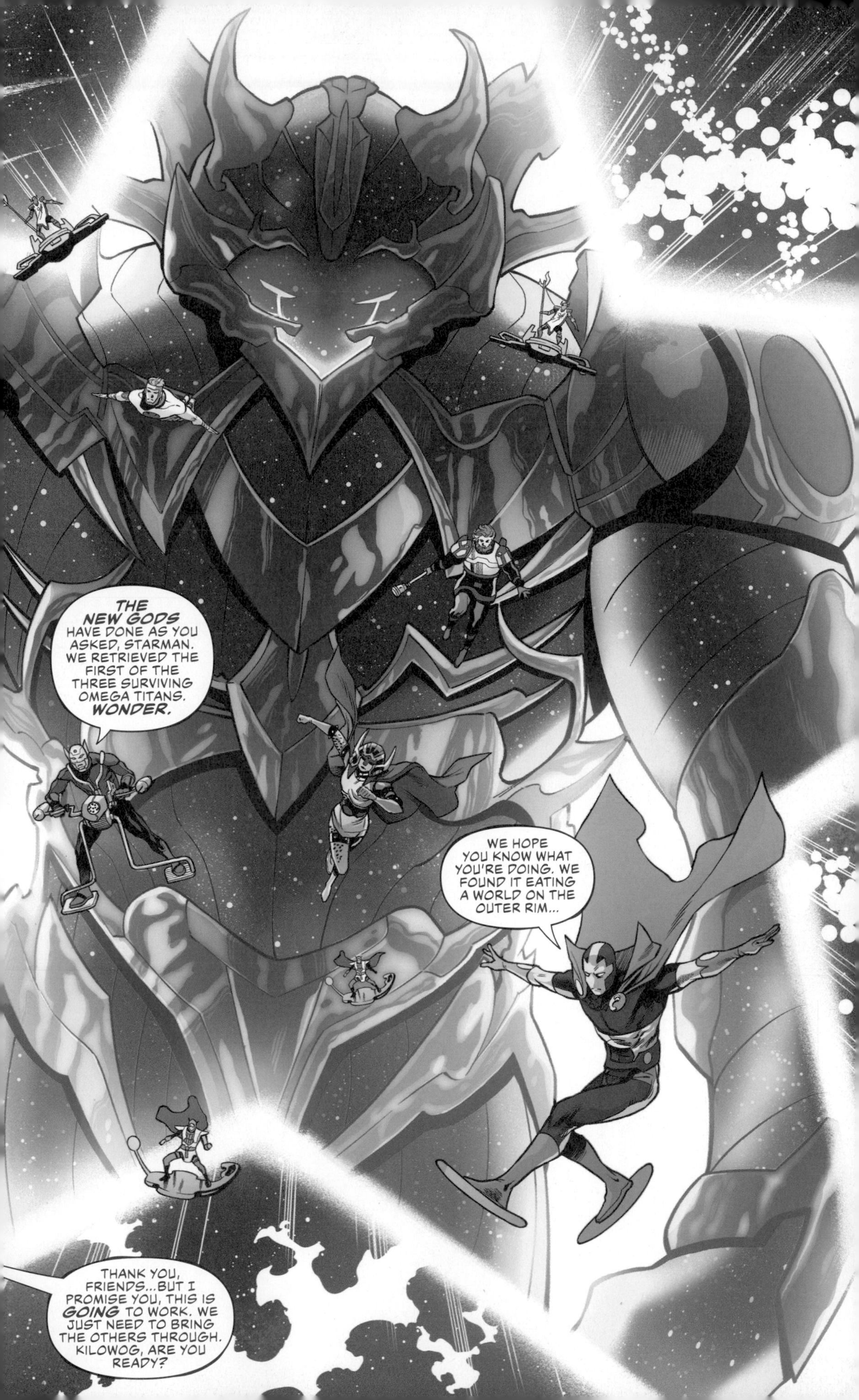
THE NEW GODS HAVE DONE AS YOU ASKED, STARMAN. WE RETRIEVED THE FIRST OF THE THREE SURVIVING OMEGA TITANS. WONDER.
WE HOPE YOU KNOW WHAT YOU'RE DOING. WE FOUND IT EATING A WORLD ON THE OUTER RIM...
THANK YOU, FRIENDS...BUT I PROMISE YOU, THIS IS GOING TO WORK. WE JUST NEED TO BRING THE OTHERS THROUGH. KILOWOG, ARE YOU READY?

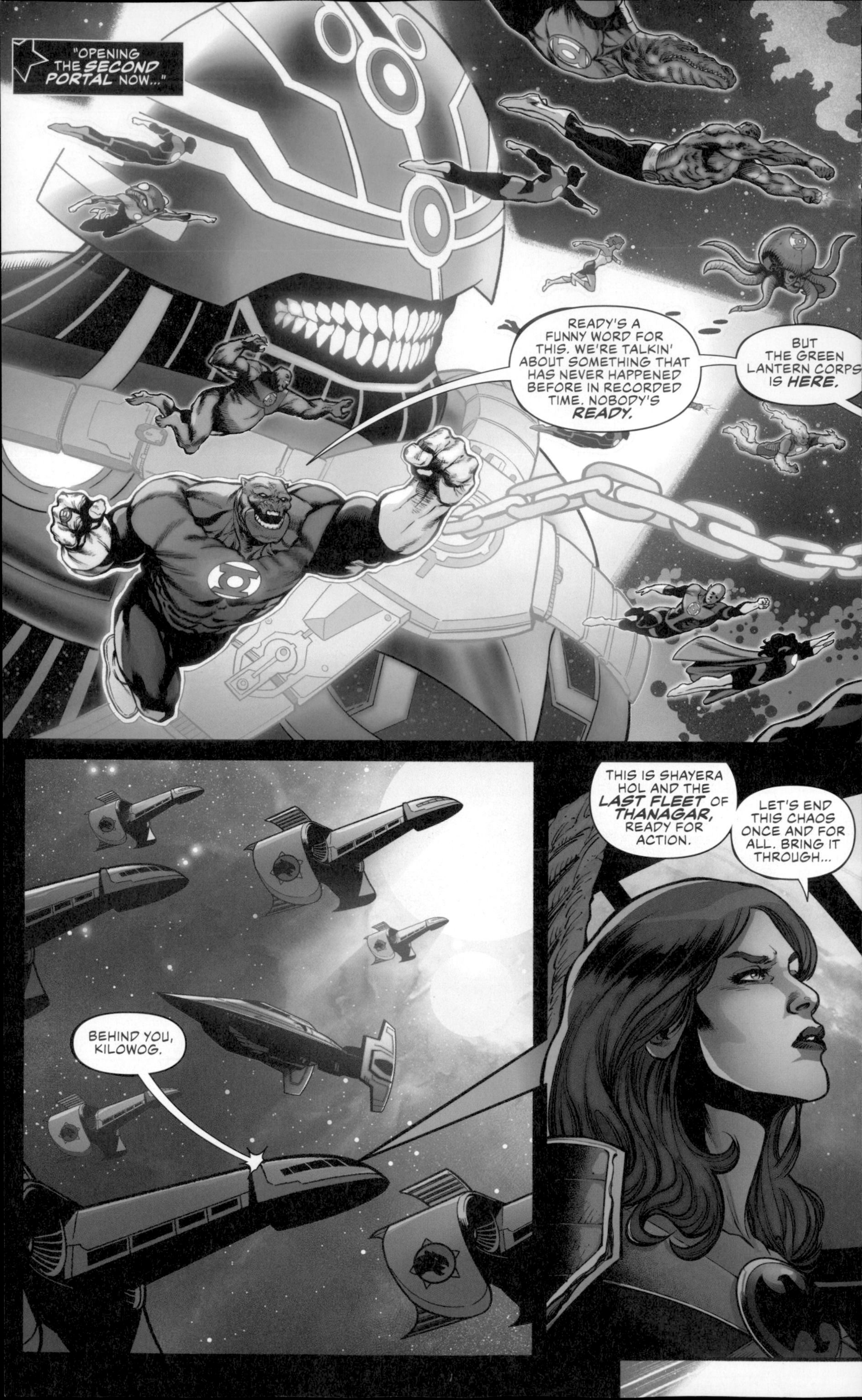
"OPENING THE SECOND PORTAL NOW..."
READY'S A FUNNY WORD FOR THIS. WE'RE TALKIN' ABOUT SOMETHING THAT HAS NEVER HAPPENED BEFORE IN RECORDED TIME. NOBODY'S READY.
BUT THE GREEN LANTERN CORPS IS HERE.
BEHIND YOU, KILOWOG.
THIS IS SHAYERA HOL AND THE LAST FLEET OF THANAGAR, READY FOR ACTION.
LET'S END THIS CHAOS ONCE AND FOR ALL. BRING IT THROUGH...

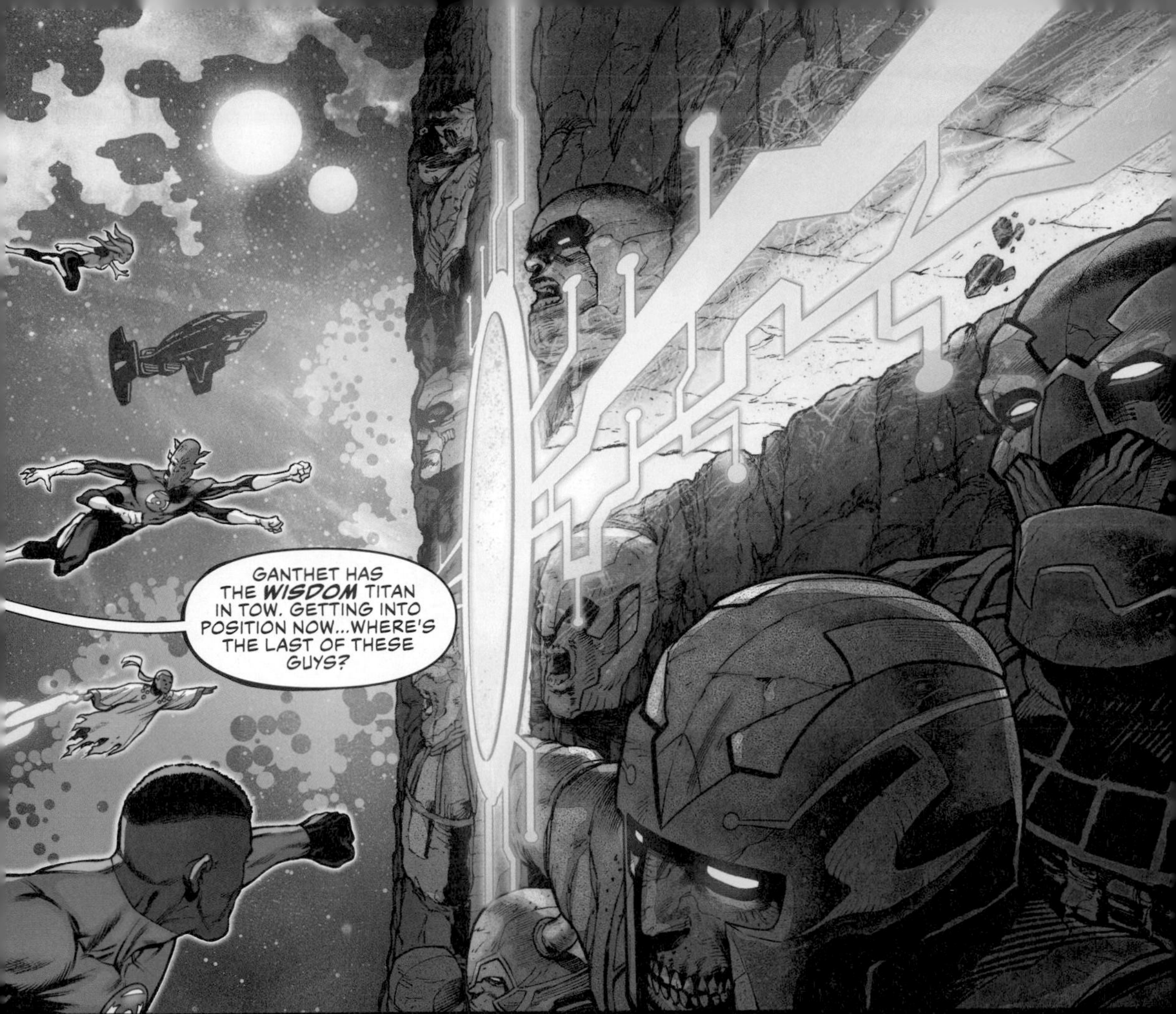
GANTHET HAS THE WISDOM TITAN IN TOW. GETTING INTO POSITION NOW...WHERE'S THE LAST OF THESE GUYS?

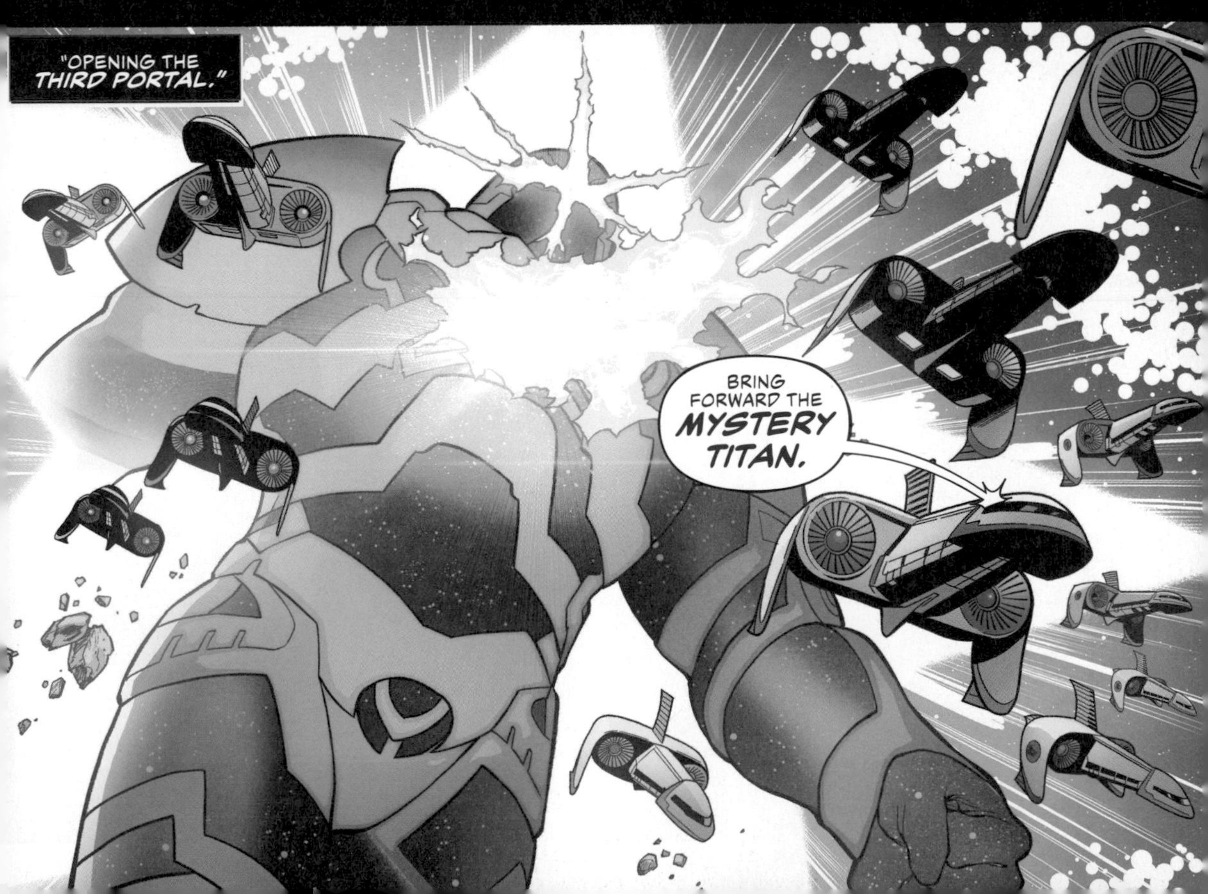
"OPENING THE THIRD PORTAL."
BRING FORWARD THE MYSTERY TITAN.

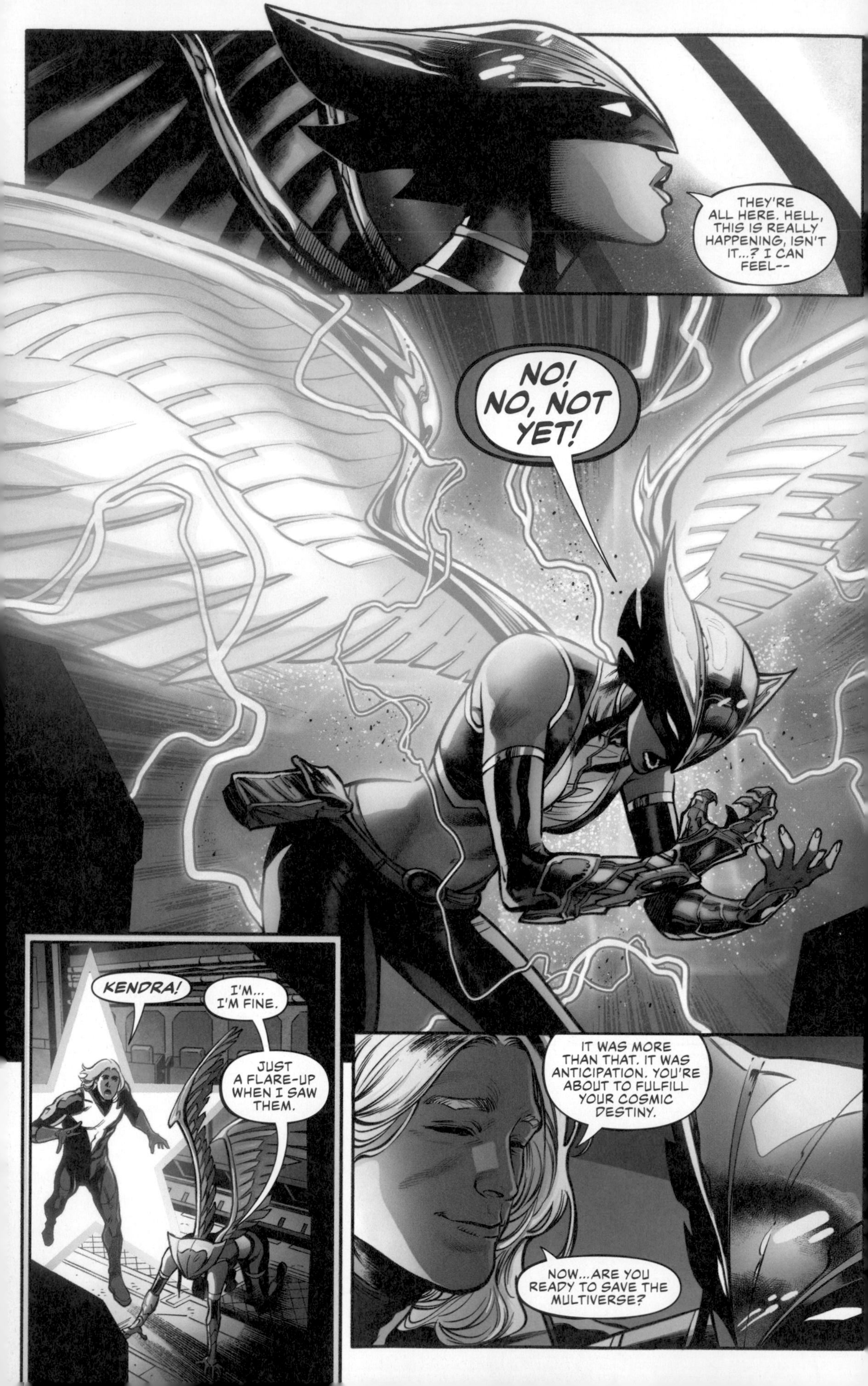
THEY'RE ALL HERE. HELL, THIS IS REALLY HAPPENING, ISN'T IT...? I CAN FEEL--
NO! NO, NOT YET!
KENDRA!
I'M... I'M FINE.
JUST A FLARE-UP WHEN I SAW THEM.
IT WAS MORE THAN THAT. IT WAS ANTICIPATION. YOU'RE ABOUT TO FULFILL YOUR COSMIC DESTINY.
NOW...ARE YOU READY TO SAVE THE MULTIVERSE?

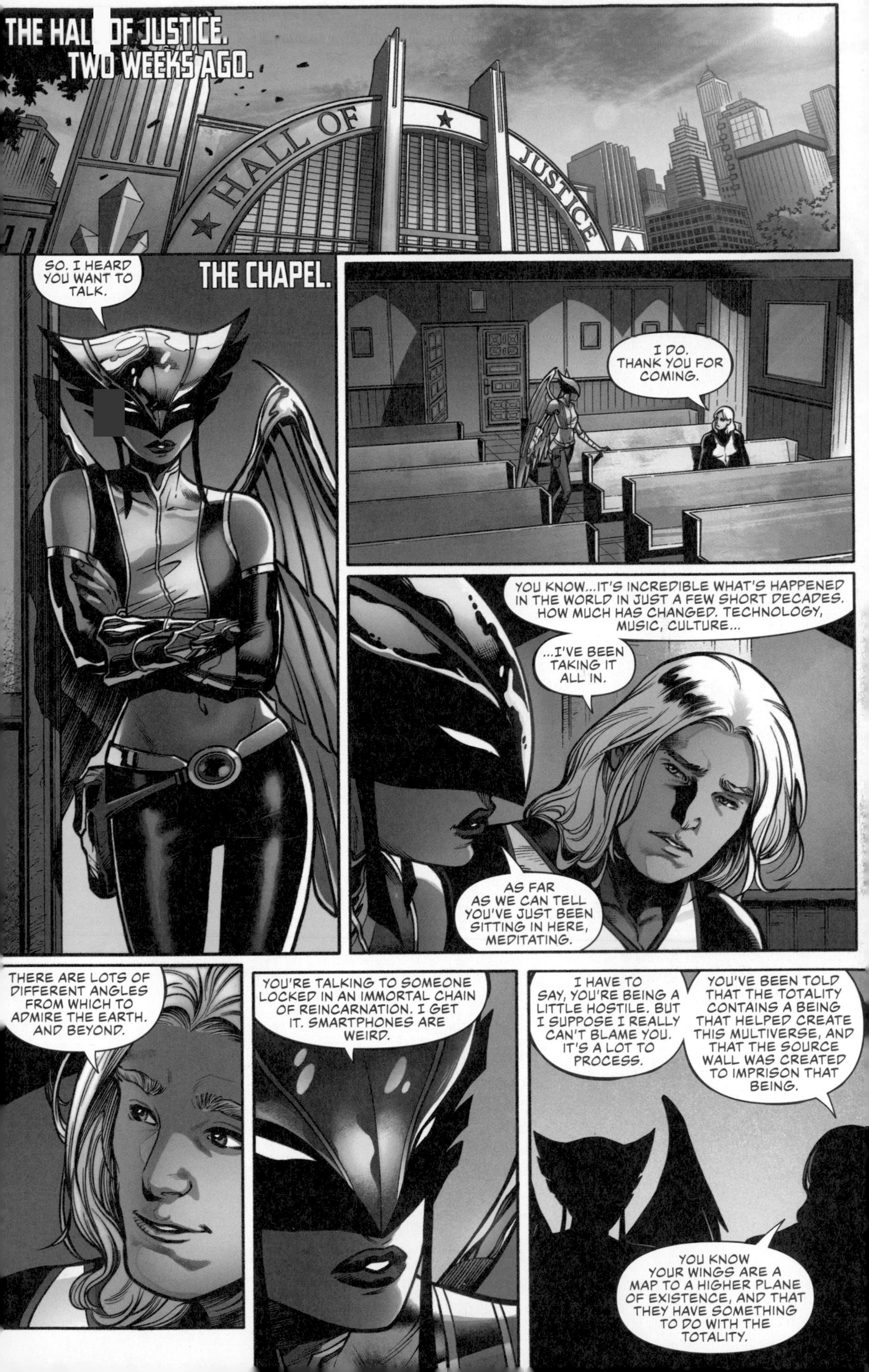
THE HAL OF JUSTICE.
TWO WEEKS AGO.
HALL OF JUSTICE
SO. I HEARD YOU WANT TO TALK.
THE CHAPEL.
I DO. THANK YOU FOR COMING.
YOU KNOW...IT'S INCREDIBLE WHAT'S HAPPENED IN THE WORLD IN JUST A FEW SHORT DECADES. HOW MUCH HAS CHANGED. TECHNOLOGY, MUSIC, CULTURE...
...I'VE BEEN TAKING IT ALL IN.
AS FAR AS WE CAN TELL YOU'VE JUST BEEN SITTING IN HERE, MEDITATING.
THERE ARE LOTS OF DIFFERENT ANGLES FROM WHICH TO ADMIRE THE EARTH. AND BEYOND.
YOU'RE TALKING TO SOMEONE LOCKED IN AN IMMORTAL CHAIN OF REINCARNATION. I GET IT. SMARTPHONES ARE WEIRD.
I HAVE TO SAY, YOU'RE BEING A LITTLE HOSTILE. BUT I SUPPOSE I REALLY CAN'T BLAME YOU. IT'S A LOT TO PROCESS.
YOU'VE BEEN TOLD THAT THE TOTALITY CONTAINS A BEING THAT HELPED CREATE THIS MULTIVERSE, AND THAT THE SOURCE WALL WAS CREATED TO IMPRISON THAT BEING.
YOU KNOW YOUR WINGS ARE A MAP TO A HIGHER PLANE OF EXISTENCE, AND THAT THEY HAVE SOMETHING TO DO WITH THE TOTALITY.

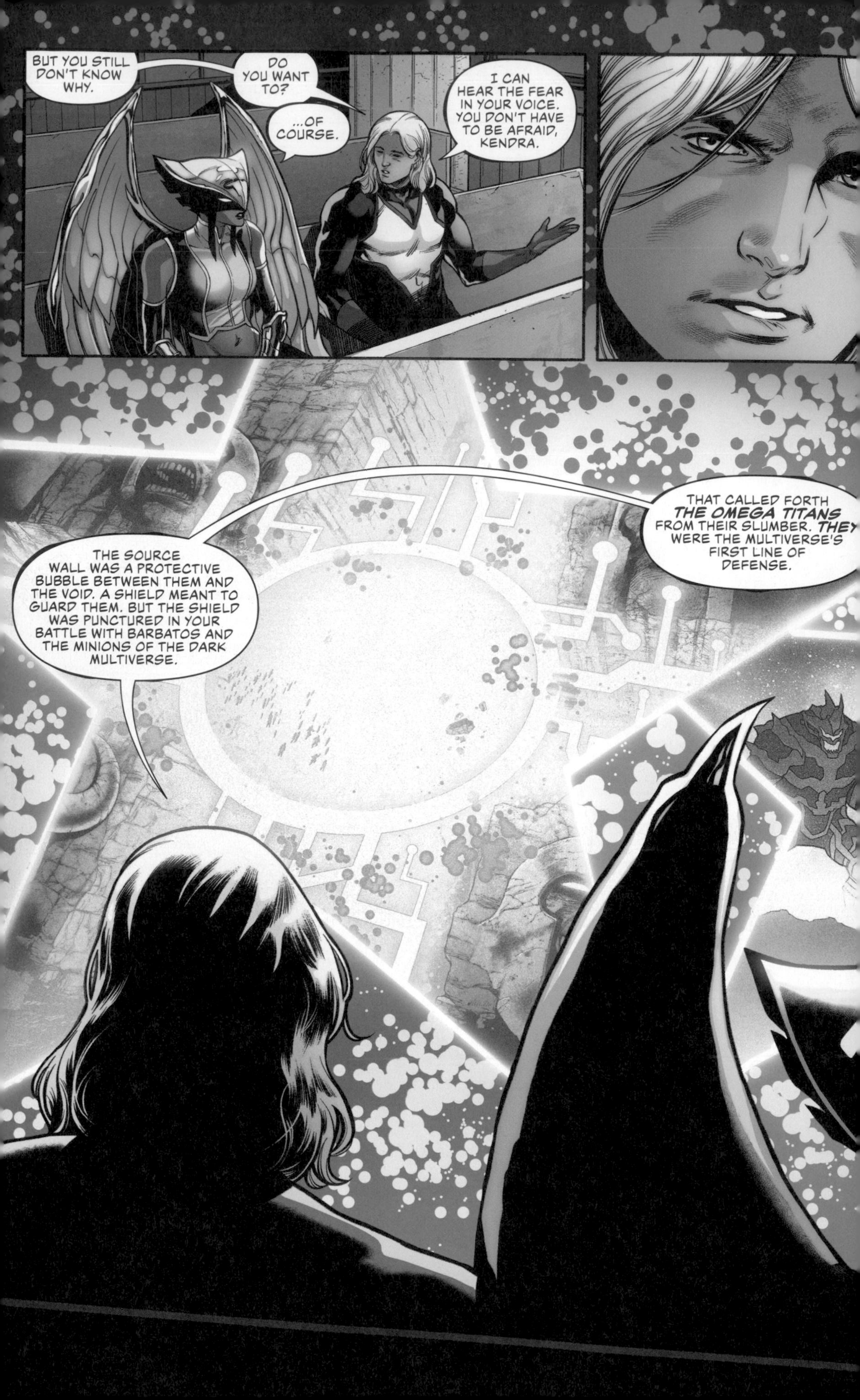
BUT YOU STILL DON'T KNOW WHY.
DO YOU WANT TO?
...OF COURSE.
I CAN HEAR THE FEAR IN YOUR VOICE. YOU DON'T HAVE TO BE AFRAID, KENDRA.
THE SOURCE WALL WAS A PROTECTIVE BUBBLE BETWEEN THEM AND THE VOID. A SHIELD MEANT TO GUARD THEM. BUT THE SHIELD WAS PUNCTURED IN YOUR BATTLE WITH BARBATOS AND THE MINIONS OF THE DARK MULTIVERSE.
THAT CALLED FORTH ***THE OMEGA TITANS*** FROM THEIR SLUMBER. ***THEY*** WERE THE MULTIVERSE'S FIRST LINE OF DEFENSE.

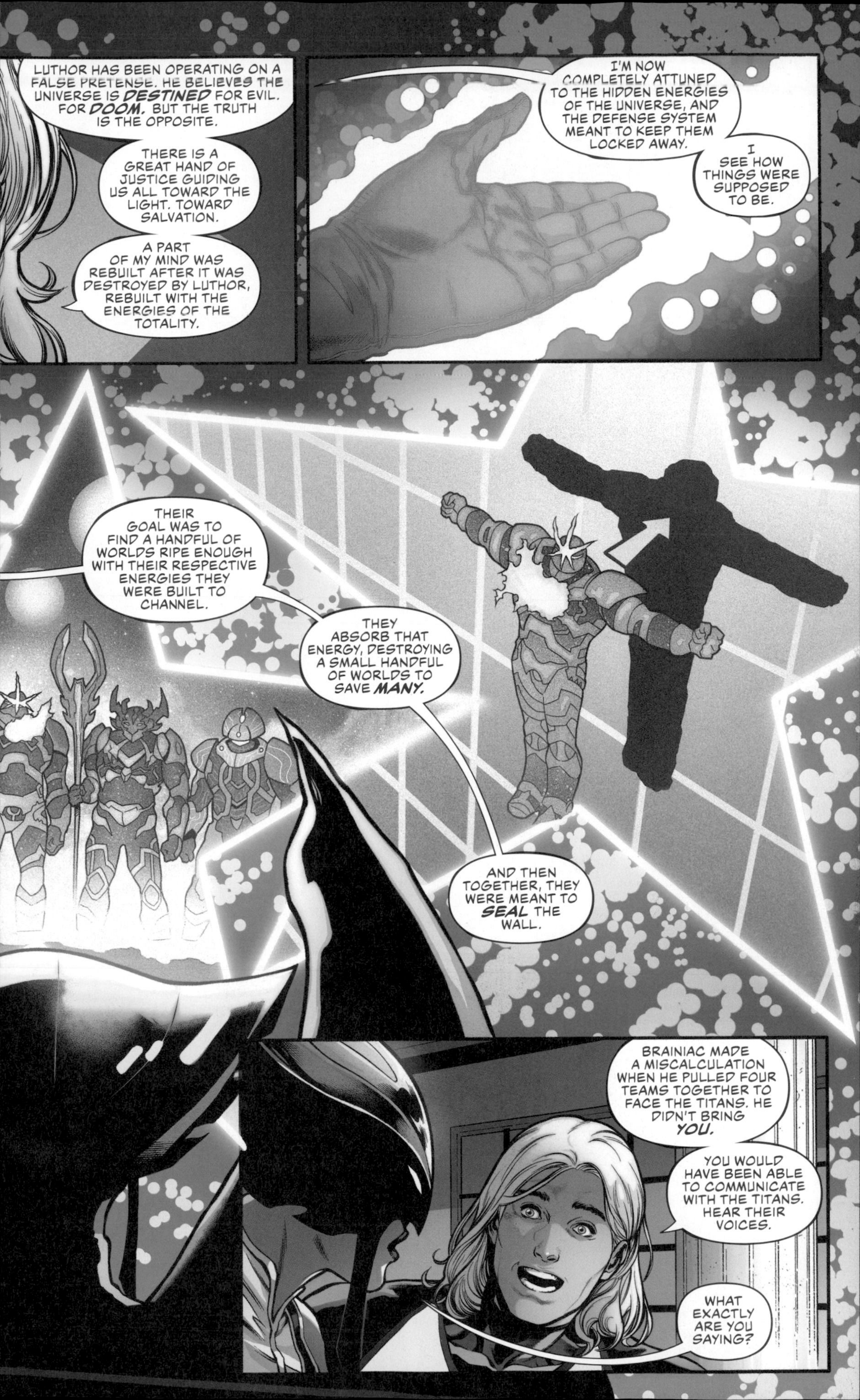
LUTHOR HAS BEEN OPERATING ON A FALSE PRETENSE. HE BELIEVES THE UNIVERSE IS DESTINED FOR EVIL. FOR DOOM. BUT THE TRUTH IS THE OPPOSITE.
THERE IS A GREAT HAND OF JUSTICE GUIDING US ALL TOWARD THE LIGHT. TOWARD SALVATION.
A PART OF MY MIND WAS REBUILT AFTER IT WAS DESTROYED BY LUTHOR, REBUILT WITH THE ENERGIES OF THE TOTALITY.
I'M NOW COMPLETELY ATTUNED TO THE HIDDEN ENERGIES OF THE UNIVERSE, AND THE DEFENSE SYSTEM MEANT TO KEEP THEM LOCKED AWAY.
I SEE HOW THINGS WERE SUPPOSED TO BE.
THEIR GOAL WAS TO FIND A HANDFUL OF WORLDS RIPE ENOUGH WITH THEIR RESPECTIVE ENERGIES THEY WERE BUILT TO CHANNEL.
THEY ABSORB THAT ENERGY, DESTROYING A SMALL HANDFUL OF WORLDS TO SAVE MANY.
AND THEN TOGETHER, THEY WERE MEANT TO SEAL THE WALL.
BRAINIAC MADE A MISCALCULATION WHEN HE PULLED FOUR TEAMS TOGETHER TO FACE THE TITANS. HE DIDN'T BRING YOU.
YOU WOULD HAVE BEEN ABLE TO COMMUNICATE WITH THE TITANS. HEAR THEIR VOICES.
WHAT EXACTLY ARE YOU SAYING?

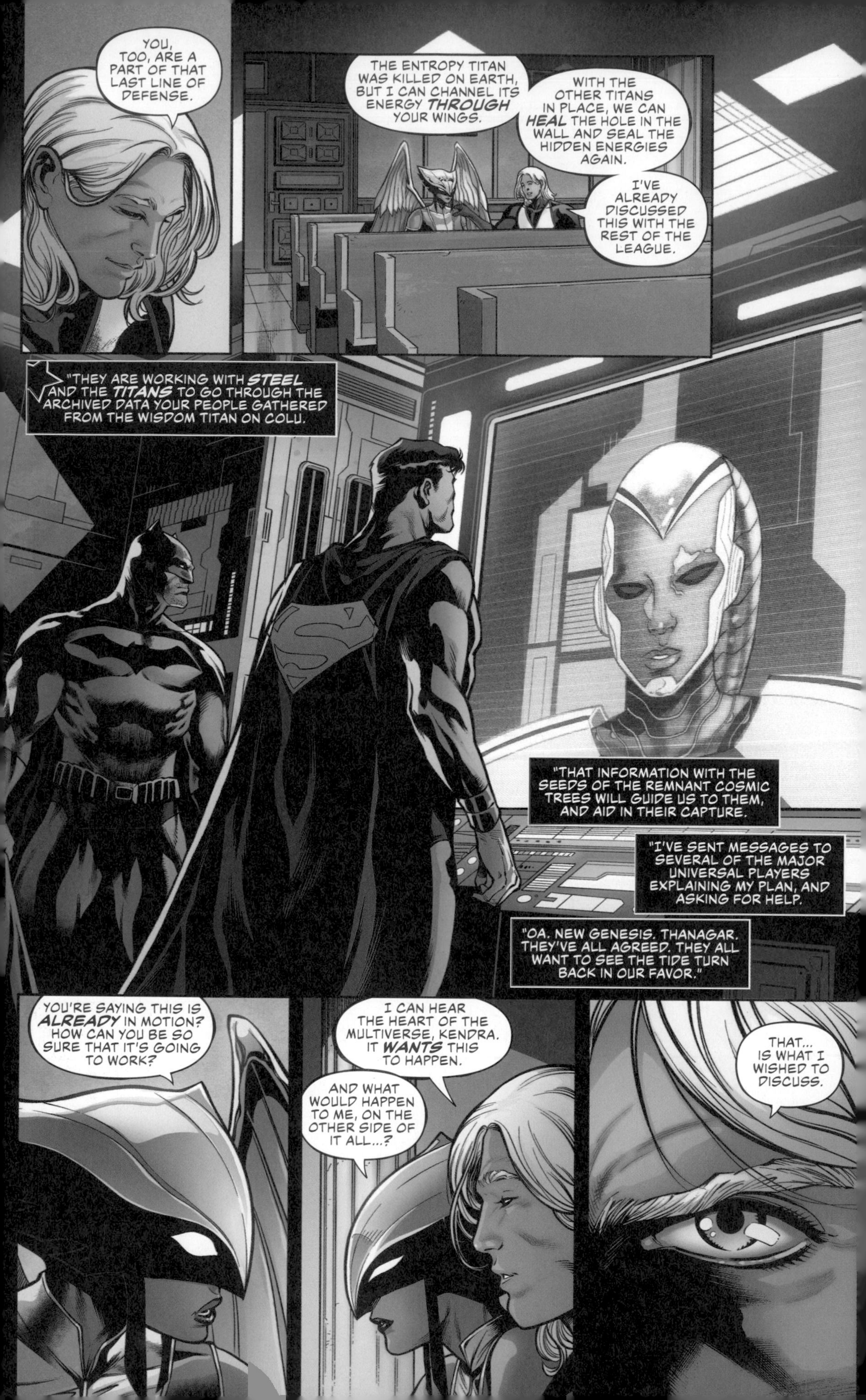
YOU, TOO, ARE A PART OF THAT LAST LINE OF DEFENSE.
THE ENTROPY TITAN WAS KILLED ON EARTH, BUT I CAN CHANNEL ITS ENERGY THROUGH YOUR WINGS.
WITH THE OTHER TITANS IN PLACE, WE CAN HEAL THE HOLE IN THE WALL AND SEAL THE HIDDEN ENERGIES AGAIN.
I'VE ALREADY DISCUSSED THIS WITH THE REST OF THE LEAGUE.
"THEY ARE WORKING WITH STEEL AND THE TITANS TO GO THROUGH THE ARCHIVED DATA YOUR PEOPLE GATHERED FROM THE WISDOM TITAN ON COLU.
"THAT INFORMATION WITH THE SEEDS OF THE REMNANT COSMIC TREES WILL GUIDE US TO THEM, AND AID IN THEIR CAPTURE.
"I'VE SENT MESSAGES TO SEVERAL OF THE MAJOR UNIVERSAL PLAYERS EXPLAINING MY PLAN, AND ASKING FOR HELP.
"OA. NEW GENESIS. THANAGAR. THEY'VE ALL AGREED. THEY ALL WANT TO SEE THE TIDE TURN BACK IN OUR FAVOR."
YOU'RE SAYING THIS IS ALREADY IN MOTION? HOW CAN YOU BE SO SURE THAT IT'S GOING TO WORK?
I CAN HEAR THE HEART OF THE MULTIVERSE, KENDRA. IT WANTS THIS TO HAPPEN.
AND WHAT WOULD HAPPEN TO ME, ON THE OTHER SIDE OF IT ALL...?
THAT... IS WHAT I WISHED TO DISCUSS.

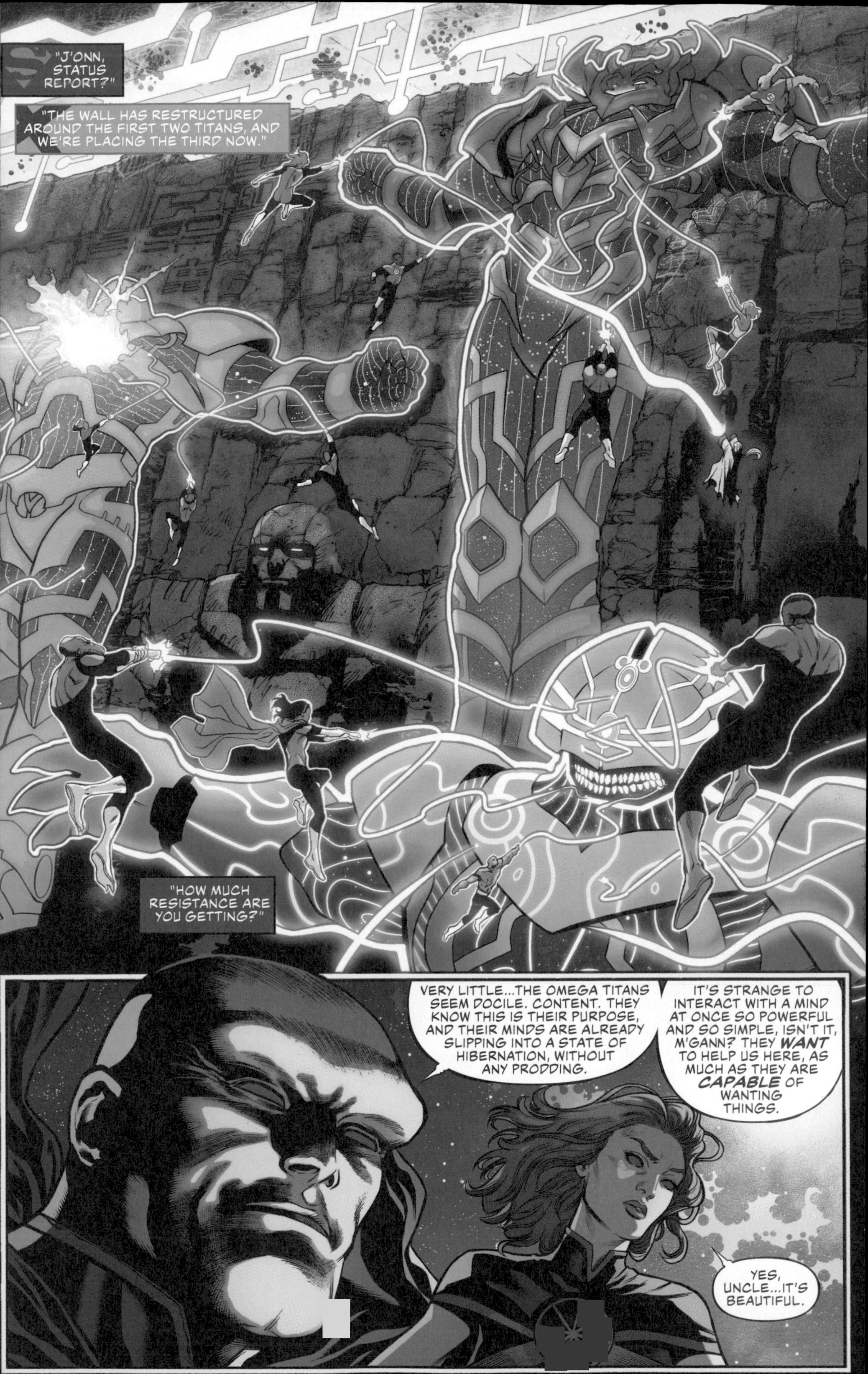
"J'ONN, STATUS REPORT?"
"THE WALL HAS RESTRUCTURED AROUND THE FIRST TWO TITANS, AND WE'RE PLACING THE THIRD NOW."
"HOW MUCH RESISTANCE ARE YOU GETTING?"
VERY LITTLE...THE OMEGA TITANS SEEM DOCILE. CONTENT. THEY KNOW THIS IS THEIR PURPOSE, AND THEIR MINDS ARE ALREADY SLIPPING INTO A STATE OF HIBERNATION, WITHOUT ANY PRODDING.
IT'S STRANGE TO INTERACT WITH A MIND AT ONCE SO POWERFUL AND SO SIMPLE, ISN'T IT, M'GANN? THEY WANT TO HELP US HERE, AS MUCH AS THEY ARE CAPABLE OF WANTING THINGS.
YES, UNCLE...IT'S BEAUTIFUL.

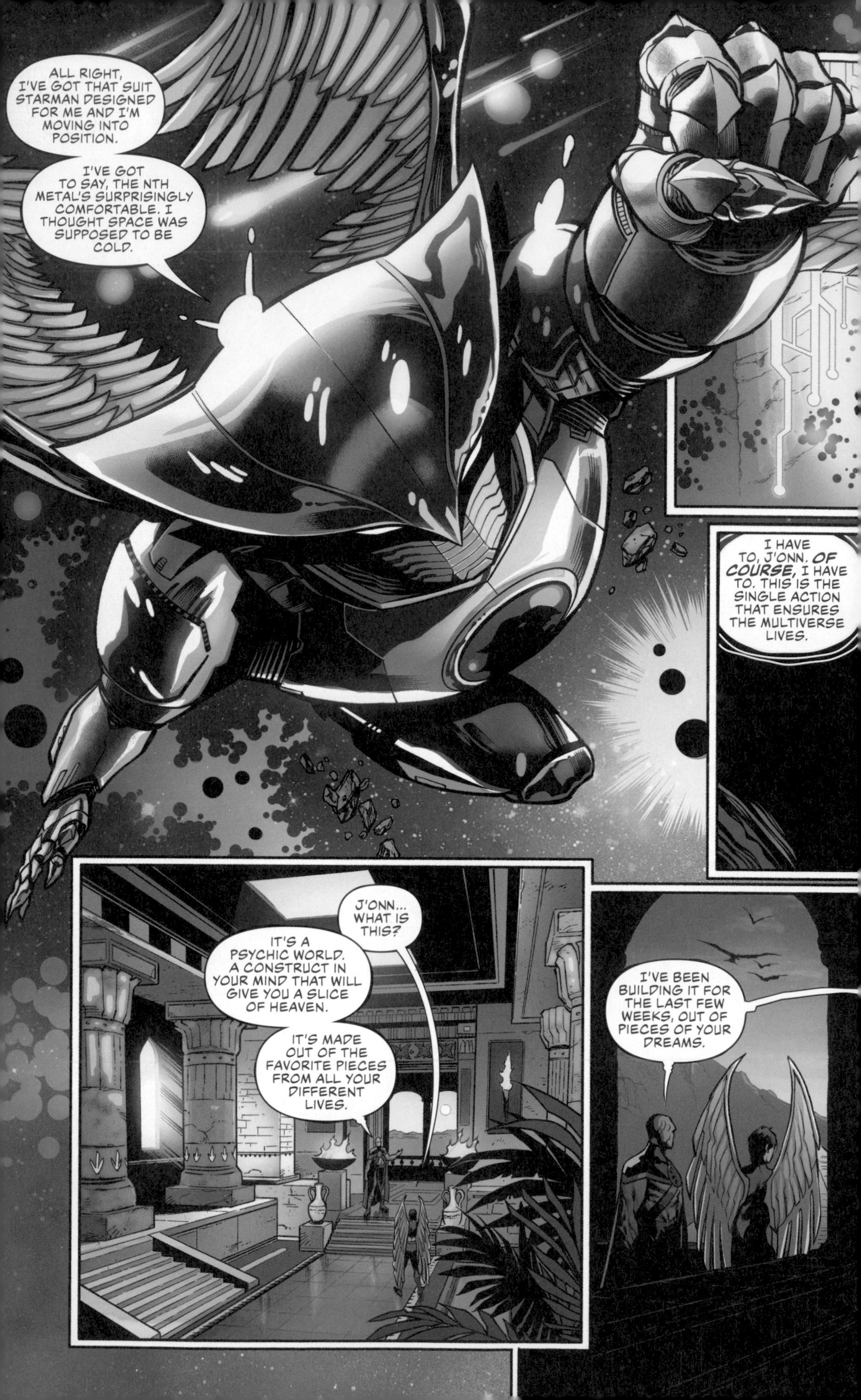
ALL RIGHT, I'VE GOT THAT SUIT STARMAN DESIGNED FOR ME AND I'M MOVING INTO POSITION.
I'VE GOT TO SAY, THE NTH METAL'S SURPRISINGLY COMFORTABLE. I THOUGHT SPACE WAS SUPPOSED TO BE COLD.
I HAVE TO, J'ONN. *OF COURSE,* I HAVE TO. THIS IS THE SINGLE ACTION THAT ENSURES THE MULTIVERSE LIVES.
J'ONN... WHAT IS THIS?
IT'S A PSYCHIC WORLD. A CONSTRUCT IN YOUR MIND THAT WILL GIVE YOU A SLICE OF HEAVEN.
IT'S MADE OUT OF THE FAVORITE PIECES FROM ALL YOUR DIFFERENT LIVES.
I'VE BEEN BUILDING IT FOR THE LAST FEW WEEKS, OUT OF PIECES OF YOUR DREAMS.

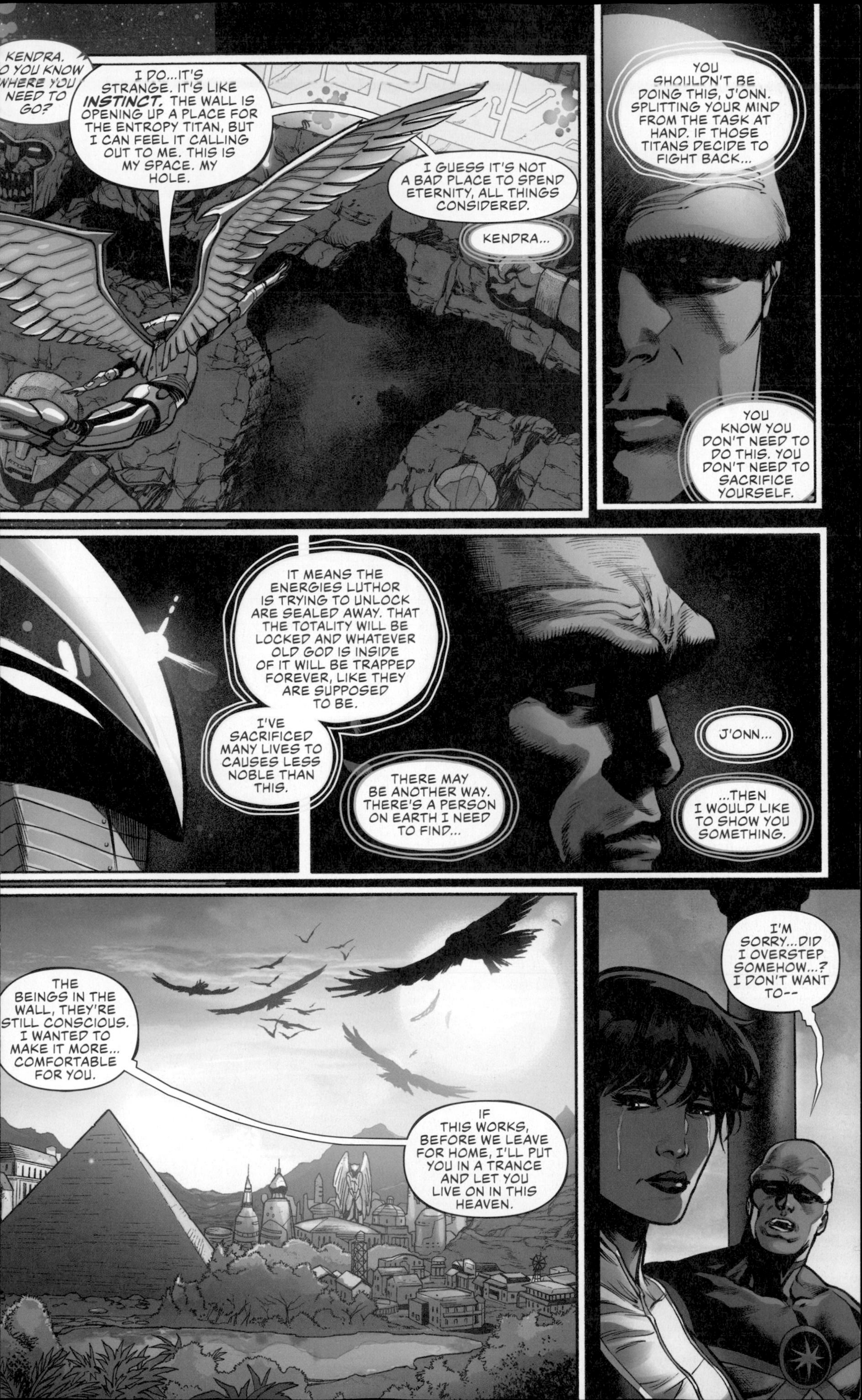
KENDRA. O YOU KNOW WHERE YOU NEED TO GO?
I DO...IT'S STRANGE. IT'S LIKE *INSTINCT.* THE WALL IS OPENING UP A PLACE FOR THE ENTROPY TITAN, BUT I CAN FEEL IT CALLING OUT TO ME. THIS IS MY SPACE. MY HOLE.
I GUESS IT'S NOT A BAD PLACE TO SPEND ETERNITY, ALL THINGS CONSIDERED.
KENDRA...
YOU SHOULDN'T BE DOING THIS, J'ONN. SPLITTING YOUR MIND FROM THE TASK AT HAND. IF THOSE TITANS DECIDE TO FIGHT BACK...
YOU KNOW YOU DON'T NEED TO DO THIS. YOU DON'T NEED TO SACRIFICE YOURSELF.
IT MEANS THE ENERGIES LUTHOR IS TRYING TO UNLOCK ARE SEALED AWAY. THAT THE TOTALITY WILL BE LOCKED AND WHATEVER OLD GOD IS INSIDE OF IT WILL BE TRAPPED FOREVER, LIKE THEY ARE SUPPOSED TO BE.
I'VE SACRIFICED MANY LIVES TO CAUSES LESS NOBLE THAN THIS.
THERE MAY BE ANOTHER WAY. THERE'S A PERSON ON EARTH I NEED TO FIND...
J'ONN...
...THEN I WOULD LIKE TO SHOW YOU SOMETHING.
THE BEINGS IN THE WALL, THEY'RE STILL CONSCIOUS. I WANTED TO MAKE IT MORE... COMFORTABLE FOR YOU.
IF THIS WORKS, BEFORE WE LEAVE FOR HOME, I'LL PUT YOU IN A TRANCE AND LET YOU LIVE ON IN THIS HEAVEN.
I'M SORRY...DID I OVERSTEP SOMEHOW...? I DON'T WANT TO--

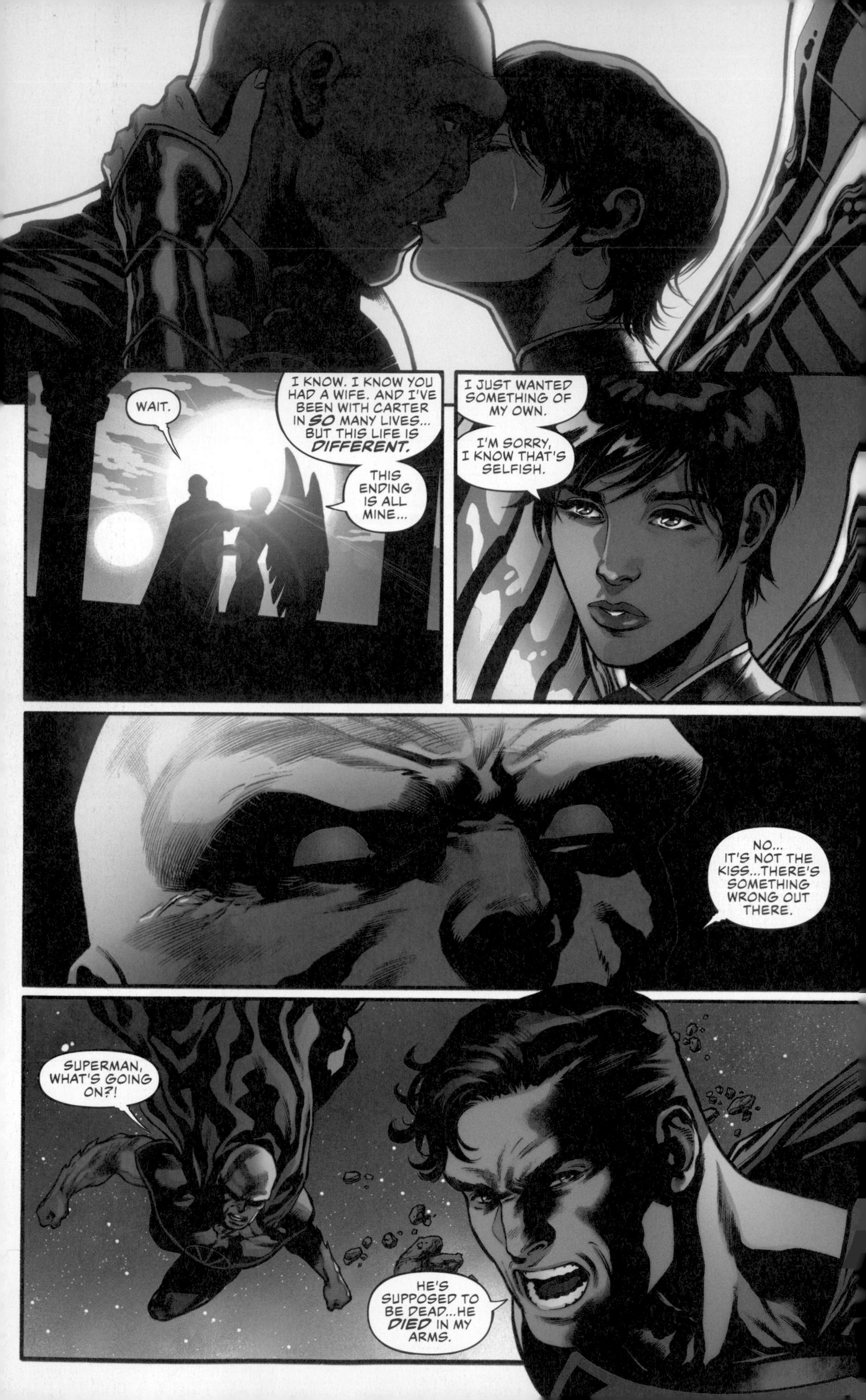
WAIT.
I KNOW. I KNOW YOU HAD A WIFE. AND I'VE BEEN WITH CARTER IN SO MANY LIVES... BUT THIS LIFE IS DIFFERENT.
THIS ENDING IS ALL MINE...
I JUST WANTED SOMETHING OF MY OWN.
I'M SORRY, I KNOW THAT'S SELFISH.
NO... IT'S NOT THE KISS...THERE'S SOMETHING WRONG OUT THERE.
SUPERMAN, WHAT'S GOING ON?!
HE'S SUPPOSED TO BE DEAD...HE DIED IN MY ARMS.

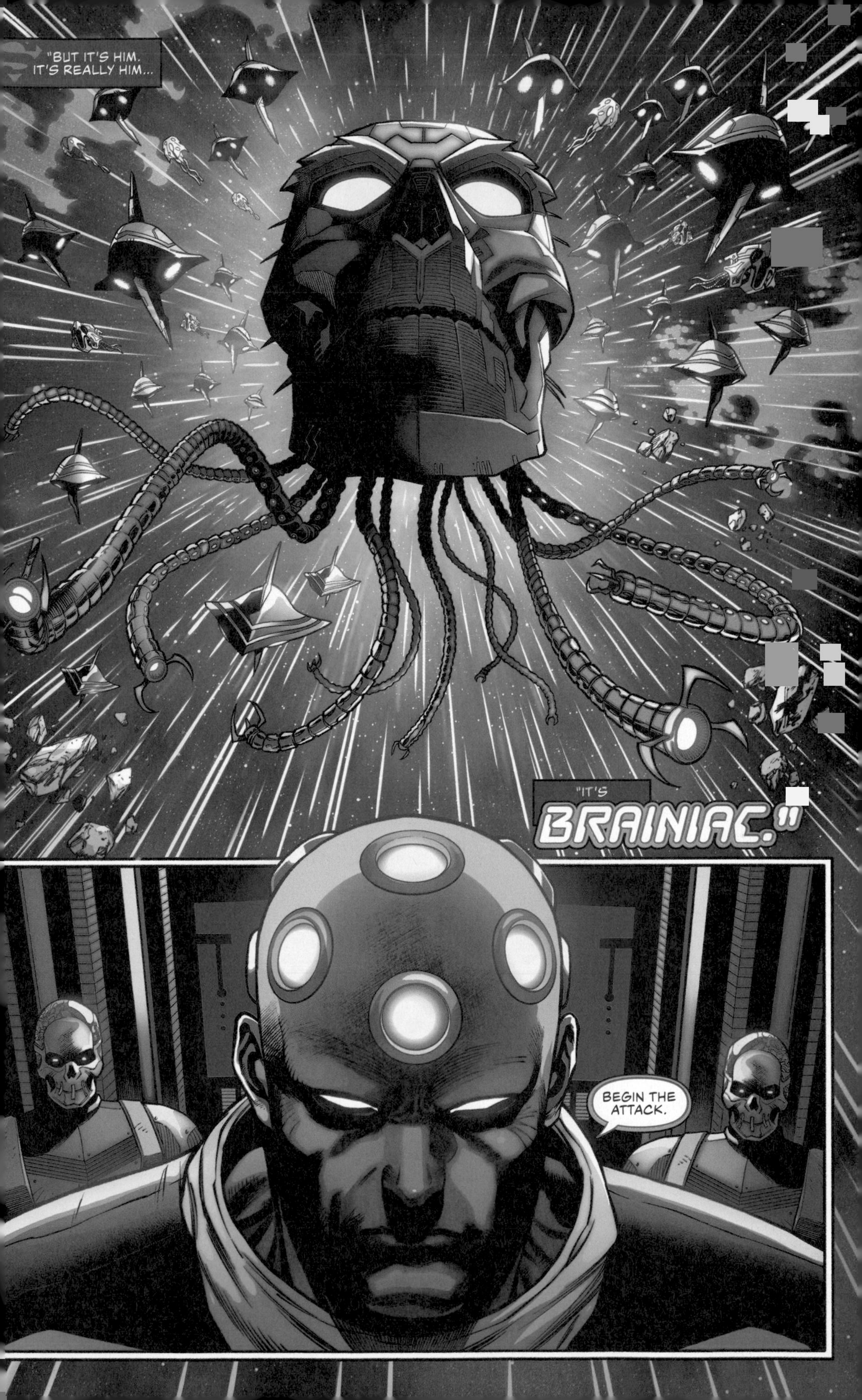
"BUT IT'S HIM. IT'S REALLY HIM...
"IT'S
BRAINIAC."
BEGIN THE ATTACK.

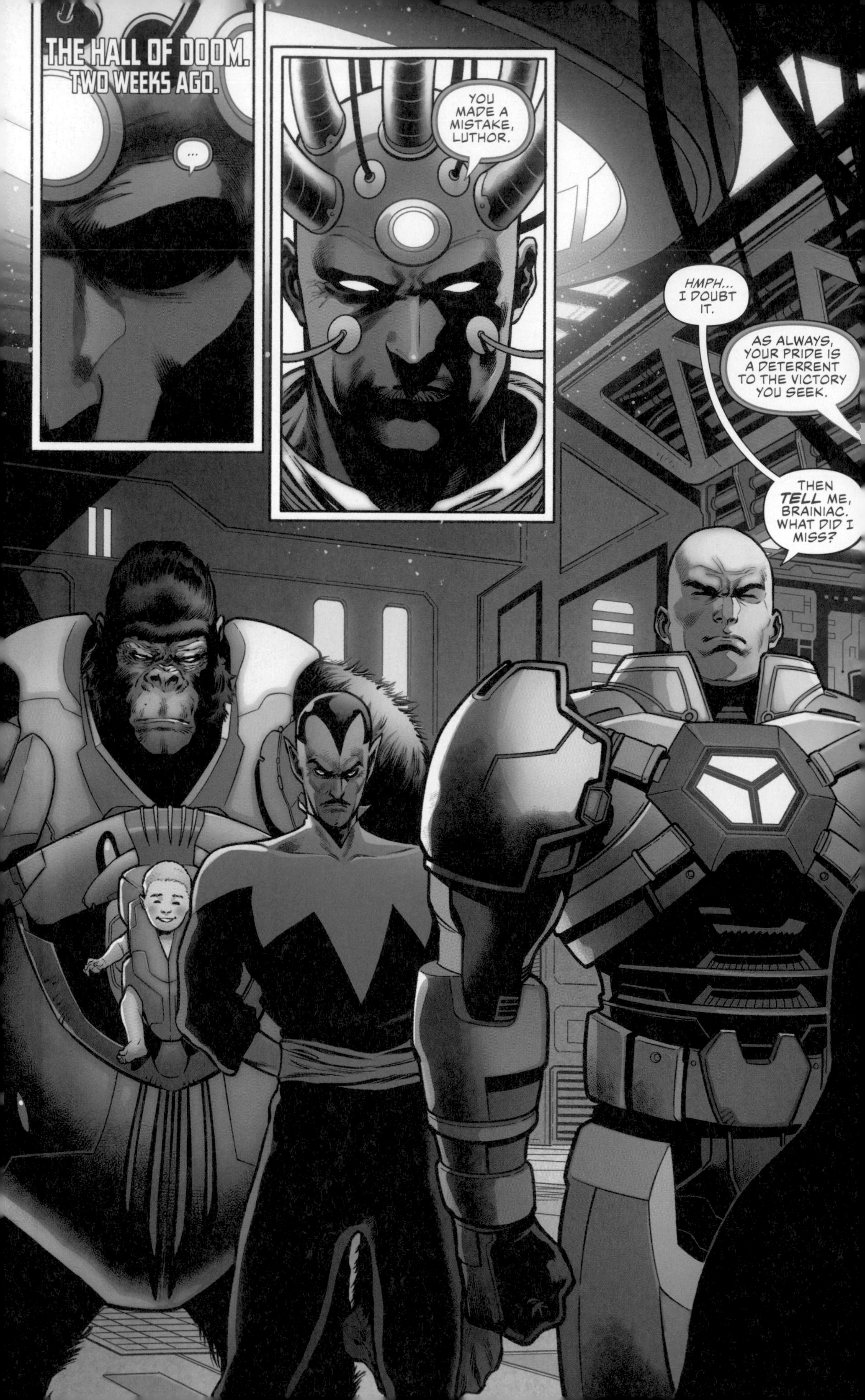
THE HALL OF DOOM. TWO WEEKS AGO.
...
YOU MADE A MISTAKE, LUTHOR.
HMPH... I DOUBT IT.
AS ALWAYS, YOUR PRIDE IS A DETERRENT TO THE VICTORY YOU SEEK.
THEN TELL ME, BRAINIAC. WHAT DID I MISS?

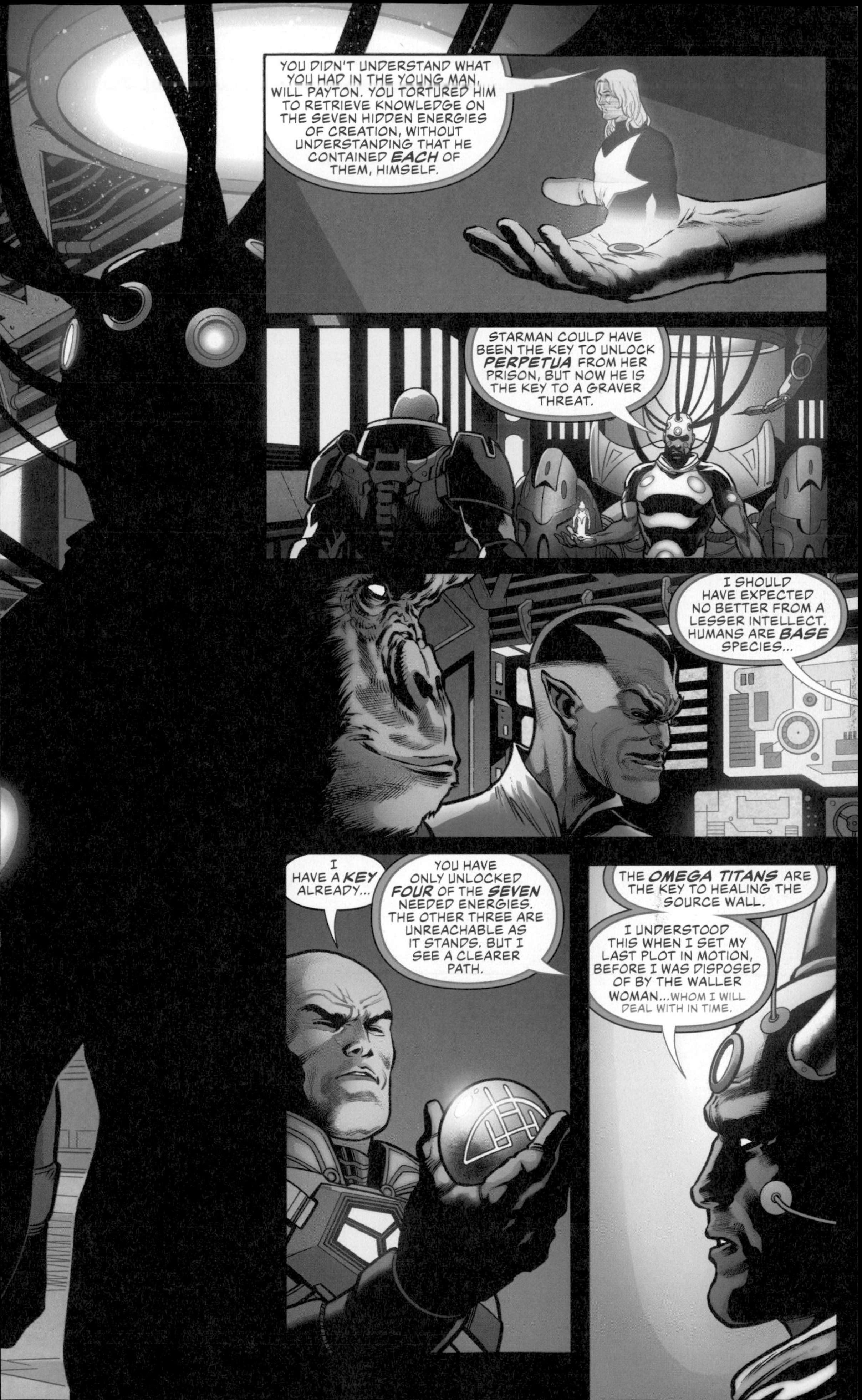
YOU DIDN'T UNDERSTAND WHAT YOU HAD IN THE YOUNG MAN, WILL PAYTON. YOU TORTURED HIM TO RETRIEVE KNOWLEDGE ON THE SEVEN HIDDEN ENERGIES OF CREATION, WITHOUT UNDERSTANDING THAT HE CONTAINED EACH OF THEM, HIMSELF.
STARMAN COULD HAVE BEEN THE KEY TO UNLOCK PERPETUA FROM HER PRISON, BUT NOW HE IS THE KEY TO A GRAVER THREAT.
I SHOULD HAVE EXPECTED NO BETTER FROM A LESSER INTELLECT. HUMANS ARE BASE SPECIES...
I HAVE A KEY ALREADY...
YOU HAVE ONLY UNLOCKED FOUR OF THE SEVEN NEEDED ENERGIES. THE OTHER THREE ARE UNREACHABLE AS IT STANDS. BUT I SEE A CLEARER PATH.
THE OMEGA TITANS ARE THE KEY TO HEALING THE SOURCE WALL.
I UNDERSTOOD THIS WHEN I SET MY LAST PLOT IN MOTION, BEFORE I WAS DISPOSED OF BY THE WALLER WOMAN...WHOM I WILL DEAL WITH IN TIME.

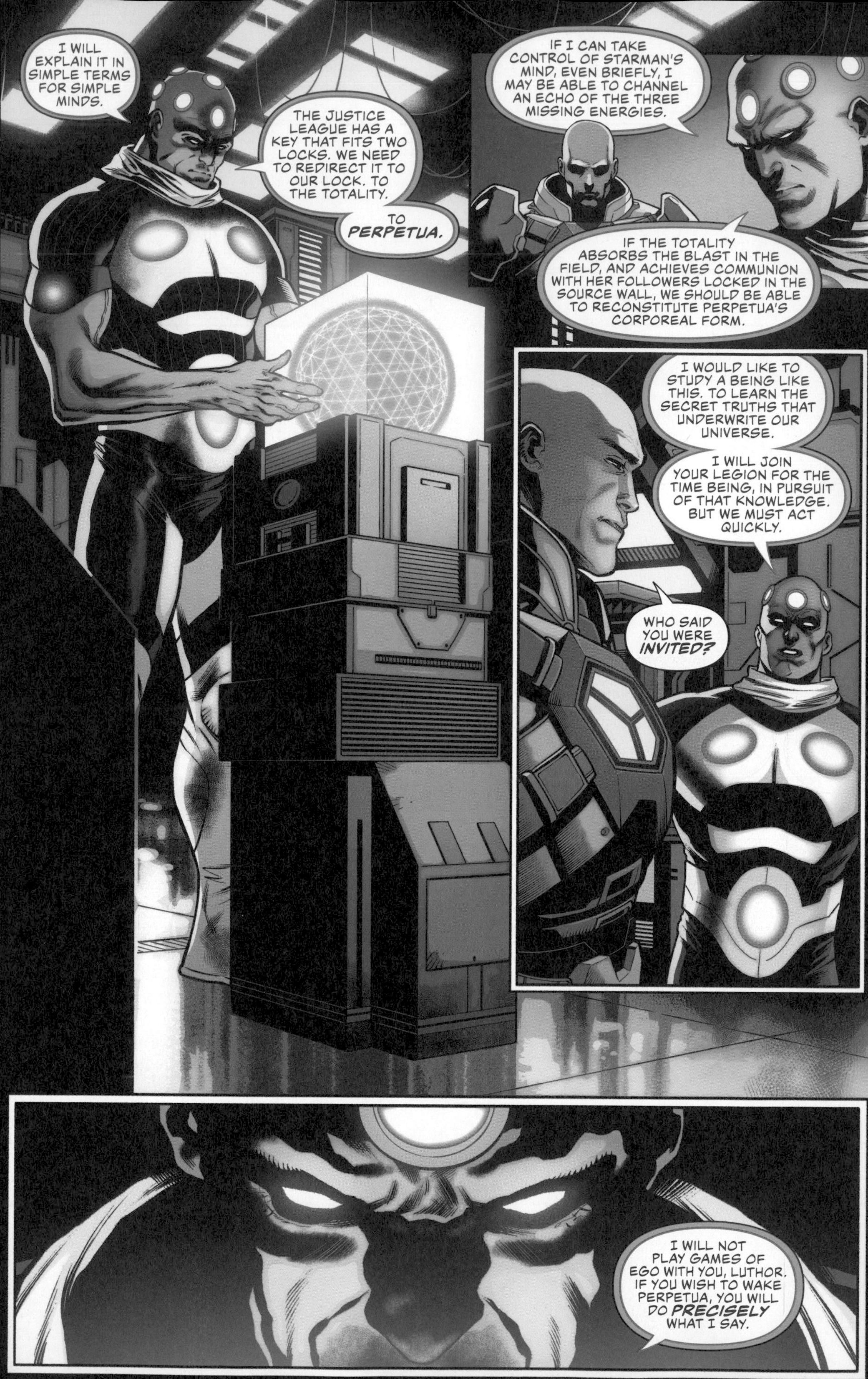
I WILL EXPLAIN IT IN SIMPLE TERMS FOR SIMPLE MINDS.
THE JUSTICE LEAGUE HAS A KEY THAT FITS TWO LOCKS. WE NEED TO REDIRECT IT TO OUR LOCK. TO THE TOTALITY.
TO ***PERPETUA.***
IF I CAN TAKE CONTROL OF STARMAN'S MIND, EVEN BRIEFLY, I MAY BE ABLE TO CHANNEL AN ECHO OF THE THREE MISSING ENERGIES.
IF THE TOTALITY ABSORBS THE BLAST IN THE FIELD, AND ACHIEVES COMMUNION WITH HER FOLLOWERS LOCKED IN THE SOURCE WALL, WE SHOULD BE ABLE TO RECONSTITUTE PERPETUA'S CORPOREAL FORM.
I WOULD LIKE TO STUDY A BEING LIKE THIS. TO LEARN THE SECRET TRUTHS THAT UNDERWRITE OUR UNIVERSE.
I WILL JOIN YOUR LEGION FOR THE TIME BEING, IN PURSUIT OF THAT KNOWLEDGE. BUT WE MUST ACT QUICKLY.
WHO SAID YOU WERE ***INVITED?***
I WILL NOT PLAY GAMES OF EGO WITH YOU, LUTHOR. IF YOU WISH TO WAKE PERPETUA, YOU WILL DO ***PRECISELY*** WHAT I SAY.

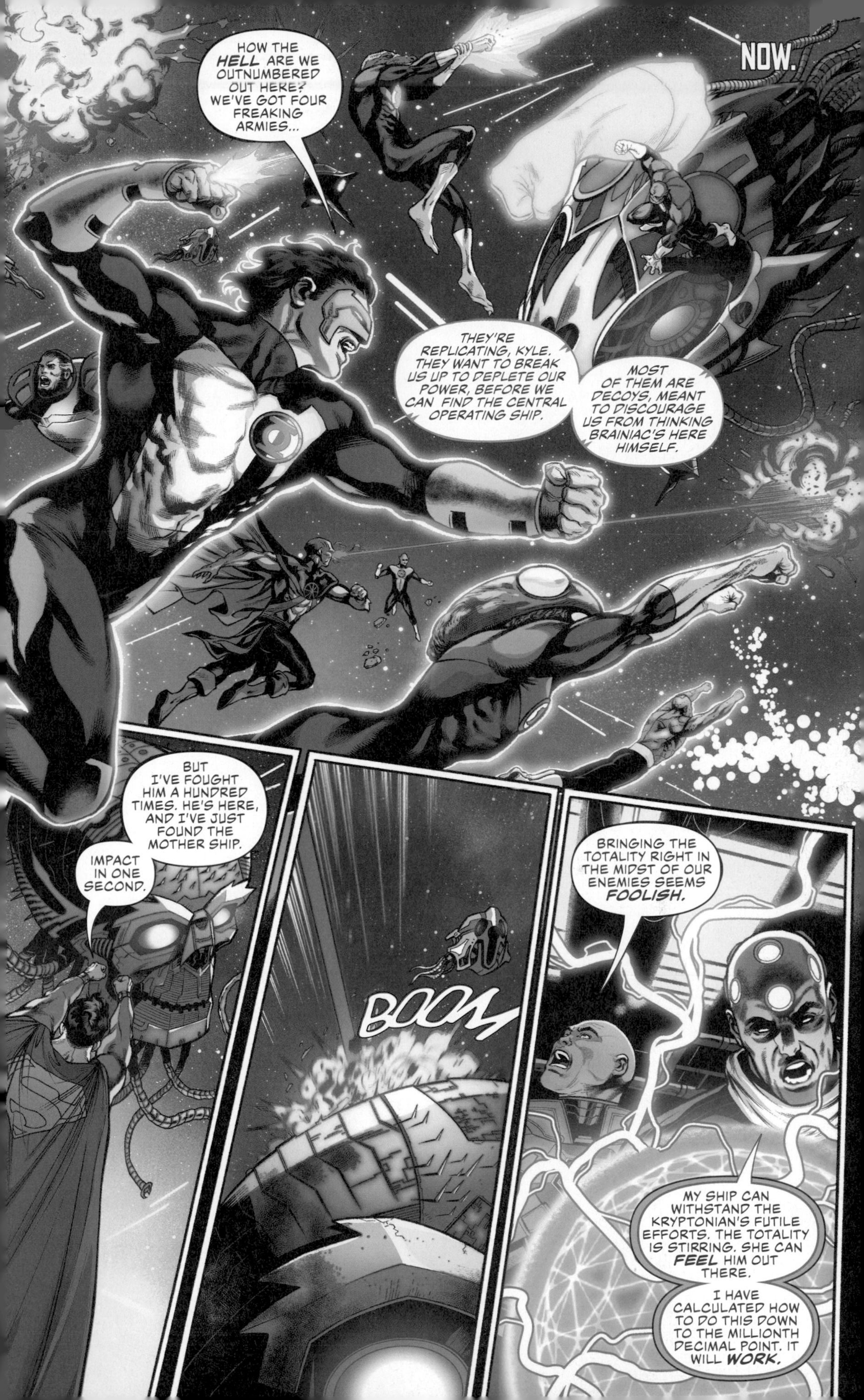
NOW.
HOW THE HELL ARE WE OUTNUMBERED OUT HERE? WE'VE GOT FOUR FREAKING ARMIES...
THEY'RE REPLICATING, KYLE. THEY WANT TO BREAK US UP TO DEPLETE OUR POWER, BEFORE WE CAN FIND THE CENTRAL OPERATING SHIP.
MOST OF THEM ARE DECOYS, MEANT TO DISCOURAGE US FROM THINKING BRAINIAC'S HERE HIMSELF.
BUT I'VE FOUGHT HIM A HUNDRED TIMES. HE'S HERE, AND I'VE JUST FOUND THE MOTHER SHIP.
IMPACT IN ONE SECOND.
BOOM
BRINGING THE TOTALITY RIGHT IN THE MIDST OF OUR ENEMIES SEEMS FOOLISH.
MY SHIP CAN WITHSTAND THE KRYPTONIAN'S FUTILE EFFORTS. THE TOTALITY IS STIRRING. SHE CAN FEEL HIM OUT THERE.
I HAVE CALCULATED HOW TO DO THIS DOWN TO THE MILLIONTH DECIMAL POINT. IT WILL WORK.

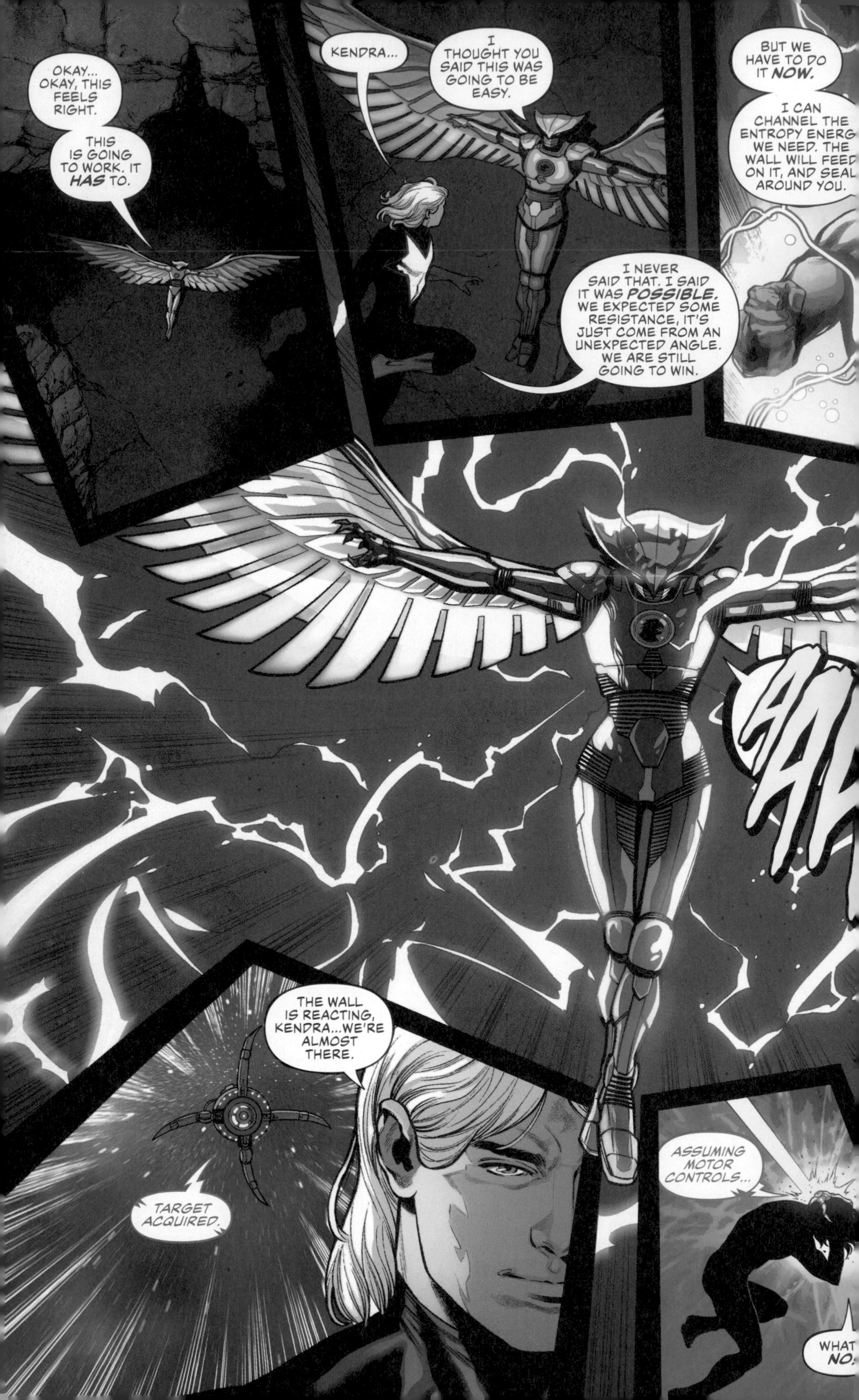
OKAY... OKAY, THIS FEELS RIGHT.
THIS IS GOING TO WORK. IT **HAS** TO.
KENDRA...
I THOUGHT YOU SAID THIS WAS GOING TO BE EASY.
I NEVER SAID THAT. I SAID IT WAS **POSSIBLE.** WE EXPECTED SOME RESISTANCE, IT'S JUST COME FROM AN UNEXPECTED ANGLE. WE ARE STILL GOING TO WIN.
BUT WE HAVE TO DO IT **NOW.**
THE WALL IS REACTING, KENDRA...WE'RE ALMOST THERE.
TARGET ACQUIRED.
ASSUMING MOTOR CONTROLS...

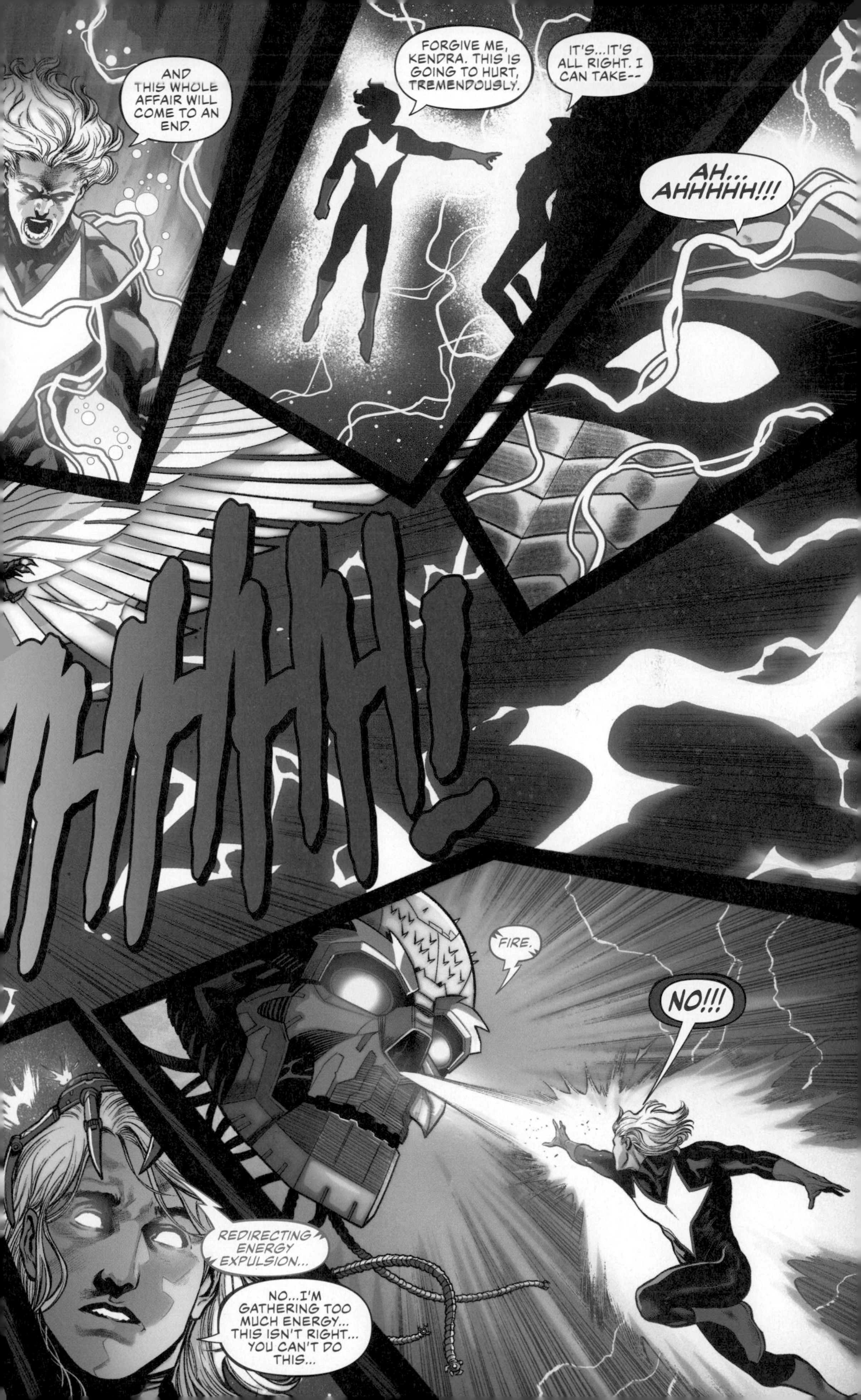
AND THIS WHOLE AFFAIR WILL COME TO AN END.
FORGIVE ME, KENDRA. THIS IS GOING TO HURT, TREMENDOUSLY.
IT'S...IT'S ALL RIGHT. I CAN TAKE--
AH... AHHHHH!!!
FIRE.
NO!!!
REDIRECTING ENERGY EXPULSION...
NO...I'M GATHERING TOO MUCH ENERGY... THIS ISN'T RIGHT... YOU CAN'T DO THIS...

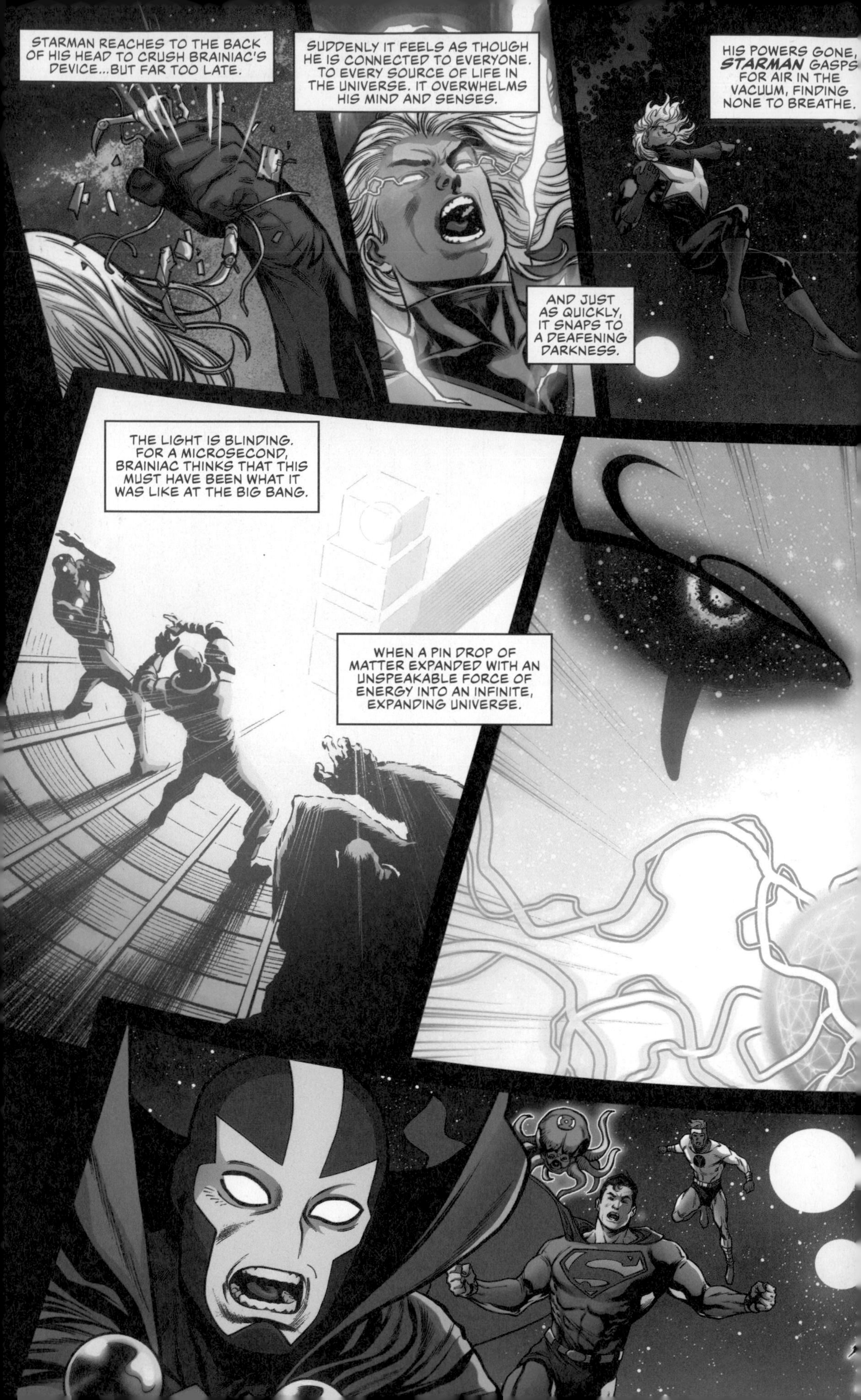
STARMAN REACHES TO THE BACK OF HIS HEAD TO CRUSH BRAINIAC'S DEVICE...BUT FAR TOO LATE.
SUDDENLY IT FEELS AS THOUGH HE IS CONNECTED TO EVERYONE. TO EVERY SOURCE OF LIFE IN THE UNIVERSE. IT OVERWHELMS HIS MIND AND SENSES.
AND JUST AS QUICKLY, IT SNAPS TO A DEAFENING DARKNESS.
HIS POWERS GONE, STARMAN GASPS FOR AIR IN THE VACUUM, FINDING NONE TO BREATHE.
THE LIGHT IS BLINDING. FOR A MICROSECOND, BRAINIAC THINKS THAT THIS MUST HAVE BEEN WHAT IT WAS LIKE AT THE BIG BANG.
WHEN A PIN DROP OF MATTER EXPANDED WITH AN UNSPEAKABLE FORCE OF ENERGY INTO AN INFINITE, EXPANDING UNIVERSE.

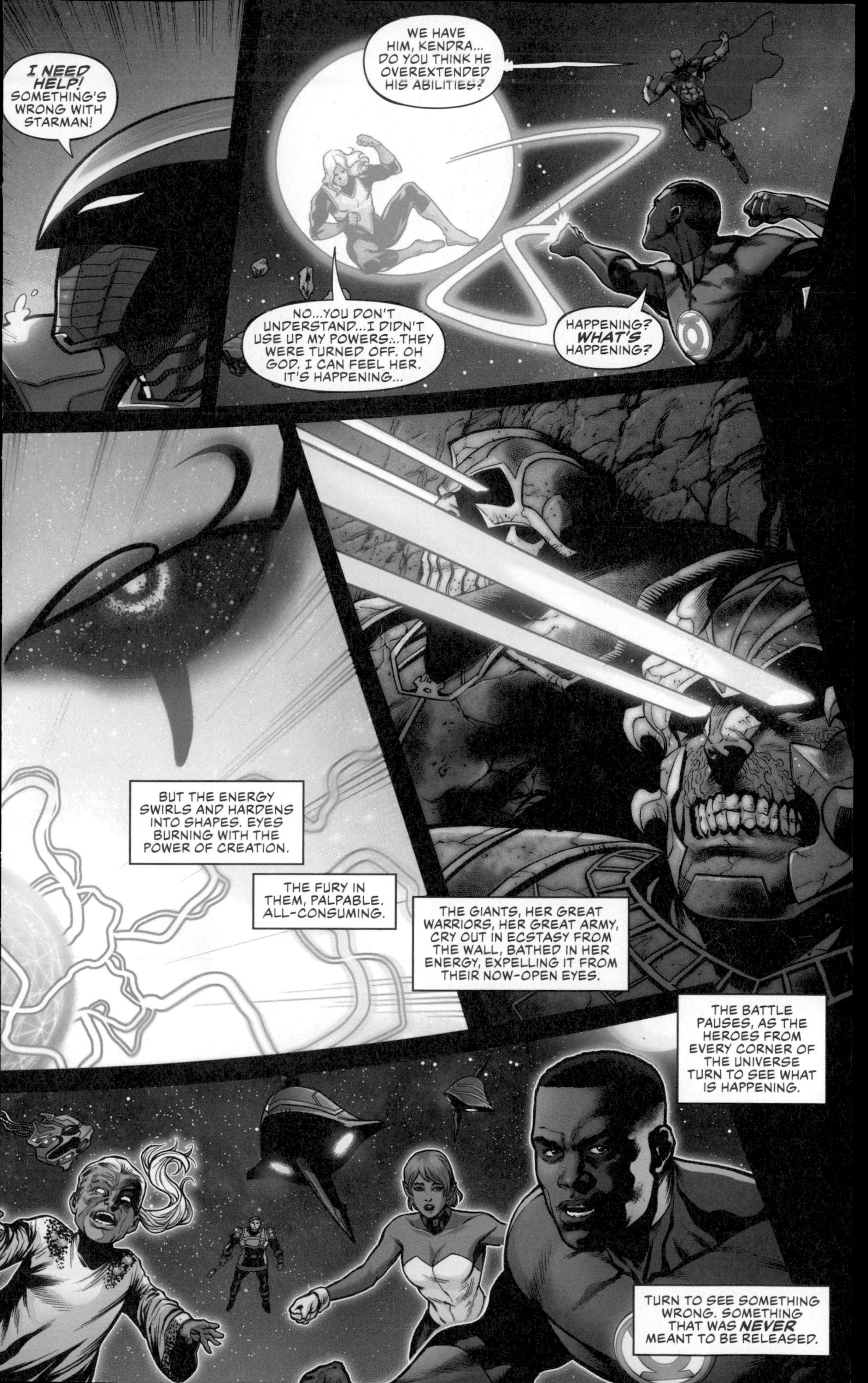

I NEED HELP! SOMETHING'S WRONG WITH STARMAN!
WE HAVE HIM, KENDRA... DO YOU THINK HE OVEREXTENDED HIS ABILITIES?
NO...YOU DON'T UNDERSTAND...I DIDN'T USE UP MY POWERS...THEY WERE TURNED OFF. OH GOD. I CAN FEEL HER. IT'S HAPPENING...
HAPPENING? WHAT'S HAPPENING?
BUT THE ENERGY SWIRLS AND HARDENS INTO SHAPES. EYES BURNING WITH THE POWER OF CREATION.
THE FURY IN THEM, PALPABLE. ALL-CONSUMING.
THE GIANTS, HER GREAT WARRIORS, HER GREAT ARMY, CRY OUT IN ECSTASY FROM THE WALL, BATHED IN HER ENERGY, EXPELLING IT FROM THEIR NOW-OPEN EYES.
THE BATTLE PAUSES, AS THE HEROES FROM EVERY CORNER OF THE UNIVERSE TURN TO SEE WHAT IS HAPPENING.
TURN TO SEE SOMETHING WRONG. SOMETHING THAT WAS NEVER MEANT TO BE RELEASED.

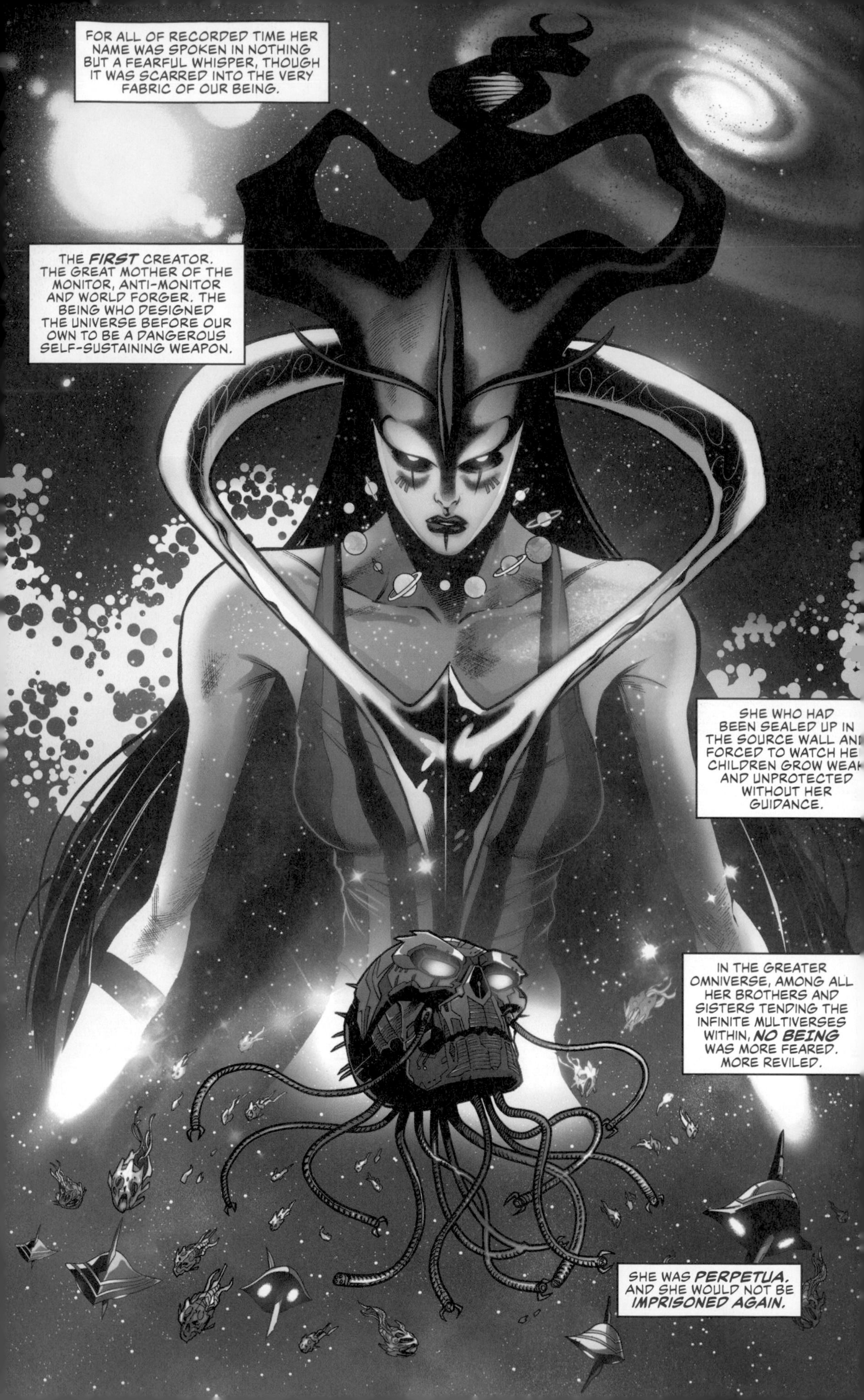
FOR ALL OF RECORDED TIME HER NAME WAS SPOKEN IN NOTHING BUT A FEARFUL WHISPER, THOUGH IT WAS SCARRED INTO THE VERY FABRIC OF OUR BEING.
THE *FIRST* CREATOR. THE GREAT MOTHER OF THE MONITOR, ANTI-MONITOR AND WORLD FORGER. THE BEING WHO DESIGNED THE UNIVERSE BEFORE OUR OWN TO BE A DANGEROUS SELF-SUSTAINING WEAPON.
SHE WHO HAD BEEN SEALED UP IN THE SOURCE WALL AN FORCED TO WATCH HE CHILDREN GROW WEA AND UNPROTECTED WITHOUT HER GUIDANCE.
IN THE GREATER OMNIVERSE, AMONG ALL HER BROTHERS AND SISTERS TENDING THE INFINITE MULTIVERSES WITHIN, ***NO BEING*** WAS MORE FEARED. MORE REVILED.
SHE WAS ***PERPETUA.*** AND SHE WOULD NOT BE ***IMPRISONED AGAIN.***

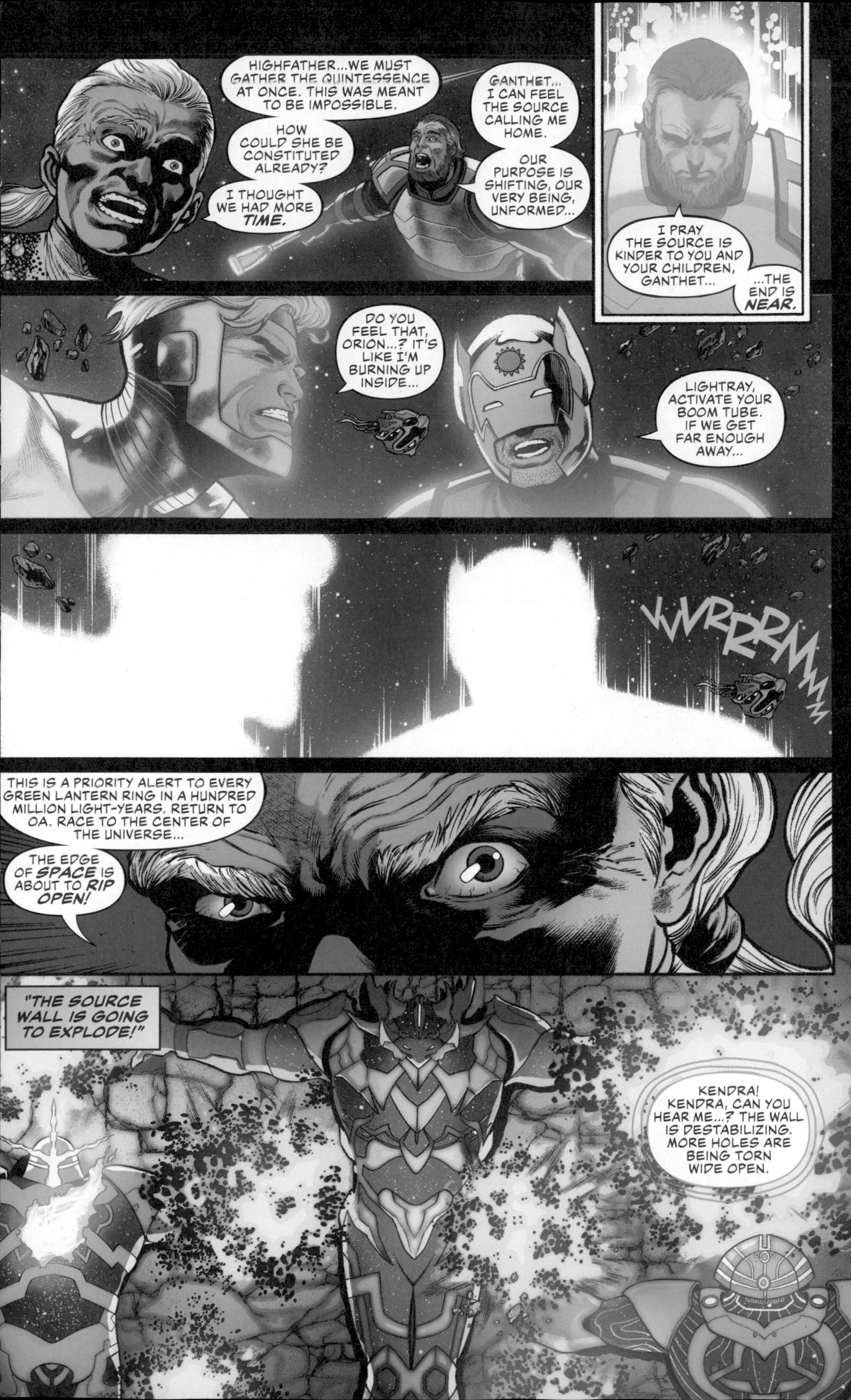
HIGHFATHER...WE MUST GATHER THE QUINTESSENCE AT ONCE. THIS WAS MEANT TO BE IMPOSSIBLE.
HOW COULD SHE BE CONSTITUTED ALREADY?
I THOUGHT WE HAD MORE TIME.
GANTHET... I CAN FEEL THE SOURCE CALLING ME HOME.
OUR PURPOSE IS SHIFTING, OUR VERY BEING, UNFORMED...
I PRAY THE SOURCE IS KINDER TO YOU AND YOUR CHILDREN, GANTHET...
...THE END IS NEAR.
DO YOU FEEL THAT, ORION...? IT'S LIKE I'M BURNING UP INSIDE...
LIGHTRAY, ACTIVATE YOUR BOOM TUBE. IF WE GET FAR ENOUGH AWAY...
VVVRRRMMMM
THIS IS A PRIORITY ALERT TO EVERY GREEN LANTERN RING IN A HUNDRED MILLION LIGHT-YEARS. RETURN TO OA. RACE TO THE CENTER OF THE UNIVERSE...
THE EDGE OF SPACE IS ABOUT TO RIP OPEN!
"THE SOURCE WALL IS GOING TO EXPLODE!"
KENDRA! KENDRA, CAN YOU HEAR ME...? THE WALL IS DESTABILIZING. MORE HOLES ARE BEING TORN WIDE OPEN.

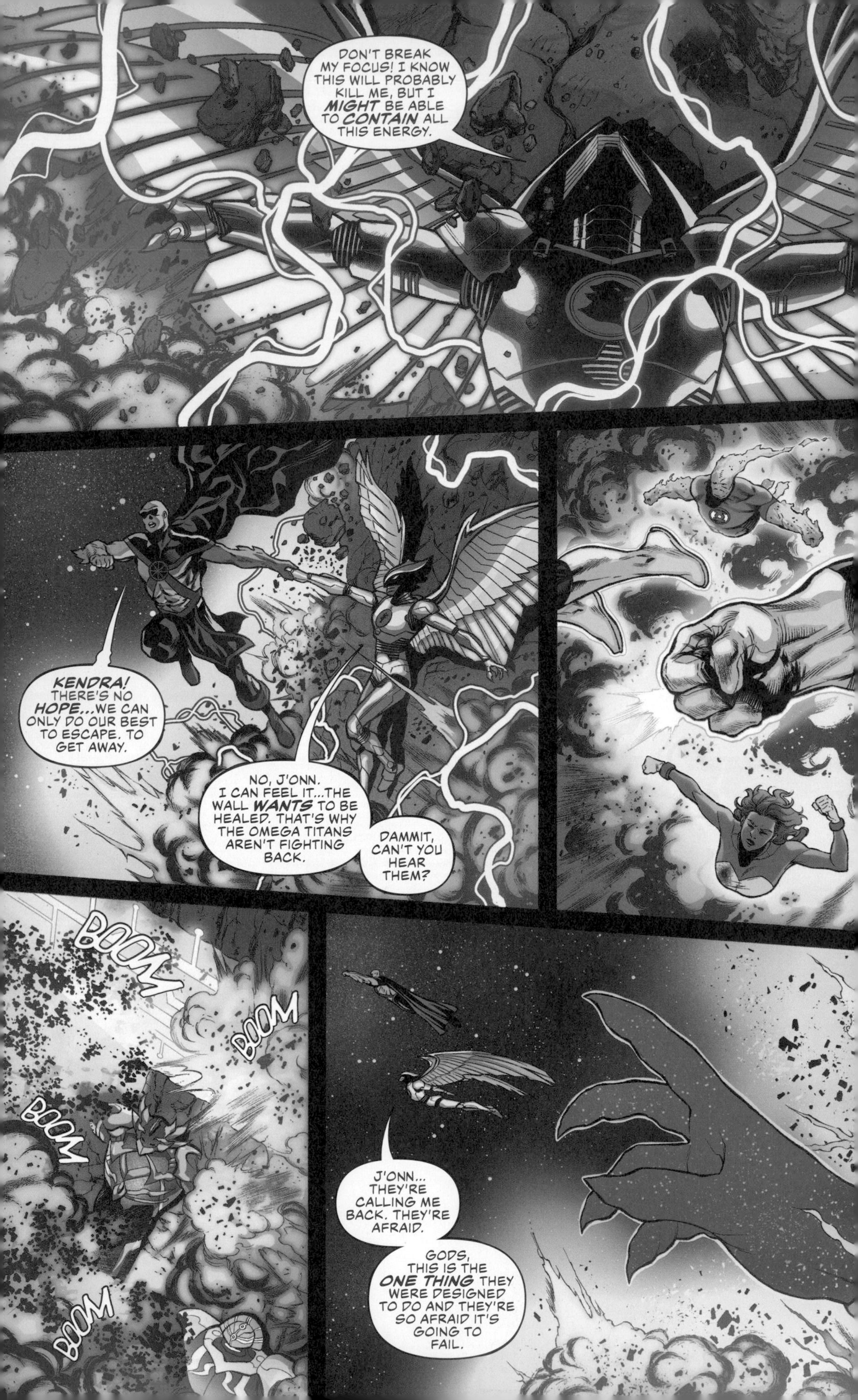
DON'T BREAK MY FOCUS! I KNOW THIS WILL PROBABLY KILL ME, BUT I MIGHT BE ABLE TO CONTAIN ALL THIS ENERGY.
KENDRA! THERE'S NO HOPE...WE CAN ONLY DO OUR BEST TO ESCAPE. TO GET AWAY.
NO, J'ONN. I CAN FEEL IT...THE WALL WANTS TO BE HEALED. THAT'S WHY THE OMEGA TITANS AREN'T FIGHTING BACK.
DAMMIT, CAN'T YOU HEAR THEM?
BOOM
BOOM
BOOM
BOOM
J'ONN... THEY'RE CALLING ME BACK. THEY'RE AFRAID.
GODS, THIS IS THE ONE THING THEY WERE DESIGNED TO DO AND THEY'RE SO AFRAID IT'S GOING TO FAIL.

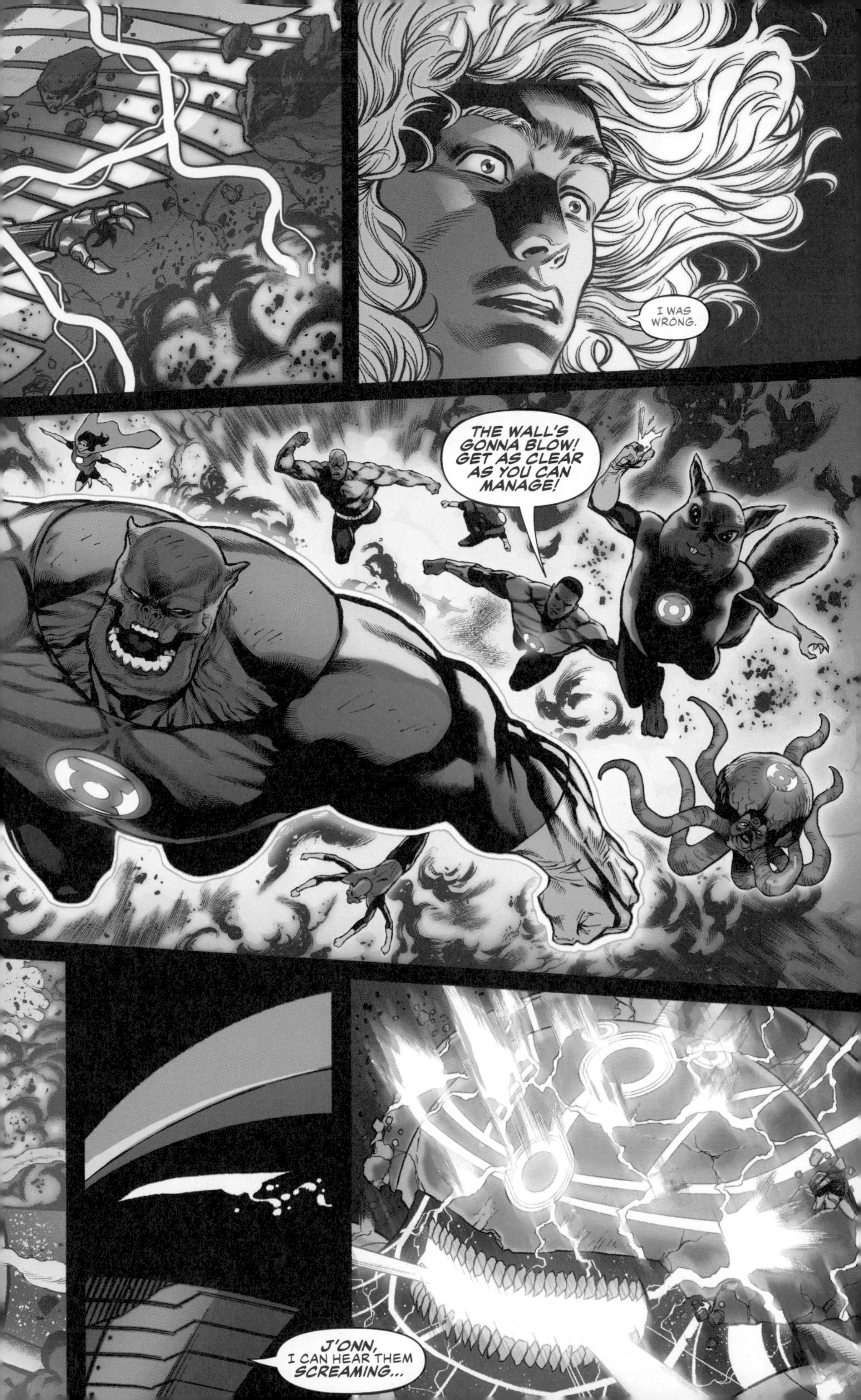
I WAS WRONG.
THE WALL'S GONNA BLOW! GET AS CLEAR AS YOU CAN MANAGE!
J'ONN, I CAN HEAR THEM SCREAMING...

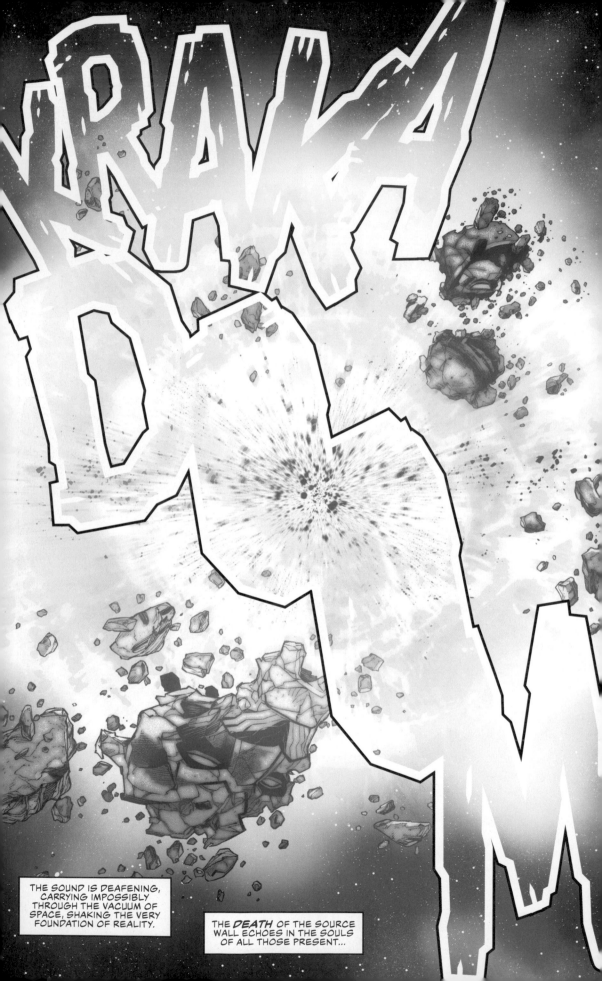

THE SOUND IS DEAFENING, CARRYING IMPOSSIBLY THROUGH THE VACUUM OF SPACE, SHAKING THE VERY FOUNDATION OF REALITY.

THE *DEATH* OF THE SOURCE WALL ECHOES IN THE SOULS OF ALL THOSE PRESENT...

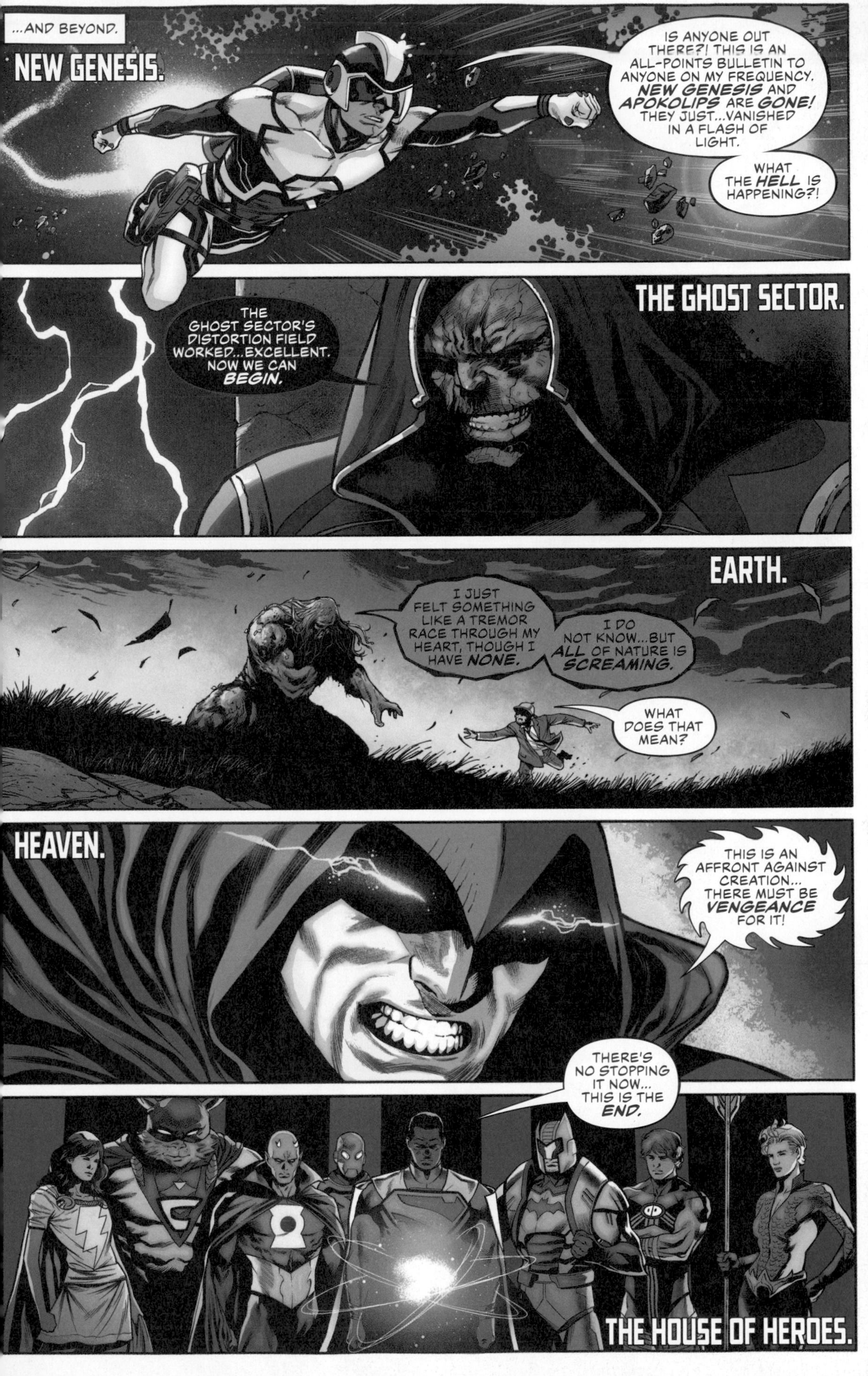

...AND BEYOND.
NEW GENESIS.
IS ANYONE OUT THERE?! THIS IS AN ALL-POINTS BULLETIN TO ANYONE ON MY FREQUENCY. NEW GENESIS AND APOKOLIPS ARE GONE! THEY JUST...VANISHED IN A FLASH OF LIGHT.
WHAT THE HELL IS HAPPENING?!
THE GHOST SECTOR.
THE GHOST SECTOR'S DISTORTION FIELD WORKED...EXCELLENT. NOW WE CAN BEGIN.
EARTH.
I JUST FELT SOMETHING LIKE A TREMOR RACE THROUGH MY HEART, THOUGH I HAVE NONE.
I DO NOT KNOW...BUT ALL OF NATURE IS SCREAMING.
WHAT DOES THAT MEAN?
HEAVEN.
THIS IS AN AFFRONT AGAINST CREATION... THERE MUST BE VENGEANCE FOR IT!
THERE'S NO STOPPING IT NOW... THIS IS THE END.
THE HOUSE OF HEROES.

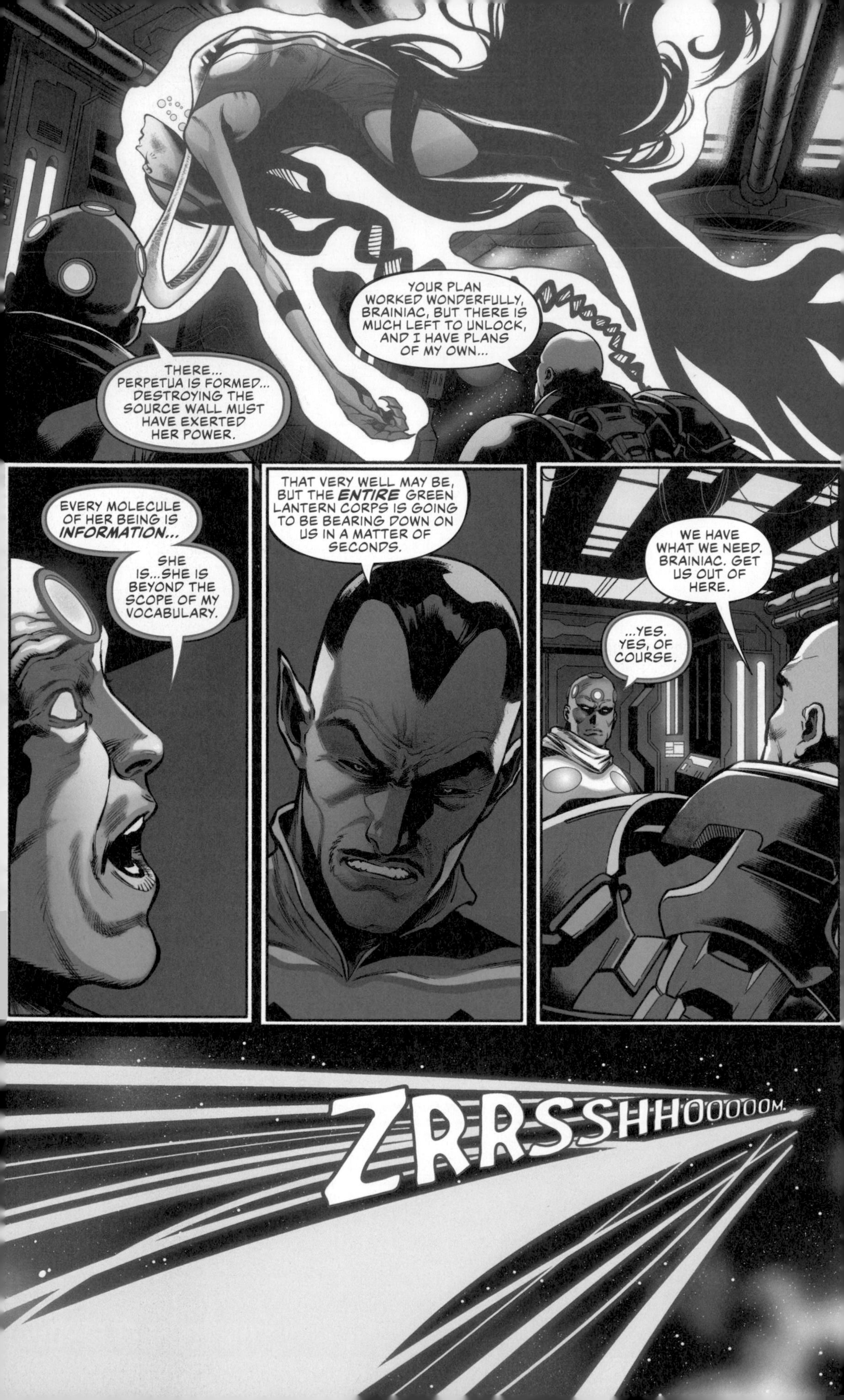
YOUR PLAN WORKED WONDERFULLY, BRAINIAC, BUT THERE IS MUCH LEFT TO UNLOCK, AND I HAVE PLANS OF MY OWN...
THERE... PERPETUA IS FORMED... DESTROYING THE SOURCE WALL MUST HAVE EXERTED HER POWER.
EVERY MOLECULE OF HER BEING IS *INFORMATION...*
SHE IS...SHE IS BEYOND THE SCOPE OF MY VOCABULARY.
THAT VERY WELL MAY BE, BUT THE *ENTIRE* GREEN LANTERN CORPS IS GOING TO BE BEARING DOWN ON US IN A MATTER OF SECONDS.
WE HAVE WHAT WE NEED. BRAINIAC. GET US OUT OF HERE.
...YES. YES, OF COURSE.
ZRRSSHHOOOOOOM.

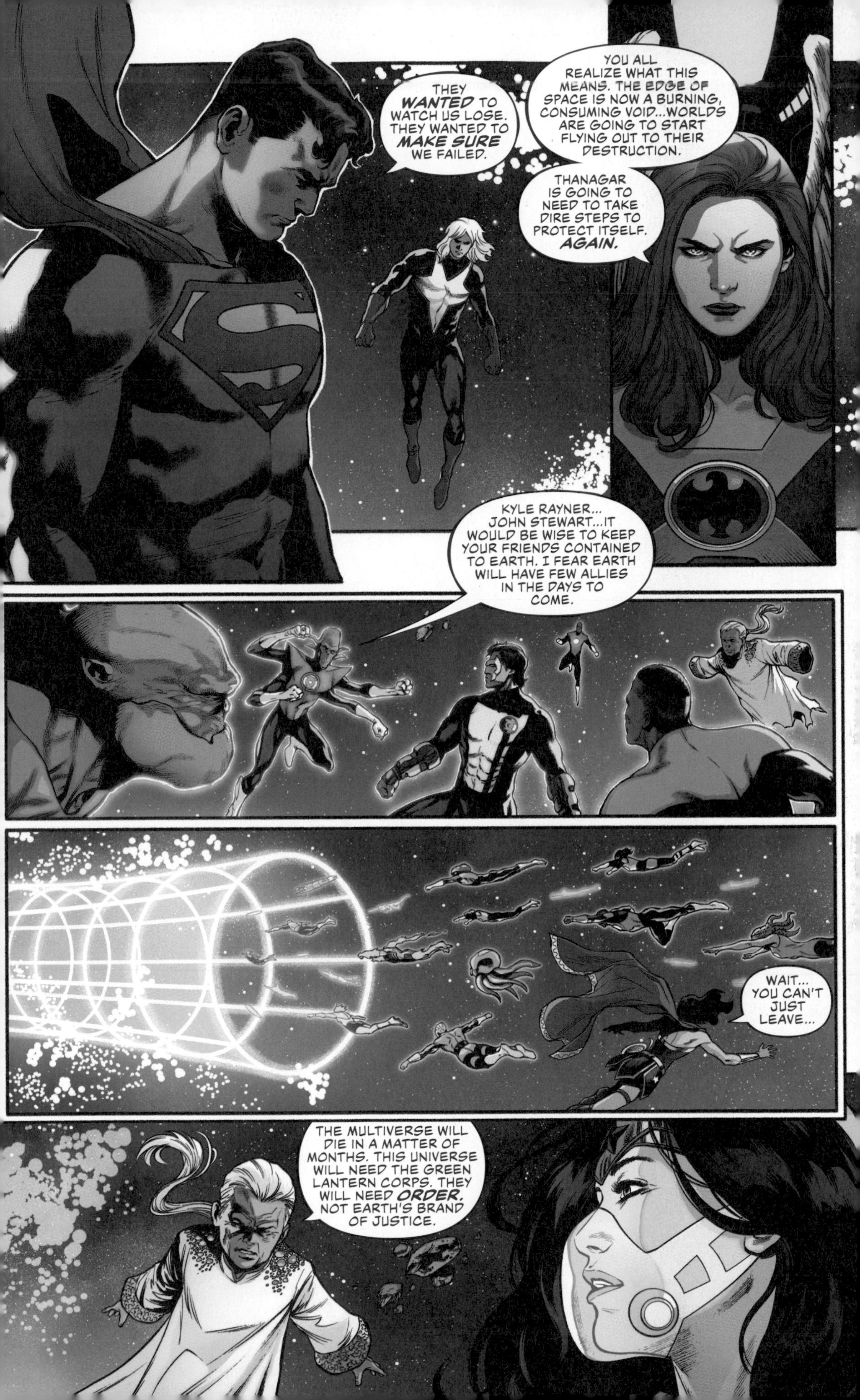
THEY WANTED TO WATCH US LOSE. THEY WANTED TO MAKE SURE WE FAILED.
YOU ALL REALIZE WHAT THIS MEANS. THE EDGE OF SPACE IS NOW A BURNING, CONSUMING VOID...WORLDS ARE GOING TO START FLYING OUT TO THEIR DESTRUCTION.
THANAGAR IS GOING TO NEED TO TAKE DIRE STEPS TO PROTECT ITSELF. AGAIN.
KYLE RAYNER... JOHN STEWART...IT WOULD BE WISE TO KEEP YOUR FRIENDS CONTAINED TO EARTH. I FEAR EARTH WILL HAVE FEW ALLIES IN THE DAYS TO COME.
WAIT... YOU CAN'T JUST LEAVE...
THE MULTIVERSE WILL DIE IN A MATTER OF MONTHS. THIS UNIVERSE WILL NEED THE GREEN LANTERN CORPS. THEY WILL NEED ORDER. NOT EARTH'S BRAND OF JUSTICE.

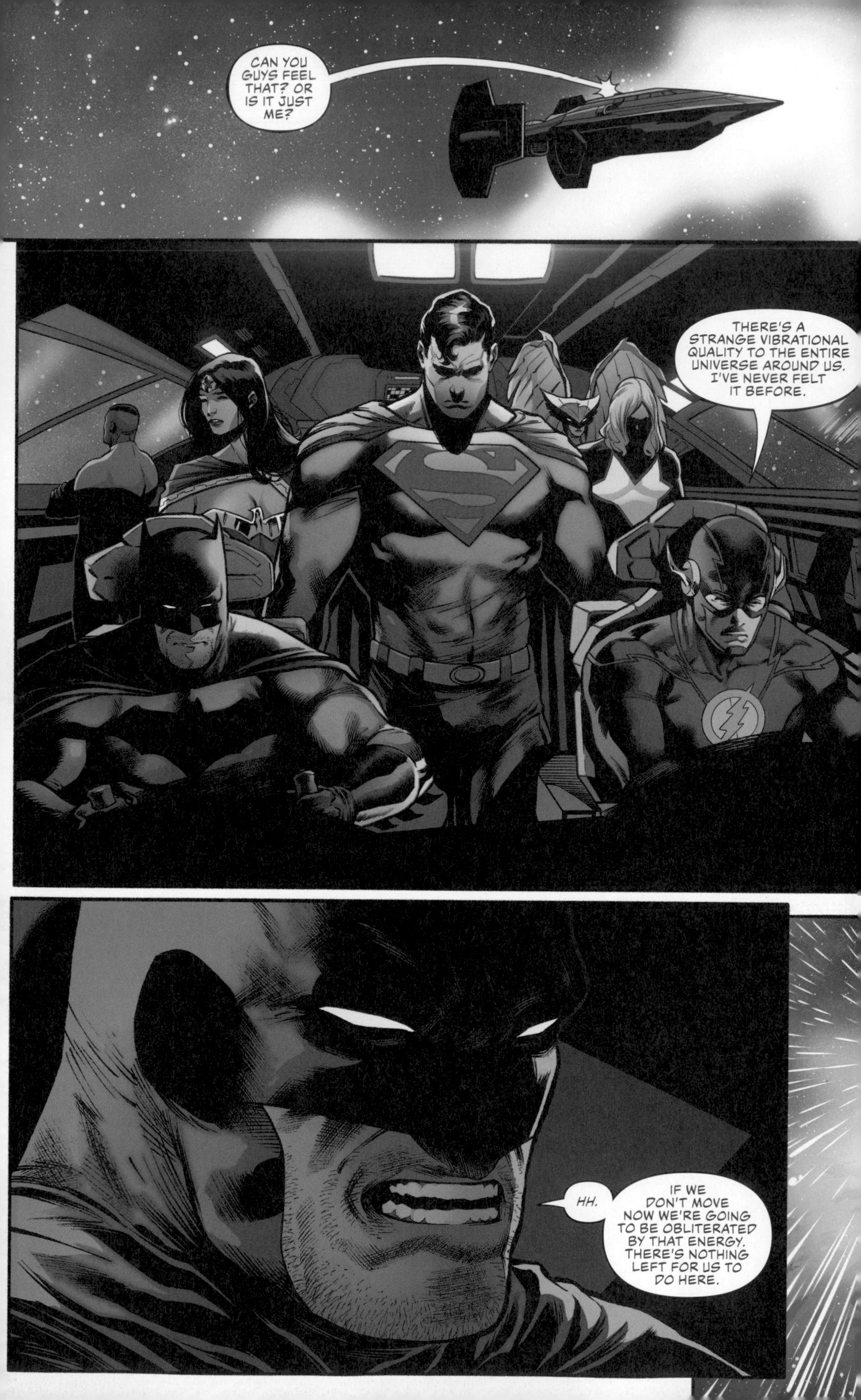
CAN YOU GUYS FEEL THAT? OR IS IT JUST ME?
THERE'S A STRANGE VIBRATIONAL QUALITY TO THE ENTIRE UNIVERSE AROUND US. I'VE NEVER FELT IT BEFORE.
HH.
IF WE DON'T MOVE NOW WE'RE GOING TO BE OBLITERATED BY THAT ENERGY. THERE'S NOTHING LEFT FOR US TO DO HERE.

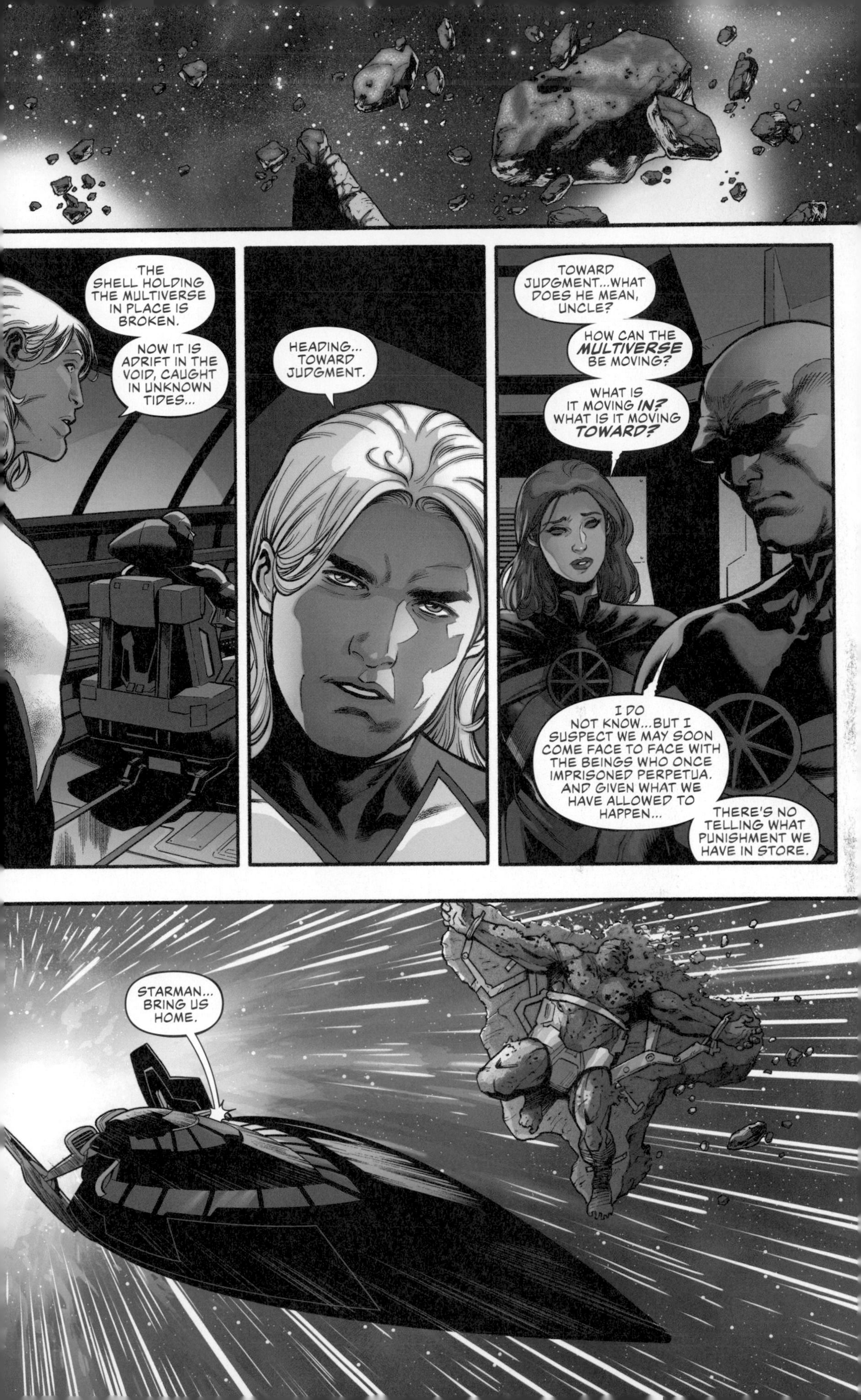
THE SHELL HOLDING THE MULTIVERSE IN PLACE IS BROKEN.
NOW IT IS ADRIFT IN THE VOID, CAUGHT IN UNKNOWN TIDES...
HEADING... TOWARD JUDGMENT.
TOWARD JUDGMENT...WHAT DOES HE MEAN, UNCLE?
HOW CAN THE MULTIVERSE BE MOVING?
WHAT IS IT MOVING IN? WHAT IS IT MOVING TOWARD?
I DO NOT KNOW...BUT I SUSPECT WE MAY SOON COME FACE TO FACE WITH THE BEINGS WHO ONCE IMPRISONED PERPETUA. AND GIVEN WHAT WE HAVE ALLOWED TO HAPPEN...
THERE'S NO TELLING WHAT PUNISHMENT WE HAVE IN STORE.
STARMAN... BRING US HOME.

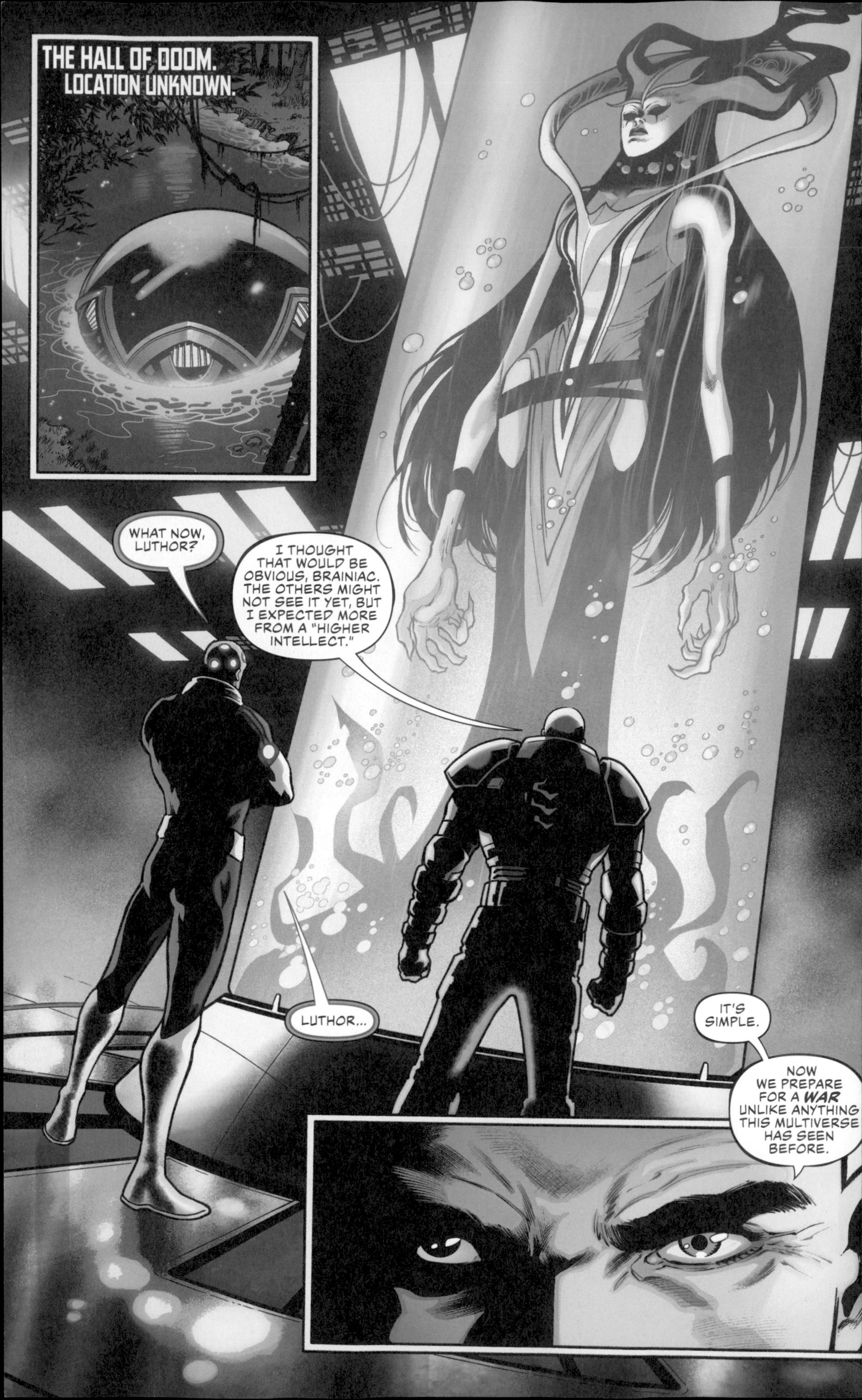
THE HALL OF DOOM.
LOCATION UNKNOWN.
WHAT NOW, LUTHOR?
I THOUGHT THAT WOULD BE OBVIOUS, BRAINIAC. THE OTHERS MIGHT NOT SEE IT YET, BUT I EXPECTED MORE FROM A "HIGHER INTELLECT."
LUTHOR...
IT'S SIMPLE.
NOW WE PREPARE FOR A WAR UNLIKE ANYTHING THIS MULTIVERSE HAS SEEN BEFORE.

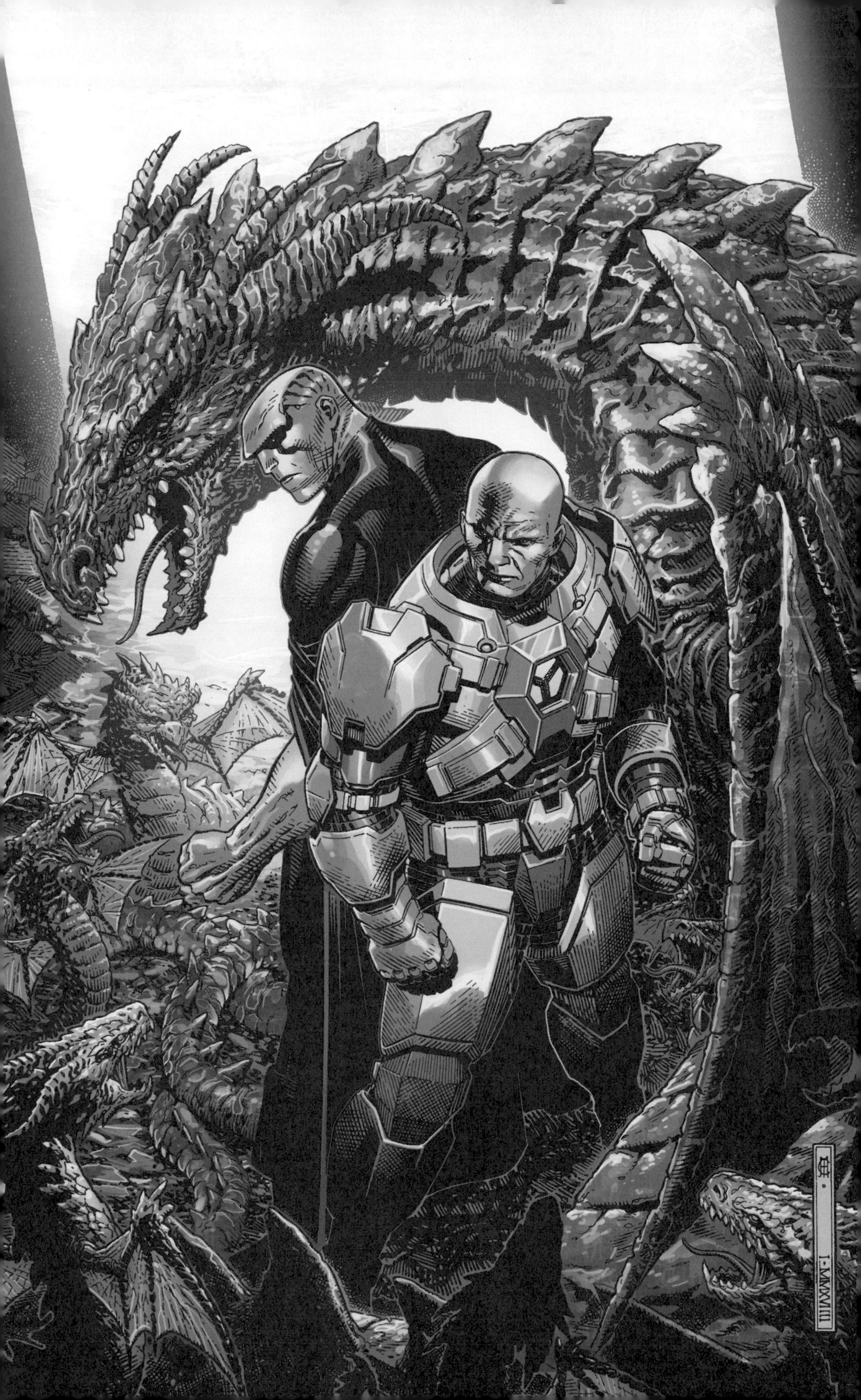

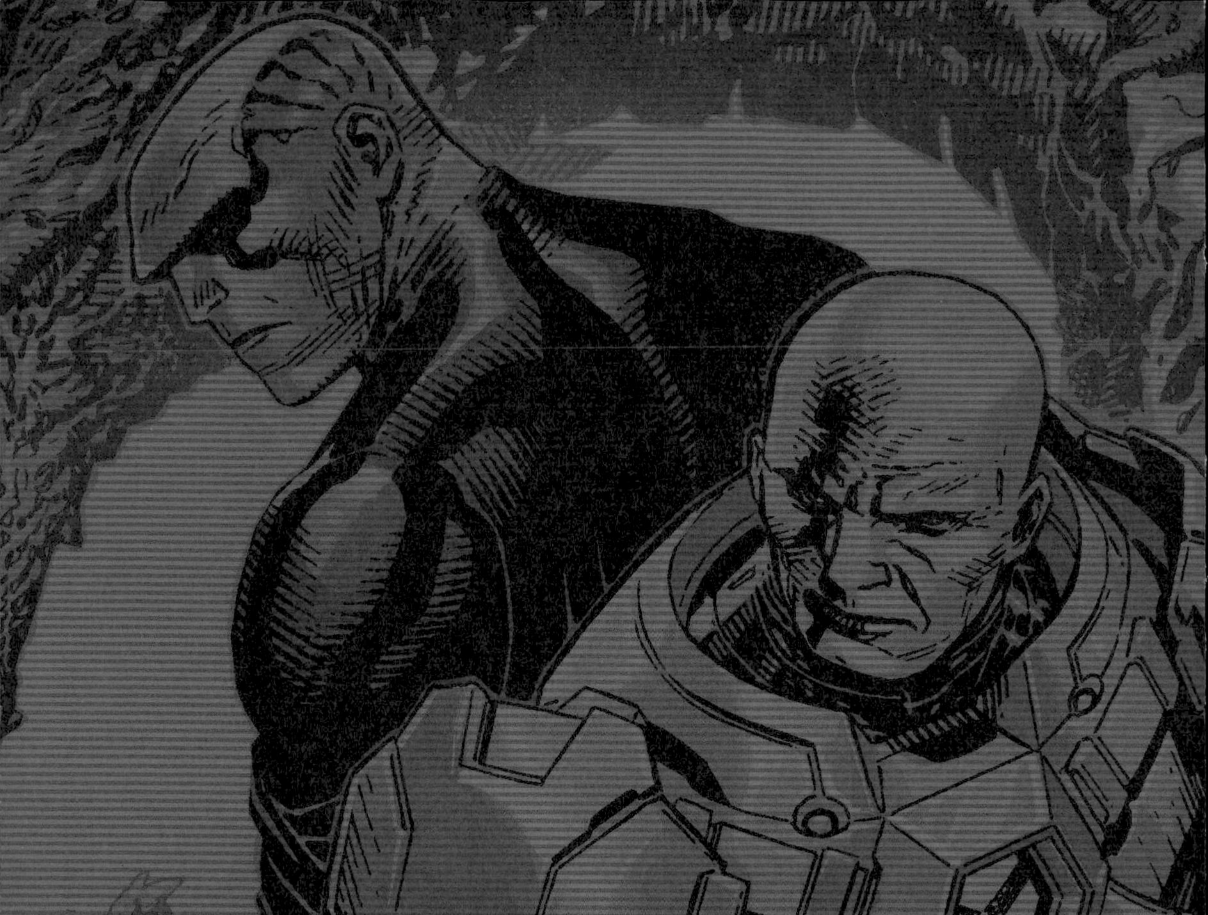

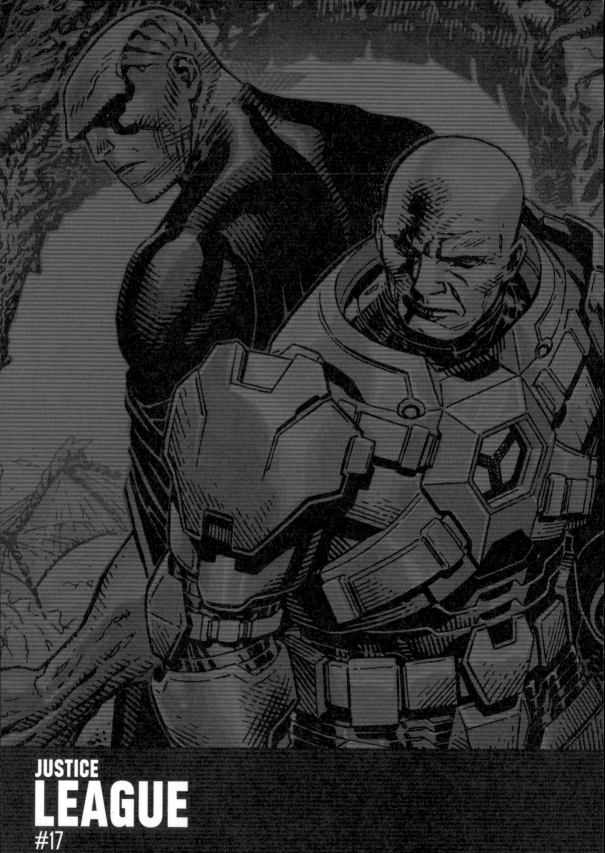

JUSTICE
LEAGUE
#17

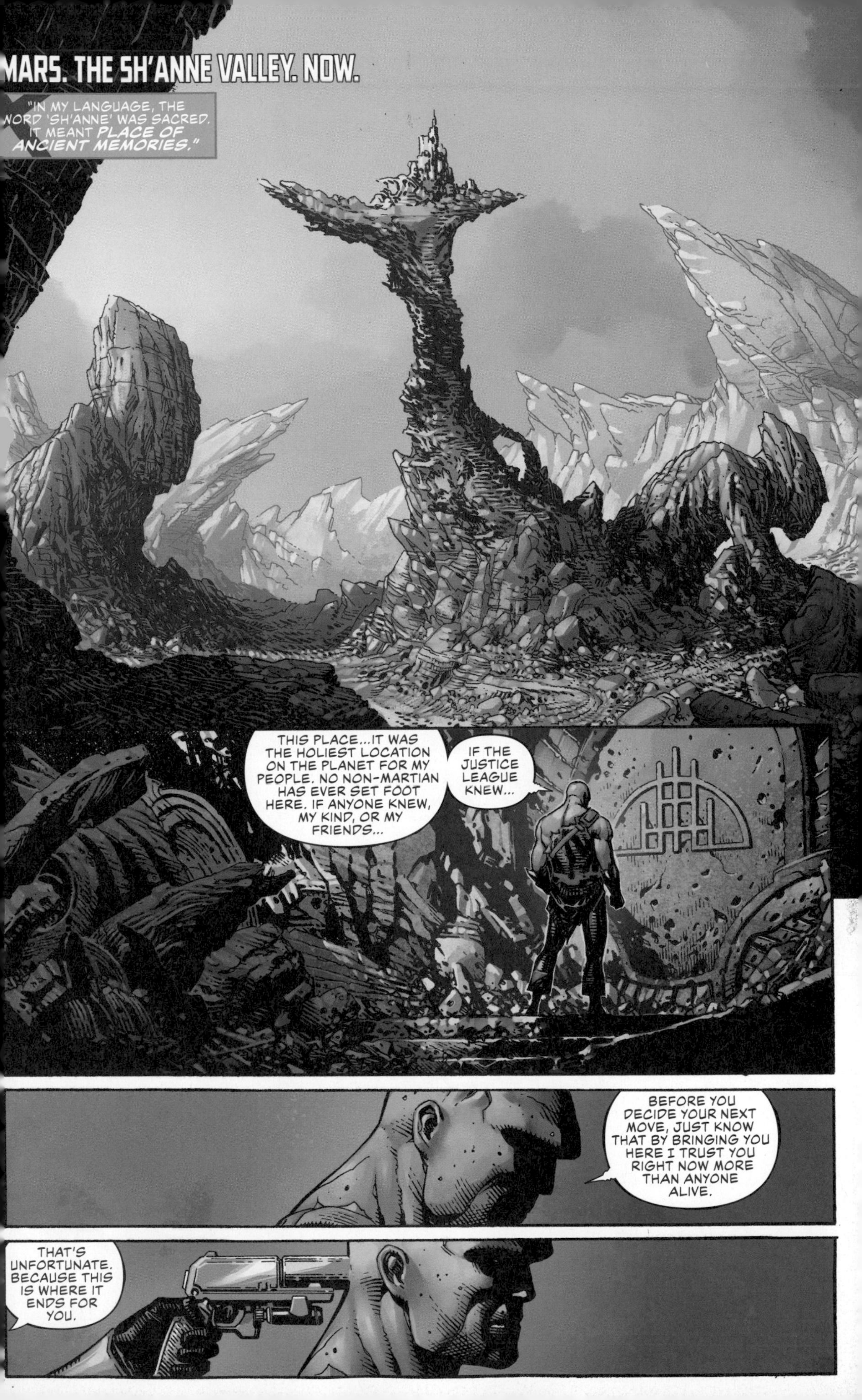
MARS. THE SH'ANNE VALLEY. NOW.
"IN MY LANGUAGE, THE WORD 'SH'ANNE' WAS SACRED. IT MEANT PLACE OF ANCIENT MEMORIES."
THIS PLACE...IT WAS THE HOLIEST LOCATION ON THE PLANET FOR MY PEOPLE. NO NON-MARTIAN HAS EVER SET FOOT HERE. IF ANYONE KNEW, MY KIND, OR MY FRIENDS...
IF THE JUSTICE LEAGUE KNEW...
BEFORE YOU DECIDE YOUR NEXT MOVE, JUST KNOW THAT BY BRINGING YOU HERE I TRUST YOU RIGHT NOW MORE THAN ANYONE ALIVE.
THAT'S UNFORTUNATE. BECAUSE THIS IS WHERE IT ENDS FOR YOU.

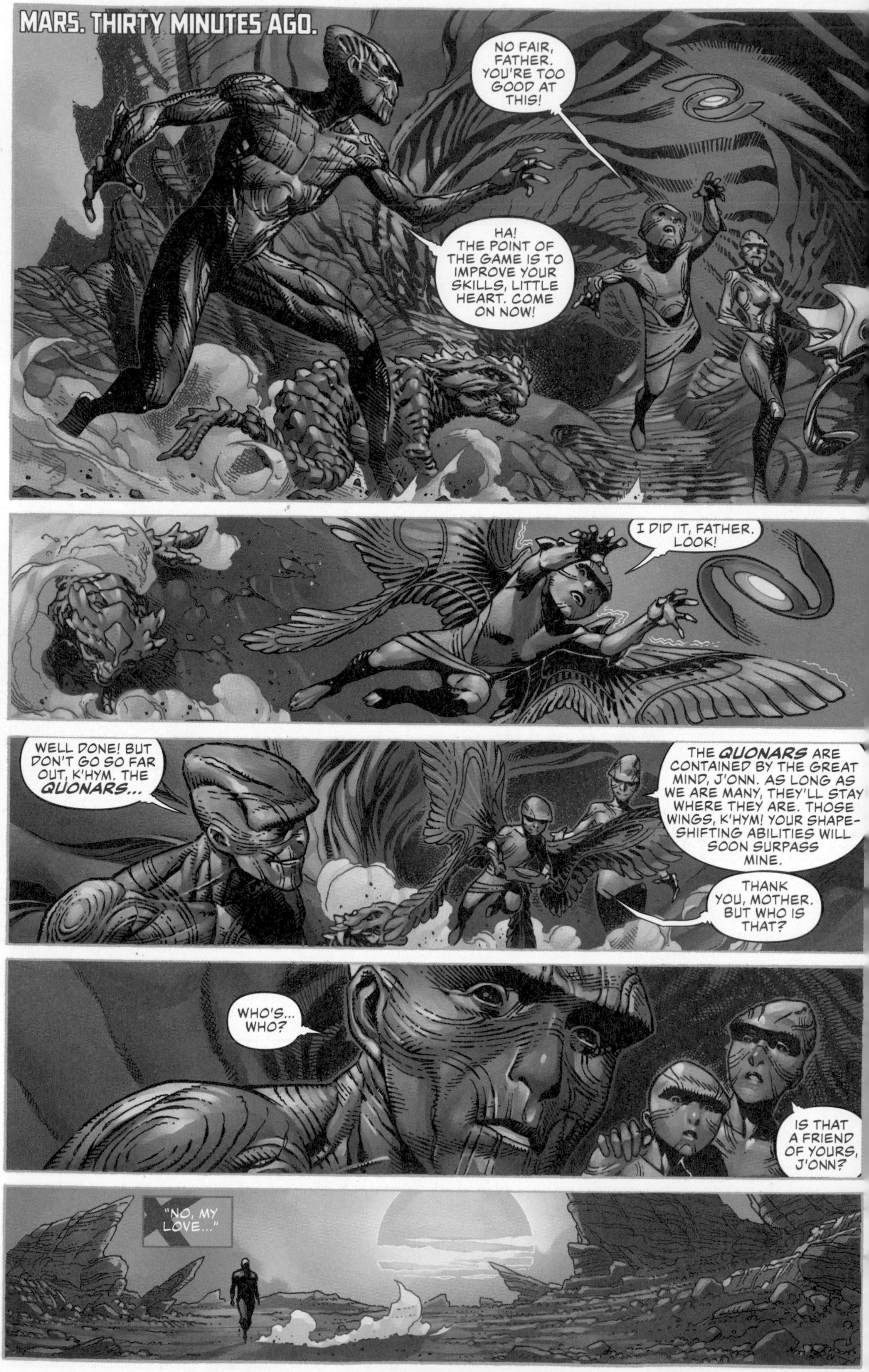
MARS. THIRTY MINUTES AGO.
NO FAIR, FATHER. YOU'RE TOO GOOD AT THIS!
HA! THE POINT OF THE GAME IS TO IMPROVE YOUR SKILLS, LITTLE HEART. COME ON NOW!
I DID IT, FATHER. LOOK!
WELL DONE! BUT DON'T GO SO FAR OUT, K'HYM. THE QUONARS...
THE QUONARS ARE CONTAINED BY THE GREAT MIND, J'ONN. AS LONG AS WE ARE MANY, THEY'LL STAY WHERE THEY ARE. THOSE WINGS, K'HYM! YOUR SHAPE-SHIFTING ABILITIES WILL SOON SURPASS MINE.
THANK YOU, MOTHER. BUT WHO IS THAT?
WHO'S... WHO?
IS THAT A FRIEND OF YOURS, J'ONN?
"NO, MY LOVE..."

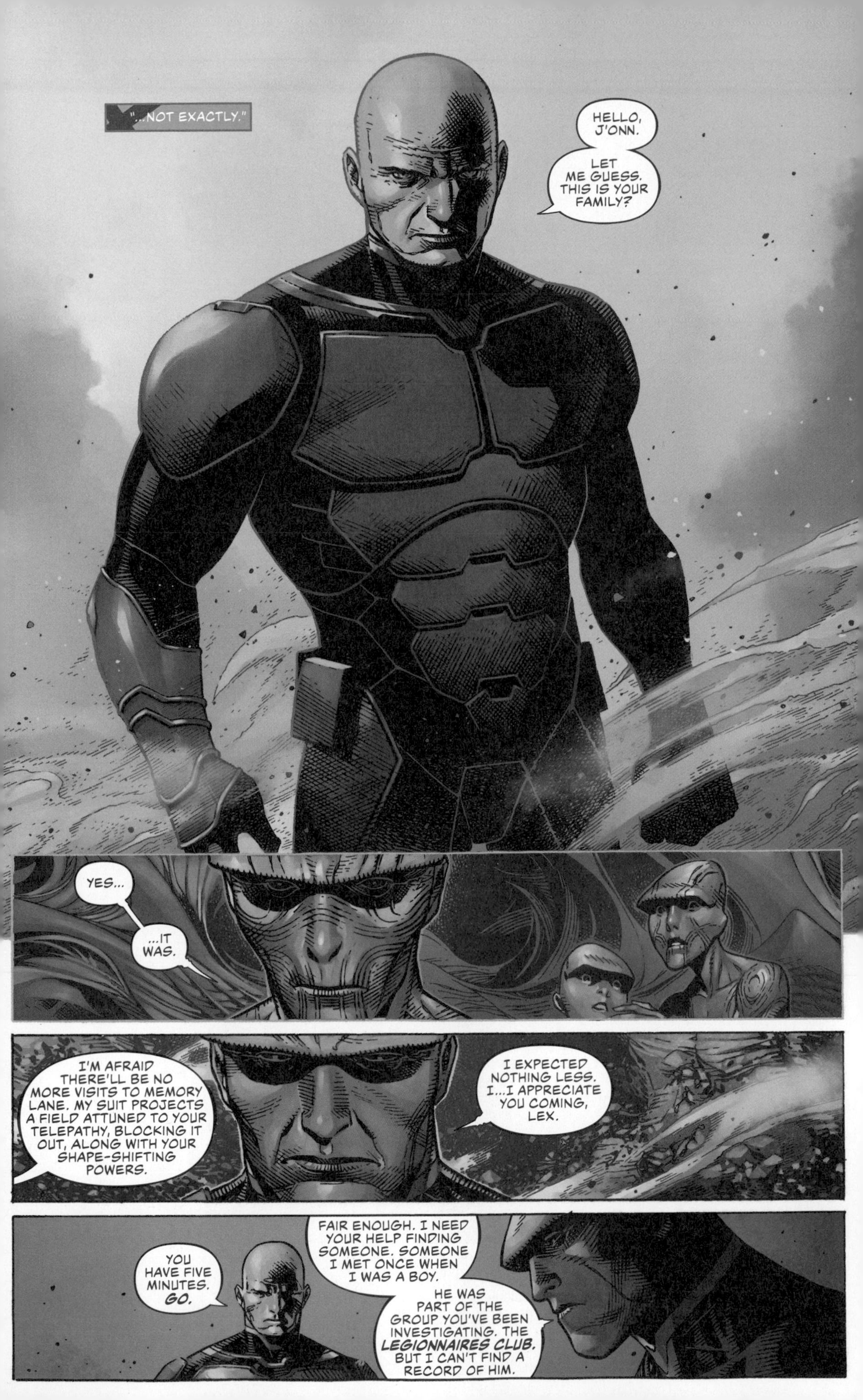
"...NOT EXACTLY."
HELLO, J'ONN.
LET ME GUESS. THIS IS YOUR FAMILY?
YES...
...IT WAS.
I'M AFRAID THERE'LL BE NO MORE VISITS TO MEMORY LANE. MY SUIT PROJECTS A FIELD ATTUNED TO YOUR TELEPATHY, BLOCKING IT OUT, ALONG WITH YOUR SHAPE-SHIFTING POWERS.
I EXPECTED NOTHING LESS. I...I APPRECIATE YOU COMING, LEX.
YOU HAVE FIVE MINUTES. GO.
FAIR ENOUGH. I NEED YOUR HELP FINDING SOMEONE. SOMEONE I MET ONCE WHEN I WAS A BOY.
HE WAS PART OF THE GROUP YOU'VE BEEN INVESTIGATING. THE LEGIONNAIRES CLUB. BUT I CAN'T FIND A RECORD OF HIM.

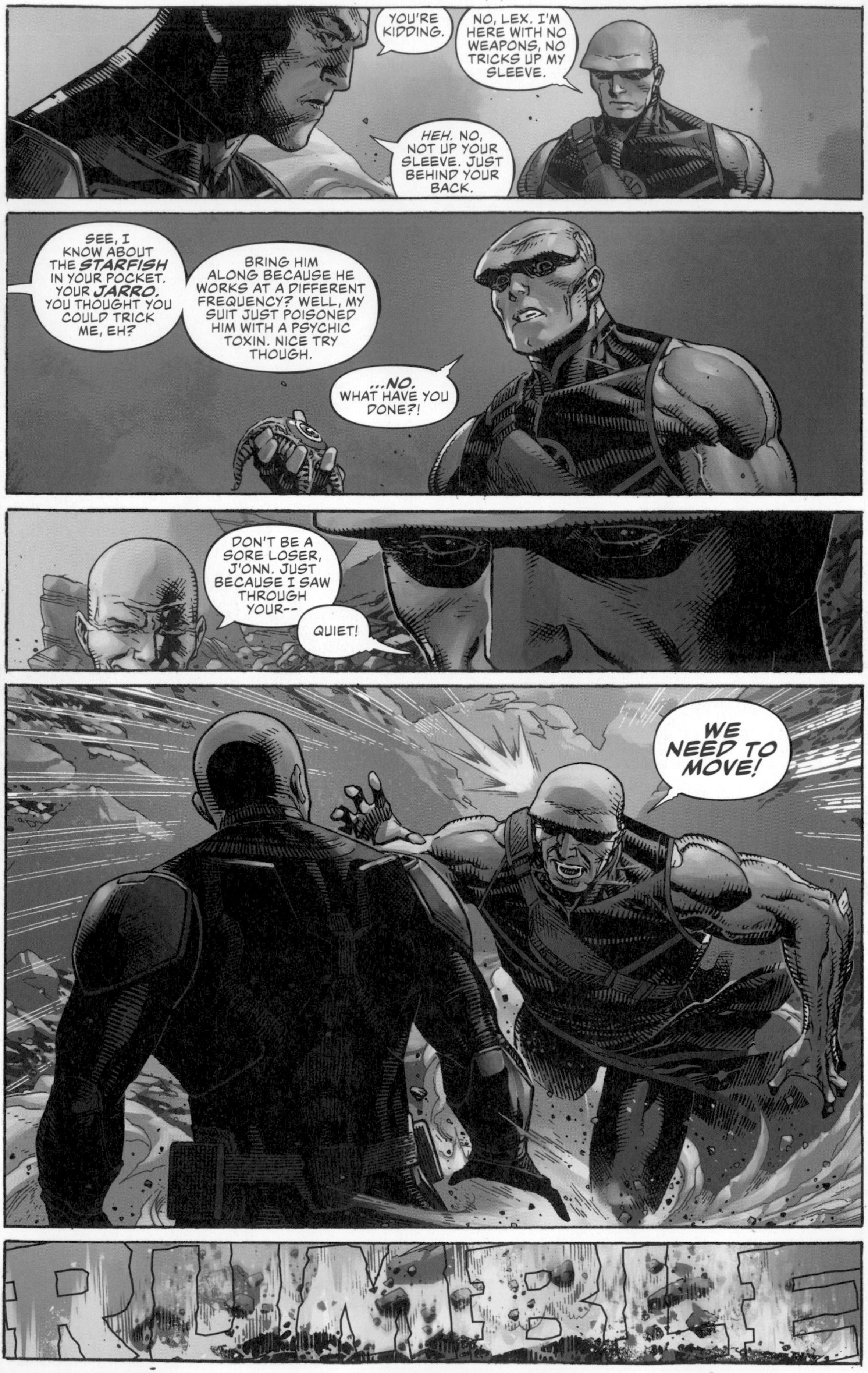

YOU'RE KIDDING.
NO, LEX. I'M HERE WITH NO WEAPONS, NO TRICKS UP MY SLEEVE.
HEH. NO, NOT UP YOUR SLEEVE. JUST BEHIND YOUR BACK.
SEE, I KNOW ABOUT THE STARFISH IN YOUR POCKET. YOUR JARRO. YOU THOUGHT YOU COULD TRICK ME, EH?
BRING HIM ALONG BECAUSE HE WORKS AT A DIFFERENT FREQUENCY? WELL, MY SUIT JUST POISONED HIM WITH A PSYCHIC TOXIN. NICE TRY THOUGH.
...NO. WHAT HAVE YOU DONE?!
DON'T BE A SORE LOSER, J'ONN. JUST BECAUSE I SAW THROUGH YOUR--
QUIET!
WE NEED TO MOVE!

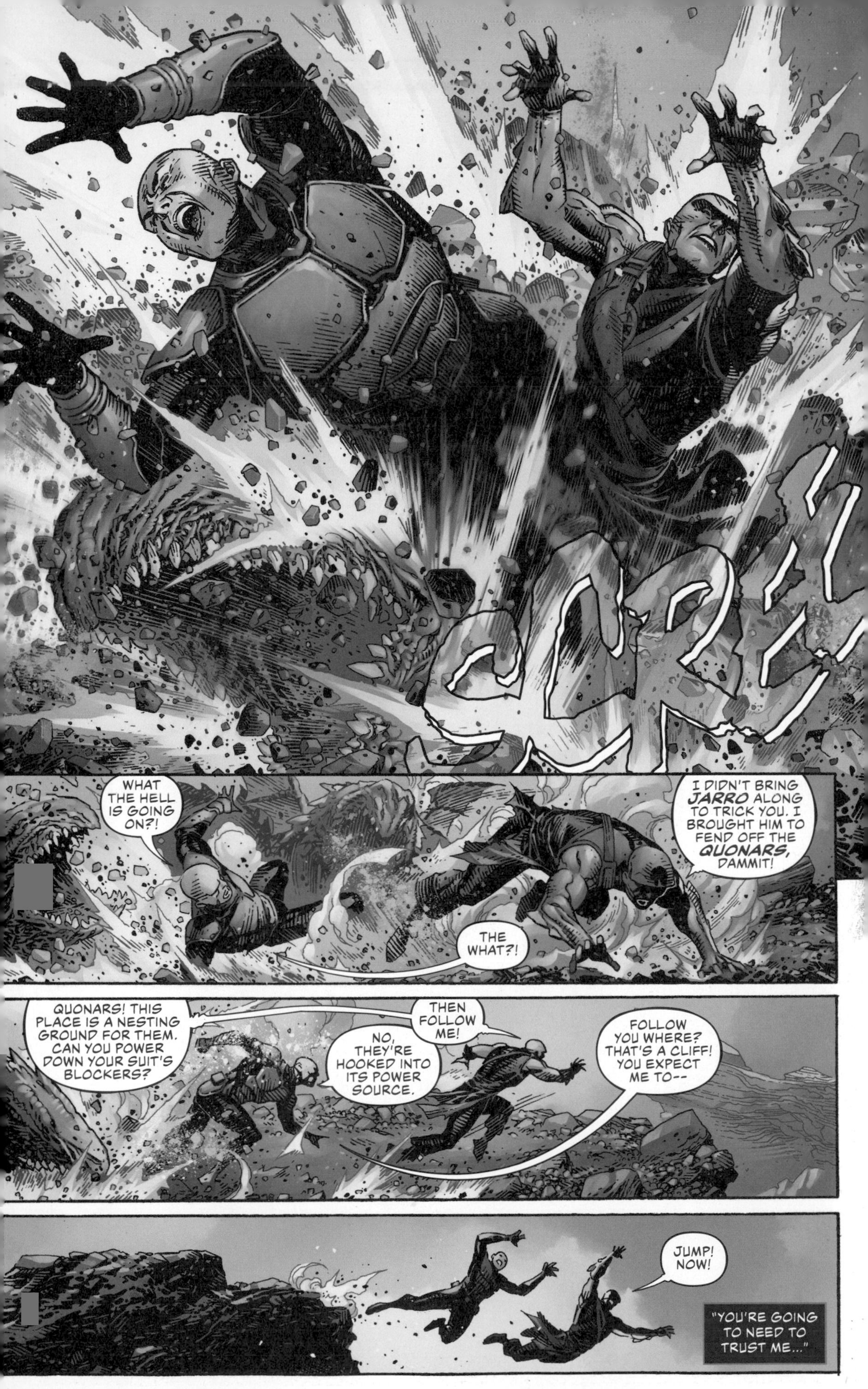
WHAT THE HELL IS GOING ON?!
I DIDN'T BRING JARRO ALONG TO TRICK YOU. I BROUGHT HIM TO FEND OFF THE QUONARS, DAMMIT!
THE WHAT?!
QUONARS! THIS PLACE IS A NESTING GROUND FOR THEM. CAN YOU POWER DOWN YOUR SUIT'S BLOCKERS?
NO, THEY'RE HOOKED INTO ITS POWER SOURCE.
THEN FOLLOW ME!
FOLLOW YOU WHERE? THAT'S A CLIFF! YOU EXPECT ME TO--
JUMP! NOW!
"YOU'RE GOING TO NEED TO TRUST ME..."

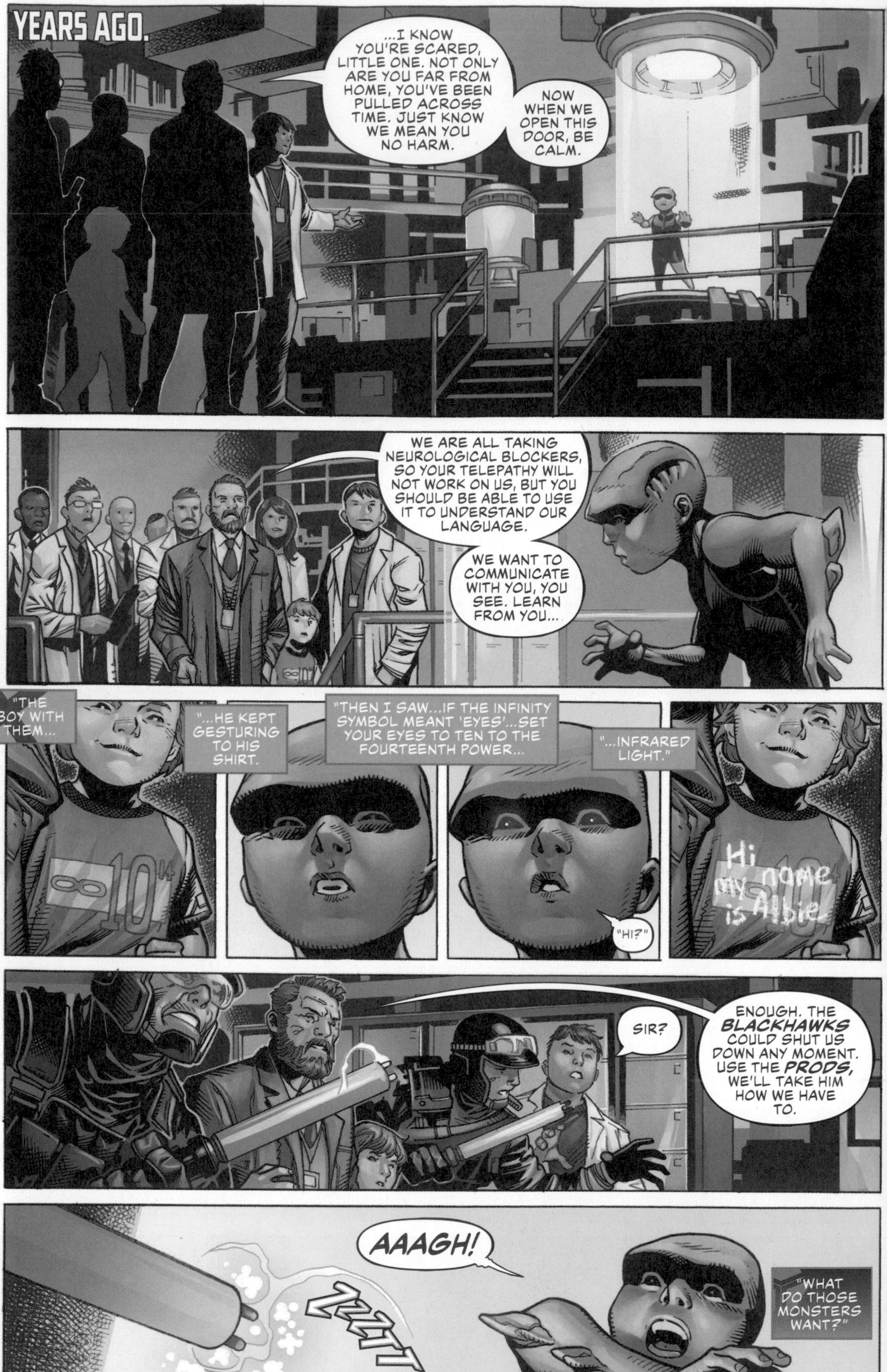
YEARS AGO.
...I KNOW YOU'RE SCARED, LITTLE ONE. NOT ONLY ARE YOU FAR FROM HOME, YOU'VE BEEN PULLED ACROSS TIME. JUST KNOW WE MEAN YOU NO HARM.
NOW WHEN WE OPEN THIS DOOR, BE CALM.
WE ARE ALL TAKING NEUROLOGICAL BLOCKERS, SO YOUR TELEPATHY WILL NOT WORK ON US, BUT YOU SHOULD BE ABLE TO USE IT TO UNDERSTAND OUR LANGUAGE.
WE WANT TO COMMUNICATE WITH YOU, YOU SEE. LEARN FROM YOU...
"THE BOY WITH THEM...
"...HE KEPT GESTURING TO HIS SHIRT.
"THEN I SAW...IF THE INFINITY SYMBOL MEANT 'EYES'...SET YOUR EYES TO TEN TO THE FOURTEENTH POWER...
"...INFRARED LIGHT."
"HI?"
Hi my name is Albie
SIR?
ENOUGH. THE BLACKHAWKS COULD SHUT US DOWN ANY MOMENT. USE THE PRODS, WE'LL TAKE HIM HOW WE HAVE TO.
AAAGH!
ZZZTT
"WHAT DO THOSE MONSTERS WANT?"

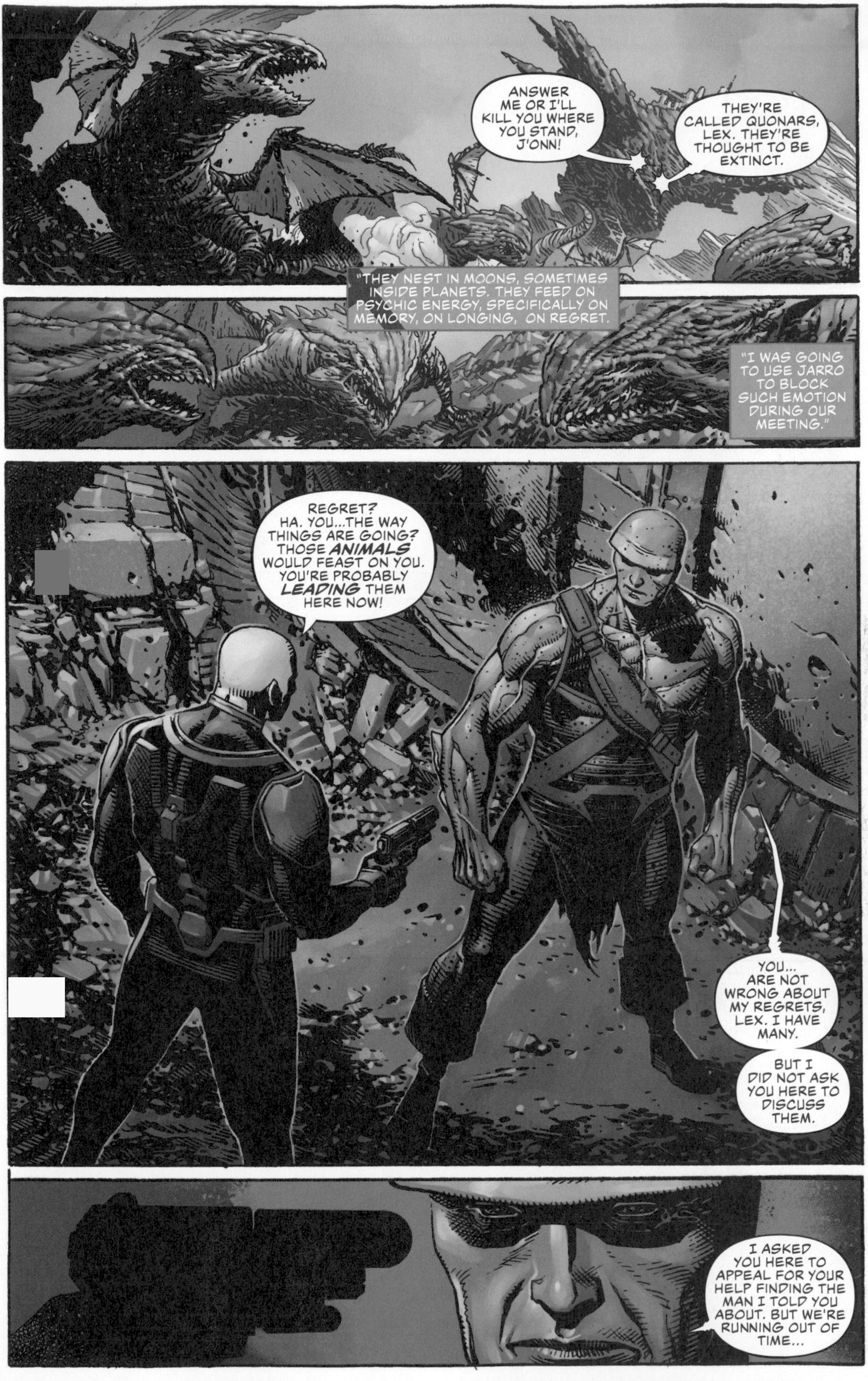

ANSWER ME OR I'LL KILL YOU WHERE YOU STAND, J'ONN!
THEY'RE CALLED QUONARS, LEX. THEY'RE THOUGHT TO BE EXTINCT.
"THEY NEST IN MOONS, SOMETIMES INSIDE PLANETS. THEY FEED ON PSYCHIC ENERGY, SPECIFICALLY ON MEMORY, ON LONGING, ON REGRET.
"I WAS GOING TO USE JARRO TO BLOCK SUCH EMOTION DURING OUR MEETING."
REGRET? HA. YOU...THE WAY THINGS ARE GOING? THOSE ANIMALS WOULD FEAST ON YOU. YOU'RE PROBABLY LEADING THEM HERE NOW!
YOU... ARE NOT WRONG ABOUT MY REGRETS, LEX. I HAVE MANY.
BUT I DID NOT ASK YOU HERE TO DISCUSS THEM.
I ASKED YOU HERE TO APPEAL FOR YOUR HELP FINDING THE MAN I TOLD YOU ABOUT. BUT WE'RE RUNNING OUT OF TIME...

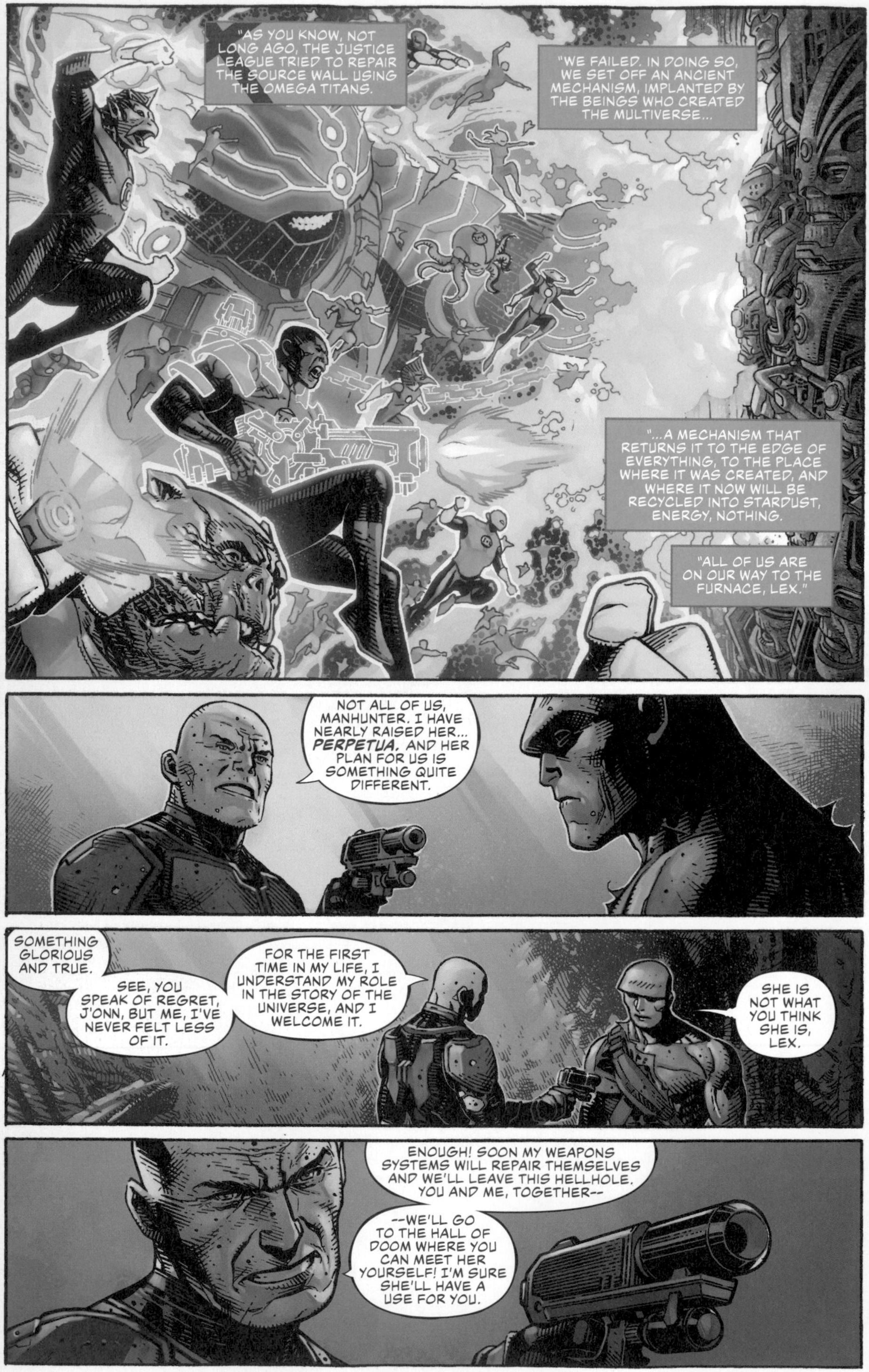
"AS YOU KNOW, NOT LONG AGO, THE JUSTICE LEAGUE TRIED TO REPAIR THE SOURCE WALL USING THE OMEGA TITANS.
"WE FAILED. IN DOING SO, WE SET OFF AN ANCIENT MECHANISM, IMPLANTED BY THE BEINGS WHO CREATED THE MULTIVERSE...
"...A MECHANISM THAT RETURNS IT TO THE EDGE OF EVERYTHING, TO THE PLACE WHERE IT WAS CREATED, AND WHERE IT NOW WILL BE RECYCLED INTO STARDUST, ENERGY, NOTHING.
"ALL OF US ARE ON OUR WAY TO THE FURNACE, LEX."
NOT ALL OF US, MANHUNTER. I HAVE NEARLY RAISED HER... *PERPETUA.* AND HER PLAN FOR US IS SOMETHING QUITE DIFFERENT.
SOMETHING GLORIOUS AND TRUE.
SEE, YOU SPEAK OF REGRET, J'ONN, BUT ME, I'VE NEVER FELT LESS OF IT.
FOR THE FIRST TIME IN MY LIFE, I UNDERSTAND MY ROLE IN THE STORY OF THE UNIVERSE, AND I WELCOME IT.
SHE IS NOT WHAT YOU THINK SHE IS, LEX.
ENOUGH! SOON MY WEAPONS SYSTEMS WILL REPAIR THEMSELVES AND WE'LL LEAVE THIS HELLHOLE. YOU AND ME, TOGETHER--
--WE'LL GO TO THE HALL OF DOOM WHERE YOU CAN MEET HER YOURSELF! I'M SURE SHE'LL HAVE A USE FOR YOU.

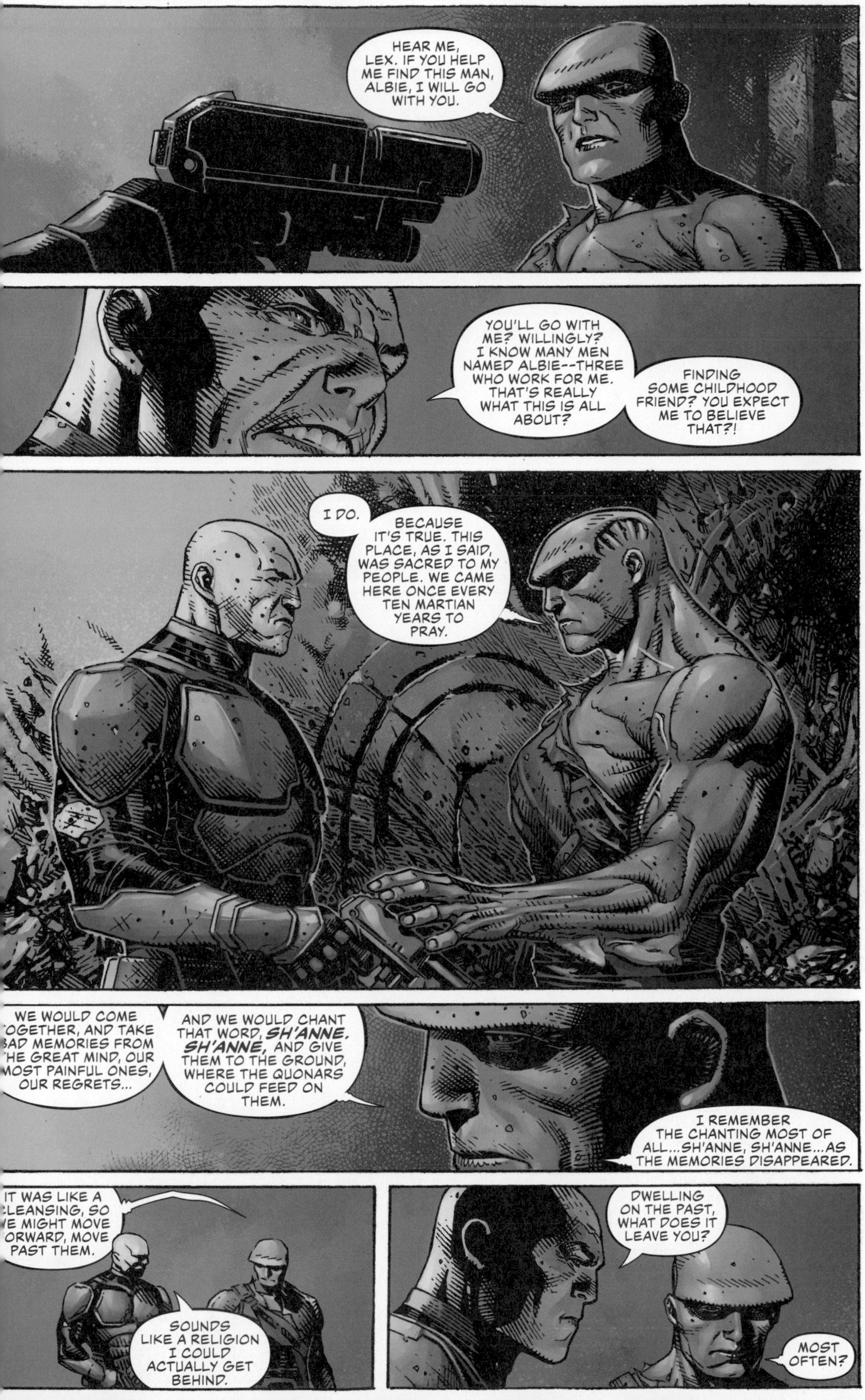
HEAR ME, LEX. IF YOU HELP ME FIND THIS MAN, ALBIE, I WILL GO WITH YOU.
YOU'LL GO WITH ME? WILLINGLY? I KNOW MANY MEN NAMED ALBIE--THREE WHO WORK FOR ME. THAT'S REALLY WHAT THIS IS ALL ABOUT?
FINDING SOME CHILDHOOD FRIEND? YOU EXPECT ME TO BELIEVE THAT?!
I DO.
BECAUSE IT'S TRUE. THIS PLACE, AS I SAID, WAS SACRED TO MY PEOPLE. WE CAME HERE ONCE EVERY TEN MARTIAN YEARS TO PRAY.
WE WOULD COME TOGETHER, AND TAKE BAD MEMORIES FROM THE GREAT MIND, OUR MOST PAINFUL ONES, OUR REGRETS...
AND WE WOULD CHANT THAT WORD, ***SH'ANNE. SH'ANNE,*** AND GIVE THEM TO THE GROUND, WHERE THE QUONARS COULD FEED ON THEM.
I REMEMBER THE CHANTING MOST OF ALL...SH'ANNE, SH'ANNE...AS THE MEMORIES DISAPPEARED.
IT WAS LIKE A CLEANSING, SO WE MIGHT MOVE FORWARD, MOVE PAST THEM.
SOUNDS LIKE A RELIGION I COULD ACTUALLY GET BEHIND.
DWELLING ON THE PAST, WHAT DOES IT LEAVE YOU?
MOST OFTEN?

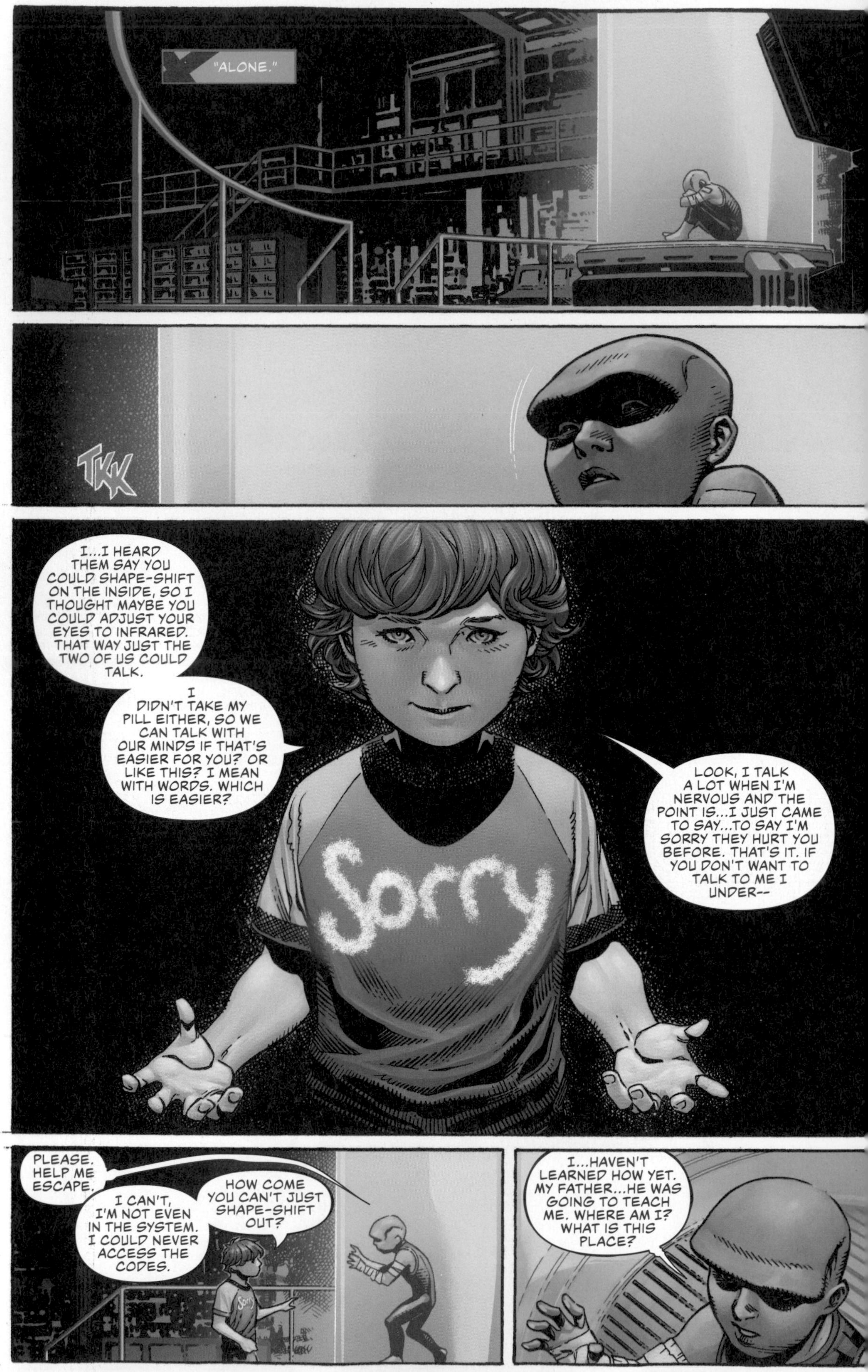
"ALONE."
TKK
I...I HEARD THEM SAY YOU COULD SHAPE-SHIFT ON THE INSIDE, SO I THOUGHT MAYBE YOU COULD ADJUST YOUR EYES TO INFRARED. THAT WAY JUST THE TWO OF US COULD TALK.
I DIDN'T TAKE MY PILL EITHER, SO WE CAN TALK WITH OUR MINDS IF THAT'S EASIER FOR YOU? OR LIKE THIS? I MEAN WITH WORDS. WHICH IS EASIER?
LOOK, I TALK A LOT WHEN I'M NERVOUS AND THE POINT IS...I JUST CAME TO SAY...TO SAY I'M SORRY THEY HURT YOU BEFORE. THAT'S IT. IF YOU DON'T WANT TO TALK TO ME I UNDER--
Sorry
PLEASE. HELP ME ESCAPE.
HOW COME YOU CAN'T JUST SHAPE-SHIFT OUT?
I CAN'T, I'M NOT EVEN IN THE SYSTEM. I COULD NEVER ACCESS THE CODES.
I...HAVEN'T LEARNED HOW YET. MY FATHER...HE WAS GOING TO TEACH ME. WHERE AM I? WHAT IS THIS PLACE?

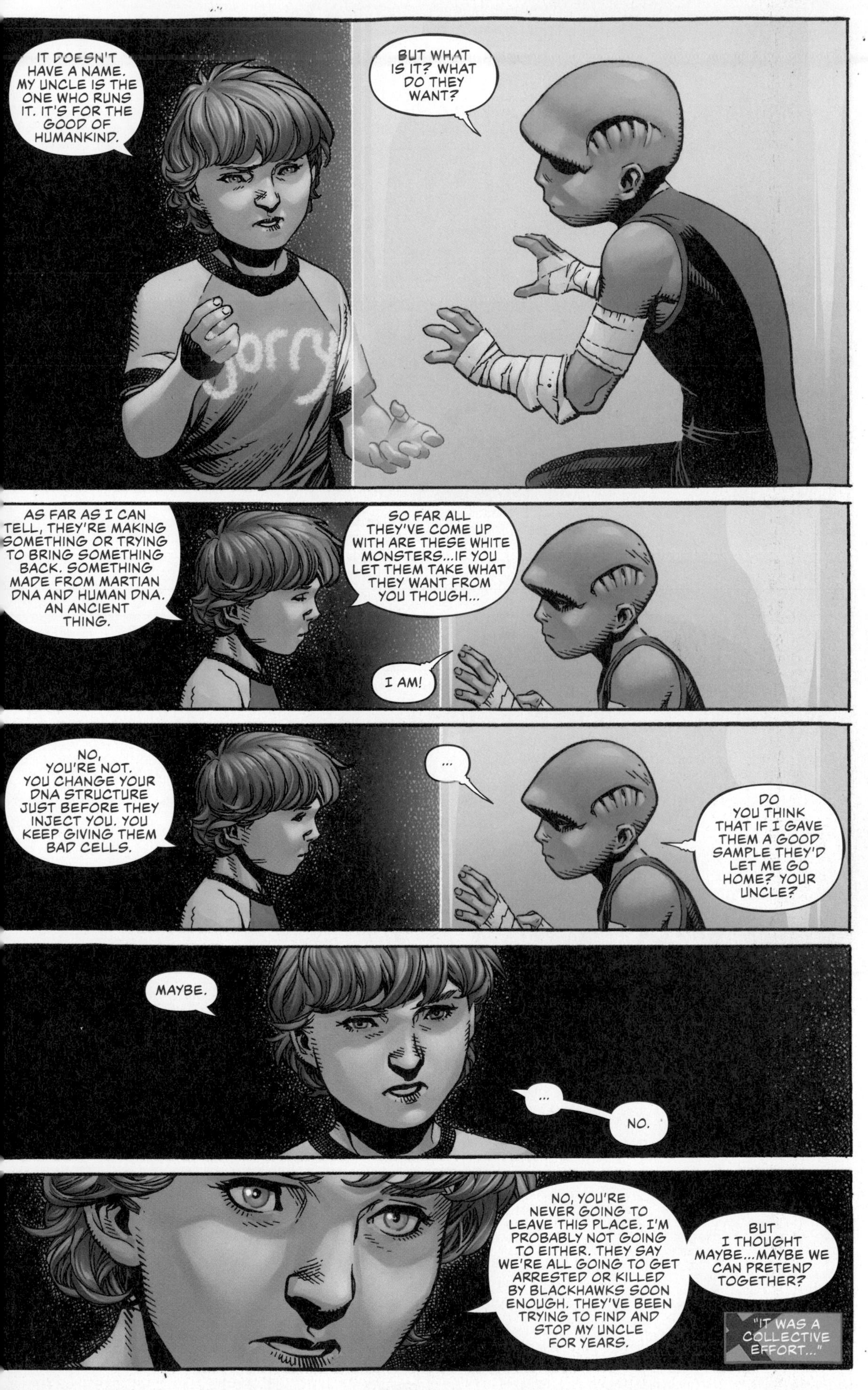
IT DOESN'T HAVE A NAME. MY UNCLE IS THE ONE WHO RUNS IT. IT'S FOR THE GOOD OF HUMANKIND.
BUT WHAT IS IT? WHAT DO THEY WANT?
AS FAR AS I CAN TELL, THEY'RE MAKING SOMETHING OR TRYING TO BRING SOMETHING BACK. SOMETHING MADE FROM MARTIAN DNA AND HUMAN DNA. AN ANCIENT THING.
SO FAR ALL THEY'VE COME UP WITH ARE THESE WHITE MONSTERS...IF YOU LET THEM TAKE WHAT THEY WANT FROM YOU THOUGH...
I AM!
NO, YOU'RE NOT. YOU CHANGE YOUR DNA STRUCTURE JUST BEFORE THEY INJECT YOU. YOU KEEP GIVING THEM BAD CELLS.
...
DO YOU THINK THAT IF I GAVE THEM A GOOD SAMPLE THEY'D LET ME GO HOME? YOUR UNCLE?
MAYBE.
...
NO.
NO, YOU'RE NEVER GOING TO LEAVE THIS PLACE. I'M PROBABLY NOT GOING TO EITHER. THEY SAY WE'RE ALL GOING TO GET ARRESTED OR KILLED BY BLACKHAWKS SOON ENOUGH. THEY'VE BEEN TRYING TO FIND AND STOP MY UNCLE FOR YEARS.
BUT I THOUGHT MAYBE...MAYBE WE CAN PRETEND TOGETHER?
"IT WAS A COLLECTIVE EFFORT..."

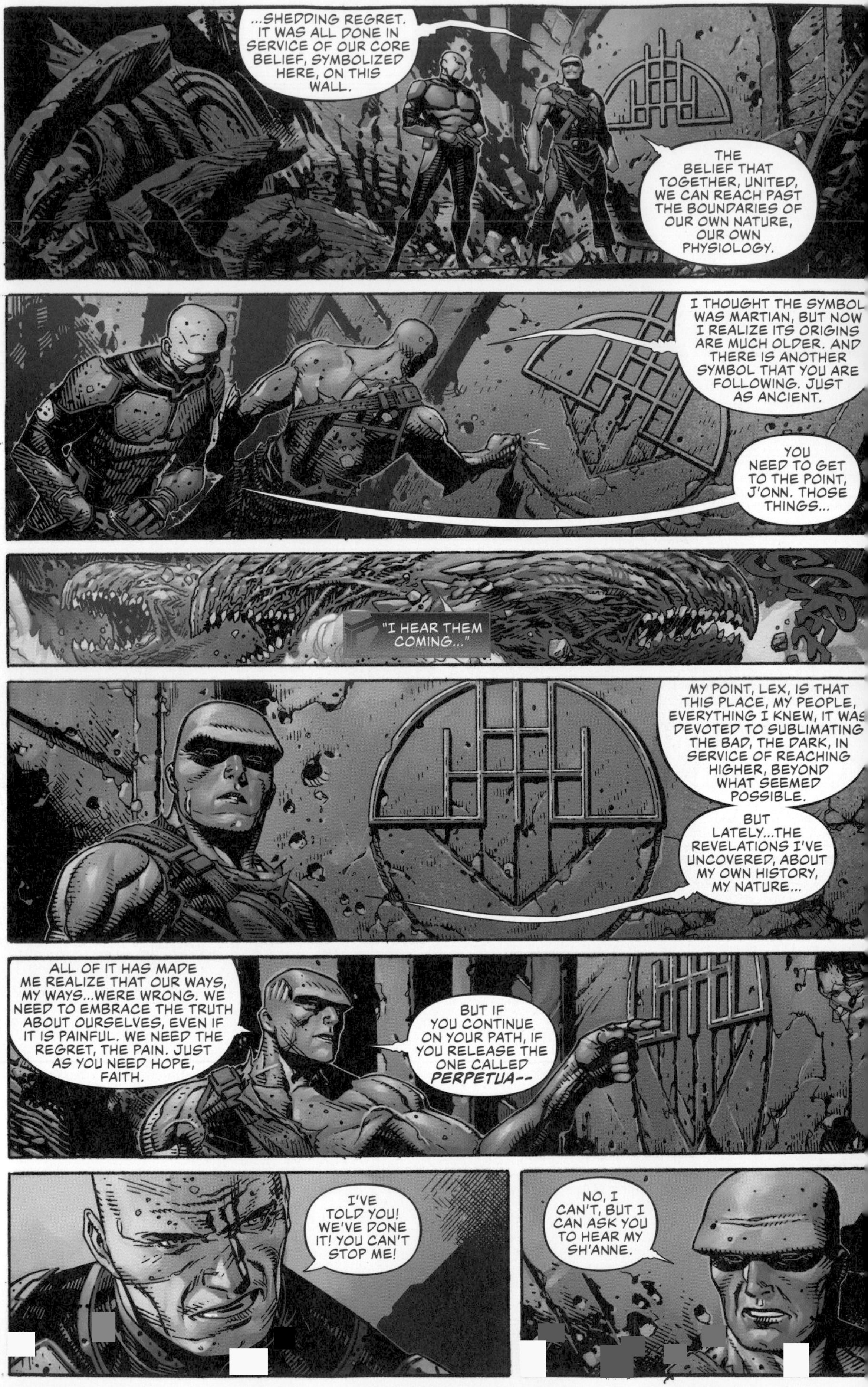
...SHEDDING REGRET. IT WAS ALL DONE IN SERVICE OF OUR CORE BELIEF, SYMBOLIZED HERE, ON THIS WALL.
THE BELIEF THAT TOGETHER, UNITED, WE CAN REACH PAST THE BOUNDARIES OF OUR OWN NATURE, OUR OWN PHYSIOLOGY.
I THOUGHT THE SYMBOL WAS MARTIAN, BUT NOW I REALIZE ITS ORIGINS ARE MUCH OLDER. AND THERE IS ANOTHER SYMBOL THAT YOU ARE FOLLOWING. JUST AS ANCIENT.
YOU NEED TO GET TO THE POINT, J'ONN. THOSE THINGS...
"I HEAR THEM COMING..."
MY POINT, LEX, IS THAT THIS PLACE, MY PEOPLE, EVERYTHING I KNEW, IT WAS DEVOTED TO SUBLIMATING THE BAD, THE DARK, IN SERVICE OF REACHING HIGHER, BEYOND WHAT SEEMED POSSIBLE.
BUT LATELY...THE REVELATIONS I'VE UNCOVERED, ABOUT MY OWN HISTORY, MY NATURE...
ALL OF IT HAS MADE ME REALIZE THAT OUR WAYS, MY WAYS...WERE WRONG. WE NEED TO EMBRACE THE TRUTH ABOUT OURSELVES, EVEN IF IT IS PAINFUL. WE NEED THE REGRET, THE PAIN. JUST AS YOU NEED HOPE, FAITH.
BUT IF YOU CONTINUE ON YOUR PATH, IF YOU RELEASE THE ONE CALLED PERPETUA--
I'VE TOLD YOU! WE'VE DONE IT! YOU CAN'T STOP ME!
NO, I CAN'T, BUT I CAN ASK YOU TO HEAR MY SH'ANNE.

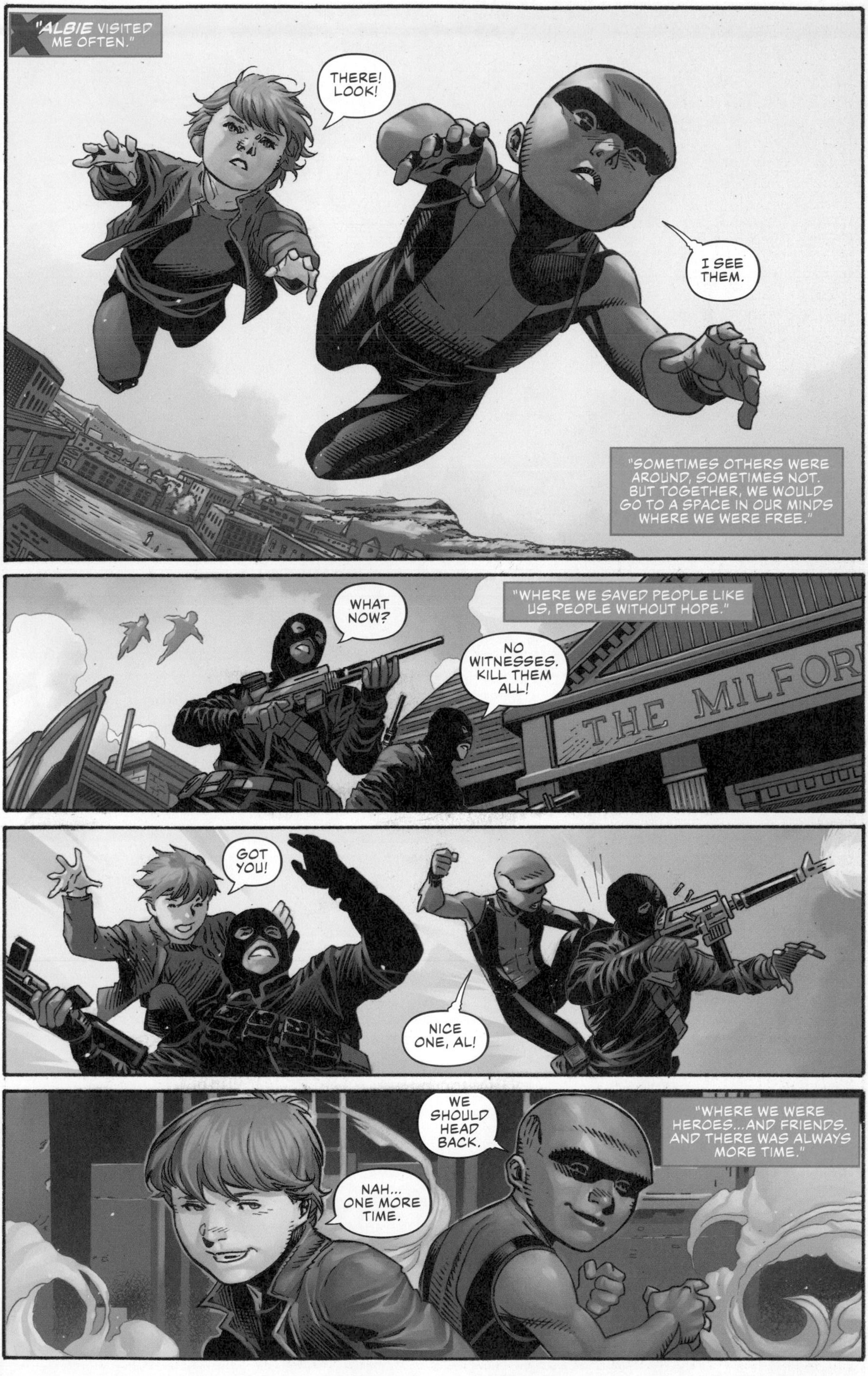
"ALBIE VISITED ME OFTEN."
THERE! LOOK!
I SEE THEM.
"SOMETIMES OTHERS WERE AROUND, SOMETIMES NOT. BUT TOGETHER, WE WOULD GO TO A SPACE IN OUR MINDS WHERE WE WERE FREE."
"WHERE WE SAVED PEOPLE LIKE US, PEOPLE WITHOUT HOPE."
WHAT NOW?
NO WITNESSES. KILL THEM ALL!
THE MILFOR
GOT YOU!
NICE ONE, AL!
"WHERE WE WERE HEROES...AND FRIENDS. AND THERE WAS ALWAYS MORE TIME."
WE SHOULD HEAD BACK.
NAH... ONE MORE TIME.

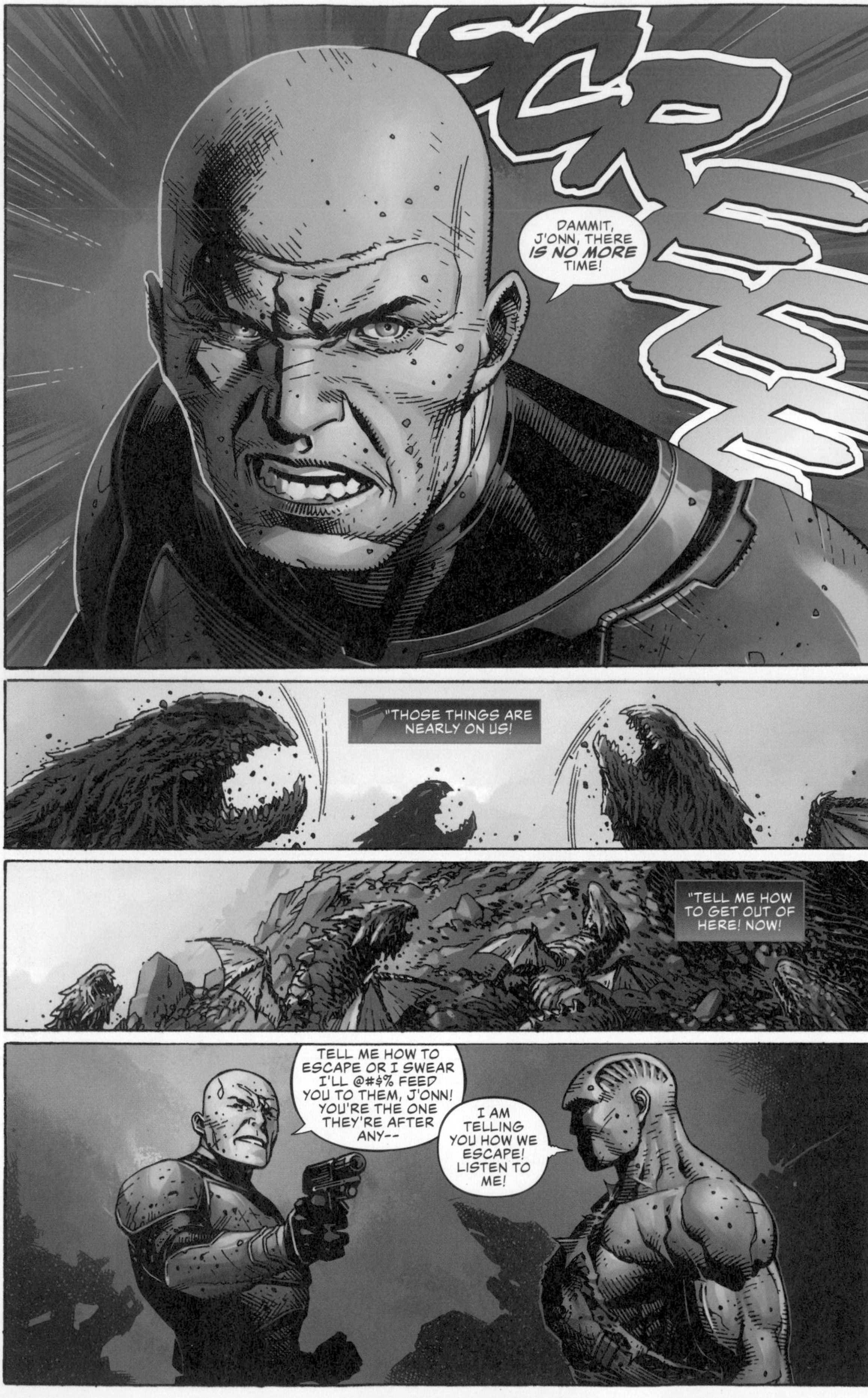
DAMMIT, J'ONN, THERE IS NO MORE TIME!
"THOSE THINGS ARE NEARLY ON US!
"TELL ME HOW TO GET OUT OF HERE! NOW!
TELL ME HOW TO ESCAPE OR I SWEAR I'LL @#$% FEED YOU TO THEM, J'ONN! YOU'RE THE ONE THEY'RE AFTER ANY--
I AM TELLING YOU HOW WE ESCAPE! LISTEN TO ME!

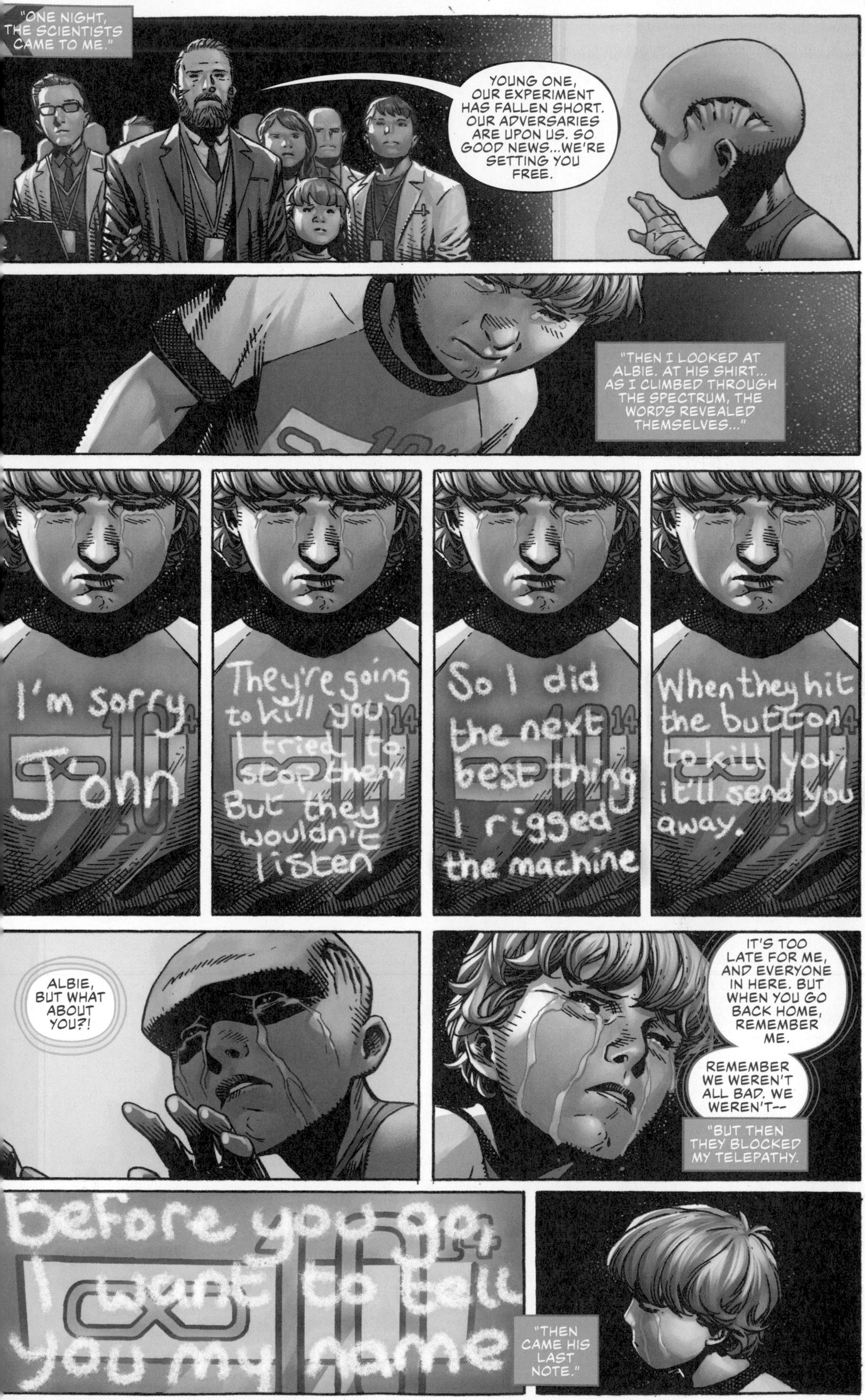
"ONE NIGHT, THE SCIENTISTS CAME TO ME."
YOUNG ONE, OUR EXPERIMENT HAS FALLEN SHORT. OUR ADVERSARIES ARE UPON US. SO GOOD NEWS...WE'RE SETTING YOU FREE.
"THEN I LOOKED AT ALBIE. AT HIS SHIRT... AS I CLIMBED THROUGH THE SPECTRUM, THE WORDS REVEALED THEMSELVES..."
I'm sorry John
They're going to kill you I tried to stop them But they wouldn't listen
So I did the next best thing I rigged the machine
When they hit the button to kill you, it'll send you away.
ALBIE, BUT WHAT ABOUT YOU?!
IT'S TOO LATE FOR ME, AND EVERYONE IN HERE. BUT WHEN YOU GO BACK HOME, REMEMBER ME.
REMEMBER WE WEREN'T ALL BAD. WE WEREN'T--
"BUT THEN THEY BLOCKED MY TELEPATHY.
before you go, I want to tell you my name
"THEN CAME HIS LAST NOTE."

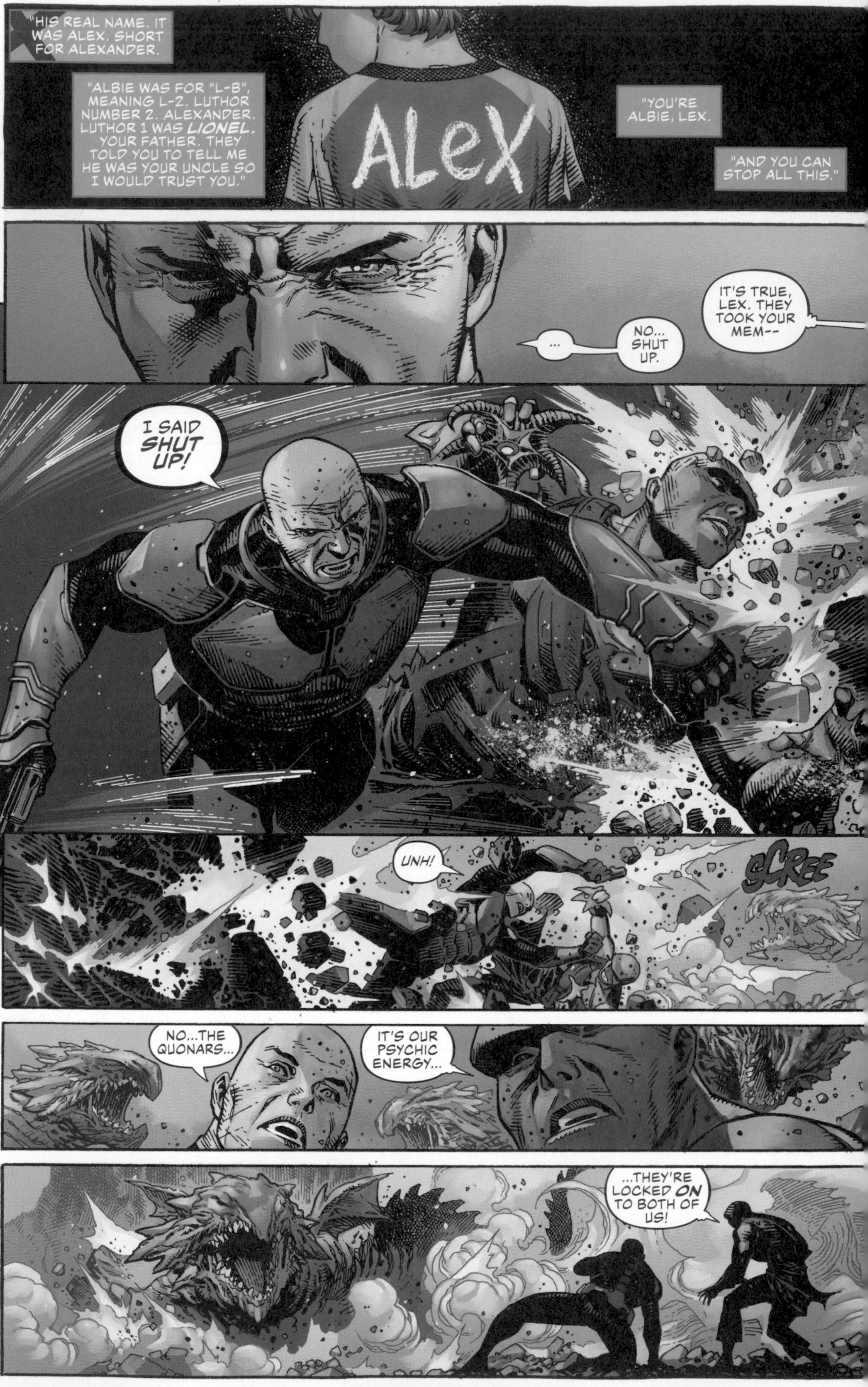
"HIS REAL NAME. IT WAS ALEX. SHORT FOR ALEXANDER.
"ALBIE WAS FOR "L-B", MEANING L-2. LUTHOR NUMBER 2. ALEXANDER. LUTHOR 1 WAS LIONEL. YOUR FATHER. THEY TOLD YOU TO TELL ME HE WAS YOUR UNCLE SO I WOULD TRUST YOU."
ALeX
"YOU'RE ALBIE, LEX.
"AND YOU CAN STOP ALL THIS."
IT'S TRUE, LEX. THEY TOOK YOUR MEM--
NO... SHUT UP.
...
I SAID SHUT UP!
UNH!
SCREE
NO...THE QUONARS...
IT'S OUR PSYCHIC ENERGY...
...THEY'RE LOCKED ON TO BOTH OF US!

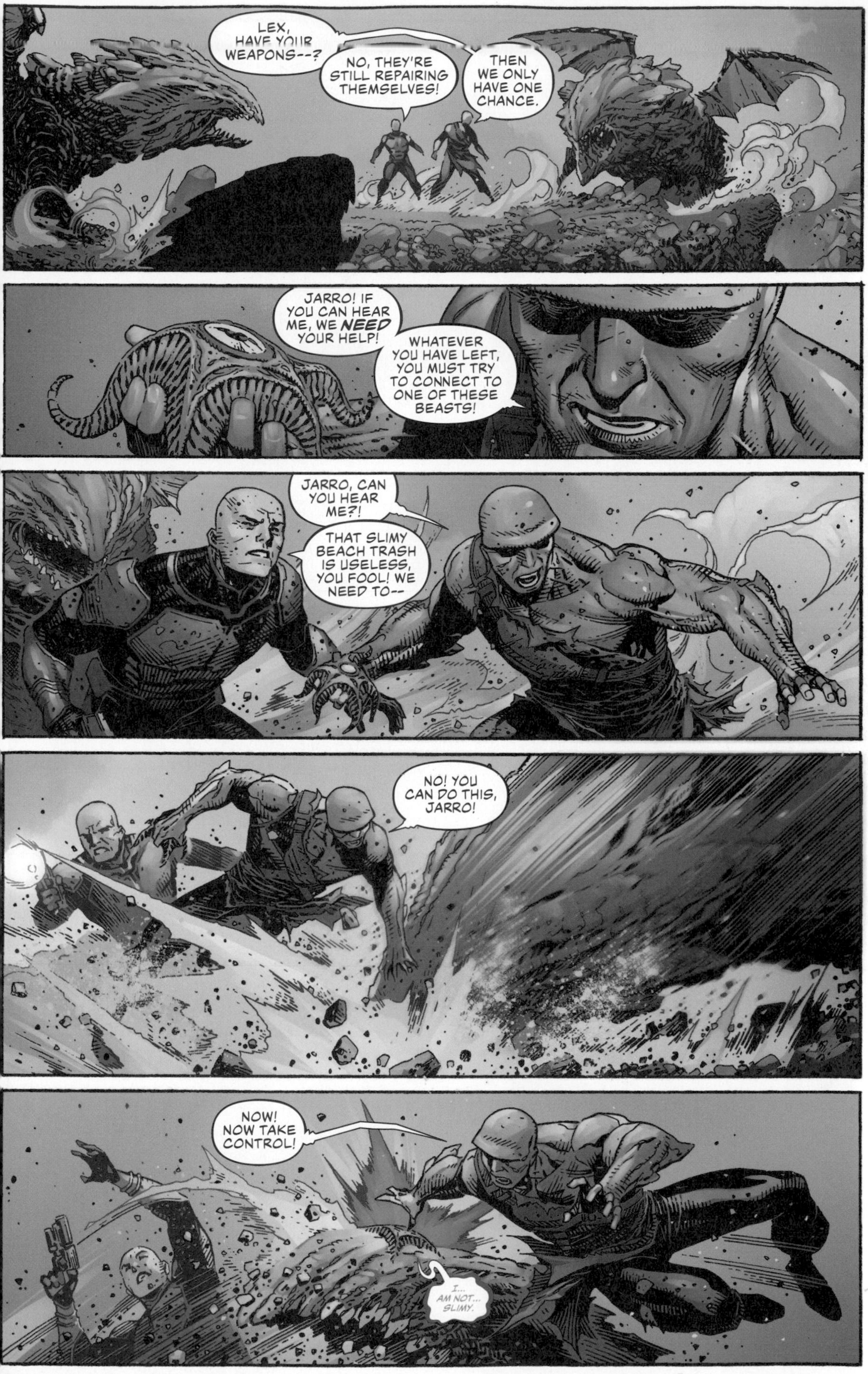
LEX, HAVE YOUR WEAPONS--?
NO, THEY'RE STILL REPAIRING THEMSELVES!
THEN WE ONLY HAVE ONE CHANCE.
JARRO! IF YOU CAN HEAR ME, WE **NEED** YOUR HELP!
WHATEVER YOU HAVE LEFT, YOU MUST TRY TO CONNECT TO ONE OF THESE BEASTS!
JARRO, CAN YOU HEAR ME?!
THAT SLIMY BEACH TRASH IS USELESS, YOU FOOL! WE NEED TO--
NO! YOU CAN DO THIS, JARRO!
NOW! NOW TAKE CONTROL!
I... AM NOT... SLIMY.

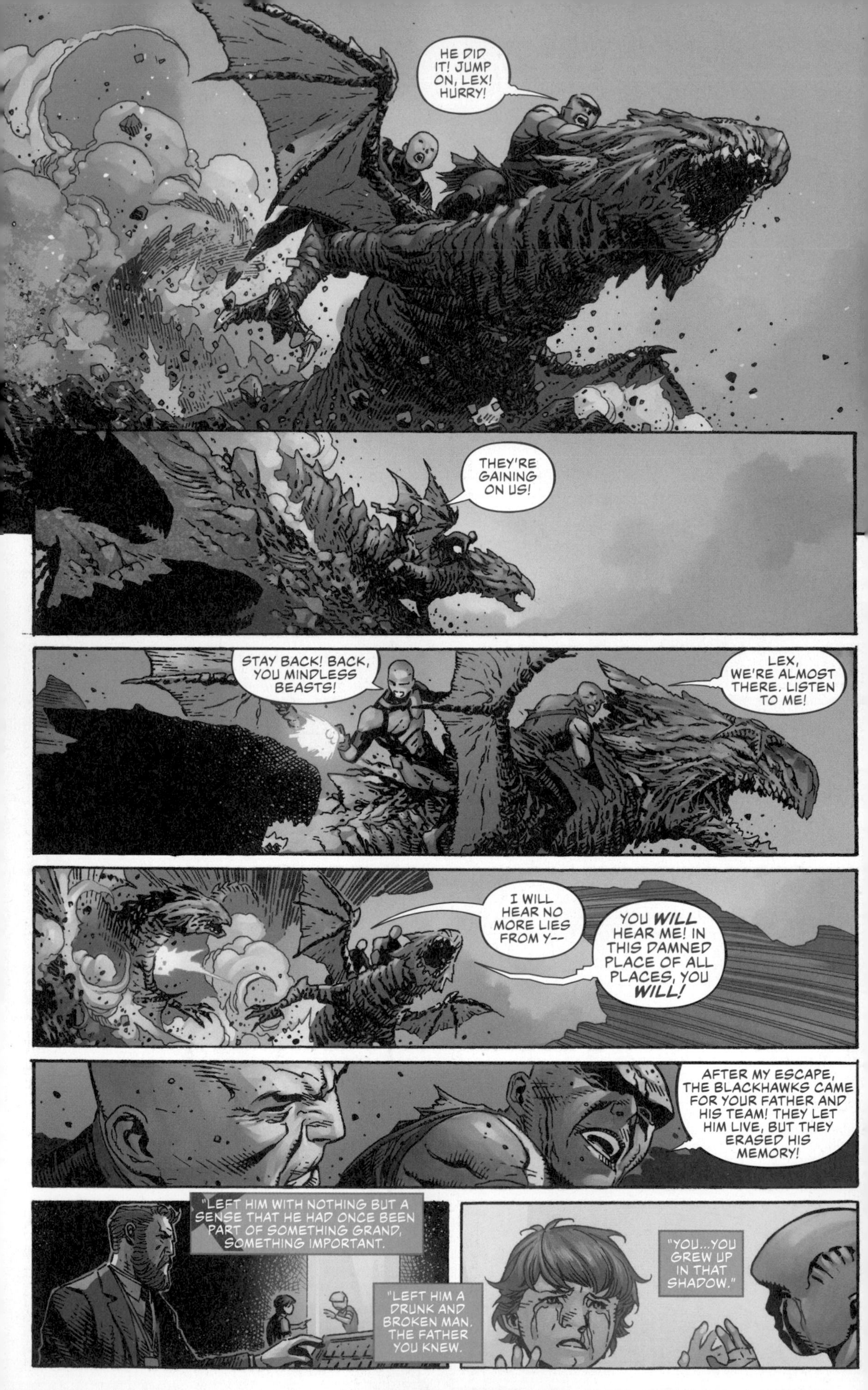
HE DID IT! JUMP ON, LEX! HURRY!
THEY'RE GAINING ON US!
STAY BACK! BACK, YOU MINDLESS BEASTS!
LEX, WE'RE ALMOST THERE. LISTEN TO ME!
I WILL HEAR NO MORE LIES FROM Y--
YOU WILL HEAR ME! IN THIS DAMNED PLACE OF ALL PLACES, YOU WILL!
AFTER MY ESCAPE, THE BLACKHAWKS CAME FOR YOUR FATHER AND HIS TEAM! THEY LET HIM LIVE, BUT THEY ERASED HIS MEMORY!
"LEFT HIM WITH NOTHING BUT A SENSE THAT HE HAD ONCE BEEN PART OF SOMETHING GRAND, SOMETHING IMPORTANT.
"LEFT HIM A DRUNK AND BROKEN MAN. THE FATHER YOU KNEW.
"YOU...YOU GREW UP IN THAT SHADOW."

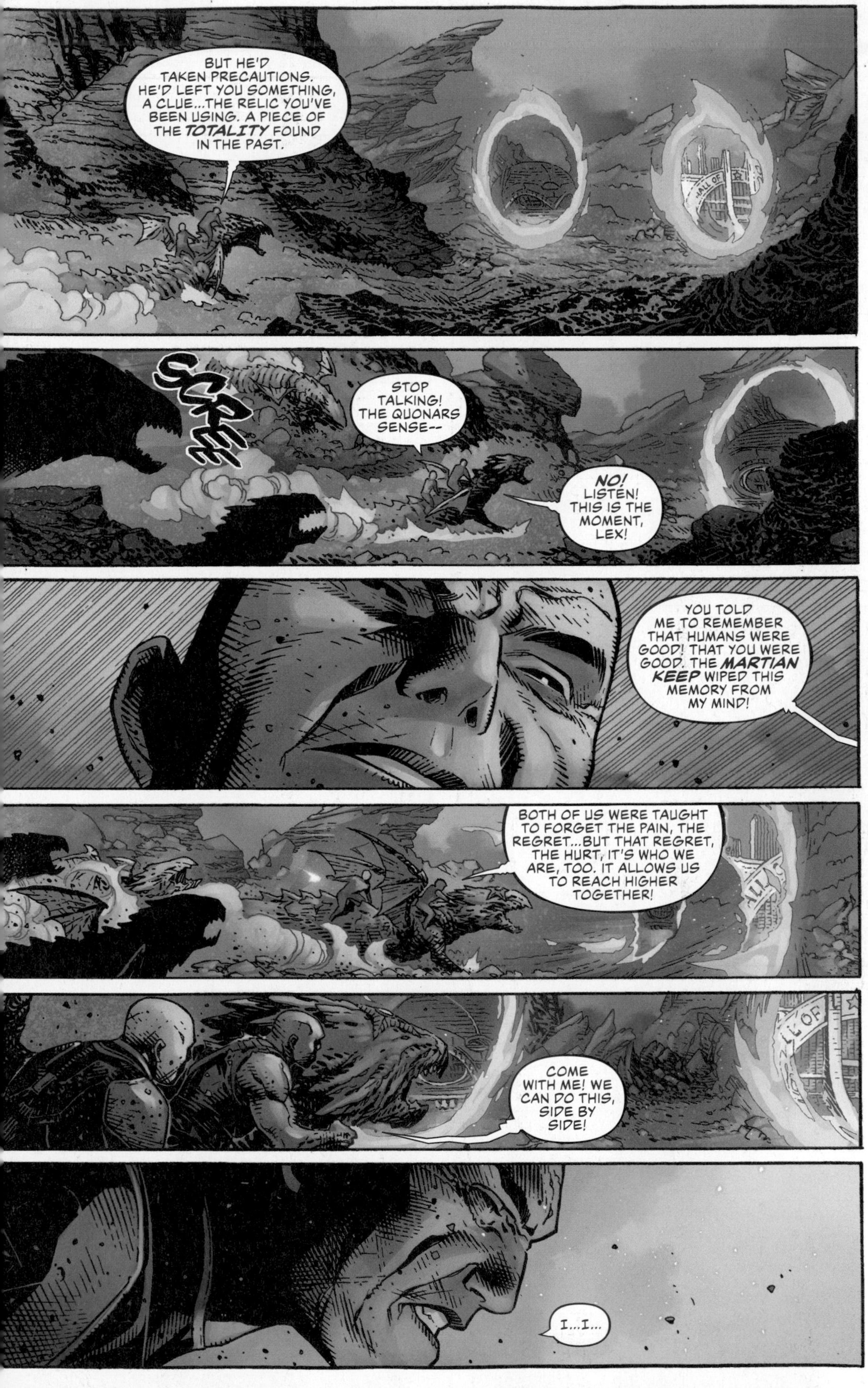
BUT HE'D TAKEN PRECAUTIONS. HE'D LEFT YOU SOMETHING, A CLUE...THE RELIC YOU'VE BEEN USING. A PIECE OF THE *TOTALITY* FOUND IN THE PAST.
SCREE
STOP TALKING! THE QUONARS SENSE--
NO! LISTEN! THIS IS THE MOMENT, LEX!
YOU TOLD ME TO REMEMBER THAT HUMANS WERE GOOD! THAT YOU WERE GOOD. THE *MARTIAN KEEP* WIPED THIS MEMORY FROM MY MIND!
BOTH OF US WERE TAUGHT TO FORGET THE PAIN, THE REGRET...BUT THAT REGRET, THE HURT, IT'S WHO WE ARE, TOO. IT ALLOWS US TO REACH HIGHER TOGETHER!
COME WITH ME! WE CAN DO THIS, SIDE BY SIDE!
I...I...

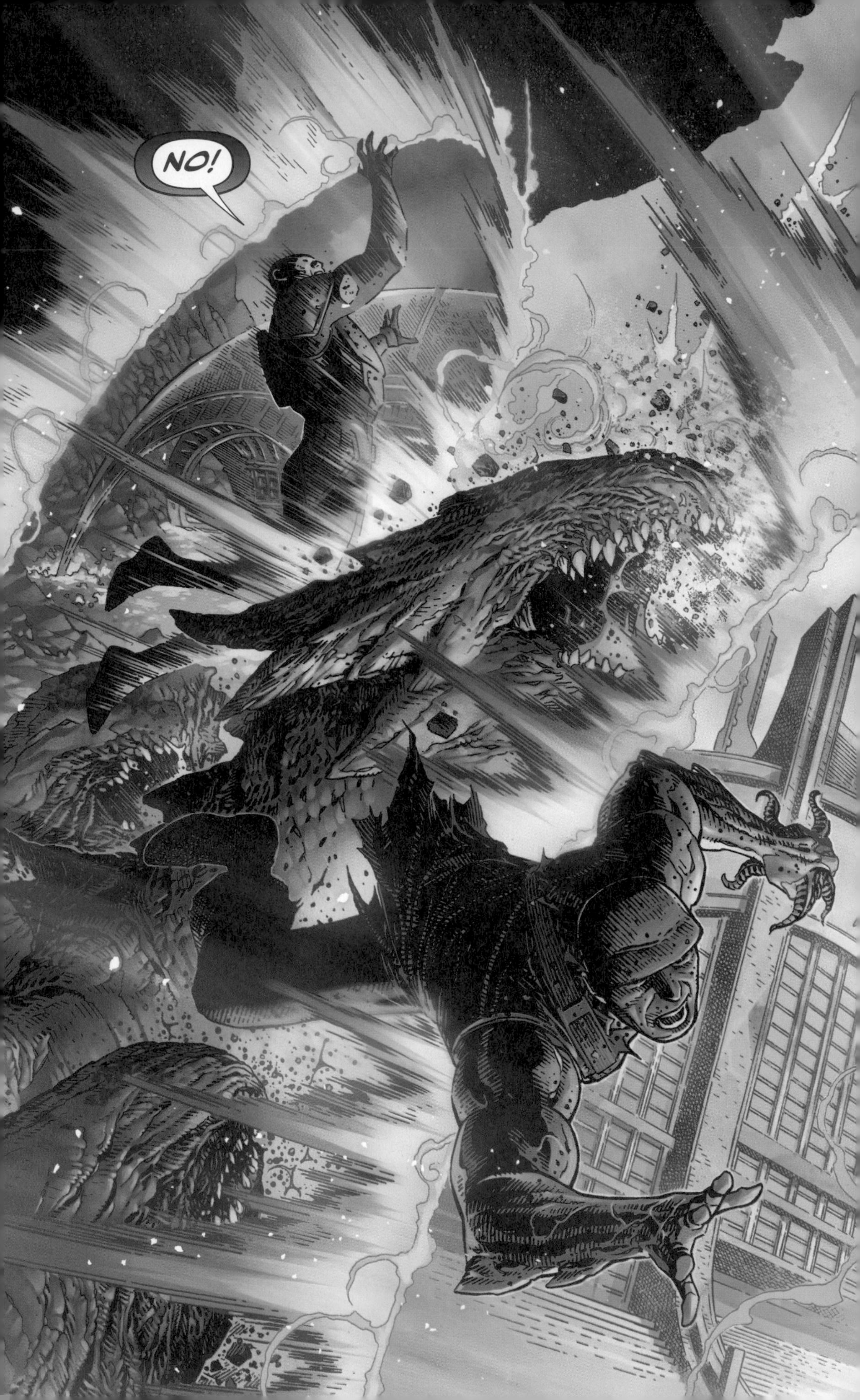
NO!

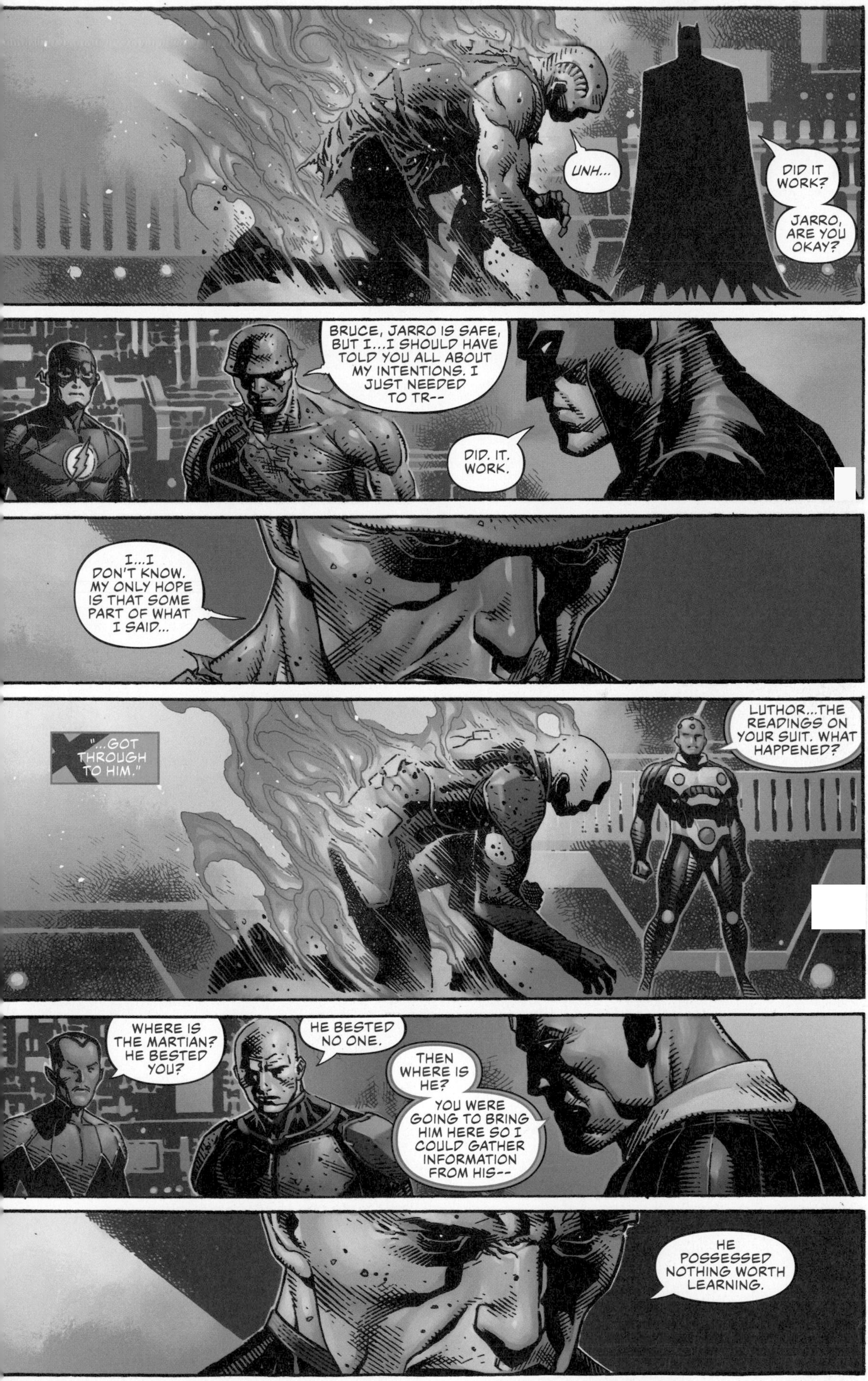
UNH...
DID IT WORK?
JARRO, ARE YOU OKAY?
BRUCE, JARRO IS SAFE, BUT I...I SHOULD HAVE TOLD YOU ALL ABOUT MY INTENTIONS. I JUST NEEDED TO TR--
DID. IT. WORK.
I...I DON'T KNOW. MY ONLY HOPE IS THAT SOME PART OF WHAT I SAID...
"...GOT THROUGH TO HIM."
LUTHOR...THE READINGS ON YOUR SUIT. WHAT HAPPENED?
WHERE IS THE MARTIAN? HE BESTED YOU?
HE BESTED NO ONE.
THEN WHERE IS HE?
YOU WERE GOING TO BRING HIM HERE SO I COULD GATHER INFORMATION FROM HIS--
HE POSSESSED NOTHING WORTH LEARNING.

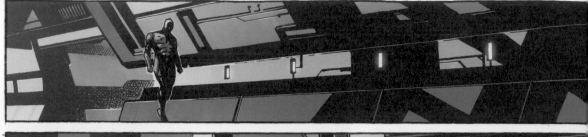

SH'ANNE...
SH'ANNE...

OLD FRONTIE

SCOTT SNYDER STORY
JIM CHEUNG PENCILS
CHEUNG WITH MARK MORALES AN
WALDEN WONG INKS
TOMEU MOREY COLORS
TOM NAPOLITANO LETTERS
CHEUNG AND
ROMULO FAJARDO JR. COVER
ANDREW MARINO ASSISTANT EDITO
MARIE JAVINS EDITOR

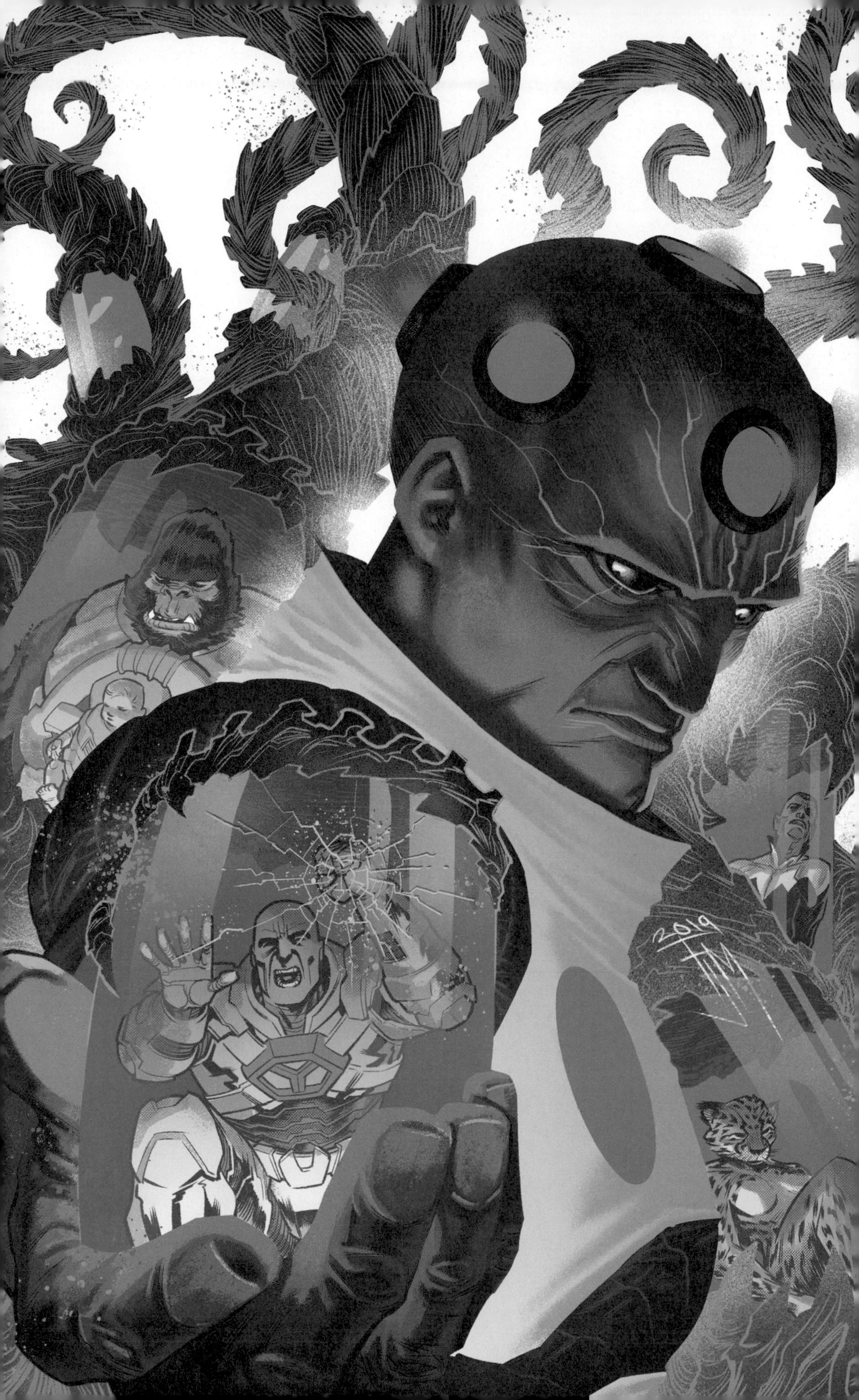
2019

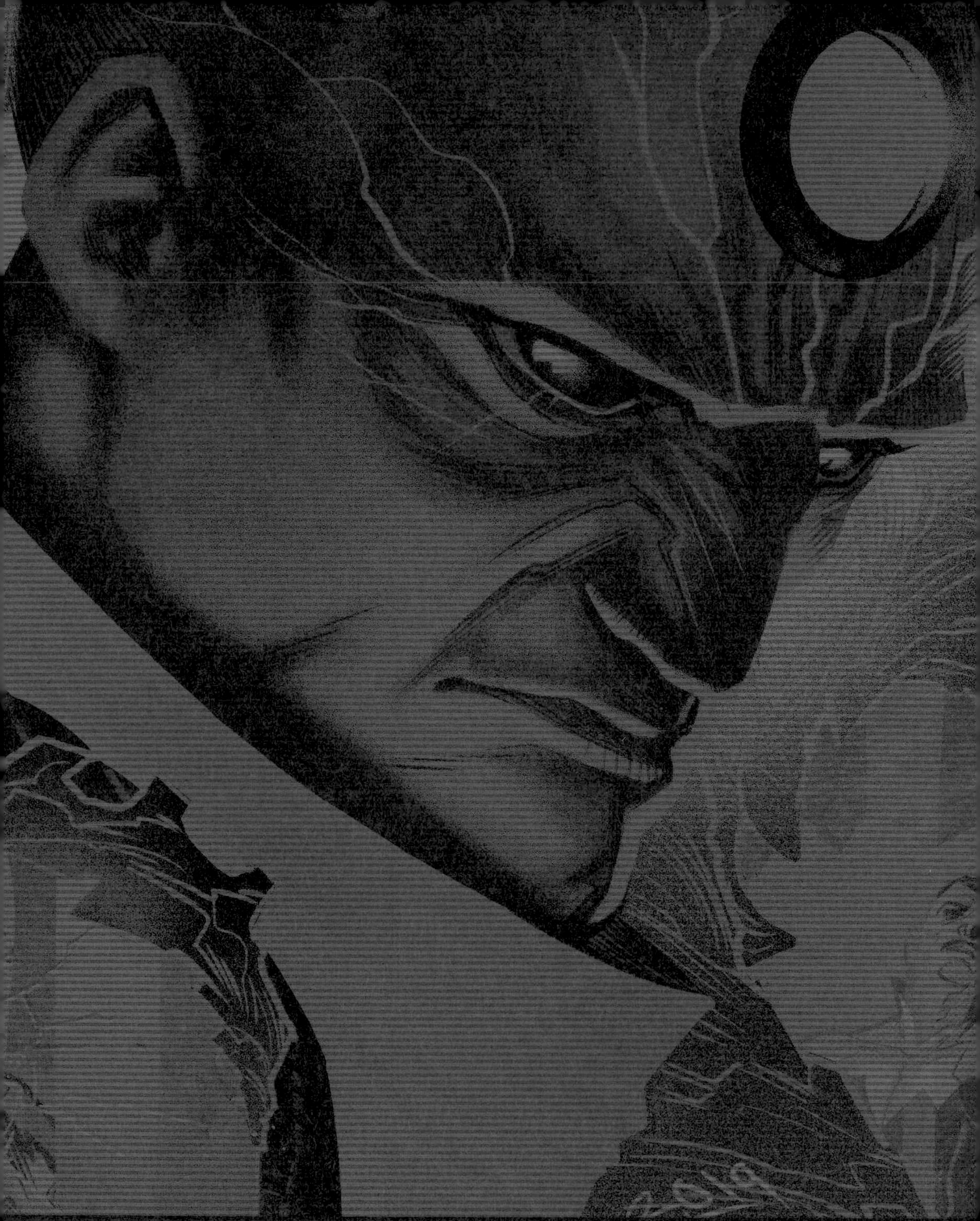

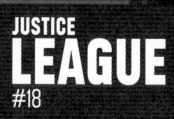

JUSTICE
LEAGUE
#18

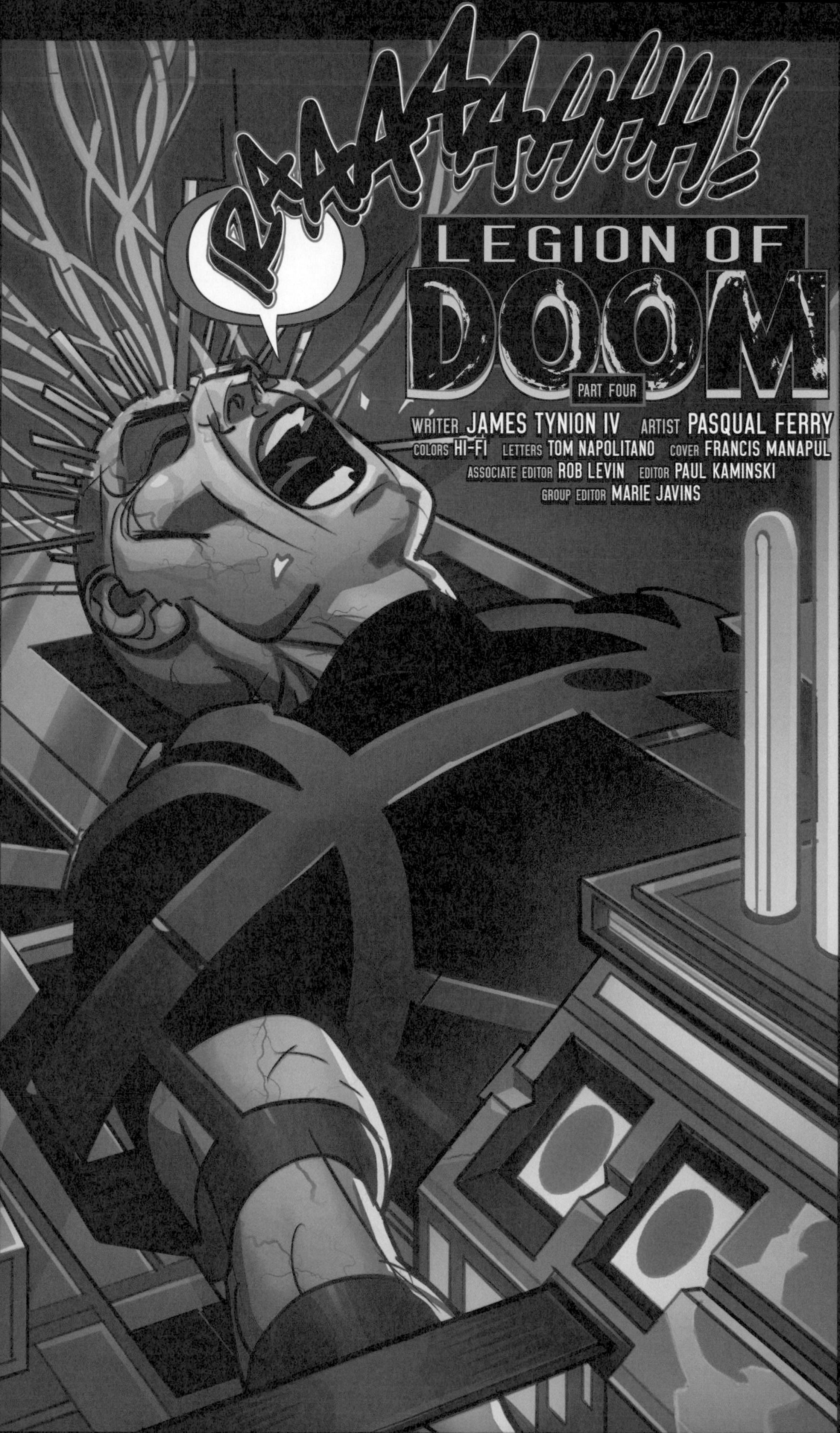
RAAAAAHH!
LEGION OF DOOM
PART FOUR
WRITER JAMES TYNION IV ARTIST PASQUAL FERRY
COLORS HI-FI LETTERS TOM NAPOLITANO COVER FRANCIS MANAPUL
ASSOCIATE EDITOR ROB LEVIN EDITOR PAUL KAMINSKI
GROUP EDITOR MARIE JAVINS

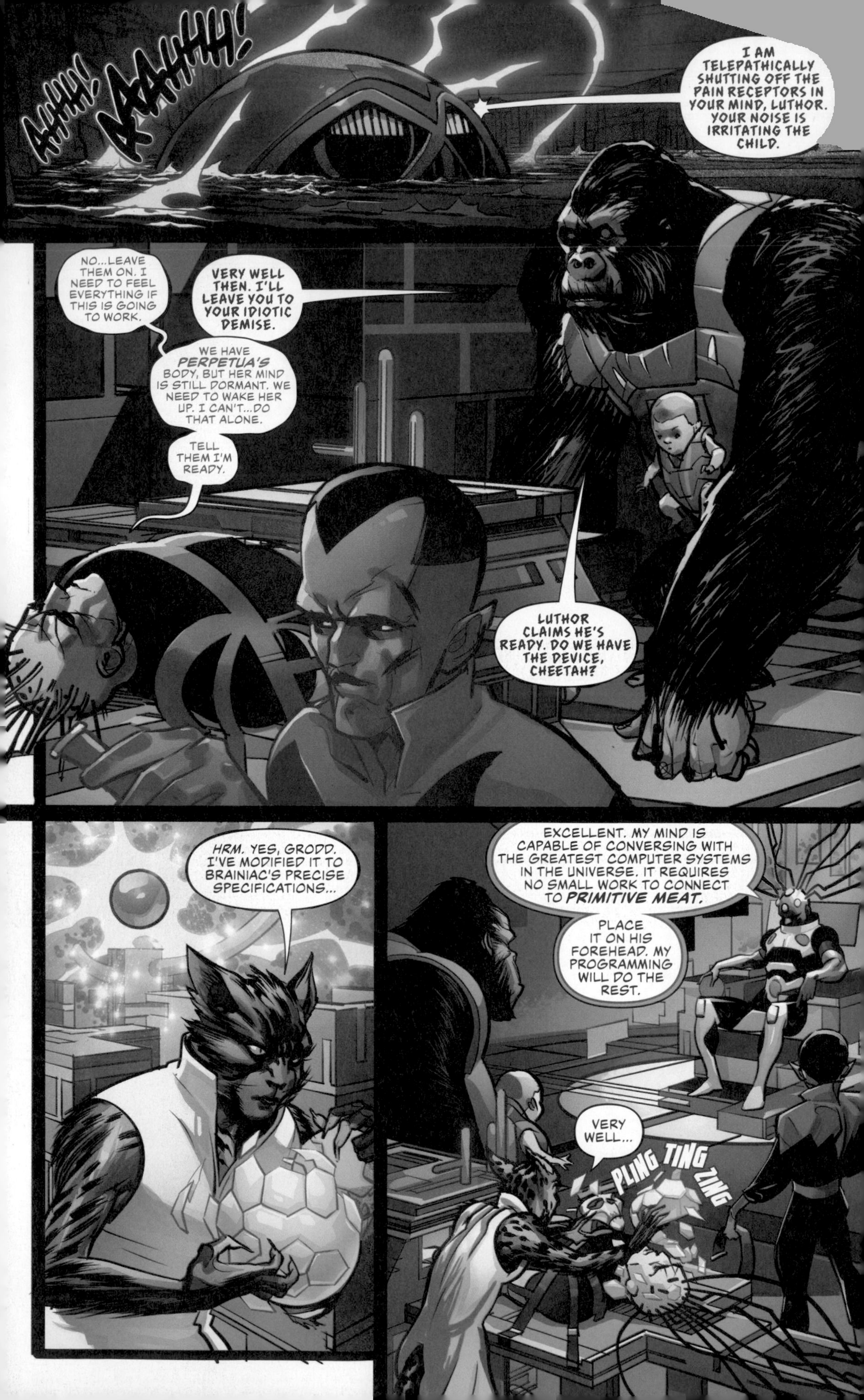
AHHH! AAAHHH!
I AM TELEPATHICALLY SHUTTING OFF THE PAIN RECEPTORS IN YOUR MIND, LUTHOR. YOUR NOISE IS IRRITATING THE CHILD.
NO...LEAVE THEM ON. I NEED TO FEEL EVERYTHING IF THIS IS GOING TO WORK.
VERY WELL THEN. I'LL LEAVE YOU TO YOUR IDIOTIC DEMISE.
WE HAVE PERPETUA'S BODY, BUT HER MIND IS STILL DORMANT. WE NEED TO WAKE HER UP. I CAN'T...DO THAT ALONE.
TELL THEM I'M READY.
LUTHOR CLAIMS HE'S READY. DO WE HAVE THE DEVICE, CHEETAH?
HRM. YES, GRODD. I'VE MODIFIED IT TO BRAINIAC'S PRECISE SPECIFICATIONS...
EXCELLENT. MY MIND IS CAPABLE OF CONVERSING WITH THE GREATEST COMPUTER SYSTEMS IN THE UNIVERSE. IT REQUIRES NO SMALL WORK TO CONNECT TO PRIMITIVE MEAT.
PLACE IT ON HIS FOREHEAD. MY PROGRAMMING WILL DO THE REST.
VERY WELL...
PLING TING ZING

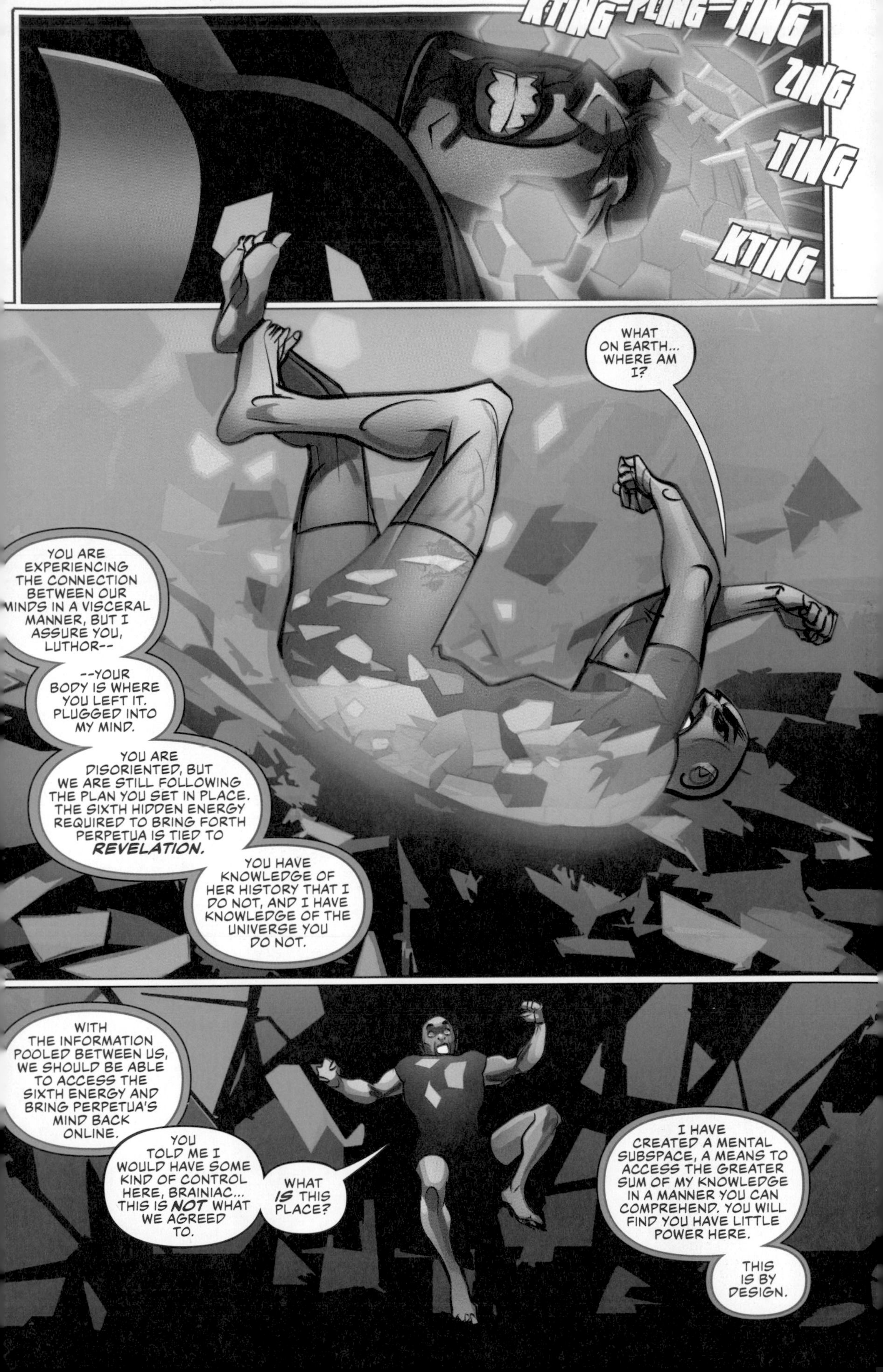
KTING-PLING-TING
ZING
TING
KTING
WHAT ON EARTH... WHERE AM I?
YOU ARE EXPERIENCING THE CONNECTION BETWEEN OUR MINDS IN A VISCERAL MANNER, BUT I ASSURE YOU, LUTHOR--
--YOUR BODY IS WHERE YOU LEFT IT. PLUGGED INTO MY MIND.
YOU ARE DISORIENTED, BUT WE ARE STILL FOLLOWING THE PLAN YOU SET IN PLACE. THE SIXTH HIDDEN ENERGY REQUIRED TO BRING FORTH PERPETUA IS TIED TO REVELATION.
YOU HAVE KNOWLEDGE OF HER HISTORY THAT I DO NOT, AND I HAVE KNOWLEDGE OF THE UNIVERSE YOU DO NOT.
WITH THE INFORMATION POOLED BETWEEN US, WE SHOULD BE ABLE TO ACCESS THE SIXTH ENERGY AND BRING PERPETUA'S MIND BACK ONLINE.
YOU TOLD ME I WOULD HAVE SOME KIND OF CONTROL HERE, BRAINIAC... THIS IS NOT WHAT WE AGREED TO.
WHAT IS THIS PLACE?
I HAVE CREATED A MENTAL SUBSPACE, A MEANS TO ACCESS THE GREATER SUM OF MY KNOWLEDGE IN A MANNER YOU CAN COMPREHEND. YOU WILL FIND YOU HAVE LITTLE POWER HERE.
THIS IS BY DESIGN.

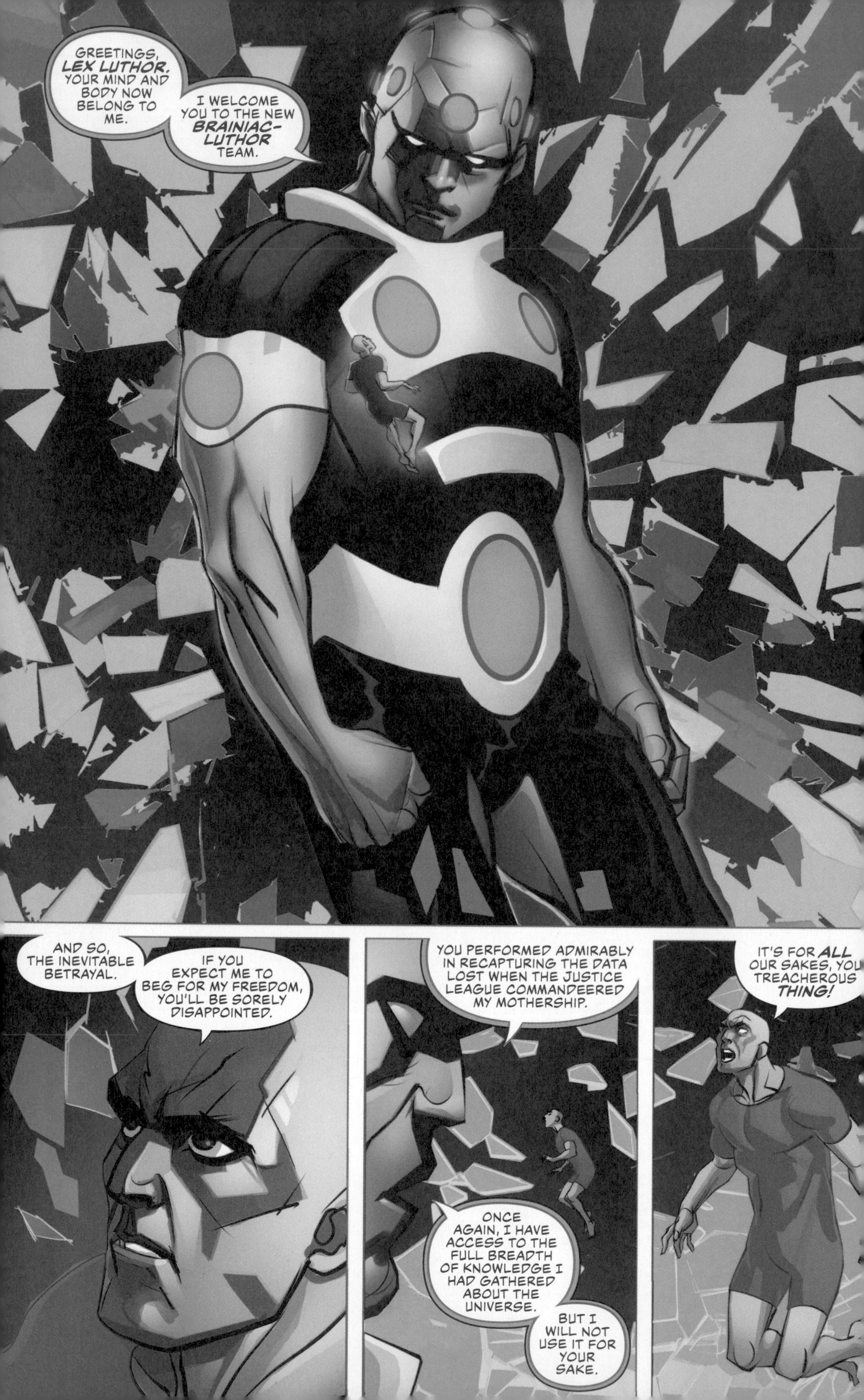
GREETINGS, LEX LUTHOR. YOUR MIND AND BODY NOW BELONG TO ME.
I WELCOME YOU TO THE NEW BRAINIAC-LUTHOR TEAM.
AND SO, THE INEVITABLE BETRAYAL.
IF YOU EXPECT ME TO BEG FOR MY FREEDOM, YOU'LL BE SORELY DISAPPOINTED.
YOU PERFORMED ADMIRABLY IN RECAPTURING THE DATA LOST WHEN THE JUSTICE LEAGUE COMMANDEERED MY MOTHERSHIP.
ONCE AGAIN, I HAVE ACCESS TO THE FULL BREADTH OF KNOWLEDGE I HAD GATHERED ABOUT THE UNIVERSE.
BUT I WILL NOT USE IT FOR YOUR SAKE.
IT'S FOR ALL OUR SAKES, YOU TREACHEROUS THING!

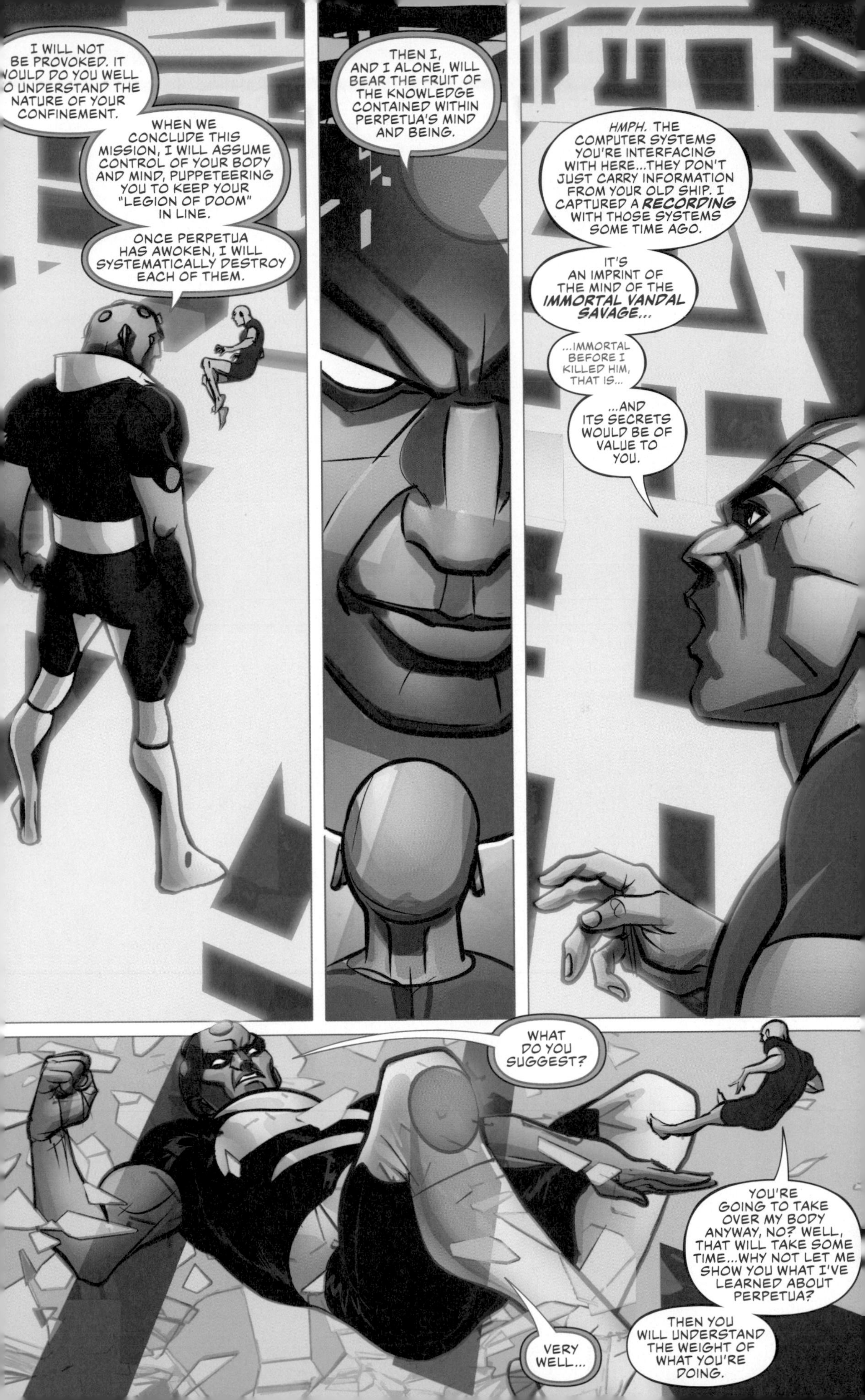
I WILL NOT BE PROVOKED. IT WOULD DO YOU WELL TO UNDERSTAND THE NATURE OF YOUR CONFINEMENT.
WHEN WE CONCLUDE THIS MISSION, I WILL ASSUME CONTROL OF YOUR BODY AND MIND, PUPPETEERING YOU TO KEEP YOUR "LEGION OF DOOM" IN LINE.
ONCE PERPETUA HAS AWOKEN, I WILL SYSTEMATICALLY DESTROY EACH OF THEM.
THEN I, AND I ALONE, WILL BEAR THE FRUIT OF THE KNOWLEDGE CONTAINED WITHIN PERPETUA'S MIND AND BEING.
HMPH. THE COMPUTER SYSTEMS YOU'RE INTERFACING WITH HERE...THEY DON'T JUST CARRY INFORMATION FROM YOUR OLD SHIP. I CAPTURED A ***RECORDING*** WITH THOSE SYSTEMS SOME TIME AGO.
IT'S AN IMPRINT OF THE MIND OF THE ***IMMORTAL VANDAL SAVAGE...***
...IMMORTAL BEFORE I KILLED HIM, THAT IS...
...AND ITS SECRETS WOULD BE OF VALUE TO YOU.
WHAT DO YOU SUGGEST?
YOU'RE GOING TO TAKE OVER MY BODY ANYWAY, NO? WELL, THAT WILL TAKE SOME TIME...WHY NOT LET ME SHOW YOU WHAT I'VE LEARNED ABOUT PERPETUA?
THEN YOU WILL UNDERSTAND THE WEIGHT OF WHAT YOU'RE DOING.
VERY WELL...

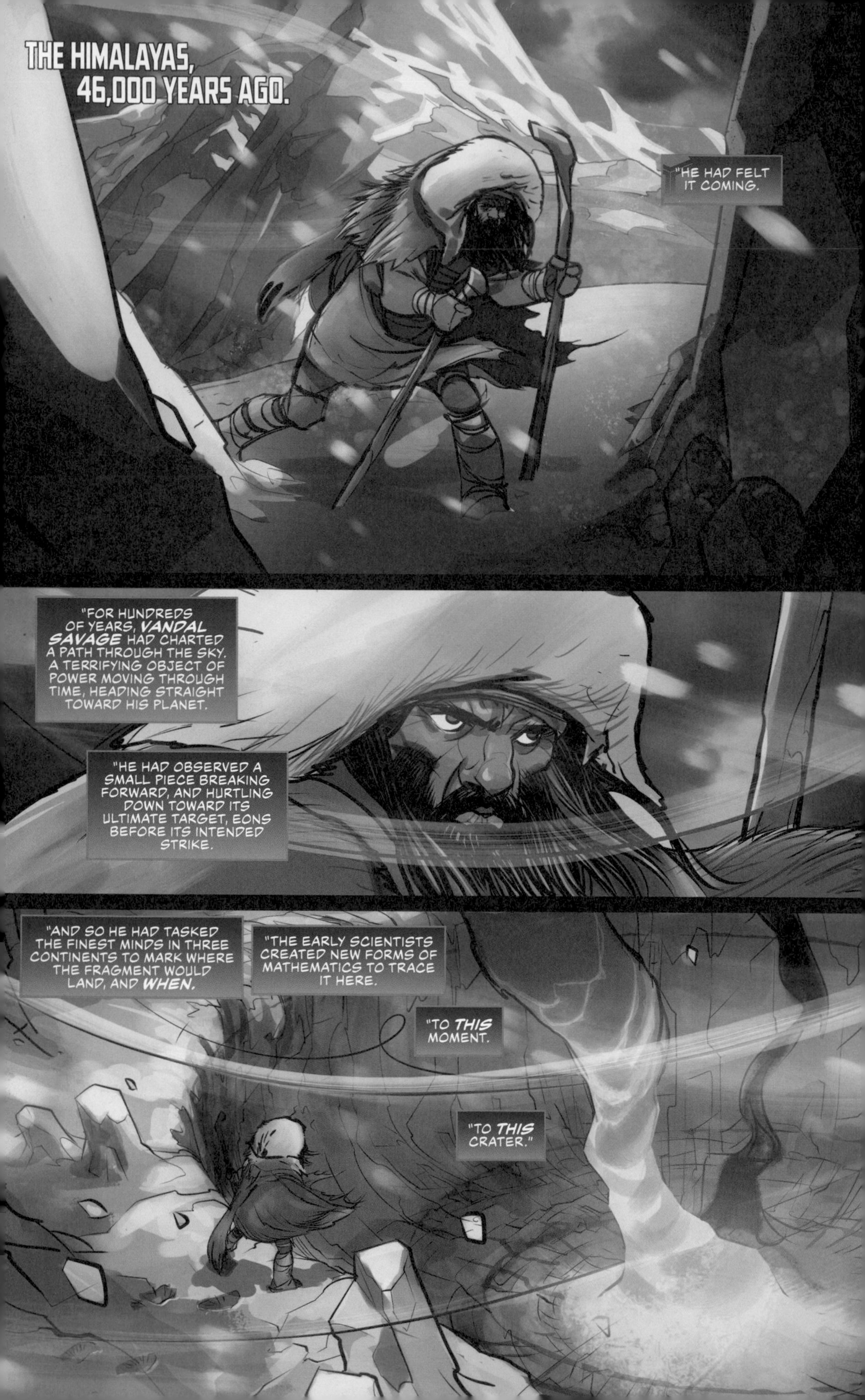

THE HIMALAYAS, 46,000 YEARS AGO.
"HE HAD FELT IT COMING.
"FOR HUNDREDS OF YEARS, VANDAL SAVAGE HAD CHARTED A PATH THROUGH THE SKY. A TERRIFYING OBJECT OF POWER MOVING THROUGH TIME, HEADING STRAIGHT TOWARD HIS PLANET.
"HE HAD OBSERVED A SMALL PIECE BREAKING FORWARD, AND HURTLING DOWN TOWARD ITS ULTIMATE TARGET, EONS BEFORE ITS INTENDED STRIKE.
"AND SO HE HAD TASKED THE FINEST MINDS IN THREE CONTINENTS TO MARK WHERE THE FRAGMENT WOULD LAND, AND WHEN.
"THE EARLY SCIENTISTS CREATED NEW FORMS OF MATHEMATICS TO TRACE IT HERE.
"TO THIS MOMENT.
"TO THIS CRATER."

"HE REMEMBERED THE COMET THAT TRANSFORMED HIM-- MANY, MANY YEARS EARLIER-- THAT MARKED HIS CHANGE FROM A CAVE-DWELLING PRIMITIVE TO AN IMMORTAL CONQUEROR.

"THAT COMET HAD POWER, BUT THIS HAD MORE. THIS WAS PART OF A *BIGGER* STORY, AND HE KNEW IT.

"HE COULD FEEL SOMETHING WITHIN THE FRAGMENT *HIDDEN* FROM HIM. HERALDING THE COMING OF A GREAT POWER.

"AND SO, VANDAL *KNEW* HE MUST UNCOVER THE TRUTH OF THIS STRANGE METAL, BEFORE IT WAS TOO LATE."

AN EARLY FRAGMENT OF THE TOTALITY STRIKING BEFORE THE DAWN OF HUMAN CIVILIZATION. I SUSPECT THIS OCCURRED ON MANY WORLDS, IN MANY TIMES.

PERHAPS.

BUT IN HOW MANY OF THOSE WORLDS DID A SINGLE MAN COVET ITS POWER SO COMPLETELY?

HE SLAUGHTERED THE WISE MEN WHO HELPED HIM FIND IT HERE.

JUST IMAGINE IF HUMANITY HAD *ALGEBRA* MILLENNIA BEFORE THE RISE OF ITS FIRST TRUE CITY. WHERE WE WOULD BE TODAY...

INSTEAD, ONE MAN HELD THE GREATEST SECRET IN THE UNIVERSE IN HIS HANDS--AND *KEPT IT TO HIMSELF.*

WHAT DOES THIS PROVE? WHAT IS THE IMPORTANCE OF A DEAD CAVEMAN?

COME NOW, BRAINIAC. IT'S NOT THE STORY OF THE *MAN.*

THIS IS THE STORY OF THE HUNK OF METAL THAT COULD OPEN THE DOOR TO PERPETUA.

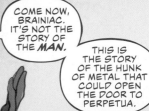

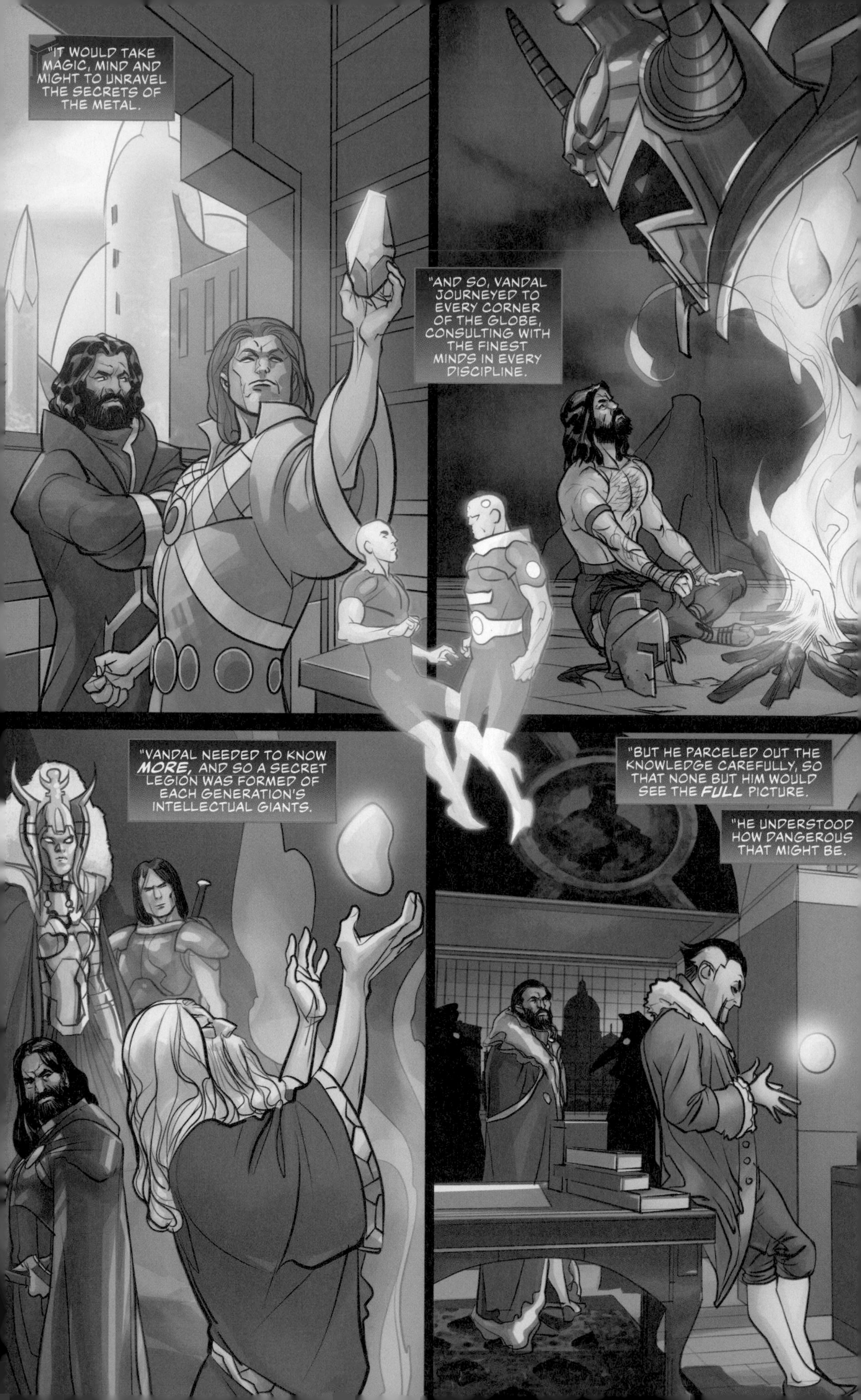
"IT WOULD TAKE MAGIC, MIND AND MIGHT TO UNRAVEL THE SECRETS OF THE METAL.
"AND SO, VANDAL JOURNEYED TO EVERY CORNER OF THE GLOBE, CONSULTING WITH THE FINEST MINDS IN EVERY DISCIPLINE.
"VANDAL NEEDED TO KNOW MORE, AND SO A SECRET LEGION WAS FORMED OF EACH GENERATION'S INTELLECTUAL GIANTS.
"BUT HE PARCELED OUT THE KNOWLEDGE CAREFULLY, SO THAT NONE BUT HIM WOULD SEE THE FULL PICTURE.
"HE UNDERSTOOD HOW DANGEROUS THAT MIGHT BE.

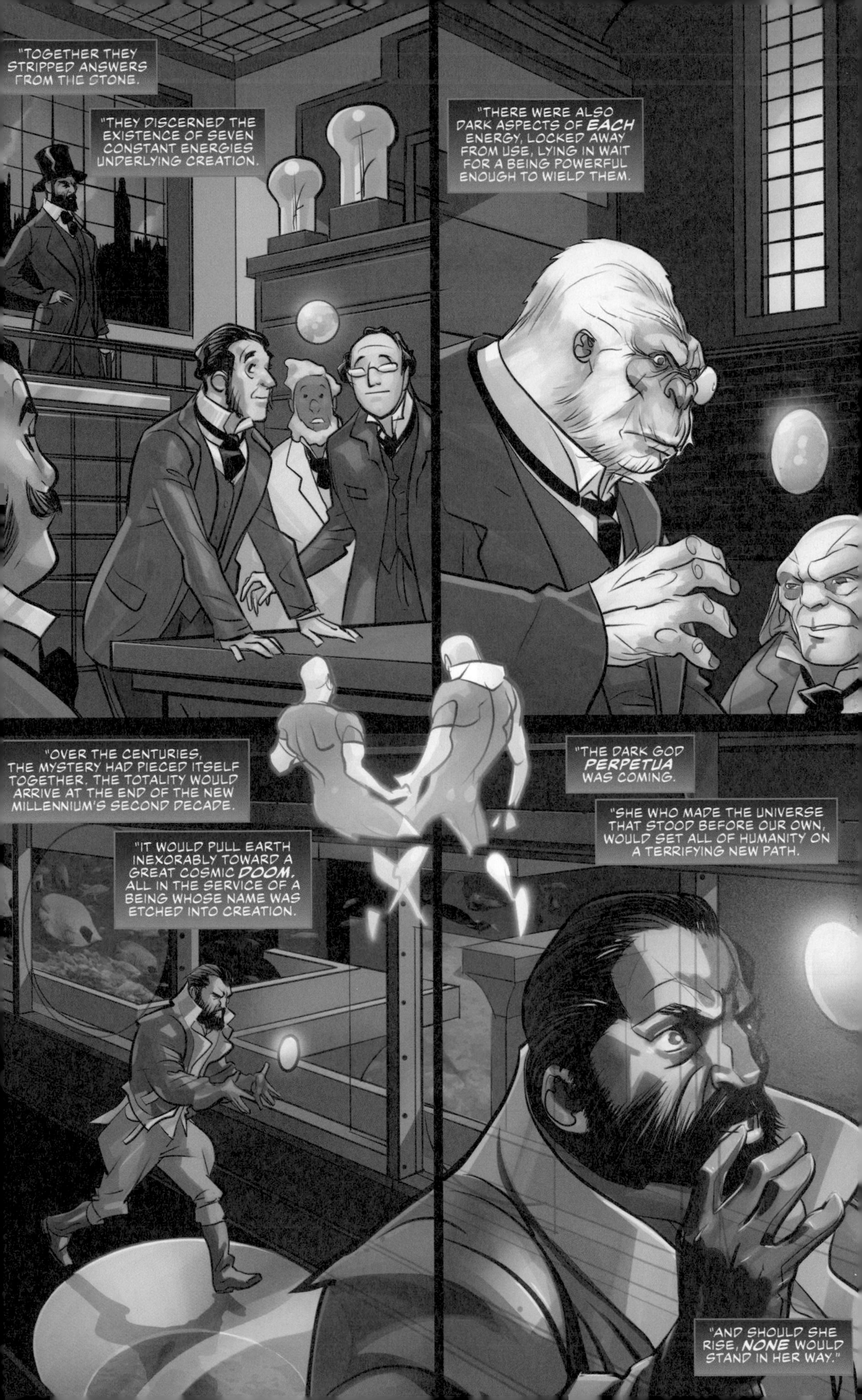
"TOGETHER THEY STRIPPED ANSWERS FROM THE STONE.
"THEY DISCERNED THE EXISTENCE OF SEVEN CONSTANT ENERGIES UNDERLYING CREATION.
"THERE WERE ALSO DARK ASPECTS OF EACH ENERGY, LOCKED AWAY FROM USE, LYING IN WAIT FOR A BEING POWERFUL ENOUGH TO WIELD THEM.
"OVER THE CENTURIES, THE MYSTERY HAD PIECED ITSELF TOGETHER. THE TOTALITY WOULD ARRIVE AT THE END OF THE NEW MILLENNIUM'S SECOND DECADE.
"IT WOULD PULL EARTH INEXORABLY TOWARD A GREAT COSMIC DOOM, ALL IN THE SERVICE OF A BEING WHOSE NAME WAS ETCHED INTO CREATION.
"THE DARK GOD PERPETUA WAS COMING.
"SHE WHO MADE THE UNIVERSE THAT STOOD BEFORE OUR OWN, WOULD SET ALL OF HUMANITY ON A TERRIFYING NEW PATH.
"AND SHOULD SHE RISE, NONE WOULD STAND IN HER WAY."

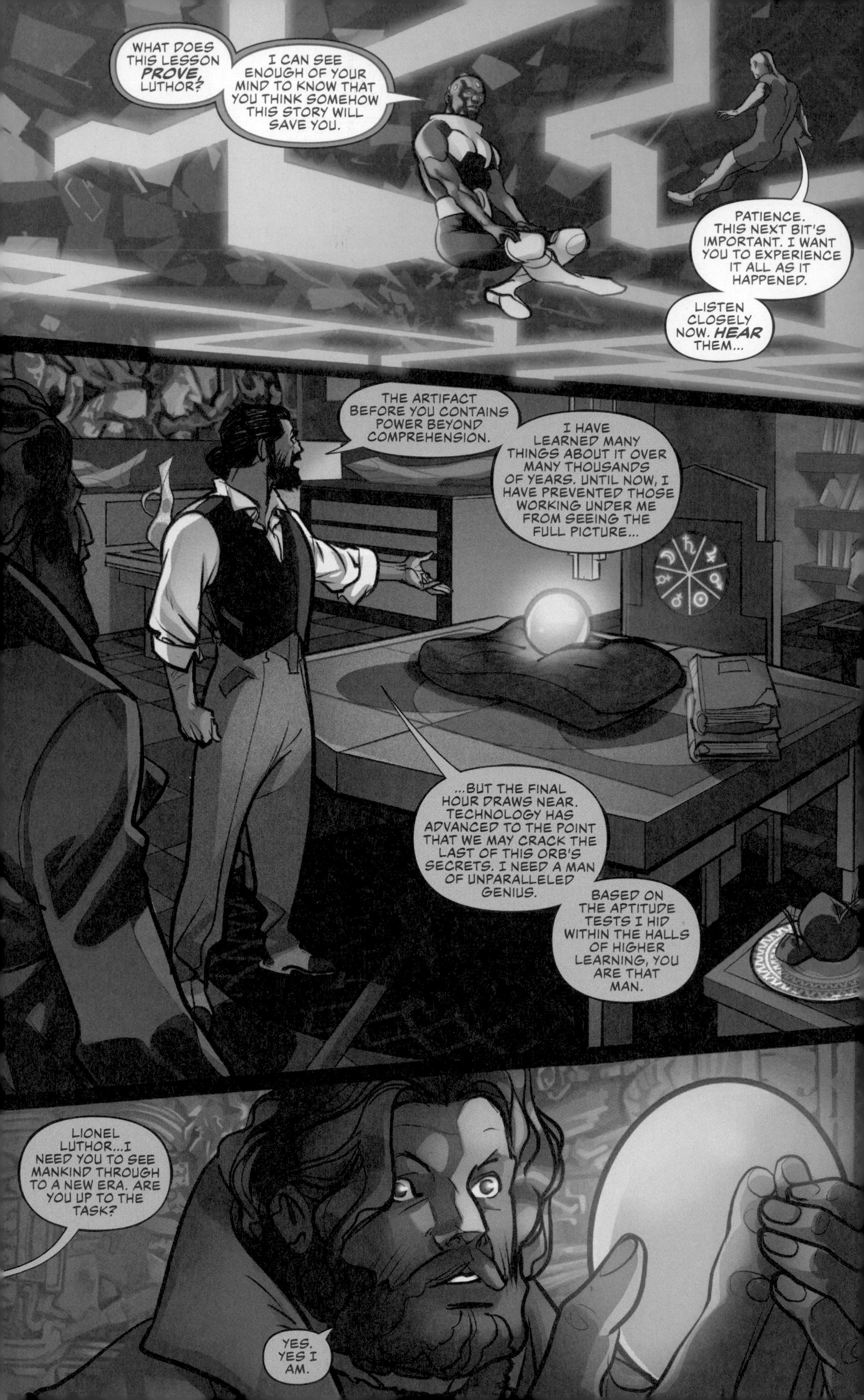
WHAT DOES THIS LESSON PROVE, LUTHOR?
I CAN SEE ENOUGH OF YOUR MIND TO KNOW THAT YOU THINK SOMEHOW THIS STORY WILL SAVE YOU.
PATIENCE. THIS NEXT BIT'S IMPORTANT. I WANT YOU TO EXPERIENCE IT ALL AS IT HAPPENED.
LISTEN CLOSELY NOW. HEAR THEM...
THE ARTIFACT BEFORE YOU CONTAINS POWER BEYOND COMPREHENSION.
I HAVE LEARNED MANY THINGS ABOUT IT OVER MANY THOUSANDS OF YEARS. UNTIL NOW, I HAVE PREVENTED THOSE WORKING UNDER ME FROM SEEING THE FULL PICTURE...
...BUT THE FINAL HOUR DRAWS NEAR. TECHNOLOGY HAS ADVANCED TO THE POINT THAT WE MAY CRACK THE LAST OF THIS ORB'S SECRETS. I NEED A MAN OF UNPARALLELED GENIUS.
BASED ON THE APTITUDE TESTS I HID WITHIN THE HALLS OF HIGHER LEARNING, YOU ARE THAT MAN.
LIONEL LUTHOR...I NEED YOU TO SEE MANKIND THROUGH TO A NEW ERA. ARE YOU UP TO THE TASK?
YES. YES I AM.

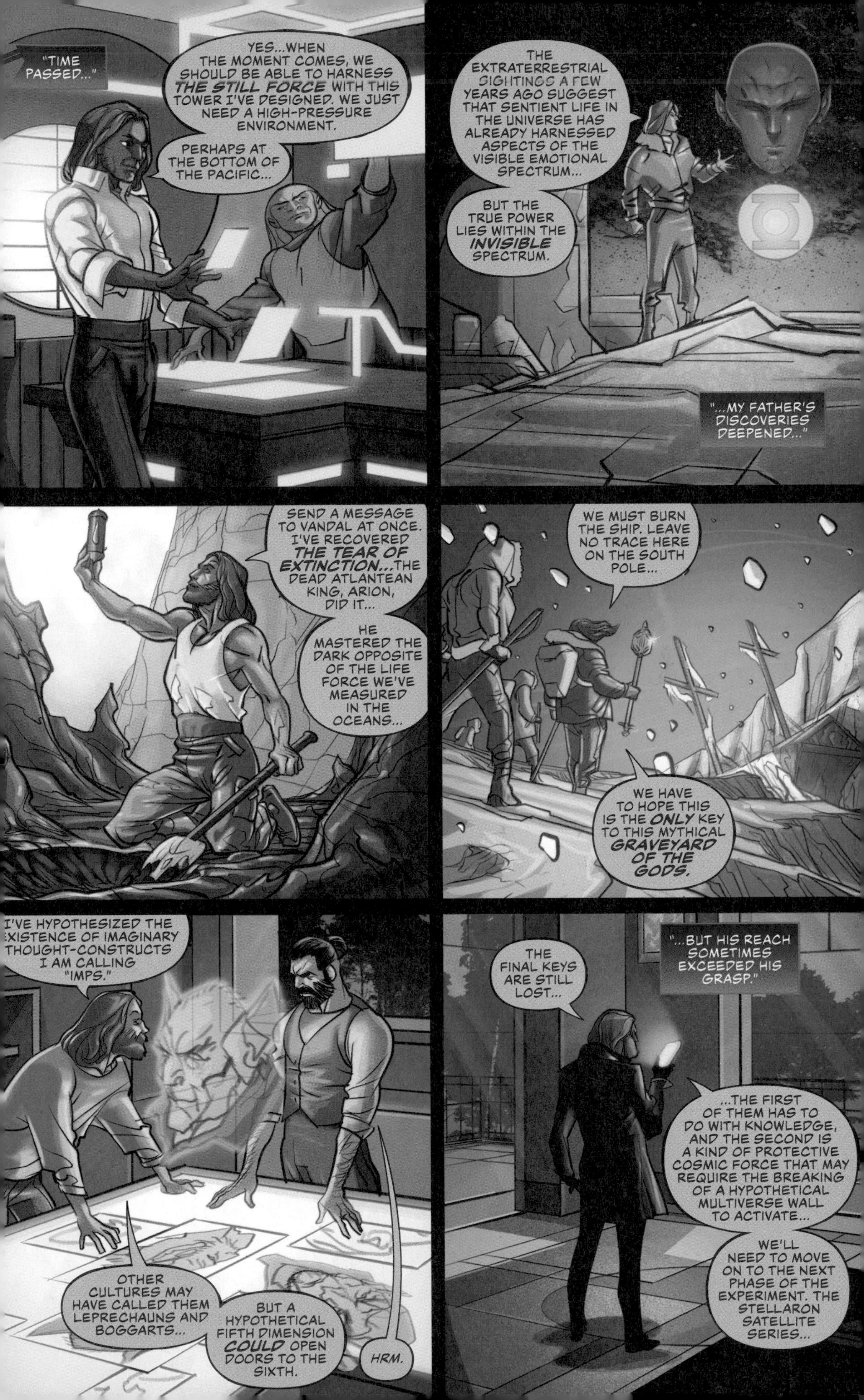
"TIME PASSED..."
YES...WHEN THE MOMENT COMES, WE SHOULD BE ABLE TO HARNESS THE STILL FORCE WITH THIS TOWER I'VE DESIGNED. WE JUST NEED A HIGH-PRESSURE ENVIRONMENT.
PERHAPS AT THE BOTTOM OF THE PACIFIC...
THE EXTRATERRESTRIAL SIGHTINGS A FEW YEARS AGO SUGGEST THAT SENTIENT LIFE IN THE UNIVERSE HAS ALREADY HARNESSED ASPECTS OF THE VISIBLE EMOTIONAL SPECTRUM...
BUT THE TRUE POWER LIES WITHIN THE INVISIBLE SPECTRUM.
"...MY FATHER'S DISCOVERIES DEEPENED..."
SEND A MESSAGE TO VANDAL AT ONCE. I'VE RECOVERED THE TEAR OF EXTINCTION...THE DEAD ATLANTEAN KING, ARION, DID IT...
HE MASTERED THE DARK OPPOSITE OF THE LIFE FORCE WE'VE MEASURED IN THE OCEANS...
WE MUST BURN THE SHIP. LEAVE NO TRACE HERE ON THE SOUTH POLE...
WE HAVE TO HOPE THIS IS THE ONLY KEY TO THIS MYTHICAL GRAVEYARD OF THE GODS.
I'VE HYPOTHESIZED THE EXISTENCE OF IMAGINARY THOUGHT-CONSTRUCTS I AM CALLING "IMPS."
OTHER CULTURES MAY HAVE CALLED THEM LEPRECHAUNS AND BOGGARTS...
BUT A HYPOTHETICAL FIFTH DIMENSION COULD OPEN DOORS TO THE SIXTH.
HRM.
"...BUT HIS REACH SOMETIMES EXCEEDED HIS GRASP."
THE FINAL KEYS ARE STILL LOST...
...THE FIRST OF THEM HAS TO DO WITH KNOWLEDGE, AND THE SECOND IS A KIND OF PROTECTIVE COSMIC FORCE THAT MAY REQUIRE THE BREAKING OF A HYPOTHETICAL MULTIVERSE WALL TO ACTIVATE...
WE'LL NEED TO MOVE ON TO THE NEXT PHASE OF THE EXPERIMENT. THE STELLARON SATELLITE SERIES...

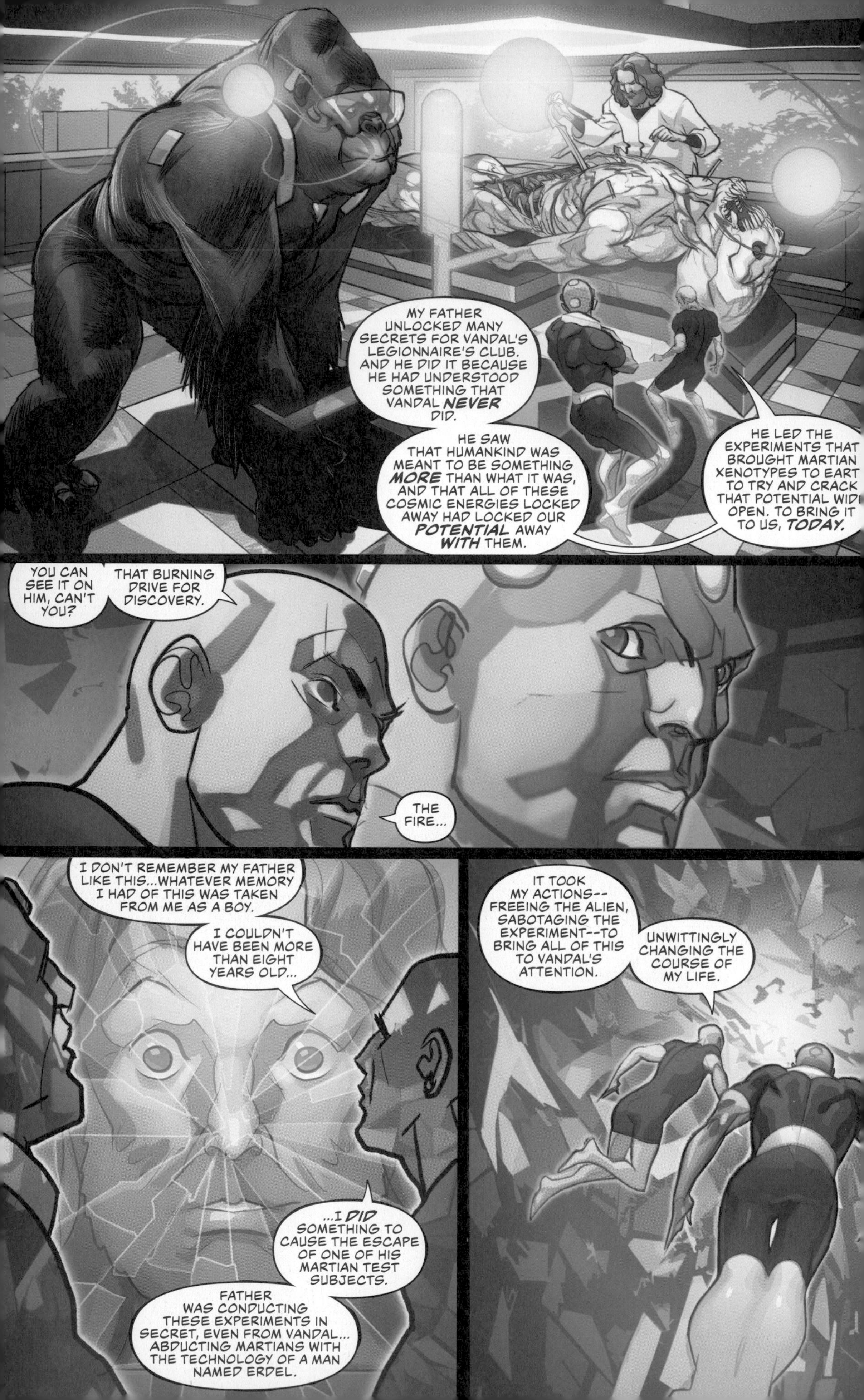
MY FATHER UNLOCKED MANY SECRETS FOR VANDAL'S LEGIONNAIRE'S CLUB. AND HE DID IT BECAUSE HE HAD UNDERSTOOD SOMETHING THAT VANDAL **NEVER** DID.
HE SAW THAT HUMANKIND WAS MEANT TO BE SOMETHING **MORE** THAN WHAT IT WAS, AND THAT ALL OF THESE COSMIC ENERGIES LOCKED AWAY HAD LOCKED OUR **POTENTIAL** AWAY **WITH** THEM.
HE LED THE EXPERIMENTS THAT BROUGHT MARTIAN XENOTYPES TO EART TO TRY AND CRACK THAT POTENTIAL WID OPEN. TO BRING IT TO US, **TODAY.**
YOU CAN SEE IT ON HIM, CAN'T YOU?
THAT BURNING DRIVE FOR DISCOVERY.
THE FIRE...
I DON'T REMEMBER MY FATHER LIKE THIS...WHATEVER MEMORY I HAD OF THIS WAS TAKEN FROM ME AS A BOY.
I COULDN'T HAVE BEEN MORE THAN EIGHT YEARS OLD...
...I **DID** SOMETHING TO CAUSE THE ESCAPE OF ONE OF HIS MARTIAN TEST SUBJECTS.
FATHER WAS CONDUCTING THESE EXPERIMENTS IN SECRET, EVEN FROM VANDAL... ABDUCTING MARTIANS WITH THE TECHNOLOGY OF A MAN NAMED ERDEL.
IT TOOK MY ACTIONS-- FREEING THE ALIEN, SABOTAGING THE EXPERIMENT--TO BRING ALL OF THIS TO VANDAL'S ATTENTION.
UNWITTINGLY CHANGING THE COURSE OF MY LIFE.

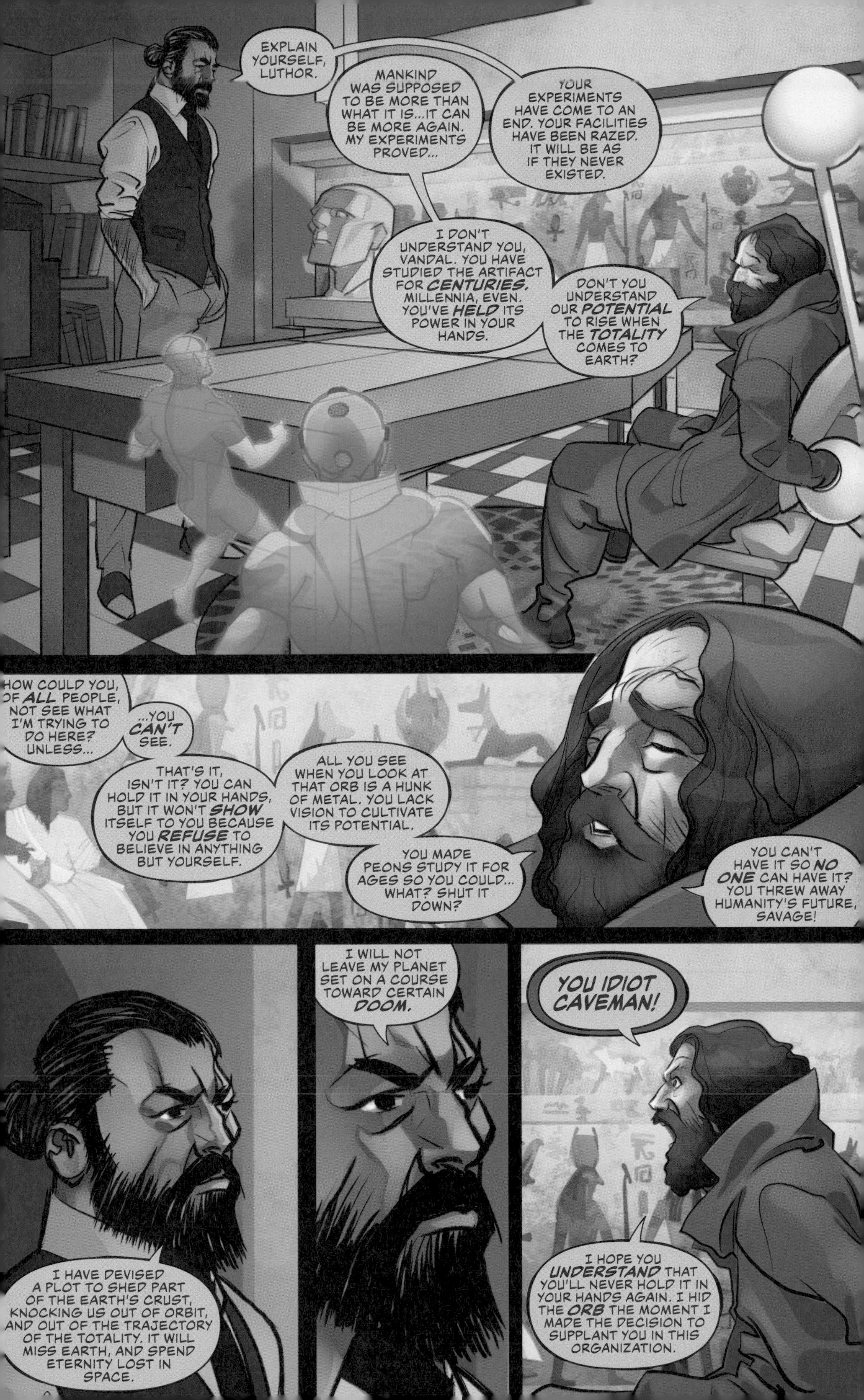

EXPLAIN YOURSELF, LUTHOR.
MANKIND WAS SUPPOSED TO BE MORE THAN WHAT IT IS...IT CAN BE MORE AGAIN. MY EXPERIMENTS PROVED...
YOUR EXPERIMENTS HAVE COME TO AN END. YOUR FACILITIES HAVE BEEN RAZED. IT WILL BE AS IF THEY NEVER EXISTED.
I DON'T UNDERSTAND YOU, VANDAL. YOU HAVE STUDIED THE ARTIFACT FOR CENTURIES, MILLENNIA, EVEN. YOU'VE HELD ITS POWER IN YOUR HANDS.
DON'T YOU UNDERSTAND OUR POTENTIAL TO RISE WHEN THE TOTALITY COMES TO EARTH?
HOW COULD YOU, OF ALL PEOPLE, NOT SEE WHAT I'M TRYING TO DO HERE? UNLESS...
...YOU CAN'T SEE.
THAT'S IT, ISN'T IT? YOU CAN HOLD IT IN YOUR HANDS, BUT IT WON'T SHOW ITSELF TO YOU BECAUSE YOU REFUSE TO BELIEVE IN ANYTHING BUT YOURSELF.
ALL YOU SEE WHEN YOU LOOK AT THAT ORB IS A HUNK OF METAL. YOU LACK VISION TO CULTIVATE ITS POTENTIAL.
YOU MADE PEONS STUDY IT FOR AGES SO YOU COULD... WHAT? SHUT IT DOWN?
YOU CAN'T HAVE IT SO NO ONE CAN HAVE IT? YOU THREW AWAY HUMANITY'S FUTURE, SAVAGE!
I HAVE DEVISED A PLOT TO SHED PART OF THE EARTH'S CRUST, KNOCKING US OUT OF ORBIT, AND OUT OF THE TRAJECTORY OF THE TOTALITY. IT WILL MISS EARTH, AND SPEND ETERNITY LOST IN SPACE.
I WILL NOT LEAVE MY PLANET SET ON A COURSE TOWARD CERTAIN DOOM.
YOU IDIOT CAVEMAN!
I HOPE YOU UNDERSTAND THAT YOU'LL NEVER HOLD IT IN YOUR HANDS AGAIN. I HID THE ORB THE MOMENT I MADE THE DECISION TO SUPPLANT YOU IN THIS ORGANIZATION.

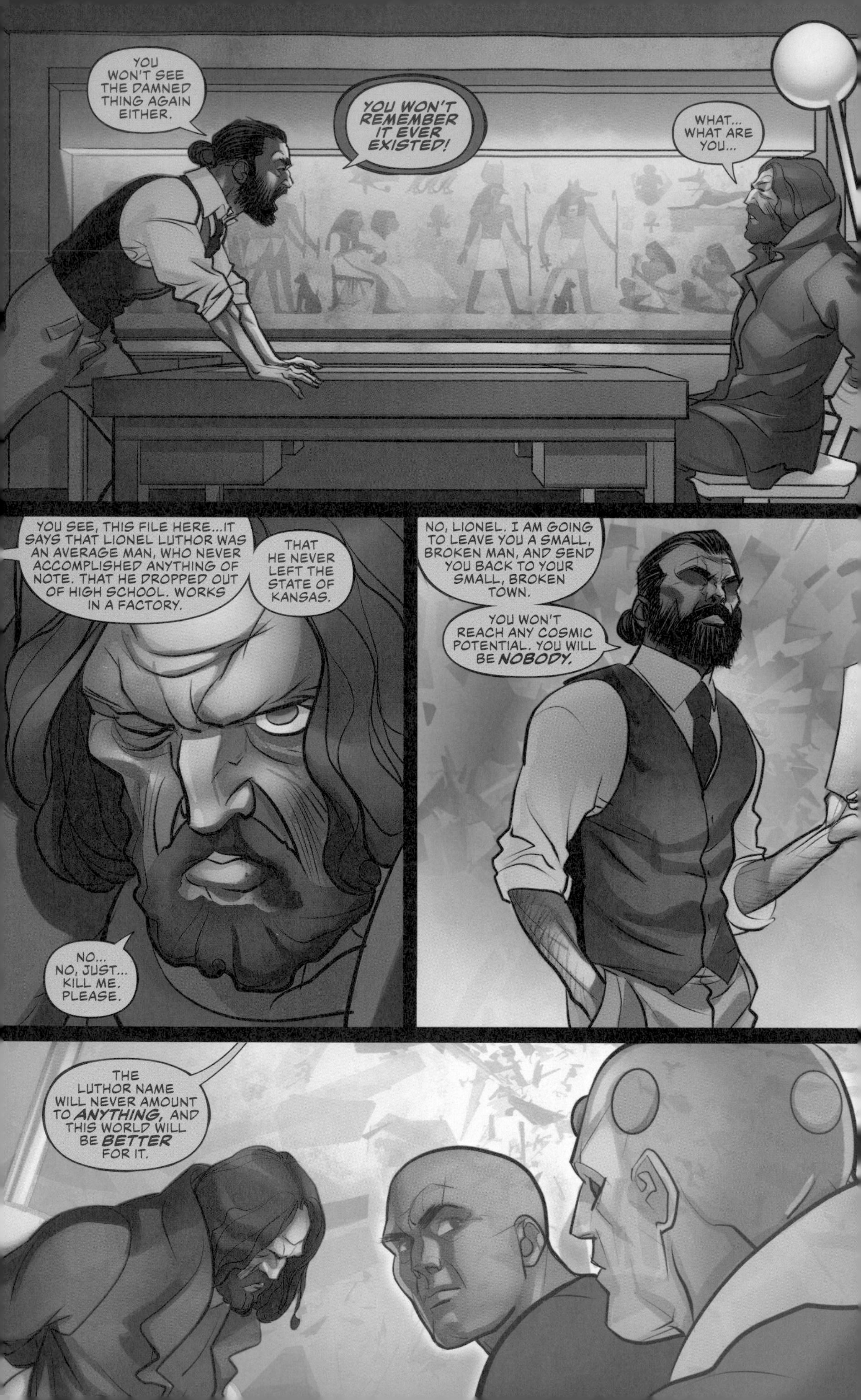
YOU WON'T SEE THE DAMNED THING AGAIN EITHER.
YOU WON'T REMEMBER IT EVER EXISTED!
WHAT... WHAT ARE YOU...
YOU SEE, THIS FILE HERE...IT SAYS THAT LIONEL LUTHOR WAS AN AVERAGE MAN, WHO NEVER ACCOMPLISHED ANYTHING OF NOTE. THAT HE DROPPED OUT OF HIGH SCHOOL. WORKS IN A FACTORY.
THAT HE NEVER LEFT THE STATE OF KANSAS.
NO... NO, JUST... KILL ME. PLEASE.
NO, LIONEL. I AM GOING TO LEAVE YOU A SMALL, BROKEN MAN, AND SEND YOU BACK TO YOUR SMALL, BROKEN TOWN.
YOU WON'T REACH ANY COSMIC POTENTIAL. YOU WILL BE *NOBODY.*
THE LUTHOR NAME WILL NEVER AMOUNT TO *ANYTHING,* AND THIS WORLD WILL BE *BETTER* FOR IT.

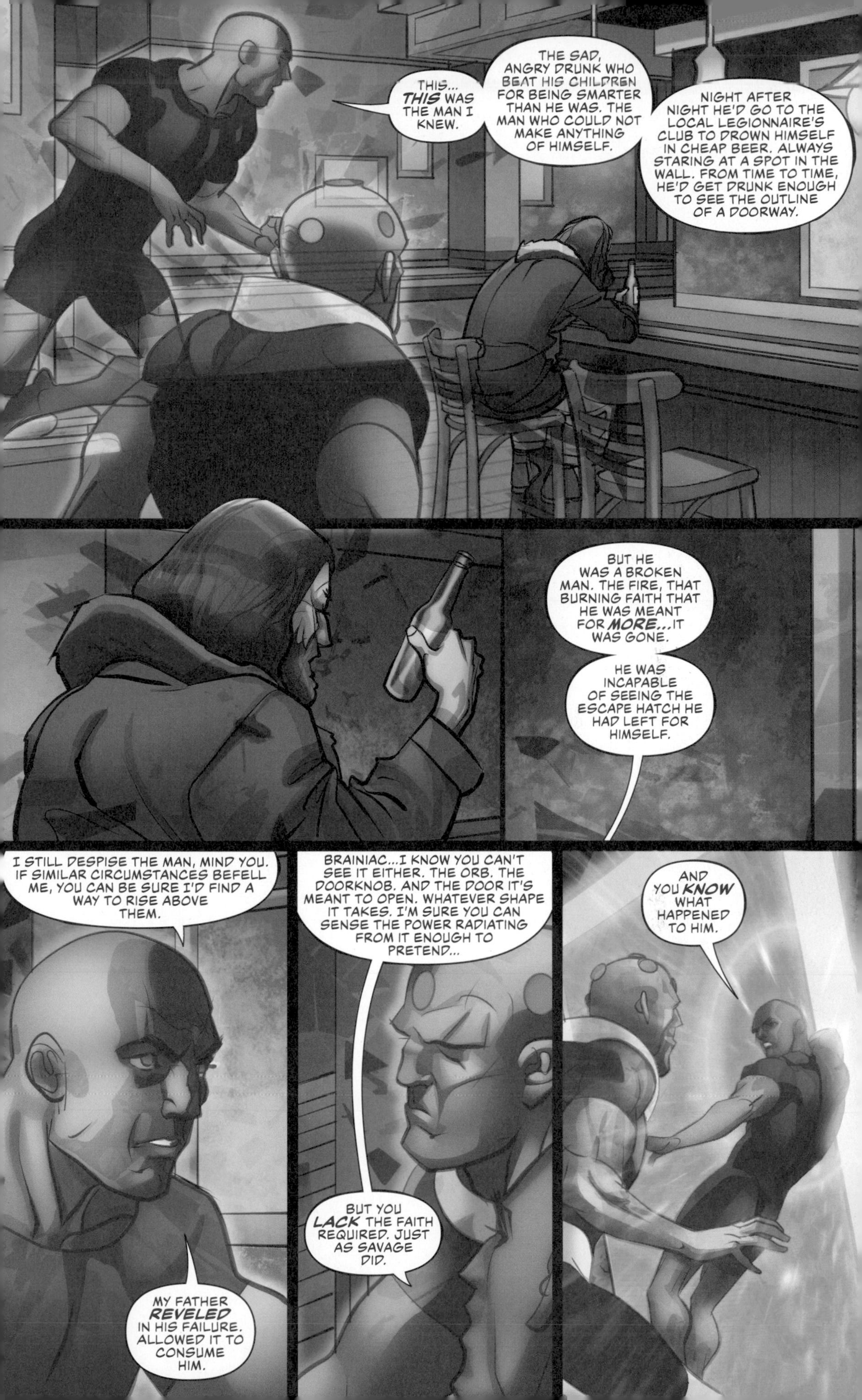
THIS... THIS WAS THE MAN I KNEW.
THE SAD, ANGRY DRUNK WHO BEAT HIS CHILDREN FOR BEING SMARTER THAN HE WAS. THE MAN WHO COULD NOT MAKE ANYTHING OF HIMSELF.
NIGHT AFTER NIGHT HE'D GO TO THE LOCAL LEGIONNAIRE'S CLUB TO DROWN HIMSELF IN CHEAP BEER. ALWAYS STARING AT A SPOT IN THE WALL. FROM TIME TO TIME, HE'D GET DRUNK ENOUGH TO SEE THE OUTLINE OF A DOORWAY.
BUT HE WAS A BROKEN MAN. THE FIRE, THAT BURNING FAITH THAT HE WAS MEANT FOR MORE... IT WAS GONE.
HE WAS INCAPABLE OF SEEING THE ESCAPE HATCH HE HAD LEFT FOR HIMSELF.
I STILL DESPISE THE MAN, MIND YOU. IF SIMILAR CIRCUMSTANCES BEFELL ME, YOU CAN BE SURE I'D FIND A WAY TO RISE ABOVE THEM.
MY FATHER REVELED IN HIS FAILURE. ALLOWED IT TO CONSUME HIM.
BRAINIAC...I KNOW YOU CAN'T SEE IT EITHER. THE ORB. THE DOORKNOB. AND THE DOOR IT'S MEANT TO OPEN. WHATEVER SHAPE IT TAKES. I'M SURE YOU CAN SENSE THE POWER RADIATING FROM IT ENOUGH TO PRETEND...
BUT YOU LACK THE FAITH REQUIRED. JUST AS SAVAGE DID.
AND YOU KNOW WHAT HAPPENED TO HIM.

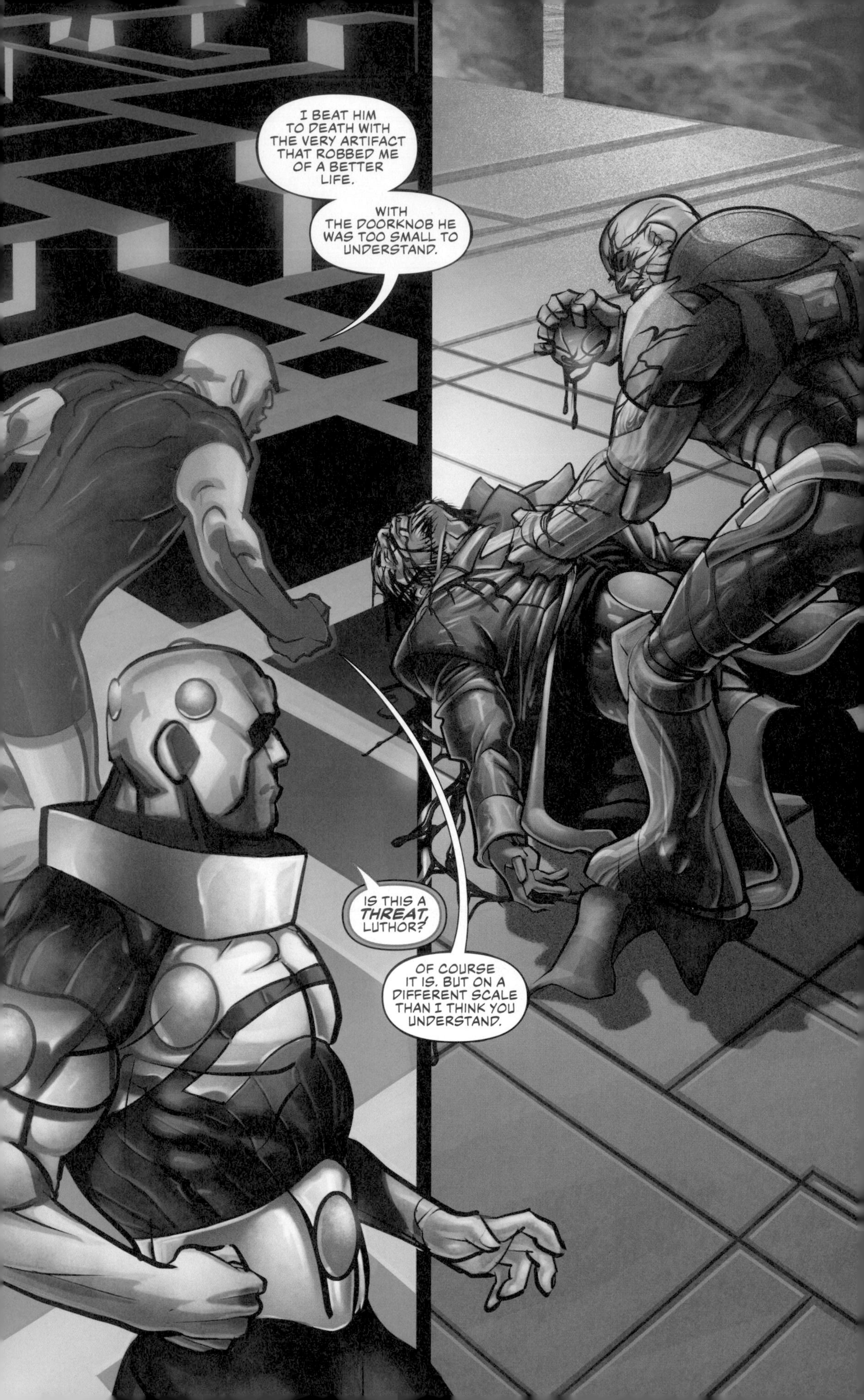
I BEAT HIM TO DEATH WITH THE VERY ARTIFACT THAT ROBBED ME OF A BETTER LIFE.
WITH THE DOORKNOB HE WAS TOO SMALL TO UNDERSTAND.
IS THIS A *THREAT,* LUTHOR?
OF COURSE IT IS. BUT ON A DIFFERENT SCALE THAN I THINK YOU UNDERSTAND.

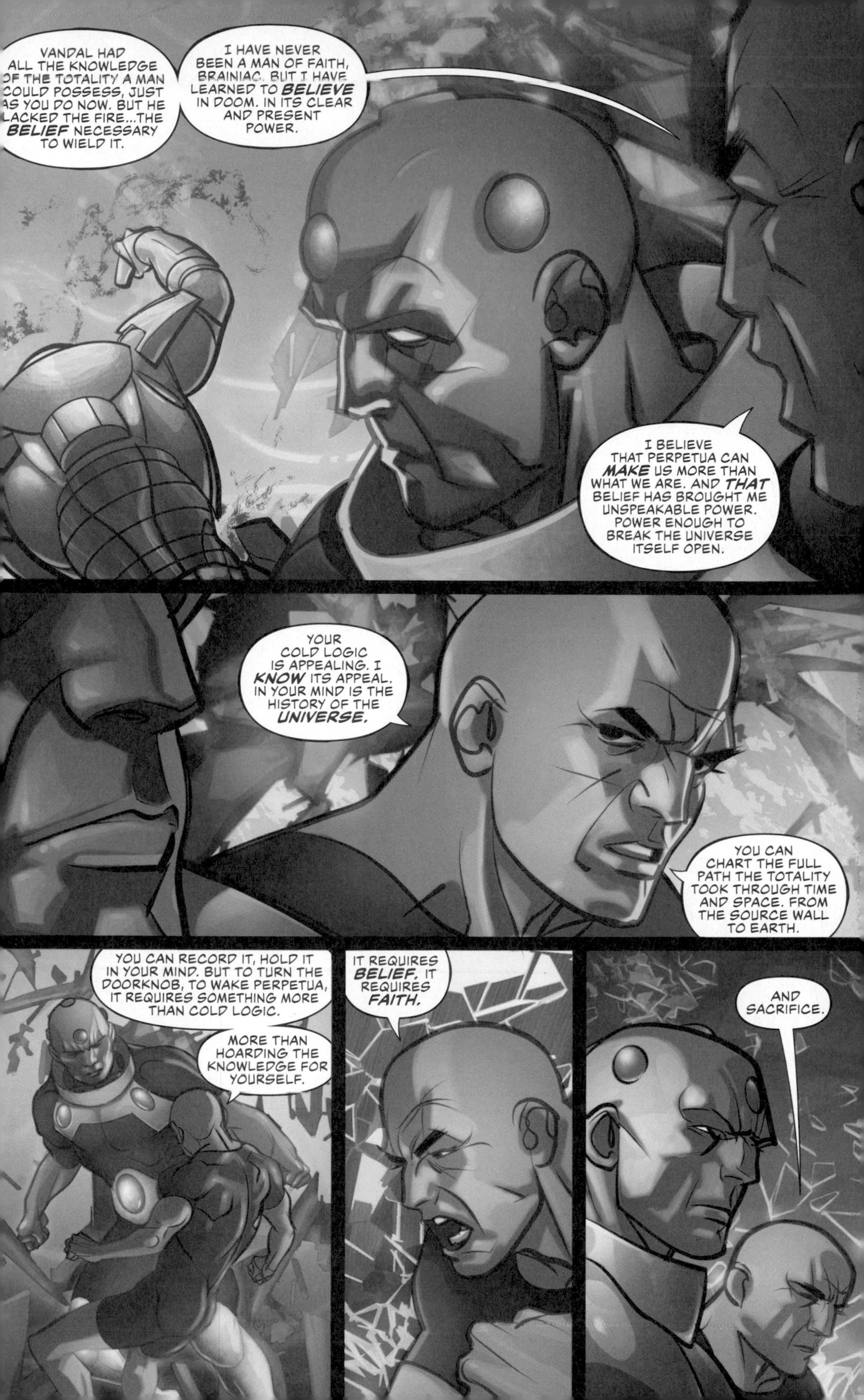
VANDAL HAD ALL THE KNOWLEDGE OF THE TOTALITY A MAN COULD POSSESS, JUST AS YOU DO NOW. BUT HE LACKED THE FIRE...THE BELIEF NECESSARY TO WIELD IT.
I HAVE NEVER BEEN A MAN OF FAITH, BRAINIAC. BUT I HAVE LEARNED TO BELIEVE IN DOOM. IN ITS CLEAR AND PRESENT POWER.
I BELIEVE THAT PERPETUA CAN MAKE US MORE THAN WHAT WE ARE. AND THAT BELIEF HAS BROUGHT ME UNSPEAKABLE POWER. POWER ENOUGH TO BREAK THE UNIVERSE ITSELF OPEN.
YOUR COLD LOGIC IS APPEALING. I KNOW ITS APPEAL. IN YOUR MIND IS THE HISTORY OF THE UNIVERSE.
YOU CAN CHART THE FULL PATH THE TOTALITY TOOK THROUGH TIME AND SPACE. FROM THE SOURCE WALL TO EARTH.
YOU CAN RECORD IT, HOLD IT IN YOUR MIND. BUT TO TURN THE DOORKNOB, TO WAKE PERPETUA, IT REQUIRES SOMETHING MORE THAN COLD LOGIC.
MORE THAN HOARDING THE KNOWLEDGE FOR YOURSELF.
IT REQUIRES BELIEF. IT REQUIRES FAITH.
AND SACRIFICE.

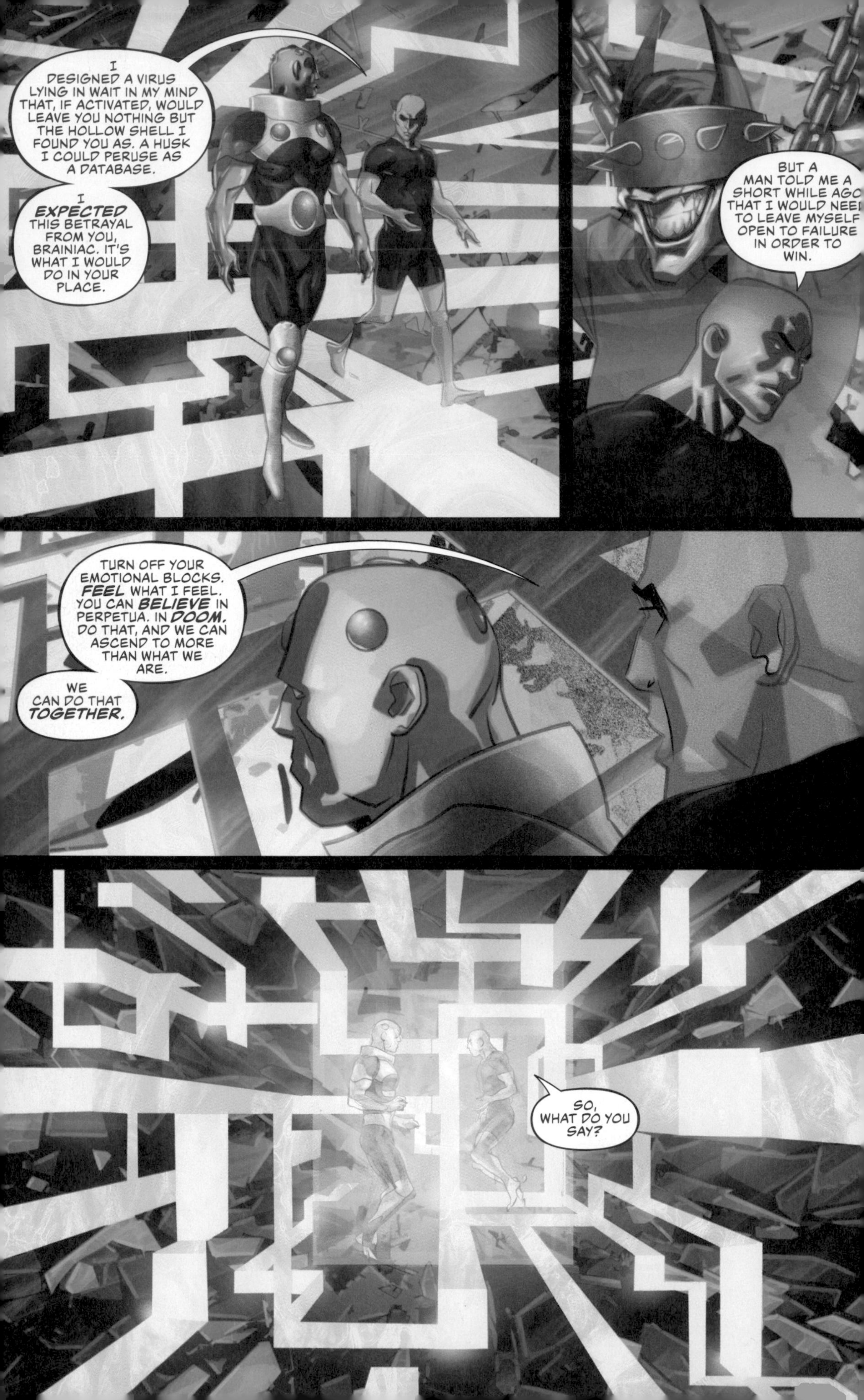
I DESIGNED A VIRUS LYING IN WAIT IN MY MIND THAT, IF ACTIVATED, WOULD LEAVE YOU NOTHING BUT THE HOLLOW SHELL I FOUND YOU AS. A HUSK I COULD PERUSE AS A DATABASE.
I *EXPECTED* THIS BETRAYAL FROM YOU, BRAINIAC. IT'S WHAT I WOULD DO IN YOUR PLACE.
BUT A MAN TOLD ME A SHORT WHILE AGO THAT I WOULD NEED TO LEAVE MYSELF OPEN TO FAILURE IN ORDER TO WIN.
TURN OFF YOUR EMOTIONAL BLOCKS. *FEEL* WHAT I FEEL. YOU CAN *BELIEVE* IN PERPETUA. IN *DOOM.* DO THAT, AND WE CAN ASCEND TO MORE THAN WHAT WE ARE.
WE CAN DO THAT *TOGETHER.*
SO, WHAT DO YOU SAY?

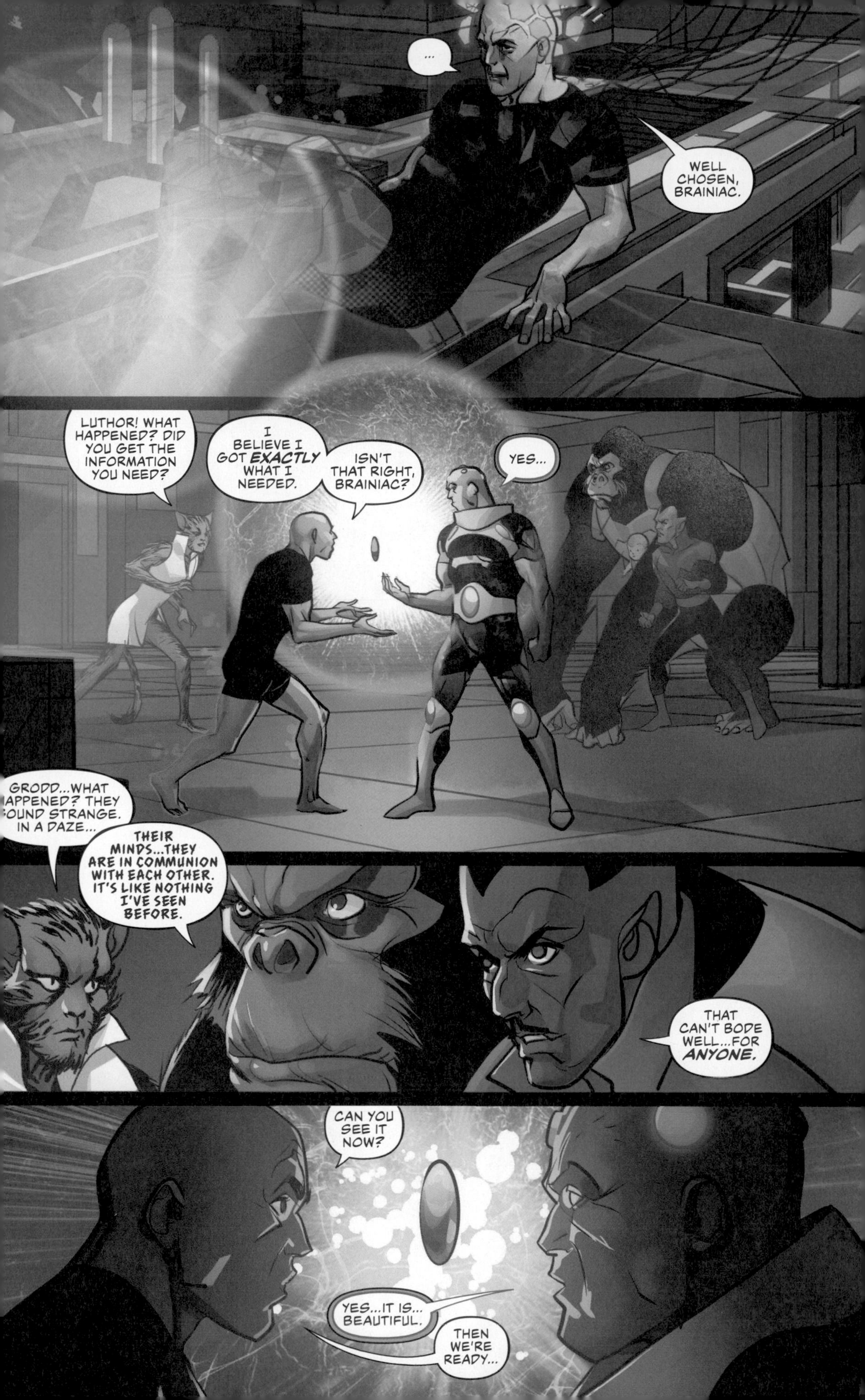
...
WELL CHOSEN, BRAINIAC.
LUTHOR! WHAT HAPPENED? DID YOU GET THE INFORMATION YOU NEED?
I BELIEVE I GOT EXACTLY WHAT I NEEDED.
ISN'T THAT RIGHT, BRAINIAC?
YES...
GRODD...WHAT HAPPENED? THEY SOUND STRANGE. IN A DAZE...
THEIR MINDS...THEY ARE IN COMMUNION WITH EACH OTHER. IT'S LIKE NOTHING I'VE SEEN BEFORE.
THAT CAN'T BODE WELL...FOR ANYONE.
CAN YOU SEE IT NOW?
YES...IT IS... BEAUTIFUL.
THEN WE'RE READY...

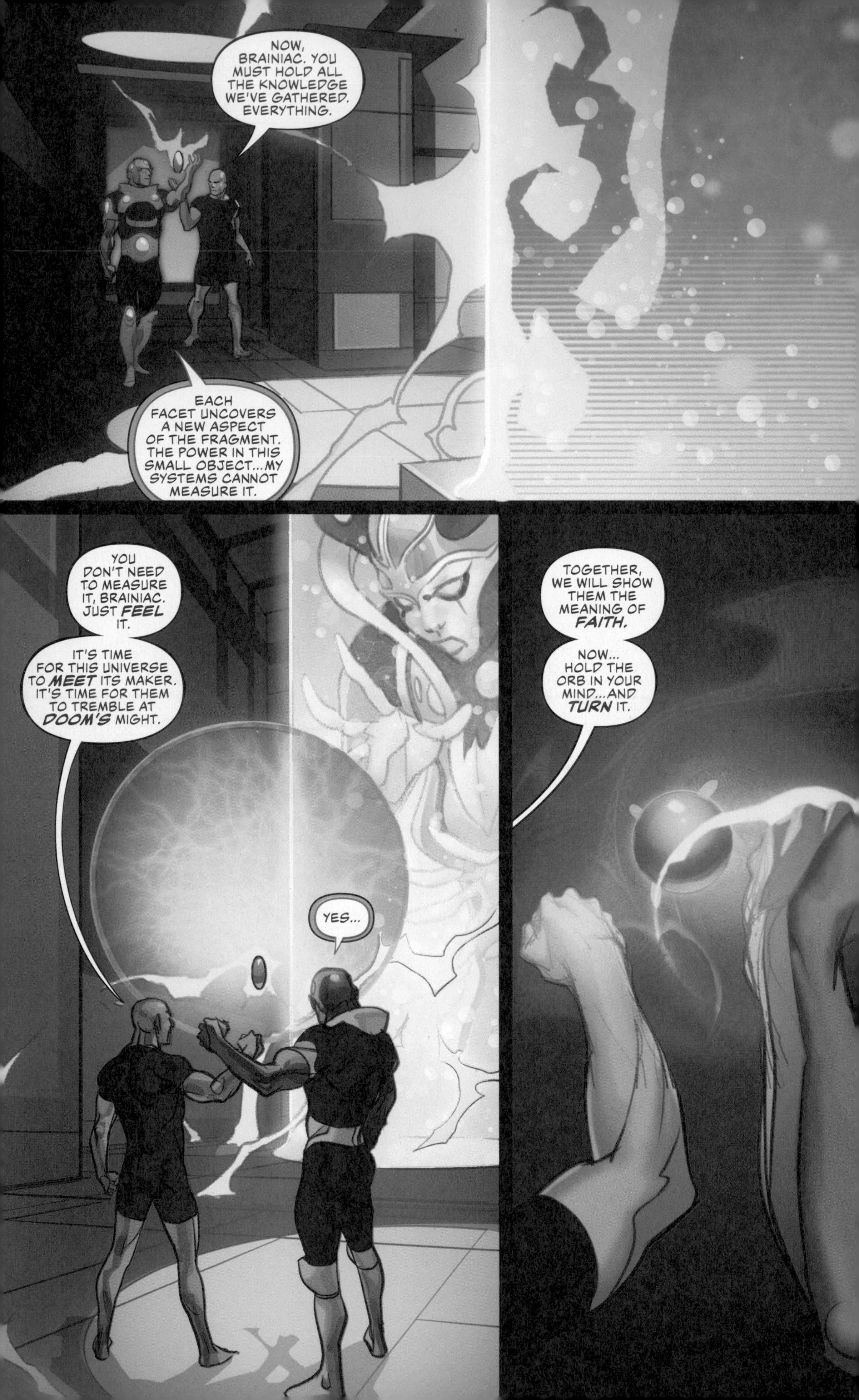
NOW, BRAINIAC. YOU MUST HOLD ALL THE KNOWLEDGE WE'VE GATHERED. EVERYTHING.
EACH FACET UNCOVERS A NEW ASPECT OF THE FRAGMENT. THE POWER IN THIS SMALL OBJECT...MY SYSTEMS CANNOT MEASURE IT.
YOU DON'T NEED TO MEASURE IT, BRAINIAC. JUST FEEL IT.
IT'S TIME FOR THIS UNIVERSE TO MEET ITS MAKER. IT'S TIME FOR THEM TO TREMBLE AT DOOM'S MIGHT.
YES...
TOGETHER, WE WILL SHOW THEM THE MEANING OF FAITH.
NOW... HOLD THE ORB IN YOUR MIND...AND TURN IT.

JUSTICE LEAGUE #13 variant cover
by JAE LEE and JUNE CHUNG

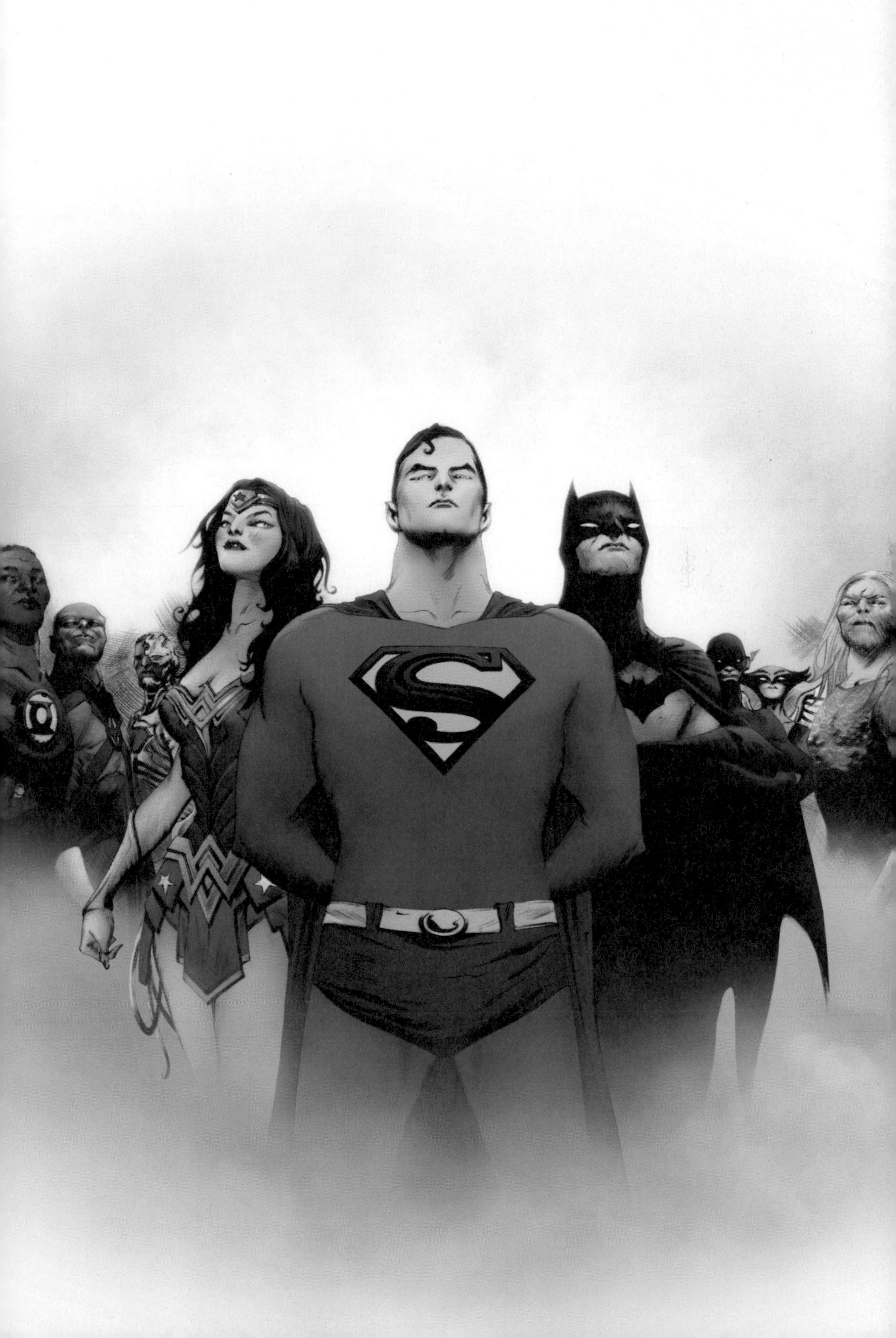

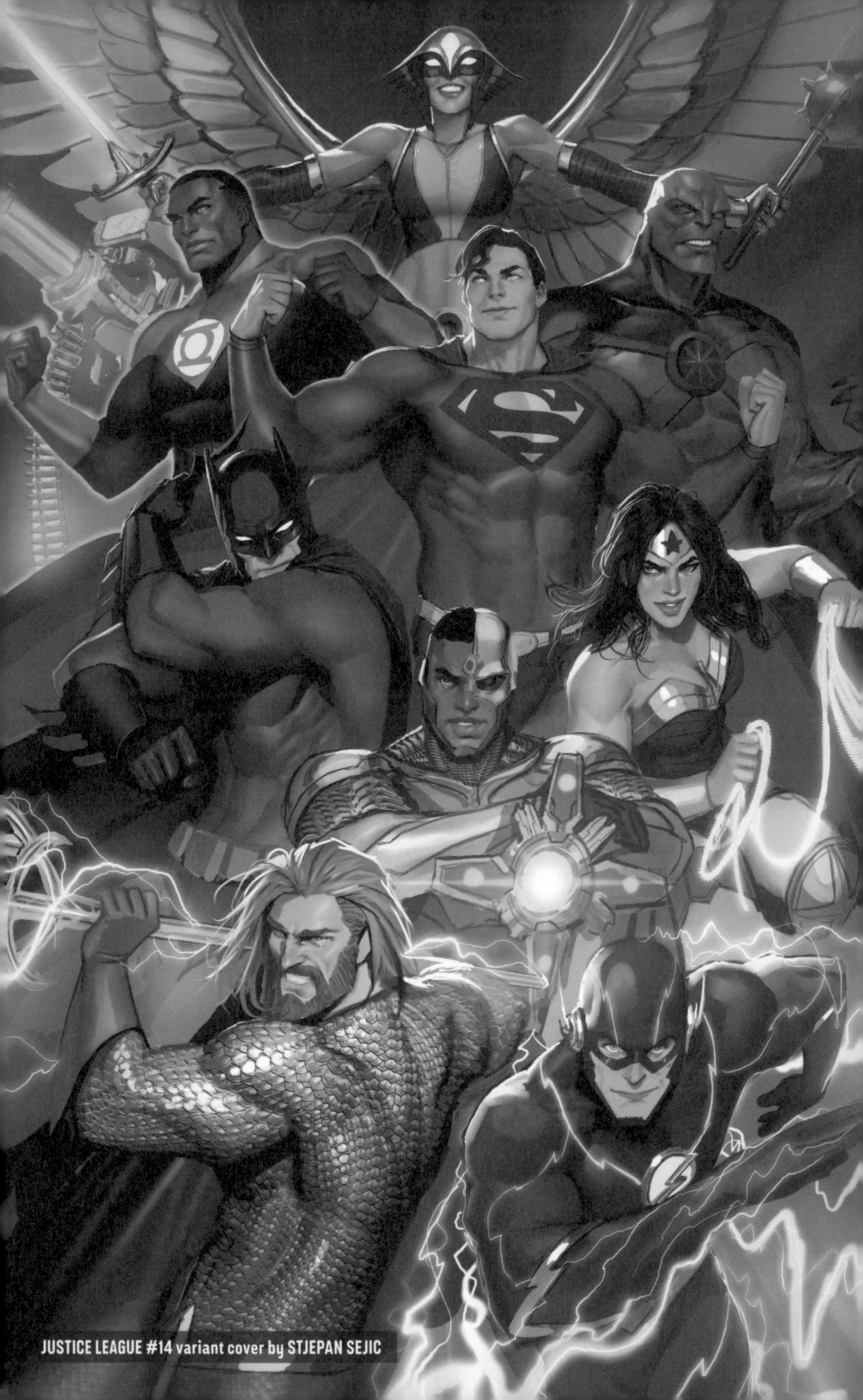

JUSTICE LEAGUE #14 variant cover by STJEPAN SEJIC

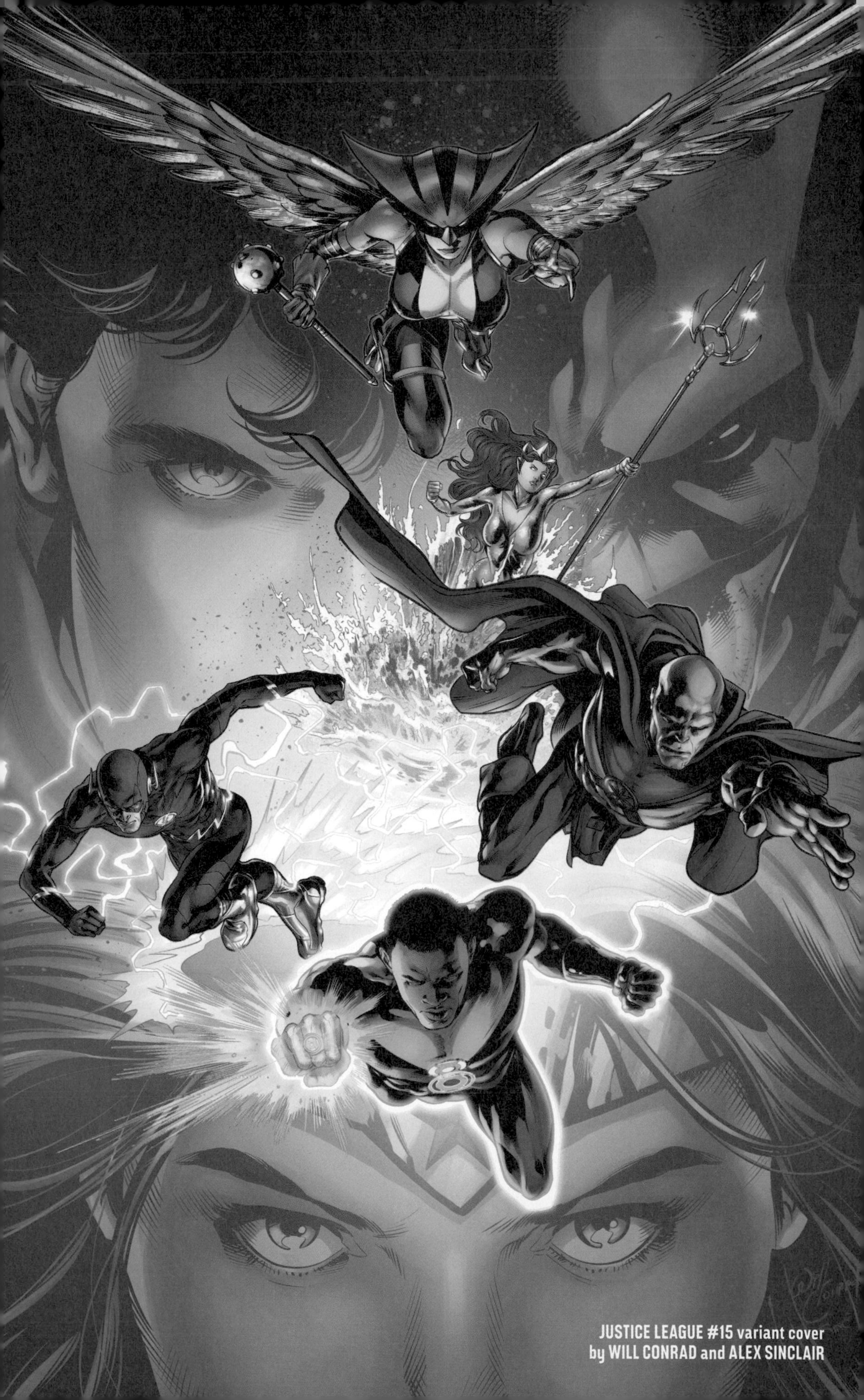

JUSTICE LEAGUE #15 variant cover
by WILL CONRAD and ALEX SINCLAIR

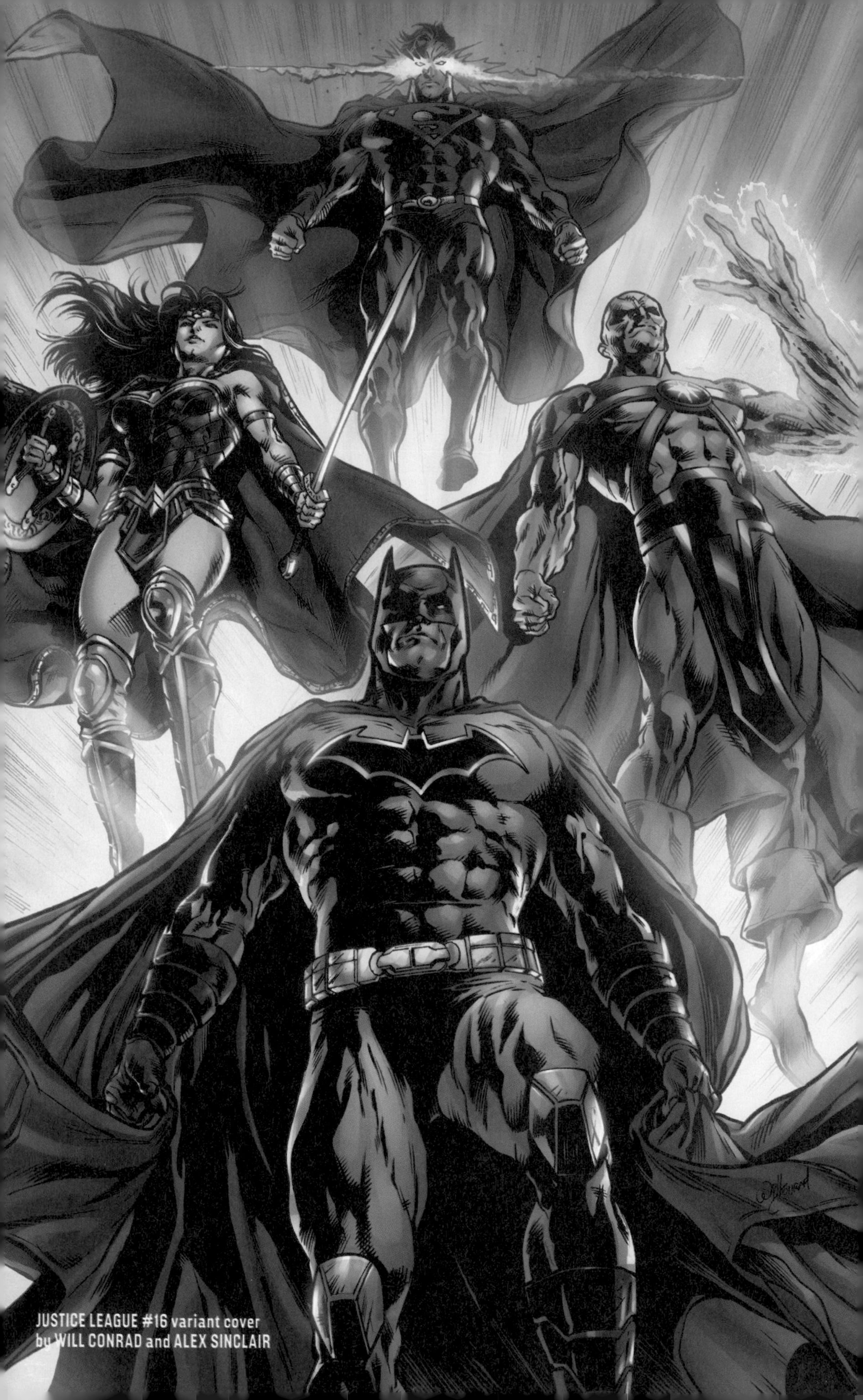

JUSTICE LEAGUE #16 variant cover
by WILL CONRAD and ALEX SINCLAIR

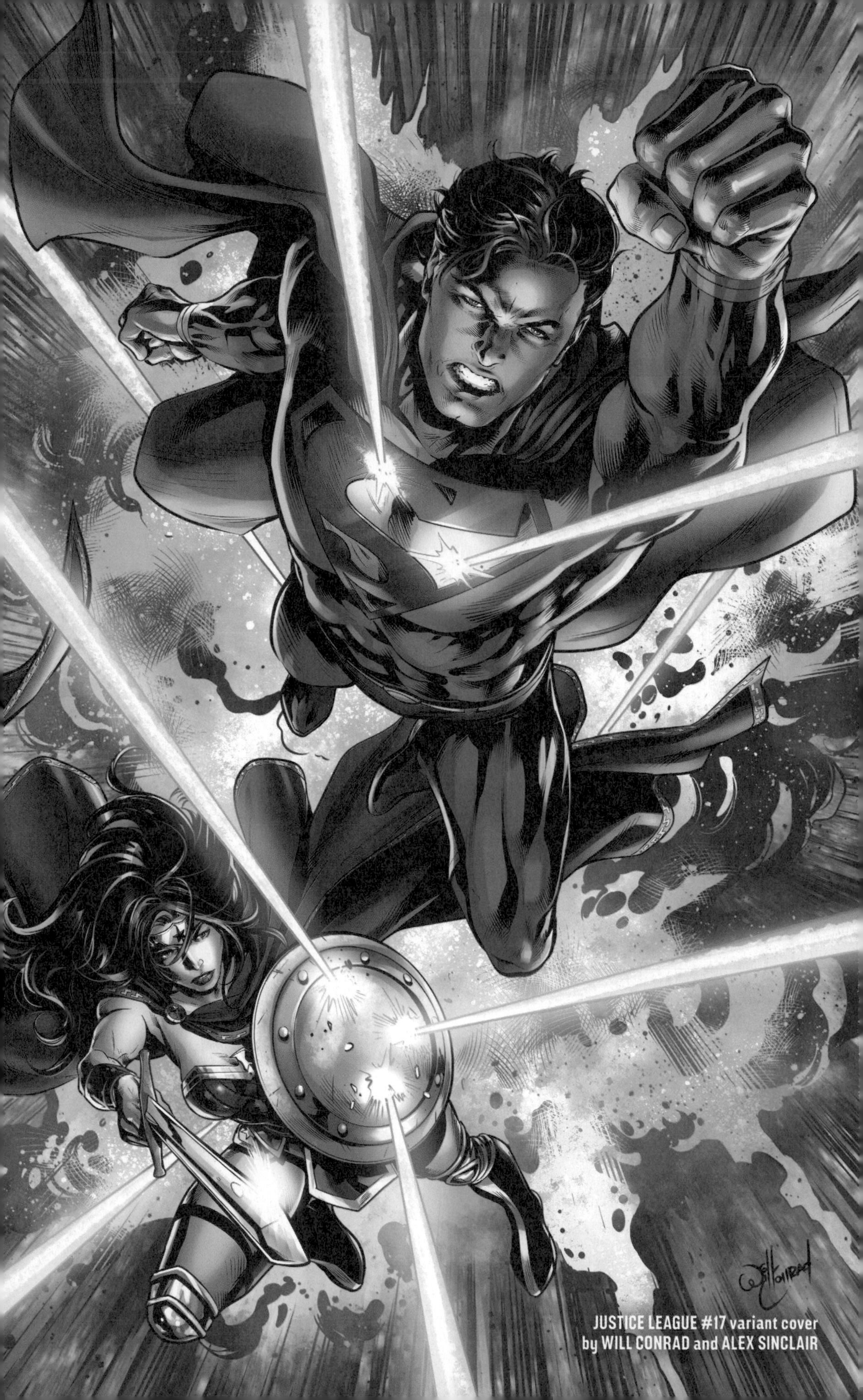

JUSTICE LEAGUE #17 variant cover
by WILL CONRAD and ALEX SINCLAIR

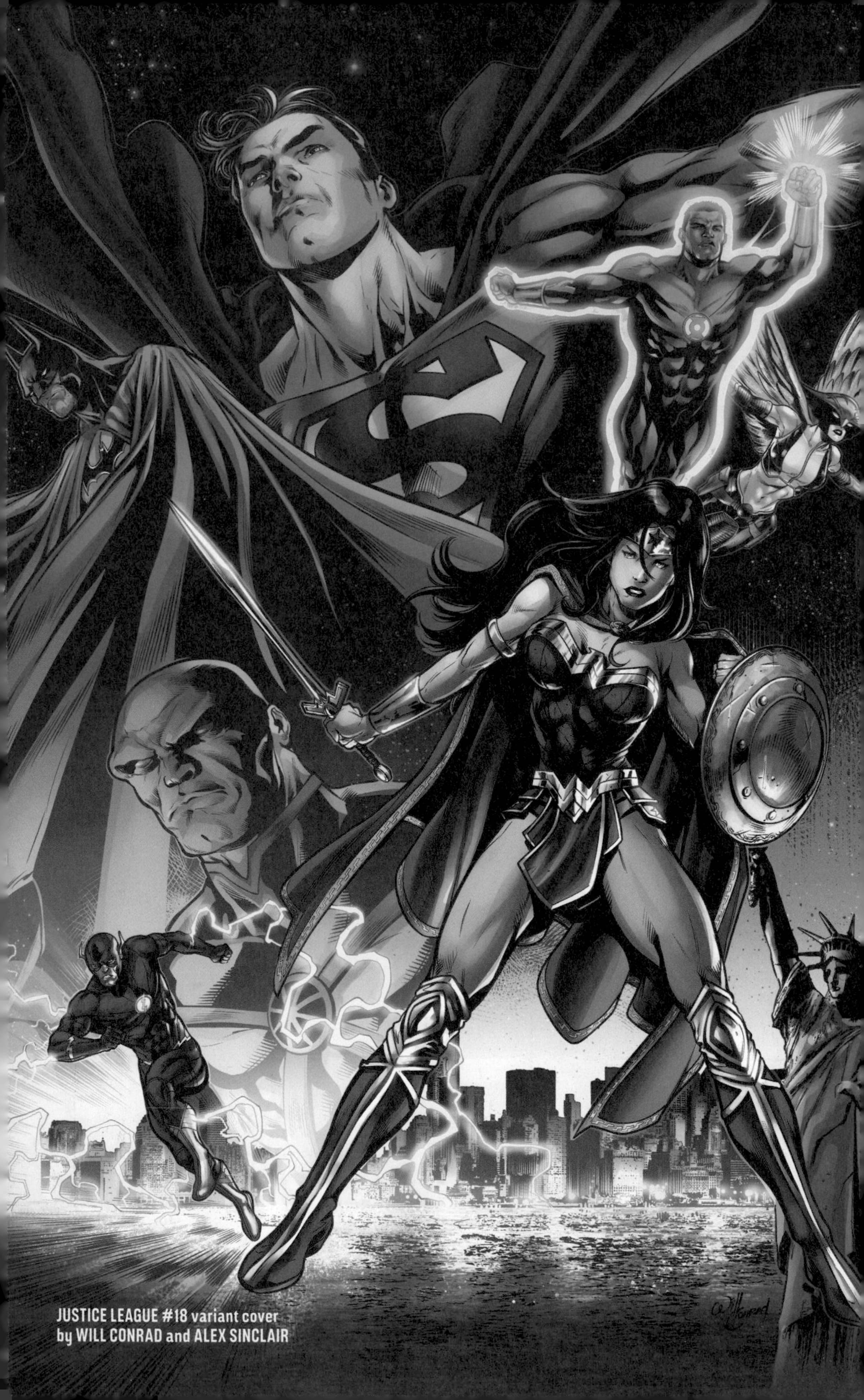

JUSTICE LEAGUE #18 variant cover
by WILL CONRAD and ALEX SINCLAIR